# Deviance & Deviants

# Deviance & Deviants

*A Sociological Approach*

William E. Thompson and Jennifer C. Gibbs

**WILEY** Blackwell

*Library of Congress Cataloging-in-Publication Data*

Names: Thompson, William E. (William Edwin), 1950– author. | Gibbs, Jennifer C., 1978– author.
Title: Deviance & deviants : a sociological approach / William E. Thompson, Jennifer C. Gibbs.
Description: Hoboken : Wiley-Blackwell, 2016. | Includes bibliographical references and index.
Identifiers: LCCN 2016007515 (print) | LCCN 2016013846 (ebook) | ISBN 9781118604595 (paperback) | ISBN 9781118604694 (pdf) | ISBN 9781118604656 (epub)
Subjects: LCSH: Deviant behavior. | BISAC: SOCIAL SCIENCE / Criminology.
Classification: LCC HM811 .T468 2016 (print) | LCC HM811 (ebook) | DDC 302.5/42–dc23
LC record available at http://lccn.loc.gov/2016007515

A catalogue record for this book is available from the British Library.

Cover image: Matt Gone, also known as "The Checkered Man". Photo © Jorge Dan Lopez/Reuters

Set in 10.5/13pt Minion by SPi Global, Pondicherry, India

Printed in Singapore by C.O.S. Printers Pte Ltd

1   2017

# Brief Contents

# Contents

•

# Preface

Too often, people are led to believe that society's norms are clearly defined, rigidly enforced, and arbitrarily followed or broken. Mass media and social media often reinforce these ideas and portray those who are labeled as deviant as being individuals who are somehow inherently different from the rest of us – social misfits, perhaps mentally, or at least morally, impaired. Indeed, some people are comforted by the notion that the world is dichotomous and can be neatly divided into *good* and *bad*, *right* and *wrong*, *conformity* and *deviance*. Because many people are curious as to what makes deviants "tick," there is a tendency for definitions of deviance and deviants to take an individualistic and pathological approach emphasizing the uniqueness of those who violate society's folkways, mores, and laws. The first wisdom of sociology, however, and the guiding principle for this book is: *things are not what they seem* (Berger, 1963). While acknowledging the uniqueness of individuals, *Deviance & Deviants: A Sociological Approach* insists that the study of deviance is not, as has been suggested, merely the study of "nuts, sluts, and preverts" (sic) (Liazos, 1972). Instead, this book places norm violation in a much broader sociological context and explores how both deviance (norm violating behaviors) and deviants (those believed to have committed those behaviors) are socially constructed and socially defined.

Some of the special features of this book include:

- Taking both a macro-level and micro-level approach to norm violating behavior, looking at how norms are socially constructed, socially defined, and socially sanctioned.
- Exploring how deviance becomes part of a person's social and personal identity.
- Looking at some of the popular notions and pseudoscientific explanations for deviance and debunking many of the myths that surround deviance and deviants.
- Providing sociological explanations for deviance based on solid social scientific research.
- Exploring areas of deviance sometimes overlooked by other books on the subject, such as deviant occupations, sexual deviance, extreme deviance, elite deviance, and cyberdeviance.
- Beginning each chapter with specific learning outcomes and ending with critical thinking questions designed to assess those outcomes.

- A subheading in each chapter that focuses on the media and how they help construct, define, and redefine that particular topic related to deviance.
- In each chapter, a box entitled "In Their Own Words" in which people who have been labeled as deviant provide their viewpoint on the particular subject of that chapter.
- Key terms and concepts appear in boldface type followed by italicized definitions. These key terms are listed in alphabetical order at the end of each chapter and again in a comprehensive glossary at the end of the book.

We invite you to open your minds as you open your books and explore the fascinating world of social deviance and social deviants. Apply your critical thinking skills as you read, asking questions and questioning answers.

# About the Companion Website

This book is accompanied by a companion website:

## www.wiley.com/go/thompson

The *Deviance & Deviants: A Sociological Approach* companion website features resources created by Christopher Michael Haraszkiewicz to help you use this book in university courses, whether you're an instructor or a student.

**For Instructors**
- Activity and project ideas
- Chapter outlines
- PowerPoint slides
- Test bank

**For Students**
- Study guide

# 1

# Defining Social Deviance and Deviants

**Student Learning Outcomes**

After reading this chapter students will be able to:

1  Define deviance from an absolutist position, from the statistical anomaly view, and from the sociological approach which focuses on the normative relativist perspective and the social construction of deviance.
2  Explain how deviance is socially constructed around a range of tolerance that is relative to culture, time, place, and situation in regard to acts, actors, and a social audience.
3  Identify the role of media in defining deviance.
4  Distinguish between crime and deviance.
5  Distinguish between diversity and deviance.
6  Identify some of the negative consequences and positive aspects of deviance.

*One of the first videos depicted live kittens being placed in sealed clear plastic bags and filmed while suffocating. Another depicted a live kitten being fed to a python. Animal rights activists demanded that the videos be removed from the internet and that the alleged creator and poster of those videos, Canadian Eric Clinton Newman, aka Luka Rocco Magnotta, be arrested and brought to justice for animal cruelty. Police investigations indicated that Newman legally changed his name in 2006 to Magnotta and had begun a fledgling acting career in both straight and gay pornographic movies. He also was allegedly linked to some white supremacist groups, and had three convictions for consumer fraud related to a stolen credit card on his*

*Deviance & Deviants: A Sociological Approach*, First Edition. William E. Thompson and Jennifer C. Gibbs.
© 2017 John Wiley & Sons, Inc. Published 2017 by John Wiley & Sons, Inc.
Companion website: www.wiley.com/go/thompson

*record. No doubt, Luka Magnotta would be defined as a "deviant" by most people's standards. Those early revelations represented only the tip of the iceberg, however, as more information surfaced about the 29-year-old Canadian. His final post was an 11-minute video of him bru- tally slaying and dismembering a 33-year-old male Chinese student attending Concordia University. The video also included scenes depicting cannibalism and necrophilia. Magnotta then allegedly mailed several severed body parts to members of various branches of the Canadian government, prompting police to launch a worldwide manhunt for one of the most deviant individuals in modern history (Magnay, 2012).*

## What is Deviance?

Animal cruelty, pornography, fraud, murder, mutilation, necrophilia – not much mystery in how and why Luka Rocco Magnotta became defined as a deviant. Most deviance, however, is much less sensational and far less clear-cut. Even some of the aforementioned acts must be socially scrutinized before being defined as deviant. Take animal cruelty for example. What Magnotta did to the kittens almost certainly qualifies as animal cruelty. But other cases are not as clear-cut. For example, several years ago England outlawed the cropping of dogs' tails and ears because it was considered to be cruel and inhumane treatment. Yet despite protests from PETA and other animal rights advocates, both procedures are still routinely performed on certain breeds in the United States by licensed veterinarians who are paid to do so by loving pet owners. Pornography has always been difficult to define, prompting the US Supreme Court to refuse to set any uniform standards deferring to "local community standards" (378 U.S. 184, 84 S.Ct. 1676). Thus, while some librarians may feel compelled to black out certain parts of the anatomy from photographs in *National Geographic*, other libraries may subscribe to far more sexually explicit magazines, and a triple XXX video store might do business only a few blocks away. Fraud is a crime in most societies, but false and misleading advertising has become widely accepted as the norm, and at least one presidential candidate declared that the United States' Social Security system is nothing more than "an elaborate Ponzi scheme." Although murder, mutilation, and necro- philia are almost universally condemned, even those acts must be socially defined. Soldiers who kill the enemy during combat are not only not viewed as being non-deviant, they might receive a medal and be hailed as heroes for doing so. Mutilating dead bodies is a ghastly act, but almost anybody who has witnessed a routine autopsy could argue that the medical procedure, while perfectly legal and sometimes required, is somewhat gruesome. No known society has promoted necrophilia, but a bill was introduced in Egypt to make it legal for a husband to have sex with his wife up to six hours after her death (Paperluss, 2012). The bill was not acted upon by the Egyptian Parliament, and some even reported that it was a hoax. Nevertheless, the point is that despite the unquestioned deviance of the heinous acts performed by Magnotta, *deviance* and *deviants* are part and parcel of the society in which they occur. Defining deviance requires people to make *judgments* – judgments about what is good or bad, right or wrong, legal or illegal. These judgments are made within personal, social, cultural, and political contexts. Let's take a look at some of the ways that deviant behavior is defined and at the social processes involved in determining if something or someone is deviant.

## The absolutist position

According to baseball legend, three umpires explained the process of calling "balls" and "strikes." The first one stated, "It's simple; some's balls and some's strikes and I calls 'em as they is." The second umpire responded, "Some's balls and some's strikes and I calls 'em as I sess 'em." The third declared, "Some's balls and some's strikes, but they ain't nothin' 'til I calls 'em" (cited in Nimmo, 1978:77). Some people, like the first umpire, believe that defining deviance is simply a matter of defining what "is." From this **absolutist position**, *some things are right, others are wrong.* Some things are good, others are bad. Some things are legal, others are illegal. Some things are deviant while others are not. This dichotomous view of the world revolves around the position that there is widespread consensus (if not unanimity) in agreement as to what is and what is not acceptable social behavior. From the absolutist position, there is no ambiguity about deviance and conformity: rules are rules, and you either conform to them or deviate from them, but you cannot do both, at least not at the same time.

An obvious weakness of the absolutist view of deviance is that it assumes widespread agreement on a common set of values that guide human behavior and lead to the creation of commonly accepted standards of what people should and should not do. Perhaps in a small homogeneous society, such consensus is possible, and the absolutist position may have merit. In any large heterogeneous society, however, there are many different sets of values and consensus about what constitute deviance and conformity is much more difficult to achieve. Consequently, an alternative view to defining deviance looks more at what most people do as being commonly accepted (*conformity*) and the behavior of only a few as being *deviant*.

## The statistical anomaly view

A somewhat less rigid, more democratic, and yet still somewhat arbitrary view of deviance is the **statistical anomaly view** which *looks at patterns of behavior, and determines what are the most common behaviors in a given social circumstance and declares them as constituting the norm. Anything deviating from the statistical norm is considered deviant.* While this perspective does not directly correlate to the second umpire's version of balls and strikes, it does allow for some judgment, and/or interpretation as to what is or is not deviant. For example, when the vast majority of young people in the United States waited until they were legally married to have sex (if there was such a time), premarital sex was considered deviant. Today, when the majority of people report that they are sexually active before marriage, a virgin on his or her wedding day might be the one who is considered deviant. Such was the theme of the popular movie *The 40-year-old Virgin* – a premise considered by many Americans to be downright ridiculous. Right-handed people comprise about 90 percent of the population, thus making left-handed people statistically deviant. In some cultures, left-handed people are considered to be unlucky, and in some cases, even dangerous; in other cultures, left-handed people are viewed as being more creative and intuitive, perhaps even having mystical powers (Haviland *et al.*, 2010). Baseball managers consider left-handers (southpaws) to be better suited to be pitchers and first-basemen, while rarely seeing them as viable catchers or third-basemen. Some basketball players consider being left-handed as an advantage since most defenders expect their opponents to dribble and shoot with their right hands. Conversely, any "leftie" who has used a pair of scissors, turned a door knob, or performed any one of a thousand other routine tasks designed for right-handers, knows that while they may not be "deviant," they certainly are in a statistical minority, and must often learn to "conform" to the expectations of a right-handed world.

**Box 1.1**   In their own words

Being deviant: A left-hander in a right-handed world
Jack E. Bynum*

I was born in 1929 and not many years passed before it became clear that I was, "different" – with a personal and peculiar physical anomaly that set me apart from other children and made me deviant. I demonstrated a decided tendency to favor my left hand over my right hand in eating and playing. My parents and neighbors noticed my developing left-handedness and exchanged hopeful projections, "Oh, it is only temporary and irrelevant in younger children" or, "The child will outgrow it in time and settle into the 'normal and acceptable' right-handed behavior."

Historically, left-handed individuals have faced serious discrimination from society. For instance, during the Dark Ages, members of this highly visible minority were stigmatized as, "unlucky," "deviant," and even "sinister" – possibly possessed by evil spirits. The superstitious maxim prevailed that, "right is right and left is wrong." Consequently, up to twelve percent of the population was assigned an aberrant, marginal, social status. However, by the dawn of the twentieth century the first medical and educational research on "handedness" suggested that the cause of left-handed dominance was neurological rather than a stubborn habit or spiritual disorder. Favoring the left hand began to be perceived as probably a natural and normal condition for some individuals. In addition, evidence accumulated that attempts to force left-handed children to comply with right-handed social expectations could have serious side effects in childhood development – such as disrupting normal patterns of speech. Slowly the intolerant rejection of left-handedness softened.

During the 1930s, as I persisted in my "deviant" childhood preference for the left hand, my parents made futile efforts to train, bribe, or cajole me into using my right hand. They soon abandoned their efforts. Aside from this minor family concern, I was a happy and healthy young boy. In elementary school I loved my teachers and classmates, and was a good student – especially in reading, spelling, and basic arithmetic. But soon, my nonconforming left-handedness received broader attention. There were still some educators who insisted that the small minority of children favoring their left hand should be encouraged to change their orientation to the right hand in order to survive socially in a right-handed world. I encountered this rigid position when elementary school teachers began teaching me to write. There were no convenient ball-point pens in those days, so penmanship involved the mastery of metal pens dipped in black ink. Teaching penmanship was standardized. Young students were instructed to grasp a pen in their right hand, dip it in ink, and transcribe their printed or cursive letters and words from left to right across a writing tablet leaving their work clearly and cleanly behind the right-moving hand and pen.

On the other hand (pun intended), left-handers, in transcribing their freshly written work from left to right on the tablet, trailed the written words with their hand – ended each sentence with ink smudged across the paper and on the offending hand. Teachers were dismayed over the resulting mess. The instructors' demand for a right-handed approach to my penmanship led to a confrontation with my mother who insisted that I be taught to write and allowed to develop my own left-handed style. So we proceeded with me making a choice between two accommodations available to left-handed writers. I could learn to write with the left hand straight and extending the pen below the emerging line of script. This would likely result in a backhanded line of occasionally overlapping letters – but safely below the advancing left hand as it moved to the right. I chose the second option. I learned to write with my left forearm and hand holding the pen crooked above the emerging line of script-thus avoiding the unsightly blotting of freshly inked words. This awkward-looking writing style does not generally produce attractive script, but it enabled me to remain left-handed while becoming literate and avoiding the original, untidy, ink-blotted alternative.

That conflict over my early writing attempts prepared me for a lifetime of struggle to satisfactorily adapt my left-handedness to a right-handed world (Rutledge and Donley, 1992). I customarily sat a little sideways in classroom chairs constructed with writing surfaces on the right side. I often encountered and learned to use tools, can openers, musical instruments, camera, computer, keyboards, and other items designed and mass-produced for the large right-handed market. Even the customer courtesy pens, attached by a short, lightweight chain at my bank cashier's window, are mounted on my right side and can inconvenience or entangle a left-handed user. A right-handed hunting rifle presented special problems for me – requiring that I reach my left hand over and across the top of the gun to activate the bolt-action mechanism. Sighting down the barrel of a right-handed rifle with my left eye, and with my left cheek resting on the stock, could produce dangerous results. Hot, spent shells were ejected from the right side of the firing chamber and stung my right cheek. Despite these handicaps, I managed to become an excellent marksman. When I went off to college, my mother taught me to do simple sewing tasks such as reattaching buttons and mending socks. Then she presented me with a pair of left-handed scissors. Later, I took those basic sewing skills and special scissors with me into the military service. I still have those left-handed scissors as a fond memory of my mother's wisdom and foresight in helping me to function in a right-handed world.

I wish I could report some noteworthy left-handed accomplishment in life that ultimately overcame all social intolerance of my deviant handedness. "Lefty" Michelangelo painted his masterpiece on the Sistine Chapel ceiling. "Lefty" Joan of Arc turned military defeat into victory for France. Five out of seven recent United States Presidents defied statistical probability by being left-handed (deKay and Huffaker, 1985). But I labored in vain to turn my handicap into full acceptance. That is – except for one brief and shining moment of public appreciation for my left-handed proclivity.

It was the beginning of my sophomore year in high school. In response to a desperate search by our coach for potential athletic ability in our small school, many male students lined up for perfunctory tryouts for the football, baseball, and basketball teams. I will never forget the moment when I was handed a baseball and told to pitch it towards home plate where a large hero from the previous year's baseball team was routinely smashing the feeble student offerings over the fence. My only experience with baseball was occasionally playing backyard "catch" with my friends. So my first pitch failed to reach home plate. My second pitch nearly hit the batter. Then, to everyone's surprise, the hulking batter flailed helplessly at my next three pitches and struck out. I was the most startled of all. Amazingly, my left-handed "affliction" – translated into an unfamiliar pitching stance and awkward windup – endowed me with an erratic throwing motion and a natural sharp-breaking curve. Somehow that combination baffled enough right-handed hitters to earn a place for me among the pitchers on the High School baseball team. My left-handedness was no longer perceived as an inferior and deviant aberration, but the source of positive attention and celebration in my small community.

I have doggedly soldiered on, learning to be resourceful over the decades in accommodating my left-handedness to the never-ending challenges of a right-handed world. Eventually, I became a University professor and spent forty years in a rewarding teaching career.

---

*Jack E. Bynum, Ph.D., is Professor Emeritus of Sociology at Oklahoma State University

Do you think being left-handed constitutes deviance? What other physical statistical anomalies might be considered deviant today? What are some of the sociological problems related to viewing "difference" as "deviance?"

Statistical anomalies may not always be discredited but they do attract a certain amount of attention. Imagine a 100-piece marching band performing at halftime. Ninety-nine of the band members are all on the left foot and one poor tuba player is on the right. In this case, right is wrong, even if the tuba player is the only one who remembered the routine and is actually standing on the correct (right) foot. There is a reason why the Medal of Honor is rarely awarded. Most soldiers do not perform the heroic deeds that merit it, although heroism is expected of all who serve in combat.

Inherent weaknesses of the statistical anomaly view of deviance is that it relies simply on numbers and patterns and does not take into account the complex social processes involved in defining behavior as either deviant or conformist. It also belies the fact that the word deviant implies a negative connotation and some behavior or quality that is disvalued by a large segment of society. The definition of deviance that we will use throughout this book is the sociological perspective which views deviance in its broadest social and cultural context understanding that conformity and deviance are socially constructed concepts.

## The Sociological Perspective

The **sociological perspective** contends that *there are no universal standards for normative behavior and, consequently, no rigid definition of either deviance or conformity*. Rather, **norms** are *socially constructed guidelines that suggest appropriate behavior in certain social situations*. As we will discuss later, these norms are relative to culture, time, place, and situation, and may vary in the way they are interpreted by various actors and social audiences. From this view, sometimes referred to as the normative/relative approach, every society creates norms and uses them to evaluate, control, and sanction human behavior in various ways. Norms can be either **prescriptive norms**, *telling us what we should do*, like the informal norm of saying "excuse me" if we burp at the table, or the formal norm that requires us to pay our federal income taxes by April 15. Or, they can be **proscriptive norms**, telling us *what we should not do*, such as the informal proscription that we should not wear white after Labor Day, or the formal laws against stealing another person's property or taking another person's life. Simply put, **conformity** is *adherence to norms* and **deviance** is *the violation of norms*. Somewhat like the third umpire's position, before any act can be determined to be *deviance* or *conformity*, and before any person is identified as a *deviant* or *conformist*, somebody has to make the call. The sociological perspective of deviance points out that deviance is socially constructed and the social construction of deviance is a much more complex process than calling balls and strikes.

## The Social Construction of Deviance

The social construction of deviance begins with **values** – *shared ideas about what is socially desirable*. In every society, people create a culture based on core principles or values that rank people, behaviors, events, objects, and social arrangements in terms of desirability. These rankings help socially define what is considered to be right or wrong, good or bad, beautiful or ugly,

**Table 1.1** Perspectives on deviance.

| Perspective | Views deviance as … |
| --- | --- |
| Absolutist Perspective | Dichotomous. Behavior is good or bad, right or wrong, legal or illegal. |
| Statistical Anomaly Perspective | Majority is conformity. Rare behavior is deviant. |
| Sociological Perspective | Deviance depends on time, place, culture, act, actors, and audience. Deviance, like beauty, is in the eye of the beholder. |

What perspective is closest to your own?

moral or immoral, just or unjust, and desirable or undesirable (Thompson and Hickey, 2011). Values logically lead to the establishment of *norms*, which we have already defined as guidelines for social behavior.

## Norms, social control, and a range of tolerance

Every society creates norms to guide people's thoughts, actions, and behaviors. Additionally, societal members create social control in the form of **sanctions** as *ways of enforcing norms*. Sociologist, Emile Durkheim (1893/1964), was among the first to point out the axiomatic quality of deviance, concluding that even in a nation of "saints," some saints would be considered "less holy" than others. When people violate social expectations there is often some type of social penalty to bear. Conversely, when people conform to norms their behavior might be rewarded, or at least not punished. There are four major types of norms: folkways, mores, laws, and taboos.

### Folkways
**Folkways** are *informal rules and expectations that guide people's everyday behavior*. Literally interpreted as "ways of the people," folkways are the most common form of norms. In American society, folkways provide us with basic social etiquette and govern such things as what we eat, when we eat, and how we eat. Most Americans have few qualms about eating beef (cows), pork (pigs), fish, or chicken, but balk at the thought of eating horses, dogs, or earthworms. Nevertheless, horses, dogs, and earthworms are excellent sources of protein and are considered perfectly acceptable cuisine in some cultures. In the United States, belching at the table is considered bad manners and should be accompanied by a brief apology, while in some Asian cultures it is considered to be the ultimate compliment to the chef or host. Although informal in nature, folkways should not be interpreted to be less important than other types of norms. In fact, violate too many folkways and people will not want to interact with you.

Informal norms usually are enforced with informal sanctions. For example, belching at the table might warrant a dirty look from a dining partner, spouse, or parent. A quiet "excuse me," would more than likely absolve the offender from any further sanction. Repeated violations, however, might cause people to choose not to dine with you in the future. A child viewed as belching on purpose to irritate a parent or guests might end up being asked to leave the table, or receive a harsher penalty such as being grounded or even spanked. Gossip, ridicule, and ostracism are other forms of informal sanctions that might be applied for violation of various types of folkways.

### Mores
**Mores,** (pronounced more-ays) are *salient norms that people consider essential to the well-being of society*. Mores are closely linked to values and usually have a moral (and sometimes religious) connotation to them. Mores against lying, cheating, stealing, harming others, committing adultery, and murder have existed since ancient times. Although mores are informal, their violation is generally considered quite serious and might result in sanctions ranging from

Arthur Boyt only eats road kill for the meat in his diet. He certainly violates some commonly held folkways, but some might contend that he also is violating mores and perhaps even crossing into the area of doing something considered taboo. Do you consider Boyt's eating habits to be deviant? If so, what types of norms is he violating? *Source*: © SWNS

being fined, ridiculed, or ostracized, to being imprisoned, tortured, or put to death. Mores are considered so important for the overall social welfare that they are often codified into laws.

### Laws

**Laws** are *formal norms established and enforced by some government entity*. Laws may or may not be closely tied to societal values. For example, mores against stealing and murder reflect such firmly entrenched values related to property and life that they are almost always encoded into laws. Conversely, laws against gambling represent such conflicts in values that some states run multi-million dollar legal lotteries and other state-supported gambling enterprises while outlawing casinos or pari-mutuel wagering. Meanwhile in some jurisdictions police officers find themselves in the unenviable position of being required to arrest private citizens playing poker for money or betting on sporting events while they are participating in an office pool on the Super Bowl or NCAA March Madness. Because laws are formal norms, their violation warrants formal sanctions ranging from written warnings to fines, imprisonment, and in extreme cases, possibly death.

### Taboos

Some actions and behaviors called **taboos**, are *acts so repugnant that their commission is considered almost unthinkable*. Cannibalism (eating of human flesh), necrophilia (sex with a dead body), and incest (sex with close blood-related relatives) are among some of the taboos found in most, if not all societies. Taboos also reflect important values and because of the intense reaction they elicit, they are often reflections of all three of the other types of norms – folkways, mores, and laws. Ironically, some taboos are viewed as so despicable that lawmakers might think them so inconceivable that they fail to make them illegal. For example, in the opening vignette about Luka Rocco Magnotta, when the Canadian government filed for extradition after he was

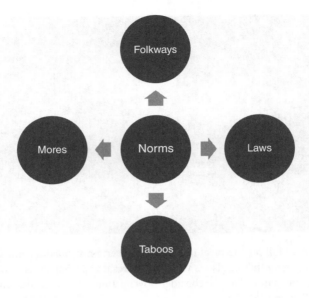

**Figure 1.1**    Four major types of norms.

arrested in Germany, the range of charges included murder, defiling a corpse, threatening the Canadian prime minister and using the mail system for delivering 'obscene, indecent, immoral or scurrilous' material (Carlson, 2012). Noticeably lacking from that list are specific charges of cannibalism, necrophilia, and mailing severed body parts as Canada had no national statutes specifically listing those unthinkable taboo offenses.

*Range of tolerance*
Although conformity to norms is expected, and often demanded, we rarely expect everybody to adhere to every single norm all the time. In fact, total rigid conformity is almost impossible. Some norms are contradictory requiring us to violate one if we attempt to conform to the other. If we should never tell a lie, but also try to never intentionally hurt somebody's feelings, then how should a husband respond when his wife asks "Do these pants make my butt look big?" Although deviance almost always elicits social control, most norms are surrounded by a **range of tolerance**, *a scope of behaviors that are considered acceptable and not considered deviant although they technically might violate a norm* (Cavan, 1961). Speed limits provide a good example of a *range of tolerance*. Even though an interstate highway may have a posted maximum speed limit of 70 miles per hour (sometimes even accompanied by a sign that says "No Tolerance"), a police officer is not likely to stop and ticket a motorist driving 71. Technically, the driver is speeding and could be issued a traffic citation, but, imagine the public relations and potential legal nightmare of doing so. Although a radar gun might be calibrated accurately enough to depict a difference of one mile per hour, very few automobile speedometers are that accurate. An officer who tickets drivers for driving one mile an hour over a 70-mile-per-hour speed limit is as likely to be considered deviant as the driver he or she ticketed. What about 72 miles per hour? Would an officer ticket a driver for that speed? Most likely not. What about 73,

74, or 75? Although each of these increments in speed are identical (one mile per hour), at some point, the speed will be viewed as excessive and not be tolerated. A driver doing 80 in a 70 mile-per-hour zone is unlikely to experience much tolerance or sympathy from a traffic officer, a judge, or even a friend or spouse. Also, other variables may enter into the equation. While driving five miles over the speed limit (75) on a 70 mile-per-hour interstate highway might be tolerated, driving 25 in a 20-miles-per-hour school zone probably would not – especially if children or a crossing guard were present. Many states now double traffic fines for speeders in work zones when workers are present, and a host of other variables such as age, race, sex, type of automobile, weather conditions, may well come into play in determining the range of tolerance for speed.

In addition to speeding, a wide range of other "deviant" behaviors are routinely tolerated, at least up to a point. Gambling was alluded to earlier and is a good example. Millions of people each year vacation in Las Vegas only to return home to states where gambling is legally prohibited. Even in many of those states, however, there are legally run state lotteries, as well as a wide range of other contests, sweepstakes, raffles, and other gambling-related activities. Almost every major newspaper prints odds and point spreads for college and professional sports, and office pools are the norm for major sporting events across the country and around the world. Ticket scalping at major sporting events is so widespread that team owners, coaches, and broadcasters openly discuss the practice. Numerous other examples abound. For example, in a society where well over half of all adults are overweight, at what point does obesity become viewed as deviant? Tattoos, once thought to be the domain of prison inmates, prostitutes, and drunken sailors, have now gone mainstream – but at what point do tattoos become excessive and perhaps viewed as extreme deviance? A certain amount of norm deviation is not only tolerated, but expected. There is a point, however, when deviance exceeds our range of tolerance, social control is warranted, and sanctions will be levied. Where that line is drawn is largely relative to culture, time, place, and situation.

## Importance of culture, time, place, and situation

Since there are no universal norms and no unanimous agreement as to what constitutes deviance and conformity, sociologists contend that it is important to analyze and evaluate human behavior within a cultural context understanding that definitions of deviance and conformity will vary relative to time, place, and situation.

### Culture
When it comes to defining deviance, no single variable is more important than **culture,** *the learned set of attitudes, values, beliefs, norms, and material goods shared by members of a society.* Consequently, it is culture that creates, defines, and validates norms in the first place. While children in the United States are being taught to eat with knives, forks, and spoons, Chinese children on the other side of the world are learning to eat with chopsticks. Women who bare their breasts in the Trobriand Islands are adhering to century-old norms while most women in the United States would never dare go topless in public. Norms vary so widely from one

culture to another that people who travel extensively often experience **culture shock** – *feelings of confusion and disorientation that occur when experiencing a different culture*. What is considered deviant in one culture may constitute conformity in another.

In a culture as diverse and heterogeneous as the United States, there are numerous **subcultures** that are *smaller cultures within a larger culture that adhere to most of the characteristics of the dominant culture, but share some set of distinctive norms that set them apart from it.* For example, the Old Order Amish is a subculture that adheres to most of the norms of American culture emphasizing honesty, hard work, and the importance of family, but rejects modern technology choosing to forego electricity in their homes and to travel by horse and buggy as opposed to driving automobiles (Hostetler, 1993). Teenagers tend to be part of a youth subculture that embraces basic adult values like freedom, independence, and individuality but expresses those values in symbolic ways that often violate norms of dress, hairstyle, and language established by their parents, schools, and other adult-run establishments. Within the youth subculture juvenile delinquents often form associations or gangs that set them even further apart from mainstream society (Thompson and Bynum, 2016). Motorcycle riders comprise a subculture and research shows that even that subculture has smaller subcultures within it consisting of one-percenters, neo-bikers, motorcyclists, women riders, and others (Thompson, 2013). Almost every major city has a large gay population that often locates in a particular area of the city where they create a *homosocial environment* replete with restaurants, shops, barbers, lawyers, doctors, real estate offices, and other businesses owned and operated by gays and lesbians who cater to the gay subculture (Thompson, *et al.*, 2016). Tattoo parlors, topless bars, adult bookstores, pawn shops, and other businesses considered outside "mainstream society" often congregate to form subcultures in certain areas of cities so that their patrons can come and go relatively unmolested by those who judge them to be deviant and disapprove of their appearance, behavior, or lifestyles.

Deviants of all types often form subcultures for their protection and so that they can be surrounded by people who share similar values and norms. Subcultures serve not only to unite and protect their members, but also help neutralize some of the negative consequences experienced by its members because of their violation of dominant cultural norms. As we explore different types of deviant behavior throughout this book we will discuss some of the deviant subcultures that exist. It is important to understand that time is also an important variable in defining deviance. The aforementioned Old Order Amish would have been much less conspicuous and judged to be conformists during the eighteenth and nineteenth centuries, but their lifestyle seems very out-of-step with today's emphasis on technology and modernity.

*Time*

Have you ever sat down with your parents and gone through old photo albums? If so, you have probably been highly amused at the hairstyles and dress styles that were popular ten, twenty, thirty, or more years ago. The first person to try any new dress style or hairstyle is almost always judged to be deviant. So is the last person to try them. Few norms seem more time-bound than those revolving around fashion and grooming. Look at portraits of America's so-called founding fathers. White powdered long wigs with ponytails, ruffled shirts, silk stockings, and buckled shoes were the norms for the time, but would be considered glaringly deviant for political leaders of today. Walk down the streets of Soho in New York City at 2.00 p.m. Go back and walk down those same streets at 2.00 a.m. and you will see what a difference time makes in what is considered normative and what is deviant.

## Place

Where things happen is extremely important. Some places can be considered deviant in and of themselves. Would you want to purchase and live in the home where Lizzie Borden slayed her parents? How about opening a child care center in what was formerly a house of ill repute? Even in "non-deviant" places, however, place becomes an important variable in evaluating the relativity of deviance and conformity. Cheering, booing, drinking beer, and yelling "kill the umpire" might be considered acceptable behavior at Yankee Stadium, but it would hardly be appropriate at a little league game. Imagine congregation members doing those things in church. Or, consider the reaction if students – or teachers – committed similar acts in class. Time and place interact in interesting ways sometimes. For example, people would not be receptive to cheering, booing, drinking beer, and shouting at Yankee Stadium during a religious crusade being held there. In that case, situation becomes an important variable.

## Situation

Would you be considered deviant if you suddenly awakened, jumped out of bed, and ran outside into the street stark naked? Before you answer, what if I added the fact that your house was on fire? Situations matter. Sleeping at home, on a train, or on an airplane is perfectly acceptable. Sleeping in class is not. Public displays of affection are generally considered deviant, and in some cases, are even illegal, yet one of the most famous photographs ever taken is that of a young sailor kissing a woman in New York City's Time Square when the end of World War II was announced. Similarly, kissing in Times Square at midnight on New Years' eve is not only acceptable, but almost mandatory.

# Importance of acts, actors, and audience

Sociologists point out that equally as important in defining deviance as culture, time, place, and situation, the *when* and *where* of deviance, are acts, actors and audiences the *what, who*, and *how* people react of deviance. Take the social context of acts for example.

## Acts

It seems obvious that a significant aspect of defining deviance resides in the act. Lying, cheating, stealing, and killing, seem inherently deviant, although as we have already pointed out, even those acts require a certain amount of scrutiny and must be put in context when judged. "Little white lies" are sometimes considered okay and even appropriate, and sometimes there is a thin line between lying and cheating and what might be interpreted as "getting a good deal." What is now referred to as "collaborative work" by two or more students was often considered "cheating" by teachers only a decade ago. Police officers, soldiers, and the state are all licensed to kill when necessary, and even everyday citizens can take another person's life in self-defense or under other legally specified circumstances. This highlights the fact that *who* commits a particular act quite often affects or determines whether it is considered conformity or deviance.

*Actors*
We have already indicated that police, soldiers, and other people in positions of authority may be allowed to do things that would be considered deviant if done by others. Sociological research also reveals that variables such as age, sex, race, and social class have tremendous impact on how people are treated and what behaviors are tolerated by them. Consider the range of tolerance for infants for example. A baby or toddler can do almost anything without suffering any consequences because, after all, they are babies and are "too young to know any better". Toddlers often reach up their mother's skirts, touch women's breasts, or punch men in the genitals without any repercussions. If a teenager or adult did the same thing, he or she would be viewed as deviant and be sanctioned in some way. Similarly, the elderly also often enjoy a very wide range of tolerance regarding norms. Old people sometimes get away with shoplifting by "forgetting" to pay for items, and elderly men in a nursing home or hospital setting may reach up and touch a female caregiver in some of the same inappropriate ways an infant might. The big difference is that the elderly male is probably very much aware of what he is doing, but knows that his behavior will be tolerated because he is "too old to know any better." There is probably no narrower range of tolerance for any age group than that of teenagers. Virtually everything that adolescents view as fun and exciting is either against the rules or illegal for them to do.

Sex is also an important variable related to norms. The United States has long held a double standard of tolerance for males and females. While "boys will be boys" has excused a lot of mischievous male behavior, the same tolerance was rarely afforded girls. For decades, if not centuries, males were allowed, if not expected and encouraged to be sexually active before marriage while women were chastised, punished, or disvalued for the same behavior. Nathaniel Hawthorne's scarlet letter was usually reserved for women.

Race plays an important role in defining deviance and conformity. The behavior of members of racial and ethnic minorities is often more highly scrutinized than that of members of the dominant racial or ethnic group. While most police departments deny the existence of racial profiling, almost any police officer will tell you that it takes place, and although "Lady Justice" the symbol for the American criminal justice system may be blindfolded, ordinary citizens, police officers, prosecutors, judges, and jurors are not.

The United States has long been associated with democracy, freedom, and equality, but from its inception, some Americans have always been more equal than others. The aforementioned variables of age, sex, and race are good examples of how categories of people have experienced differential and unequal treatment. The rights of due process, privilege of voting, signing contracts, owning property, and others have always been restricted by age, and up until the late nineteenth and early twentieth centuries were restricted by sex and race as well. Today, social class may be one of the more important variables related to life chances and life experiences. Members of the upper class tend to live longer, have better health care, and enjoy a broader range of tolerance for behavior than their counterparts in the middle and lower classes. Moreover, the upper class own and control the media, powerful forces in helping to define what and who is deviant.

# The Role of Media in Defining Deviance

On a flight to Las Vegas, one of the authors was amused when a flight attendant came over the intercom and announced as the plane landed, "remember, what happens in Vegas, stays in Vegas – and, often ends up on YouTube, Facebook, and all over the Internet and television." Today, virtually all parts of the world are linked by media that include music, newspapers, magazines, books, radio, television, motion pictures, computers, smart phones, video games, and a host of other technologies. Consequently, the audience who may be involved in defining deviance and deviants can range from as small as one or two people to as large as several million – perhaps a billion people or more. Very little deviance goes unnoticed and very few deviants remain anonymous.

How do media portrayals affect our definitions and perceptions of deviance? In one word: significantly. In the late 1970s, Michael Real (1977) pointed out that we live in a mass-mediated culture and the fact that the media, particularly television, constituted not only the "first draft of reality" for many, but the "only draft of reality" for some. Traditional mass media have always been a powerful social force in shaping values, influencing norms, and affecting people's definition of reality, and today, they along with a wide array of social media are perhaps more influential than ever. Two well-known expressions in journalism tell us: "If it bleeds, it leads;" and "If a dog bites a person, it's not news, but if a person bites a dog, it is." Consequently, we are inundated with stories about the most bizarre and sensational forms of deviance because those are the stories that sell newspapers, attract television audiences, and go "viral" on the Internet. These atypical acts of deviance reflect what Felson and Boba (2010) call the *dramatic fallacy*, or *horror–distortion sequence*, in which the media grab a horrifying story and then entertain the public with it creating misinformation, misconceptions, and a distorted view of deviant behavior. A major motivation for this sensationalism is the reliance on selling advertisements/commercials to pay the costs of printing newspapers and television programming. Can you imagine any newspaper editor, newscaster, or blogger not jumping at the opportunity to tell the story of Luka Rocco Magnotta? Book contracts and movie deals are almost certainly part of his future. Media sensationalism belies the fact, however, that most deviance is fairly mundane and often of little consequence. Moreover, media portrayals of deviance tend to reinforce the notion that we can neatly dichotomize people into categories of deviant/conformist, good/bad, right/wrong, moral/immoral, and criminal or law-abiding citizen. As sociology reminds us, however, life is not nearly that simple, and things are seldom what they seem.

## Moral entrepreneurs, moral crusades, and moral panics

Mainstream media are prominent sources for moral entrepreneurship, the promotion of moral crusades, and the creation of moral panics. Howard Becker (1963) reminds us that rules, or norms, are the products of people's efforts to define deviance and deviants. He calls these rule creators **moral entrepreneurs**: *social reformers who are not satisfied with existing rules because they believe that some type of behavior is taking place that should be controlled or eliminated.* Moral entrepreneurs often have an absolute view of right and wrong, and believe that what they view as wrong is not only deviant, but truly evil. Such strong feeling often evokes the need for a **moral crusade**, *an effort to identify wrongdoing, inform others of its existence and potentially dire consequences, and establish rules or laws to eliminate the behavior and punish the wrongdoer.* Effective moral crusades rely on the creation of **moral panic,** *the belief that the very survival of society is threatened by a particular type of deviant or deviance.* The Salem witch hunts of seventeenth century New England are a prime example, but one need not go back four centuries to witness widespread moral panics. Stanley Cohen (2011) pointed out in the early 1970s the hysteria surrounding elements of the youth subculture (most notably music) and how newspapers, magazines, and television helped create an image that music popular among youths was inspiring sex, murder, and mayhem that threatened society as we know it. This phenomenon did not begin in the 1970s, as earlier generations had been warned about the potentially dangerous effects of listing to jazz, the crooners, Elvis, the Beatles, and others that came before that time. More recently, smoking, drunk driving, violence on television, abortion, AIDS, same-sex marriage, and even the election of Barack Obama, have inspired certain members of the media to rally citizens to unite against such "obvious" threats to American civilization. Although some of these moral panics may be based on behaviors that may indeed be dangerous and potentially harmful (e.g. smoking and driving while intoxicated) their prevalence and the extent of harm caused by them has been exaggerated. Still other behaviors cited, may pose no actual threat to society at all.

## Confusing crime and deviance

Partly because of media portrayals, and sometimes just due to misunderstanding, many people equate deviance with crime. When we ask our students on the first day of class to identify some deviant behaviors, they often cite murder, rape, child molestation, theft, and other criminal activities. All of those acts are indeed examples of deviance, and these forms of deviance often dominate the attention of the media. They represent, however, only a very small segment of deviant behaviors – **crime,** or those *acts that involve the violation of formally codified norms that we have previously defined as laws.* More specifically, crimes involve only the violation of one type of laws: criminal laws. There are also a large number of *civil laws* involving contracts, and other non-criminal matters the violation of which may constitute deviance, but does not involve the commission of a crime, and rarely attract media attention. The vast majority of deviance, however, involves neither the violation of criminal nor civil laws. Rather, most deviance involves the contravention of informal folkways and mores that govern our everyday behaviors, and are the norms that are far more likely to be violated by most of us who may rarely or never commit a crime. Cheating on a spouse, lying to a teacher, dressing in opposite sex clothing, performing everyday activities in the nude, covering one's entire body and face in tattoos, abusing legally prescribed drugs, being an alcoholic, or hundreds of other norm-violating activities may be considered deviant, but they are not crimes. Consequently, it is accurate to state that *all crime is deviance,* but *not all deviance is crime.* In fact, is probably safe to say that *most deviance is not crime.* The media often confuse deviance with crime, however, and consequently, so do many consumers of the media. That is one of the reasons we challenge you to think critically about what you see, read, and hear in various forms of media. In later chapters of this book the distinctions between crime and deviance will be further explored as we study and analyze behaviors that fit into one or sometimes both of those categories.

## Equating diversity with deviance

Another source of confusion, exacerbated by the aforementioned statistical anomaly view of deviance and the focus of media attention, is the idea that being different is deviant. Up to this point, our discussion of conformity and deviance has been related to behaviors that are judged to either comply with or violate social norms. But conformity and deviance represent much broader categories, and often people are considered to be deviant, not for something they *do*, but simply for being *who or what they are*, especially if who or what they are is considered to be a bit too different. For example, while individuality and autonomy are highly valued in American society, especially if they involve unique skills or talents, persons who "go against the grain," question mainstream beliefs, or otherwise challenge the status quo, may very well be judged to be deviant and suffer the personal and social consequences that accompany that status. Media attention is often focused on the "oddball" in society, the social outcast, the person that they often lead us to believe may be dangerous simply because he or she is different.

Sometimes entire categories of people are viewed as being deviant because of their age, race, social class, sexual orientation, religious beliefs, or other physical or mental characteristics by those who are intolerant of social and cultural differences. **Prejudice** – *negative attitudes based on pre-judgments*, and **discrimination** – *negative actions toward a category of people*, are but two of the negative consequences faced by those considered to be too different from those who are judging them. These negative judgments often lead to **stereotypes** which are *static and oversimplified ideas about entire categories of people*. Nowhere are stereotypes more prevalent or powerful than in the media. Think of the way racial and ethnic minorities are often portrayed on television or in motion pictures. Although these portrayals have changed over the years, there still is a propensity for portraying minorities and those who are different in some way as villains and as threats to mainstream society.

Diversity is a social reality in large heterogeneous societies like the United States, but this fact notwithstanding, does not mean that differences are always acknowledged, understood, embraced, or even tolerated. Racism, sexism, ageism, and other forms of both institutionalized and informal prejudice, bigotry, and discrimination have been well documented in America's past and present. In smaller more homogeneous societies, being different can take an even heavier toll as the range of tolerance tends to be smaller and diversity is more likely to be defined as deviant. Conversely, in larger and more heterogeneous societies, diversity is often the norm and the range of tolerance for differentness is usually larger, especially when the positive aspects of diversity are both portrayed and promoted by various forms of media.

## Negative and Positive Results of Deviance

Violating social and cultural norms can have both negative and positive results both for society and for the deviant. Almost everybody is familiar with some of the negative consequences of deviance. After all, even though we have pointed out the differences, many people equate deviance with criminal and/or evil behavior, and think that violating norms must be inherently bad. Although that is not necessarily the case, let us first turn our attention to some of the negative consequences of deviance.

## Negative consequences of deviance

Indeed, deviance can and often does have negative consequences, some of which are fairly obvious and others that are not so apparent or well-known. Some of the negative consequences of deviance include, but are not limited to, the following (Thompson and Bynum, 2013:22–23).

*Personal harm*
Deviance often hurts people. Violence such as murder, assault, rape, robbery, abuse, and other forms of aggression results in real victims, physical injury, and sometimes even death. Deviance often takes an emotional toll as well. Consider family members of alcoholics, drug addicts, the mentally ill, or someone who has committed suicide. In its various forms, deviance can cause guilt, anguish, fear, distrust, and sometimes causes widespread panic among groups and even entire societies. The norm violator and sometimes his or her family also often experience personal harm in the form of retaliation, stigma, and ostracism.

*Threatens norms*
Any act of norm violation may call into question the validity of the norm being violated. In some cases, when one norm is questioned, others may be as well, especially if there is no discernible harm or recognized sanction. Hence, the old adage, "Give 'em an inch, and they will take a mile."

*Costs*
Deviance can be extremely expensive, both literally and figuratively. Think of the time, money, and energy spent on law enforcement, courts, probation and parole, prisons, mental institutions, drug and alcohol treatment programs, medical costs for addictions, and on and on. In addition to the financial costs, also think of the emotional and social costs when people fear one another, distrust each other, and devalue fellow members of society for who they are or what they do.

*Threatens social order.*
Deviance can be very disruptive and threaten social stability. Even isolated acts of deviance can destroy families and disrupt social order; widespread deviance can result in mobs, riots, and revolutions.

Because people are aware of the negative consequences of deviance, every society attempts to control its members' behavior to some extent. Both informal and formal sanctions are created, and efforts are made to prevent, control, and eliminate norm violating behavior, although the elimination of deviance is impossible. Although most people are well aware of the negative consequences of deviance, fewer are cognizant of the potentially positive aspects of deviance.

## Positive aspects of deviance

Despite the fact that all deviance is a result of norm violation, that does not mean that all deviance is bad, or even harmful. Emile Durkheim (1938) was among the first to point out the functional properties of deviance, a line of thinking that numerous sociologists have further developed over the years. Some of the positive aspects of deviance include (Thompson and Bynum, 2013:23–24).

### Reaffirms norms
We indicated that deviance threatens norms, but at the same time, deviance also can reaffirm norms. When the harm from deviance is apparent, people realize the need to reaffirm and perhaps even strengthen that norm to avoid future potential harm. The alcoholic reinforces the need for moderation in drinking, and the morbidly obese serve as examples for why people should eat more nutritionally sound.

### Social solidarity
It has been said that "nothing unites people like a common enemy." Deviance can unite people both on behalf of, and against, the deviant. Families sometimes come together to help an alcoholic or otherwise addicted member, and people often combine to help the mentally ill, substance abusers, or others who may be considered deviant for some reason. Conversely, people also join forces to track down and punish rapists, sex offenders, or others who threaten the safety of a neighborhood or community.

### "Safety valve"
Some people believe that small and non-threatening forms of deviance may be functional for "blowing off steam," or otherwise relieving some of the pressures of everyday life, that if left to build, might result in a larger more serious form of deviance later. Halloween, Mardi Gras, vacations in Las Vegas, and other such "time outs" from otherwise routine conformity may serve such a purpose.

### Creates jobs
We indicated that part of the tremendous costs of deviance includes the millions of dollars spent each year on law enforcement, courts, probation and parole, prisons, mental institutions, treatment programs, medical expenses for addictions, and other aspects of social control and deviance prevention. All of those areas represent college majors and career opportunities for millions of people, probably some of whom are reading this book in anticipation of someday working with deviance or deviants in some form or fashion.

### Social and cultural change
Those who forge their own path, cut through the red tape, or otherwise violate norms to make things happen often provide leadership for social and cultural change. Whether it be fads, fashions, innovations in technology, or other norm violations, social and cultural change would never come about if everybody conformed to existing norms and never tried anything new, challenging, or non-traditional.

# Summary

We began this chapter by looking at three different ways of defining deviance: the absolutist position, the statistical anomaly view, and the sociological perspective. Absolutists believe that there is a clear distinction between right and wrong, good and bad, conformity and deviance. They focus on rules believing that any behavior that violates a norm is deviance, period. Those who hold the statistical anomaly view see anything out of the ordinary or in a numerical minority as deviant. Consequently, left-handed people, members of minority religions, and geniuses all qualify as being deviant. The sociological perspective takes a much more comprehensive and complicated view of deviance and deviants leading us to understand that deviance, like most social and cultural phenomena, is socially constructed. This social construction of deviance looks at the creation of norms, social control, and a range of tolerance. Moreover, the sociological perspective emphasizes the importance of culture, time, place, and situation in defining deviance and how those definitions may vary according to the acts, actors, and audience. The sociological perspective will be the focus of understanding deviance and deviants throughout this book.

The media play an important role in defining deviance. Both traditional mass media and newer forms of social media are instrumental in shaping public attitudes about norms and behaviors and defining who is and who is not deviant. The media provide a forum for moral entrepreneurs and help to create and promote moral panics by defining so-called threats to social order and the very "moral fabric" of society. The media regularly blur the distinction between deviance and crime and often equate diversity with deviance.

Although almost everybody is familiar with many of the negative consequences of deviance – creates personal harm, threatens norms, is expensive, and threatens social order – far fewer people are aware of some of the positive aspects of deviance. Deviance can reaffirm norms, increase social solidarity, act as a safety valve, create jobs, and bring about meaningful social and cultural change.

# Outcomes Assessment

1   Define deviance from an absolutist position, from the statistical anomaly view, and from the sociological approach which focuses on the normative relativist perspective and the social construction of deviance. Explain the major distinctions among these three different approaches to defining deviance.

2   Explain how deviance is socially constructed around a range of tolerance that is relative to culture, time, place, and situation in regard to acts, actors, and a social audience.

3   Explain the role of traditional mass-media and newer forms of social media in defining deviance. What is meant by the terms moral entrepreneurs and moral panics?

4   Distinguish between crime and deviance. Define each of these terms and explain what they have in common as well as what makes them different

5   Define diversity and explain how it is different from deviance.

6   Identify and list some of the negative consequences and positive aspects of deviance.

## Key Terms and Concepts

absolutist view of deviance
conformity
crime
culture
culture shock
deviance
discrimination
folkways

laws
moral crusade
moral entrepreneurs
moral panic
mores
norms
prejudice
prescriptive norms

proscriptive norms
range of tolerance
sanctions
statistical anomaly view of
   deviance
stereotypes
subcultures
values

# 2

# Deviance and Social Identity

**Student Learning Outcomes**

After reading this chapter students will be able to:

1   Explain the process of becoming deviant.
2   Define master status and explain how deviance can become a master status.
3   Distinguish between primary and secondary deviance, and how deviants can get caught up in role engulfment.
4   Define stigma and explain the various types of stigma.
5   Explain how deviants attempt to manage a spoiled identity.
6   Discuss how the media help create, promote, and sustain deviant identities.

*In Ms Jones' kindergarten class, each student has a calendar with his or her name on it posted on the wall. At the end of each day, Ms. Jones puts either a "smiley" face ☺ if the student has been "good" or conforming, a "neutral" face ☺ if the student conformed most of the time, but perhaps violated a rule or two, or a "frowny" face ☹ , if the student misbehaved. At the end of each week, five smiley faces earns some type of reward — perhaps a few more minutes of recess, a cookie or other tasty snack, or a small prize. Even one neutral face negates the reward, but as long as there are more smiley than neutral faces, the student had a "good" week. Conversely, only one frowny face during the week warrants a small penalty — perhaps a minute or two less recess, maybe staying inside when the other children go out to play, or perhaps not getting to participate in one of the games played in class. More than one frowny*

*Deviance & Deviants: A Sociological Approach*, First Edition. William E. Thompson and Jennifer C. Gibbs.
© 2017 John Wiley & Sons, Inc. Published 2017 by John Wiley & Sons, Inc.
Companion website: www.wiley.com/go/thompson

*face can elicit a missed recess and a note being sent home to parents, and any week that ends with more frowny than smiley faces results in a parent–teacher conference. Not surprisingly, only a few weeks into the school year, Ms. Jones, and the entire kindergarten class for that matter, can readily anticipate who will earn all "smiley" faces and whose parents will be making visits to school. The "good" students and "bad" students have been identified. A few little five-year-olds are well on the path to becoming deviant.*

## Becoming Deviant

As we discovered in Chapter 1, the concepts of deviance and conformity are far more complex than they seem at first glance. A myriad of social variables come into play when determining what norms are in place, whether a norm has been violated, and how members of society will interpret that norm violation. Consequently, becoming deviant is a *process*, not an *act*. In Chapter 1 we looked at how members of society go about determining what constitutes deviance; in this chapter we focus on how people *become* deviant.

If we were somehow able to keep some type of giant ledger sheet for each individual in society, placing a smiley face on the "Conformity" page for every time he or she conformed to a social norm and a frowny face on the "Deviance" page for every single time he or she violated one, almost everybody in the world would have far more smiley faces than frowny faces. Even the most deviant of deviants tend to conform to more norms than they violate. But, what if we applied Ms. Jones' score card by creating a huge calendar for each individual, awarding a smiley face only on the days he or she went all day long without violating a single norm, and a frowny face on the days when he or she misbehaved in any minor or major way? How many people do you think would end the week with all smiley faces? How would your calendar look? Probably most of us would be identified as deviant. So what is a deviant? And how do we become one?

The answers to these questions are inherently social in nature. As a result, in order to understand the social processes involved in becoming deviant we must place deviance within a sociological context.

## Deviance as a Status

Being deviant is a social **status**, *a relative position in society that becomes part of our social identity.* Deviance can be either an **ascribed status**, *assigned to us by others through no effort on our part,* such as our sex, race, ethnicity, initial social class, or some other inherited or innate characteristic – such as being born deaf or blind. Or, deviance can be an **achieved status**, *based on something an individual does to earn it,* such as being a high school dropout, a liar, a cheater, an abusive parent, a promiscuous teacher, or a criminal. Each individual in society holds a wide array of statuses, what sociologists call a **status set**, that include *a combination of all of a person's different statuses.* Our status set, to a large extent, determines who we are, as our statuses are a major source of our identities. Most people's status sets include what could be considered both conforming and deviant statuses. Among the Queen of England's status set are Queen and female, both of which are ascribed statuses, and neither of which would ordinarily be

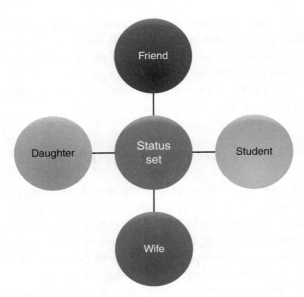

**Figure 2.1**    Status set. What are the statuses in your status set? Which are ascribed? Which are achieved?

considered deviant. Yet, given the fact that the British monarchy is patriarchal, the fact that the Queen is on the throne is somewhat deviant in itself. If she had either an older or younger male sibling, he would be the King of England and his wife would be the Queen. The current queen would be some type of duchess. The Queen also holds the achieved statuses of being a wife and a mother – neither of which is considered deviant. The Queen no doubt holds a myriad of other statuses, many of which most people are unaware, and it is possible that even she may not be aware of some of them. If any of those statuses are deviant they are yet to have been made public, something that in today's world of media awareness almost certainly would have happened.

More often than not, deviance is an achieved status as a deviant usually has committed some act that violated a norm, earning him or her the deviant status. Murderer, rapist, robber, and burglar are but a few examples of achieved deviant statuses, as are liar, cheater, alcoholic, drug addict, habitual gambler, and philanderer. Some types of deviance can be ascribed, however, such as being born into a religious cult, or being a member of a racial or ethnic group that is considered deviant by the dominant group. And, as we saw in Chapter 1, even the harmless physical anomaly of being left-handed can be considered deviant as described in Box 1.1, or at least until a baseball team needs a pitcher to face right-handed hitters. As we will see in Chapter 6, there is some controversy as to whether homosexuality is an ascribed deviant status or an achieved one, not to mention the debate over whether it should even be considered as deviant at all.

## Deviance as a master status

All statuses in a person's status set are not considered equal. For example, in the United States, a major source of an adult's identity is connected to his or her occupation or profession. In other words, to some extent, *what we do* is *who we are*. Often, when two strangers meet, after the exchange of names and initial pleasantries, one of the first questions asked is, "What do you do?" Sometimes the question is unnecessary, as many adults include that information in their introduction. For example, "Hello, I'm Fred Smith, I'm an orderly at the city hospital." Or if some third party is making the introductions, the individuals' jobs are often included as part of their identity. "Sam, I'd like you to meet Mary Jones, she is a professor of sociology at the university." When two college students meet or are introduced for the first time, the scenario is quite similar with the question, "What do you do?" most often being replaced with, "What is your major?" In essence, the question is the same, in that the person is essentially asking, "What are you *going to do* after you graduate from college?"

*When one status somewhat overpowers or supersedes other statuses in a person's status set,* it becomes that individual's **master status**. No doubt, Queen is the master status of the aforementioned Queen of England. Similarly, Barack Obama is a male, a husband, and a father, but since November of 2008, he will forever be known as President of the United States – something that would have been true even if he had not been re-elected in 2012. In fact, the status of president is so overpowering of other statuses that long after presidents have left office, they are still addressed as "Mr. President." When George Herbert Walker Bush visits his son, George W. Bush, we can only wonder if they greet each other with, "Hello, Mr. President." More importantly, once a master status is established, virtually everything that individual does from that point on is interpreted in reference to that status. For example, when President Obama is shown on television playing a game of pick-up basketball in shorts, tank top, and tennis shoes, some people question if that is appropriate behavior and attire for a president. When the elder president Bush parachuted from an airplane on his 80th birthday, many people wondered aloud if that was an appropriate thing for a president or an eighty-year-old to do. He provided his answer to that question when he repeated the feat on his 83rd birthday.

Do not be misled in thinking that master statuses are always positive or that they are always associated with prestigious occupations or positions. When a person is labeled as deviant, that status often supersedes all other statuses the person holds, even previous master statuses. Take for example the case of Orenthal James Simpson. After the 1968 college football season, O.J. "the Juice" Simpson's master status was that of Heisman Trophy winner and one of the greatest running backs in NCAA history. Shortly thereafter, he became known as one of the greatest running backs in the National Football League (NFL), and later, his master status became that of NFL "Hall of Famer." He had brief stints as sports announcer and as an actor in a few movies, but on June 17, 1994 after millions of Americans watched O.J.'s white Ford Bronco being chased by the police through the streets of Los Angeles, Simpson's master status changed dramatically. Depending on one's perspective, O.J. Simpson will probably forever be known either as the man who got away with brutally murdering his ex-wife Nicole and her friend Ron Goldman, or as the man who was framed by the L.A. police, but beat all odds and was found not guilty despite the overwhelming evidence pointing toward his guilt. A few years later, when Simpson was convicted on some unrelated criminal charges and sentenced to prison, his deviant master status was publicly and permanently confirmed.

Similarly, the late coach Joe "JoePa" Paterno held the master status of head coach of the Penn State Nittany Lions from 1966–2011. His fame was legendary, leading the university to erect a bronze statue in his honor in front of the university stadium – something usually reserved for very few if any football coaches, and then, usually only after their death. Paterno's celebrated coaching career ended in shame, however, in 2011 when he was dismissed from the university as a result of being linked to a child sex abuse scandal involving one of his long-time assistant coaches. Shortly thereafter, the Paterno statue was removed from the campus, and despite his reputation as one of the greatest college football coaches of all time, "JoePa's" master status was forever altered in the minds of millions of people. Deviance has a way of doing that to people.

We discussed how being President of the United States is such a compelling master status, yet there are at least two modern-day examples where the master status of president was trumped by being negatively labeled as deviant. Richard Milhous Nixon was elected the 37th president of the United States in 1968, and re-elected in a landslide victory in 1972. Previously a member of the US House of Representatives and the US Senate, and formerly a vice-president of the United States, Nixon's master status as President of the United States seemed unshakeable. Yet, only two short years after one of the most lopsided re-election margins in US history, as a result of the Watergate scandal, Nixon became the first US President to resign in disgrace in order to avoid impeachment proceedings and almost certain removal from office. Similarly, yet remarkably different, William Jefferson Clinton may be simultaneously one of the most beloved and hated of American presidents. Inaugurated at age 46, Clinton was the third youngest US president to take office, and almost certainly one of the most popular and polarizing figures in modern history. A member of Phi Beta Kappa and a former Rhodes Scholar, Clinton was most known for his good looks, boyish smile, and charismatic personality. Then, after a scandal involving a White House intern became public, Clinton became only the second president in American history to be impeached, although not convicted and removed from office – a deviant status that could easily have been his master status and permanent legacy. That was not to be the case, however. Clinton served out the remainder of his second term with the Congressional Budget Office reporting record budget surpluses, and he left office with the highest approval rating of any American president since World War II (Gallup, 2012). After leaving office, Bill Clinton became one of the most sought after and highest paid public speakers in America, and he established the Clinton Foundation whose philanthropic and humanitarian work helped keep him in the positive public spotlight. Clinton was selected twice as *Time* magazine's Person of the Year, in 1993 and again in 1997. The former president was actively engaged in both of President Obama's presidential campaigns, and a Pew Research Poll showed that many viewers contended that his speech was the highlight of the 2012 Democratic National Convention (Edwards-Levy, 2012).

Despite the Clinton example to the contrary, deviance as a master status often alters a person's identity to the point that all of his or her subsequent actions become interpreted in light of the deviant status. Even actions committed prior to the known deviance may be reinterpreted retrospectively in order to fit the new deviant identity. Not only will we probably never trust the word of a known liar or cheater in the future, but we may very well go back and reinterpret previous interactions with them wondering if perhaps they had lied to us or cheated us at other times without our knowledge. Olympians have been stripped of medals long after they won them, sports heroes have been denied hall of fame honors after their careers ended, and men and women have divorced seemingly devoted spouses for indiscretions they may have committed long before the pair was married. In 2013, Lance Armstrong went on television with Oprah Winfrey and confessed to using banned substances which led to his being stripped of his record-breaking seven Tour de France victories, and in 2014 a series of domestic assault charges among a few professional football players inundated the media, and almost overnight turned some popular heroes into disgusting high-profile deviants in the eyes of the general public.

## Primary and secondary deviance

Even though deviance often becomes a person's master status, it does not always alter the way that an individual views himself or herself. Some people have the ability to participate in deviant acts, yet not perceive themselves as being deviant. Sociologists call this **primary deviance**, *a situation in which a person violates norms, but does not internalize the self-concept of being deviant* (Lemert, 1951). Primary deviance is not limited to the first time a person violates a norm, as norm violation could be part of people's routine, yet they do not consider themselves to be deviant. For example, every year, thousands (perhaps millions?) of Americans fudge on their income tax returns, failing to report earned income or taking illicit deductions, all the while considering themselves to be decent, law-abiding citizens. Probably some of the students reading this book have mowed lawns, babysat, or received tips as a waiter or waitress, and not reported those monies as earned income. Although the amounts may seem trivial, technically, the norm violation is the same as if an individual was failing to report millions of dollars. Furthermore, if the seemingly trivial amounts are added up, they may indeed amount to millions or possibly even billions of dollars (Venkatesh, 2009; Wiegand, 1992).

Research indicates that student cheating has increased over the years, with more and more students indicating that they see nothing wrong with it (Perez-Pena, 2012). Box 2.1 illustrates how one student rationalizes cheating in his own words, and perceives himself to be an "honest person" and a "good student."

In many cases, however, when people violate norms, their concept of self is altered which results in **secondary deviance** *causing them to internalize a deviant identity* (Lemert, 1951). Sometimes even the first act of deviance results in the altering of self-concept. For example, if a husband flies into a jealous rage and murders his wife, it is highly unlikely that he is ever going to think of himself as a good and loving husband again. Most certainly, the rest of society will not see him as such. In less dramatic cases, a similar altering of self-concept can take place and a deviant identity can be internalized. For example, the Petrified Forest National Park in Arizona posts signs everywhere indicating that removing any of the petrified wood or other fossils is illegal. Inside the park's museum is an exhibit that features returned fossils along with hand-written notes from thieves confessing (usually anonymously) that they stole relics from the park and later felt so guilty about their deviant behavior that they felt compelled to return them in order to clear their conscience and restore their non-deviant identity.

Although students who cheat on homework or an exam may be able to rationalize their dishonesty and not accept a deviant identity, that probably would not be the case with a student who was expelled from school and publicly humiliated. Take for example a cadet at one of the military academies who violates the academic honor code. This student not only would be confronted by the instructor and the administration of the school, but most likely would also be featured in major newspapers and online, not only being labeled as a cheater in school, but also as sacrificing his or her military career and disgracing a branch of the United States

**Box 2.1    In their own words**

## Primary deviance: Student cheating*

Sure I've cheated. Everybody has. I don't make it a habit, but sometimes it's necessary in order to stay competitive. It's kind of like in the NFL or in major league baseball, or something. If everybody is taking steroids, and you're not, it doesn't matter how great an athlete you are, you don't stand a chance. Sometimes you have to cheat just to make things fair.

My dad is an attorney and my mom is a high school English teacher, and both of them have always taught me to be honest, not to lie, cheat, or steal. And I've learned that since I was a child. I believe in those things, and think I am a very moral and decent person. But at the same time, I've always felt a lot of pressure to excel, especially in school. For as long as I can remember, my dad has told me how important it is to be the best, to achieve, to win. He says that he missed the boat in high school because even though he was really smart, he didn't really know how to "play the game." He felt like if he had sucked up a little more to some of his teachers, that he probably could have been valedictorian, or at least near the very top of his class. As it was, even though he was smart and made good grades, he didn't get any scholarships. He had to work part-time to help pay for school, and he thought that made his grades suffer in college. As a result, he didn't get into the law school that he really wanted to. He had to settle for a less prestigious school, and he thinks that his career has suffered because of that. Don't get me wrong. He never told me to cheat, in fact, just the opposite. He always tells me how important it is to be honest. But just the same, he puts on the pressure. Be the best, get straight As … over achieve.

I'm pretty smart and I've always made really good grades. I wasn't the valedictorian, but I made almost all As in high school and graduated like fourth or fifth in my class of about 300. I received a couple of pretty good scholarships and, with help from my parents, I don't have to work while I'm in school. I've earned my good grades and most of the time I do all of my own work. But sure, a few times in high school I copied some friend's homework or something like that. Sometimes I let other people copy off me. It really isn't that big of a deal – especially in high school. In college, I've done almost all of my own work. My parents would die if I ever got caught cheating, and I wouldn't take the chance of like taking in a cheat-sheet, or writing something on my hand, or something stupid like that. Still, I've copied a few paragraphs out of a research paper, or taken some stuff directly offline without citing it. I really don't think of that as cheating. Everybody does it, and it's no big deal. I guess the worst thing I've done is one time I wasn't prepared for a test, so I skipped the class and told the professor I was sick. My roommate went and took the test and then came back and told me all the questions on it that he could remember. That helped a lot. I still had to study, but at least I knew what most of the questions would be. I went in the next day and took the test and aced it. The professor asked me if I had talked to anybody in the class about the test, and I said no. He knows I'm an A student and didn't really question it. He gave me the same test as the rest of the class, and it was really easy. I hadn't wasted a lot of time studying stuff that wasn't on the test. But, I probably would have made an A anyway with the extra day of studying. I don't think that makes me a bad person, or even a cheater. I'm an honest person and a good student.

---

*This interview involved a 20-year-old male honor student at a medium-sized regional state university.

How do the comments of this student reflect primary deviance? If this student had been caught cheating, given a failing grade and expelled from school, do you think he would still view himself as "an honest person and a good student?"

military. Such a deviant label would be difficult if not impossible to avoid internalizing. At the very least, it would damage chances of transferring to another university and would not make for pleasant conversation at a job interview when the prospective employer would almost certainly ask, "Why did you leave the military academy?"

## Deviant career

When people internalize a deviant identity, they are more likely to become involved in what sociologists call a **deviant career**, or *a progression through various stages of deviance from novice to fully established deviant*. Howard Becker (1963) described this process as it related to marijuana smokers, who first must be introduced to the drug, then be taught how to smoke it as well as to identify what effects they should feel during and after smoking it, and finally, how they adopt an identity as a marijuana smoker fully capable of introducing the drug to others and socializing them in the same way they were taught to use the drug. Because there is little or no pharmacological basis for the idea that marijuana is a "gateway drug" that leads to the use of other harder and more dangerous drugs, a better explanation of why some marijuana users may go on to use other drugs may be that once people experiment with marijuana and become experienced at using the drug, they may then view themselves as being part of the "drug scene." Considering the drug scene includes a wide array of other illegal drugs, the person who has already adopted a deviant identity, may be more willing and more likely to experiment with other drugs as part of developing a deviant career. As with legitimate careers, deviant careers often involve an evolutionary process that leads to a person *becoming* what they do. College professors usually proceed through stages of career development that include starting out as a graduate teaching assistant, and perhaps being a part-time adjunct, before becoming an untenured assistant professor, a tenured associate professor, and eventually a tenured full-professor. Concurrently, it is not unusual for his or her sense of identity to evolve from that of "I am a graduate student who teaches at the university" to "I am a college professor." The new status becomes so ingrained in his or her sense of identity that long after retiring from college teaching, like former presidents, many of them still refer to themselves as professors, or at least retired professors. There is even a rank beyond full professor for those who have retired: Professor Emeritus.

Many deviants follow a similar career path moving from experimenters to new initiates into extensive participation in a deviant subculture to perhaps tapering off their deviant behavior later in life. Nevertheless, the deviant status may remain. Take, for example, the first time petty criminal who may be placed on probation, but after repeated offenses ends up doing time in prison. As a "newbie" in prison, he or she may undergo much hazing and perhaps brutality, but the new inmate also may be mentored by more experienced convicts on how to survive a stint in prison. After a while, the new initiate becomes a seasoned veteran, and may become the mentor for younger and less experienced inmates. After a few releases and returns to prison, ex-cons may decide to "turn their lives around," take advantage of some of the counseling and training programs in prison, and eventually be released never to commit a crime. Nevertheless, the former prisoner's identity (master status) has only shifted from "convict" to "ex-con," and to some extent, even in "retirement," this deviant identity and deviant career persists.

## Deviance as a Role

We have established that being deviant is a status. Consequently, similar to any other status, it is accompanied by a **role**, *a set of expectations that are associated with that particular status*. If our status defines *who we are*, our role tells us *what we do*. Using the analogy of theater, we can think of the status of deviant as being the part for which we are cast and the role of deviance as the way we play the part. For example, we expect the person with the status "student" to fulfill certain roles: attend class, take notes, complete term papers, take exams, and do other things associated with being a student. Similarly, we expect the person who holds "professor" status to attend every class, lecture, follow the assigned syllabus, return papers and exams on time, and more. Just as we expect college professors, police officers, nurses, carpenters, and plumbers to look a certain way, dress a certain way, and behave a certain way so too is the case with deviants. When Jeffrey Dahmer, a tall, blonde, blue-eyed, "boy next door" type dressed in a suit entered the courtroom, many Americans could not believe that he could possibly be the deviant who had lured gay men back to his residence, killed them, had sex with their corpses, and then mutilated their bodies, froze some of their body parts, and later cooked them for a meal. Conversely, when Charles Manson was led into the courtroom in handcuffs with his scraggly beard, disheveled hair, and the outline of a swastika carved in his forehead with a jailhouse spoon, very few spectators doubted that he was capable of being the "mastermind" behind the Tate and LaBianca murders. Just as individuals occupy more than one status and therefore have a role set, people also must play a multitude of roles as part of their **role set,** the *different roles that accompany each of their statuses.*

### Role-taking, role embracement, role merger, and role engulfment

It should be obvious at this point that becoming a deviant involves more than simply committing a deviant act. **Role-taking** is *the process of adopting and fulfilling the expectations associated with a particular status*. For example, as we will see in Chapter 6, becoming a homosexual involves far more than merely committing a homosexual act and, in Chapter 7, that being an alcoholic involves far more than simply consuming liquor. When people in a particular status fulfill the role expectations associated with it, they are said to embrace the role. **Role embracement** occurs *when a person's sense of identity is influenced by the role*. Embracement of a deviant role invariably leads to secondary deviance as the individual's sense of identity is altered to be that of a deviant. Even though the deviant may embrace the deviant role, however, that does not mean that they cannot also embrace a variety of other roles in their repertoire. For example, Hollywood movies and even some research would lead us to believe that while the Godfather of an organized crime family clearly embraces that deviant role, he may also see himself as a good husband, father, and business person who adheres to a strong code of ethics, and always puts his family first.

Deeper commitment to a deviant role may lead to **role merger** in which *the individual becomes the role*. This is more indicative of the career deviant described earlier and is an important step in the process of becoming deviant. For example, nudity is part of almost every individual's daily life. Babies are born naked and little children have no innate modesty or shame about being nude. They certainly do not associate nudity with sexuality. Through the process of socialization, however, children soon learn that they should not expose certain body parts, except in private (in fact many of them refer to their genitals as their "privates"). Some people might decide that they enjoy the freedom of sleeping in the nude, and perhaps decide to practice nudity in the privacy of their own homes behind drawn shades and closed doors. If they decide that on a vacation it might be enjoyable to visit a nudist camp, then they are beginning to embrace the role of nudist and probably starting to view themselves as at least a part-time nudist. If their visit to a nudist camp turns out to be something they think they would enjoy as a lifestyle, then they probably will move from role embracement to role merger, declaring at some point: "I am a nudist."

What happens when a person becomes so absorbed in a role that it somewhat overwhelms them? Sociologists call this phenomenon **role engulfment**, *a situation in which a role becomes such an important part of a person's identity that it supersedes all other roles*. Just as deviance often becomes a person's *master status*, playing the part of a deviant often becomes a *master role*. Role engulfment often accompanies a master status, because once a person has been identified as a deviant, all of his or her subsequent behavior may be evaluated in terms of a deviant identity (Schur, 1971). A middle-aged male who volunteers to be a scout master or little league baseball coach may be viewed by friends and neighbors as an altruistic person willing to give up some of his personal time and energy to help others, especially if he has a son involved in those activities. If that same middle-aged man had been convicted of taking indecent liberties with a minor, however, his interest in young boys involved in scouting and little league would probably be interpreted quite differently. More importantly, the middle-aged man himself might view his interest in scouting and little league not as altruism, but reflective of his deviant attraction to young boys.

Role embracement, role merger, and role engulfment are not only linked to deviant roles. For example, most adults in the United States embrace both their familial and occupational roles, readily identifying themselves as wives, husbands, mothers, fathers, butchers, bakers, and candlestick makers. Being a parent and a medical doctor are not mutually exclusive and most people can simultaneously fulfill and identify with both their familial and occupational roles with little difficulty. Yet, in some cases, role embracement can evolve into role merger and role engulfment, permanently altering a person's identity and overpowering all of their other role expectations. Professional athletes, entertainers, and political leaders quite often get caught up in their celebrity status and role much to the detriment of all of their other status and role responsibilities. Children of hall of fame athletes, movie stars, ex-presidents, and other prominent celebrities often indicate that their parents were so busy giving to the team, the public, their fans, and other constituencies, that they had little time left for parenting. Consequently, even embracement and engulfment associated with positive roles can lead to a deviant status. As the 1981 biographical film *Mommy Dearest* portrayed, while Joan Crawford may have been one of the greatest actresses in American history, her parenting skills would not win any awards.

### Role distance: The deviant deviant

Can a person occupy a deviant status, be thrust into a deviant role, and yet not necessarily internalize a deviant identity or embrace the deviant role? The answer is yes, but it is not an easy accomplishment. **Role distance** occurs *when people play a role but remain detached from it in order to avoid any negative aspects associated with the role.* Erving Goffman (1961) used as an example, adults riding a merry-go-round with their children. Because their status as an adult might be threatened if they appeared to enjoy the ride, they often express their detachment by yawning or looking bored, indicating that they are really only there to fulfill their parenting role. Because being deviant involves both occupying a social status and performing a social role, people generally expect deviants to act in certain ways. These expectations may vary widely based on the nature of both the deviant and the deviance, but in most cases, people expect deviants to confess their deviance, be somewhat remorseful, and to make some type of conciliatory gesture of renewed commitment to conformity. For example, juries tend to be much more lenient toward criminals who have made confessions, seem genuinely regretful, and ready to make amends for their wrongdoing than they do the defendant who belligerently contends that he or she is innocent, shows absolutely no contrition, and is obviously unrepentant (Reid, 2011). Think over the past few years how many powerful public figures have appeared before the media to confess their infidelity, apologize to their spouse and constituents for violating their trust, and promise to be a better person in the future.

As alluded to earlier in the case of Jeffrey Dahmer, when deviants do not appear to "fit" public perceptions of a deviant, there is some confusion and the person's deviant status may be questioned. Conversely, if they fulfill the deviant role expectations, their deviant status is confirmed and, in that sense, they become a deviant who conforms to our expectations of deviance. But the deviant deviant is another situation altogether. What if the death row inmate who loudly proclaims innocence is truly innocent? What if the accused child molester was really only altruistically helping children? More often than not, deviants who refuse to accept and, at least to some extent, embrace their deviance are very problematic for the rest of society. At the very least, regardless of how they play it, deviants, and even suspected deviants are very likely to experience social stigma.

## Deviance, Deviants, and Stigma

Because deviants have questioned the values and violated the norms of society, not only is their behavior devalued and discredited, but also so are they, hence the title of this book: *Deviance and Deviants.* Committing deviance changes a person's **social identity** – *the way he or she is perceived by others,* making him or her a deviant and the potential subject of ridicule, disgrace, and dishonor. In that sense, the deviant is stigmatized, often experiencing shame and humiliation. **Stigma** is usually defined as *any attribute that discredits an individual from full social acceptance* (Goffman, 1963). Deviants experience stigma in a variety of ways. Informally, they may become the objects of gossip, humor, ridicule, hazing, bullying, or ostracism. Formally, they might be fined, imprisoned, exiled, or in severe cases, even put to death.

One of the most comprehensive sociological analyses of stigma can be found in the work of Erving Goffman (1963). He divided stigma into three types:

1  *Abominations of the body* – Physical aberrations that might include scars, birthmarks, missing limbs, blindness, baldness, tattoos, obesity, or various other potentially stigmatizing bodily attributes.
2  *Blemishes of character* – Perceived personality or behavioral traits such as lying, cheating, dishonesty, infidelity, or mental disorders.
3  *Tribal stigma* – being a member of a race, nationality, ethnic group, or religion that can discredit both the individual and his or her family members (Goffman, 1963: 4).

According to Goffman (1963) people with stigmatizing attributes generally fall into one of two categories. Either people know about the stigmatizing characteristic(s) and the individual is identified as being deviant and therefore is *discredited*. Or, people do not know about the potentially stigmatizing attribute(s), so the person is not yet labeled as deviant, but is *discreditable* – always running the risk of the potential defect being discovered.

How does a discreditable person become a discredited deviant? Often because of **stigma symbols** – *identifying marks, or characteristics that provide hidden social information* – such as scars on the wrist that might reveal an attempted suicide, track marks on the arm that might suggest illegal drug usage, or tattoos that identify criminal gang members. Another way that the discreditable become discredited is by bits and pieces of information leaking out until the deviant is either "outed," or decides it is best to reveal his or her deviance before others learn of it. Whether already discredited, or potentially discredited, deviants and potentially stigmatized individuals usually try to alleviate some of the negative social sanctions that accompany a deviant status.

## Managing a Spoiled Identity

Once identified as deviant, a person's social identity is at least temporarily harmed, and sometimes permanently destroyed. One of the ways that deviants attempt to overcome this problem is through various techniques of information control. One of the most common techniques for controlling information is **passing**, or *attempting to conceal the potentially stigmatizing attribute from others so that the person is not identified as being deviant*. Although passing puts a deviant in a situation of being discreditable, if their stigmatizing attribute is not highly visible or obtrusive, they may be able to pass without people noticing it. For years in the antebellum south, many light-skinned African-Americans passed for white to avoid the widespread racial prejudice and discrimination that not only was common social and cultural practice, but also legally sanctioned. Similarly, for decades closeted homosexuals hid their sexual orientation from family members, employers, and others to avoid the social stigma associated with homosexuality and the homosexual lifestyle. During the height of Nazi Germany, millions of Jews suffered imprisonment, torture, and death, while thousands of others escaped those indignities by passing as Gentiles. Laud Humphreys (1970) discovered in his research that one of the ways that deviants pass for being non-deviant is by donning a "breastplate of righteousness," openly condemning the very stigmatizing behavior or trait that threatens their conformist identity.

Another technique of information control is to divide the social world into two categories: those who know and those who do not know about the deviance. Cheating spouses may confide in a close friend, nudists may only practice nudism around other nudists, marijuana smokers only partake alone or with others who partake of the drug, and college professors with tattoos may wear long sleeved shirts to cover their deviance, only revealing their tattoos to close friends and family members. Often, one of the correlates of having this "inside knowledge" is the expectation to help the covert deviant remain undetected. Deviant subcultures often help individuals to hide their deviance by providing a social sanctuary where they can openly practice their deviance among others who share their values and behaviors, while hiding their stigmatizing attribute from those who disapprove.

Passing and dividing the social world are risky endeavors and pose a potential threat, however, in that an individual never knows when the potentially stigmatizing attribute might be discovered. Numerous politicians have "passed" as loving husbands and family men only to have one or more mistresses surface during a critical phase of a campaign. Reaching across the table to accept the butter plate could expose hidden scars on the wrist from a suicide attempt, and a sudden gust of wind could send even the best toupee flying across the street. In order to prevent such a social catastrophe, some deviants choose to disclose their stigmatizing attribute in order to control the timing and the amount of information that is released to others. This could involve *partial disclosure*, where an individual divulges only some of the potentially stigmatizing information: "Honey, before we get married, I think you should know that I am not a virgin," to *full disclosure*, where an individual reveals everything, "Honey, before we get married, I think you should know that I used to be a prostitute." Regardless of the level of disclosure, the deviant has the opportunity to frame the release of information, put it into a more favorable context, and somewhat control the definition of the situation, or at least get his or her version of the story out first. In a society of twenty-four hour news coverage, reality television, YouTube, smartphones, and hidden cameras, however, covert deviants always face the prospect of having their stigmatizing attribute revealed at the most inopportune time and in the most unflattering and life shattering ways.

## Deviance, Identity, and The Media

There is no place on earth or in cyberspace where deviance is simultaneously more celebrated and castigated than in the media. In today's media-saturated world, sudden disclosure of deviance can be transmitted to a worldwide audience in nanoseconds. Reputations can be made and careers as well as lives can be destroyed in less than one twenty-four hour news cycle. As we noted in Chapter 1, the media thrive on sensationalism, and deviance provides some of the most extraordinary and titillating stories available. The media, especially television and various forms of social media, have unprecedented ability to create instant cultural heroes and/or social villains.

When sudden deviance erupts in the form of mass shootings, high-speed car chases, or the taking of hostages, many so-called first responders such as police officers, firefighters, and medical personnel find that they must navigate through a crowd of media people who have somehow beat them to the scene. During high profile crimes and high-speed car chases, some police departments have chosen not to put police helicopters in the air in order to avoid possible collisions with a bevy of television news and traffic helicopters that are quick to arrive on the scene and are often equipped with better cameras and tracking equipment than routinely available to law enforcement. The competitive zeal to air high-speed car chases or to be first on the scene to record live crimes and other deviance can sometimes provide deviant scenarios of their own, as in the case of a carjacker who committed suicide on a Fox News live broadcast (Goldman, 2012). Despite widespread criticism from other media outlets and a publicly broadcast apology for airing the gruesome event, ratings for such dramatic portrayals of deviance remain quite high and the viewing public's appetite for them seems to be virtually insatiable (Kerbel, 2000). Today, news media are not only competing with each other, but also with average citizens who, equipped with smartphones and other forms of social media, may beat even the most efficient news crews to the scene and broadcast photos, video, and other information before it makes the institutionalized media outlets.

The media also play an important role in the process of defining deviance as well as assigning and reinforcing deviant identities. Deviant role models abound in the media and research indicates that media have powerful influence on shaping the way people view reality and how they perceive others (Alexander and Hanson, 2013; Real, 1977). Consequently, media can have a powerful influence over a person's social identity. For example, in the case of O.J. Simpson cited earlier in this chapter, the media played a powerful role in defining him first as a national sports hero, later as a television and movie celebrity, and ultimately as a convicted felon. Since most Americans and other media consumers around the world have never met or interacted with O.J. Simpson, clearly their perceptions of him are largely, if not exclusively, based on media portrayals of him.

What is less known, however, is the extent to which media also help shape our **personal identity**, that is to say, a *person's image of self.* Charles Horton Cooley's social psychological concept of the **looking-glass self** tells us that to a large extent, *a person's self is a reflection of other people's perceptions of him or her* – as society acts as a mirror reflecting a person's identity. The looking-glass self has three distinct stages. First, a person gives off an impression to others; second, those people respond to the actor reflecting back a judgment of him or her; the original actor responds to the judgment made by others and develops feelings of self, based on how he or she interprets those judgments. Consequently, the fact that media help shape and define a person's social identity implies that media also can play an important role in helping to determine a person's personal identity. Probably most people are aware of how positive media attention can boost a person's ego and self-esteem helping them to gain confidence and develop a better self-image. There are numerous examples of cases where athletes, musicians, and entertainers have gone from relative obscurity to relatively instant fame, and have been dramatically changed by the process. If fame and fortune can boost ego and enhance self-image, then it is reasonable to assume that sudden defamation and misfortune can have equally powerful opposite effects. How many Hall of Fame athletes, former Olympians, and washed-up actors and musicians have become homeless, alcoholic, drug addicted, or committed suicide?

In perhaps less dramatic, but equally important fashion, media can shape the self-identities of non-celebrities. Research suggests, for example, that ideal body images projected in magazines help promote unrealistic expectations among both males and females leading to possible eating disorders and steroid use (Dworkin and Wachs, 2009). Young men and women, who may not realize that many of the images in magazines have been enhanced by silicone, cosmetic cover-ups,

Why do the media promote ideal body images that may be near impossible for people to accomplish in reality? What impact does this have on people's personal and social identities? *Source*: © Peter Barrett/ Masterfile/Corbis

Photoshop, airbrushing, computer augmentation, and a variety of other artificial techniques, may believe that they are overweight, under-muscled, too blemished, or otherwise physically inadequate and therefore fall short of cultural standards of beauty and attractiveness. Those images are further emphasized and reinforced in motion pictures and television where movie stars and celebrities, many of whom have had surgical work done, have personal nutritionists and trainers, and benefit from professional makeup artists and special effects, define ideal standards of beauty and attractiveness. Few people without those advantages can measure up.

Conversely, so-called reality television provides us with yet another version of deviance that may make the average person feel very good about himself or herself. Housewives cursing and fighting, toddlers insulting their parents and other adults, and rednecks catching fish with their bare hands bring a whole new meaning to conformity and deviance. On a more serious level, some of the programs shot inside maximum security prisons demonstrate the potential consequences of serious norm violation, pointing out the disheartening, demoralizing, and dehumanizing aspects of deviance and social control. These media portrayals provide a framework, albeit a distorted one, for people to compare their own situations and lives and draw conclusions about their relative successes and failures, as well as their proclivities toward conformity and deviance.

## Summary

Becoming deviant is a process, not an act. In order to understand this process it is helpful to place deviance in a sociological context realizing that being deviant is a social status, or position in society. As with any social status, being deviant can be ascribed through no effort on our part, or it can be achieved based on something that we have done, or at least allegedly done. Because members of society place so much emphasis on conformity, deviance often becomes a master status that overpowers all the other identities that all of us have as part of our status set. As a result, committing a deviant act, being identified as deviant, and deviance becoming our master status, transforms being deviant from something we do, to who we are.

Every social status is accompanied by a social role, or set of behavioral expectations. Through socialization and role-taking, norm violators often embrace their deviant roles, sometimes to the point of role merger and role engulfment. If deviants fail to acknowledge, embrace, and fulfill their deviant role expectations, they may very well be viewed as *deviant* deviants, a type of double jeopardy that may result in even more social ridicule and other negative repercussions.

Deviance is generally a stigmatizing attribute that identifies people as less desirable and unworthy of full social acceptance. Consequently, many deviants struggle with trying to keep their deviant actions secret, or known only to a few who may share similar stigmatizing characteristics. Managing a spoiled social identity is no easy feat, especially in a media saturated world where even the slightest norm violation can be called to the attention of millions of people almost instantaneously. The full impact of becoming deviant on a person's personal and social identities is difficult to assess, but social science research suggests that being identified as a deviant has very powerful ramifications for those involved.

## Outcomes Assessment

1  Explain the process of becoming deviant.
2  Define master status and explain how deviance can become a master status.
3  Distinguish between primary and secondary deviance. Define role engulfment and give examples of how deviants can get caught up in role engulfment.
4  Define stigma and explain the various types of stigma.
5  Explain how deviants attempt to manage a spoiled identity.
6  Discuss how the media help create, promote, and sustain deviant identities. Give some specific examples.

## Key Terms and Concepts

| | | |
|---|---|---|
| achieved status | primary deviance | role set |
| ascribed status | role | secondary deviance |
| deviant career | role distance | social identity |
| looking-glass self | role embracement | status |
| master status | role engulfment | status set |
| passing | role merger | stigma |
| personal identity | role-taking | stigma symbols |

# 3

# Popular Notions and Pseudoscientific Explanations for Deviance

---

**Student Learning Outcomes**

After reading this chapter students will be able to:

1 List and explain some of the popular notions used to explain deviance.
2 Trace the evolution of explanations of deviant behavior from pseudoscience and demonic possession to the development of positivism which sought to link deviance to biological and genetic causes.
3 Explain the medical model of deviance and how it led to the medicalization of deviance.
4 Explain the popularity of violence in various forms of media and the potential influence of media on violent and aggressive forms of deviance.
5 Point out many of the fallacies associated with popular notions and pseudoscientific explanations for deviance.

---

*When little nine-year-old Elizabeth and her cousin Abigail, age 11, began having "fits," their parents were understandably concerned. The girls complained of feeling like they were being pinched and stuck with pins, but according to the girls' doctor, their bouts of screaming, throwing things, and contorting their bodies into unusual positions were not the results of any diagnosable medical disorder. Clearly, only one thing could logically explain the girls' affliction: they were victims of witchcraft. Within weeks, three witches were identified and arrested: Sarah Good, a homeless woman who begged on the streets for food and shelter, Sarah Osborne, who*

*Deviance & Deviants: A Sociological Approach*, First Edition. William E. Thompson and Jennifer C. Gibbs.
© 2017 John Wiley & Sons, Inc. Published 2017 by John Wiley & Sons, Inc.
Companion website: www.wiley.com/go/thompson

*almost never attended church services, and a slave by the name of Tituba. The women, already considered to be deviant by many members of the community, were interrogated, jailed, and ultimately executed. So began the most notorious period in Massachusetts Bay colony history: The Salem Witch Trials* (Karlsen, 1998; Roach, 2004).

What on earth would lead people to believe that the deviant behavior of two little girls could possibly be the result of some evil spell cast on them by witches? Several possible explanations emerge. First, we must consider the important sociological variables discussed in Chapter 1 regarding the definition of deviance and how they relate to this particular incident: *time, place, situation,* and *culture.* The time was the seventeenth century, and the place was in colonial America at a time when the Puritans tended to explain virtually all human behavior within a religious context. The situation was very bad economic times when the colonists were plagued with a variety of hardships. Belief in the supernatural was a common element of the Massachusetts Bay colony culture and many of the colonists believed that their particularly tough social, political, and economic situation, especially their agricultural woes, could be blamed on the waning faith of some colonists and the persistent presence of the devil among their midst (Roach, 2004). Thus, fear, superstition, and the absence of rational scientific thought combined to fuel a moral panic that resulted in scapegoating some of the most vulnerable members of society.

The Massachusetts Bay colonists were neither the first, nor were they alone in their belief in witchcraft or their association of negative situations and deviant behavior with witches, demons, or other supernatural sources of evil. There is evidence from prehistoric times, throughout ancient recorded history, during the middle ages, and even today that some people believe that the explanation for deviance resides within the deviants, who either must be possessed by demons or be under some type of supernatural spell that causes them to commit evil acts. Historian Michael Shermer (1997) postulates that fear, superstition, "… theological imaginations, ecclesiastical power, scapegoating, the decline of magic, the rise of formal religion, interpersonal conflict, misogyny, gender politics, and possibly even psychedelic drugs" may all contribute to the belief that deviance is caused by Satan, witches, ghosts, devils, demons, or other supernatural forces.

## Demonology: "The Devil Made Me Do It"

**Demonology** is *the systematic study of the belief in demons or super humans who are not considered to be deities.* There is some evidence that Stone Age humans drilled holes in the skulls of wrong-doers and those perceived to be mentally ill so that evil spirits could escape. It is theorized that the piece of removed bone may have been worn around the neck to keep evil spirits away (Brothwell, 1963). Ancient Hebrews, Greeks, and Romans all practiced rituals of exorcism, as do some modern-day Roman Catholics and members of various other religious sects (Olson, 2011). There is mention of fallen angels, devils, demons, evil spirits, or other supernatural forces associated with evil in almost every major religion found in the world today (Matthews, 2012). Despite remnants of belief that deviant behavior is caused by supernatural evil forces, however, many references to attributing wrongdoing to witches, demons, and devils today are made more in jest than in earnest.

In the 1970s, a popular comedian by the name of Flip Wilson hosted a prime time variety show on which he wrote and performed a variety of skits. One of the most popular characters he portrayed was that of Geraldine Jones, a sassy young woman who popularized the catchphrase, "The devil made me do it." Although twenty-first century America was hardly dominated by belief in witchcraft or demonic possession (or men who dressed as women), that tagline struck a popular chord with television viewers and became a popular slogan among both children and adults. More importantly, the phrase was even uttered more than once in courtrooms, as demonic possession was attempted to be used as part of legal defense strategies in a few sensational murder trials. Probably one of the most famous examples occurred in 1977, when Richard David Falco, who was going by the name of David Berkowitz and became known worldwide as the .44 Caliber Killer or the "Son of Sam," was arrested for the murders of six women and the wounding of seven others. Berkowitz indirectly claimed that the devil made him do it by insisting that his neighbor's dog was possessed by demons who told him (Berkowitz) to commit the murders (Brody, 2013). In another incident, in Galveston, Texas, a preacher who put his baby daughter in a microwave oven and "cooked" her for twenty seconds told authorities that he did it because, "Satan attacked him and saw him as a threat" (AP Galveston, 2007). As can be seen by just these few examples, the linking of deviance and deviants to morality, immorality, and sin has a very long history in western culture, and persists among some groups and individuals today (Shermer, 1997).

Various forms of media have capitalized on the popular notion that deviance may be linked to witches, demons, and devils. Popular movies and television shows have featured witches, werewolves, vampires, and the like and during the 1980s and 1990s several television talk shows focused on witchcraft, Satanism, and the occult, especially implying that there was a major increase in the involvement of teenagers in those types of activities. Geraldo, Jenny Jones, Maury Povich, Jerry Springer, and others invited noted Satanist Anton LaVey to appear on their programs as police officials, counselors, and beguiled parents all attested to the increased involvement of teens in witchcraft, Satanism, and other occult activities including bestiality, animal sacrifices, human torture and mutilation, and even human sacrifices, although almost all of the testimonies were anecdotal and contradicted by social science research, facts, and official data (Victor, 1996). Nevertheless, a moral panic fed by the media gained momentum as local school districts, police departments, and community advocates launched a movement to identify teen witches and Satanists and to curtail their occult activities. The media were not nearly as interested when sociologist Kathleen Lowney (1995) published her research findings after spending approximately five years conducting ethnographic field research on a satanic adolescent subculture she called *The Coven* that, contrary to popular belief, most of the youths involved in this so-called Satanic group were not "mentally disturbed," did not engage in any major criminal activities, and were not seriously committed to an occult ideology. To the contrary, television talk shows continued to promote the idea that legions of teenagers were being lured into witchcraft, Satanism, and other demonic cults, despite there being no supporting evidence for such allegations (Lowney, 2003). Box 3.1 features an interview with a twenty-year-old self-professed witch who talks about some of the myths and realities associated with modern witchcraft.

**Box 3.1   In their own words**

## Interview with a twenty-year-old wiccan

**INTERVIEWER:**   So, you are a modern-day witch.

**SARAH*:**   First of all, I do not like being called a "witch." I am a Wiccan. I worship Wicca, the goddess of the earth and nature. Some Wiccans believe Wicca is both male and female, but I see her as female.

**INTERVIEWER:**   But, in class when the topic came up, you identified yourself as a "modern-day witch," did you not?

**SARAH:**   Well, yes, but that's only because I knew that the rest of the class wouldn't know the difference between Wiccans and witches and that they didn't know anything about what they were talking about – just parroting what they had seen and heard on TV or somewhere. Plus, in some ways, Wiccans are a form of witch, in that we practice what most people consider to be witchcraft.

**INTERVIEWER:**   So, what is the difference, and why are the two confused by most people?

**SARAH:**   There are lots of different types of witches and warlocks, and different covens believe in different things. I don't profess to know everything about witches or witchcraft. I can tell you about modern-day Wiccans though, and what we believe, or at least what I believe. I don't profess to speak for all Wiccans. Wicca is like any religion – it means different things to different people.

**INTERVIEWER:**   Okay, let's start there. What is a Wiccan, and what do Wiccans believe? Or at least, what do you believe?

**SARAH:**   Being a Wiccan is not a whole lot different from being a Protestant, a Catholic, or a member of some other established religion, except we don't base our beliefs on the Bible or some other man-made contrived b.s. We don't need a church building or anything like that. We believe in nature, and we believe that we can be more in touch with nature to make magick potions and conduct magick rituals in order to make things better. We use our witchcraft and magick for good, not for evil – and that's magick with a k at the end, not m-a-g-i-c.

**INTERVIEWER:**   Okay, but you just used the term "witchcraft," so we seem to be back to the differences or similarities between witches and Wiccans, and also, can you explain how magick with a k at the end is different from m-a-g-i-c? And, what role does magick play in your religion?

**SARAH:**   This is what I was afraid of when I opened my mouth in class in the first place. All of this is more complicated than just is it witchcraft or isn't it? Let's just say that being a Wiccan is one type of modern day witchcraft, and leave it at that. I just don't want people to think that we are like Halloween witches, wearing pointed hats and flying on broomsticks or whatever (laugh). We are just like everybody else, except we understand the human connection to nature and the powers that nature can give us. That's where magick comes in. What is magick and how does it work? I guess, first of all, that magick with a k is mostly just a different way of spelling magic, but it also is a way of distinguishing us from "magicians" or people who do "magic tricks." Wiccans don't perform tricks. We have rituals that put us in direct contact with nature and all of its power. Magick can help heal, it can give people peace and understanding, and it connects us to psychic abilities that probably everybody has but do not know how to invoke or interpret. Especially if they believe in some other religion that teaches them not to be in tune with their bodies and nature. That's what most religions do. They put some artificial god between people and nature and teach people not to believe in their intuition, dreams, or ability to perform miracles. I have used magick to help my sister who tried for years to get pregnant and was told by doctors that she could never have a baby. I performed several incantations with my sister and I now have a 3-year-old nephew as a result. That's a classic example of using magick to invoke nature. I've done a few other things, but that's probably the most important one. It's more difficult to perform these rituals individually. Wicca works best in a group and outside in nature if possible. And, yes, like some of the movies suggest, we usually practice our rituals in the nude – that's one way of getting closer to nature, but let's not go there.

**INTERVIEWER:** Wow, that's a lot to digest. (After a long pause, and not knowing what to say next) I notice that you have a 5-pointed star tattooed on your hand. Is that a Wiccan symbol?

**SARAH:** Yes. The pentagram is used by most Wiccans as a symbol of our faith. The pentagram represents the five elements: earth, wind, fire, water, and spirit. We see all five as interconnected and important for achieving harmony in life. I have a pentacle too, a necklace with a five-pointed star on it, that I wear when I am practicing my magick. It makes me sick when I see where a bunch of teenagers who don't know the first thing about Wicca or our religion go around spray painting pentagrams on barns or buildings and then kill a cat or something and make everybody think that they are some type of modern-day witches. They are just mixed-up kids and juvenile delinquents trying to get attention. Wicca is a serious belief system and a lifestyle. It's way too complicated to explain in just a few minutes, especially to somebody who either knows absolutely nothing about it, or worse, somebody who has watched some television program and thinks they know all about it. I guess if I was to try to sum it up in one or two neat sentences, I would say, being a Wiccan is a way of believing and a way of life that believes in the superiority of nature. We worship Wicca, the goddess of nature, and invoke her power to try to make our lives better and to make the world a better place.

---

\* Sarah is a pseudonym. At the time of the interview Sarah was a 20-year-old junior in college who had been named to the Dean's honor roll each semester.

## Morality, Immorality, and Deviance

For those who do not necessarily believe that deviance is caused by witches, demons, or demonic possession, many still believe that there are natural links between morality and conformity as well as a strong connection between immorality and deviance. During the Middle Ages in Europe and the early colonial days in America, the church and/or religious doctrines dominated almost every aspect of society. Consequently, deviant behavior of almost any type was viewed as an example of, or a potential threat to, personal, community, and societal morality. Even today, for some people, the explanation for deviance is as simple as this: deviance equals sin. These people tend to adhere to the absolutist definition of deviance explained in Chapter 1, believing that there are at least some, and perhaps many, fundamental moral values to which everybody should adhere. According to them, any behavior that displays deviation from those values constitutes deviance, and anybody who does not strictly adhere to the norms those values represent is a deviant. Even natural and manmade disasters have been linked to immorality and sin as religious leaders such as Jerry Falwell, Pat Robertson, and others have contended that Hurricane Katrina's devastation of the gulf coast was most likely evidence of God punishing the sinners of New Orleans, and other major hurricanes, floods, tornadoes, and other so-called "acts of God," have been cited as being God's punishment for everything from abortion to same-sex marriage (Marley, 2007). Years earlier, Falwell and Robertson attributed the 9/11 attacks on the World Trade Centers and various other terrorist attacks to America's abandonment of God and morality (Marley, 2007). Well-known author and avowed atheist Christopher Hitchins discovered during his terminal bout with esophageal and throat cancer that several devout Christians attributed his illness to his sin of blasphemy noting that it was no mere coincidence that his throat and vocal chords were the main targets of the disease (Hitchins, 2012). For others, the presumed link between immorality and deviance is much more complex than simply being a result of "God's wrath," believing that deviance may be more about the violation of dominant social and cultural mores not necessarily connected to religious teachings than about sinning or violating religious doctrine.

From a social scientific standpoint, deviance is not linked to sin or evil, and is not a result of immorality. Nevertheless, many sociologists contend that the concept of deviance cannot be understood without linking it to societal and individual definitions of morality. As we noted in Chapter 2, Erving Goffman (1963:4), for example, linked one of his three types of stigma to what he called "blemishes of character," which included things such as "unnatural passions, ... treacherous beliefs, ... homosexuality, ..." and other characteristics, traits, or behaviors that might be viewed as immoral by so-called "normals." Similarly, Edwin Lemert (1982) maintained that defining something as deviant is primarily a moral judgment about the *rightness* or *wrongness* of it. Consequently, what he called **moral differentiation**, *the ability to promote some selected norms and values over others*, plays a significant role in the defining of both deviance and deviants. This phenomenon, especially with the advent of modern media, leads to the development of moral entrepreneurship, moral panics, and moral crusades against selected forms of deviance and deviants as discussed in Chapter 1. Even in a society that is dominated by logical, rational, and scientific thinking, or perhaps because of that very fact, few things can create moral panic more quickly than the suggestion of demonic possession, the supernatural, or other-worldliness.

Today, especially in western cultures, people are more likely to turn to scientific, or in many cases, pseudoscientific explanations for human behavior than to supernatural ones. **Science** is *knowledge based on empirical evidence gained through direct, systematic observation.* The growing influence of science, especially developments in biology and the emphasis on medicine has helped transform explanations for deviance from supernatural forces, sin, or moral character flaws into medical analogies with deviance being compared to disease. Along the way, the increasing development of science also gave rise to numerous pseudoscientific explanations for deviance.

## Positivism, Pseudoscience, and the Medical Model of Deviance

During the eighteenth century, a period that became known as the "age of enlightenment," the "age of reason," or the "age of science," people turned from primarily supernatural and theological explanations to scientific thinking to account for human behavior. This development gave rise to **positivism**, *a philosophy of science based on the assumption that true knowledge requires positive verification.* Auguste Comte, who first posited the study of society as *positivistic philosophy*, later coined the term **sociology**, to describe *the scientific study of society, social groups, and human behavior.* Comte insisted that just as phenomena in the physical world can be explained by natural laws of cause and effect, so can human social behavior. These social laws, he believed, could only be discovered through positivistic research and verification based on the scientific method.

Since the natural sciences preceded the social and behavioral sciences in development, early sociologists and psychologists often turned to biology as a model for scientific research and explanation. This eventually gave rise to the **medical model** which *compares deviance to illness or disease* for explaining human behavior, especially behavior that seemed "abnormal," abhorrent, or deviant.

### Early biological and physiological theories of deviance

Biology literally translates as the study of life, and has roots that date back to ancient times in Mesopotamia, Egypt, and parts of Asia. The study of medicine, which relies heavily on biology, can be traced back to Hippocrates and the fourth century BC in ancient Greece. To this day, virtually every medical school graduate in the United States takes the *Hippocratic Oath* to honor Hippocrates' important contributions to medical science. Modern biological science and medical practice gained very little headway throughout most of the world, however, until the advent of the microscope in the nineteenth century. Suddenly, scientists could see into a world that most humans could not even imagine existed, and the discovery of cells, bacteria, and other microscopic organisms replaced witches, fallen angels, and demons as the major cause for disease, death, and deviant behavior.

The notion that human physical and biological traits could be linked to human behavior has been around for quite some time. Franz Joseph Gall (1758–1828), a medical doctor in the late eighteenth and early nineteenth centuries, believed that human attributes and traits were directly linked to a person's brain. By dissecting cadavers, scientists had discovered that the brain consisted of several different lobes, each of which could be linked to specific functions of the body, and perhaps to personality traits. Since it was virtually impossible to actually study the brains of living people, Gall speculated that studying the human skull, the container of the malleable brain, was the next best thing. Using what appeared to be valid scientific assumptions, Gall created one of the first pseudoscientific explanations for delinquency with the development of **phrenology**, *a system for studying the shape, bumps, and indentations of the skull in order to determine the cerebral functions that would govern human behavior.* For example, a large protruding forehead would be evidence of an overly developed frontal lobe, the part of the brain that can be linked to violent and aggressive behavior. Similarly, the occipital lobe and the parietal lobes could be linked to other character traits that might translate into criminal or other deviant behavior. Although phrenology seemed based on science, it can more accurately be described as a **pseudoscience** – *a claim or belief system that is presented as scientific, but lacks the rigor of reliability, validity, and testability demanded by adherence to the scientific method.* Pseudoscience is sometimes difficult to distinguish from science, especially by non-scientists, because it usually poses as science and is characterized by exaggerated and contradictory claims that cannot be proven scientifically, but are also somewhat difficult to refute. For example, while many people view the earlier claims of demonic possession and witchcraft as ridiculous and superstitious, it is virtually impossible to scientifically *prove* that somebody is not possessed by demons, or is not a witch. Demonology and witchcraft, however, never pretended to be scientific. Phrenology, however, posed as a "scientific" explanation of deviance and seemingly possessed many of the outward appearances of "science." After all, Franz Joseph Gall was a surgeon – a man of science. He also conducted "research" by physically examining skulls and carefully charting and mapping all of the bumps, protrusions, and irregularities. Then, by applying some genuine science, the knowledge that the brain controls human behavior, he drew the mostly erroneous, but seemingly logical conclusion that the shape of the skull determines the shape of the brain, and that human behavior could be predicted by studying the shape of the skull. Gall was not some type of charlatan traveling with a circus pretending to read minds or guess people's weight, but he did use some of the same techniques of exaggerating his findings and drawing conclusions from his research that were neither scientifically provable nor refutable.

Another medical doctor who attempted to link deviance to genetics and biology was the Italian army physician and surgeon, Cesare Lombroso (1835–1909), who is often referred to as the "father" of **criminology**, *the scientific study of crime and criminal behavior.* Lombroso (1911:365) concluded that there is a "born criminal type" that is "bestial" in appearance and characterized by "low cranial capacity; retreating forehead; highly developed frontal sinuses; … early closing of the cranial structures; … tufted and crispy hair; and large ears … [and] relative insensibility to pain." Lombroso viewed the *born criminal* as being a manifestation of **atavism**, *a biological throwback to a more savage earlier phase of human evolution.* These *Homo delinquens*, Lombroso argued, were biological and social misfits in a society composed of modern more fully evolved people (Homo sapiens) where there are restrictions on the more aggressive, violent, and savage behaviors associated with atavism. Lombroso later refined and expanded his theory to distinguish between the *born criminal* and the *criminaloid*, who was different from the born criminal in that his predatory behavior was more occasional and less savage. Lombroso also described the *insane criminal*, whose deviant behavior was purportedly linked to diseases or abnormalities of the mind. Lombroso's theory of atavism, much like Gall's phrenology, relied more on pseudoscience than science. There is some evidence that Lombroso may have "fudged" some of his research findings by throwing out cases that did not seem to validate his theory and by exaggerating those cases that seemingly confirmed it. Either way, atavistic theory was shortlived, but had some lasting influence on the field of criminology by identifying possible links between biology, physiology, and deviant behavior.

Early positivism and what became known as the "Classical School" of criminology added the concept of **free will**, or *self-determination*, to the causation formula for deviant behavior, insisting that people make rational choices as to how to behave. Although the focus on free will remained strong in early criminological and sociological theories developed by social and behavioral scientists as we will see in Chapter 4, initially, that concept was somewhat overshadowed by the rapid development of the so-called "hard sciences" of biology, genetics, and physiology, which stimulated numerous other theories that focused on biological and physiological explanations for crime, delinquency, and other forms of deviant behavior. In the mid-twentieth century, for example, William Sheldon and his research associates believed that their study, which compared 200 juvenile boys petitioned to juvenile court with 4,000 males in college, showed that personality and character traits could be equated with body type (Sheldon *et al.*, 1949). Sheldon and associates believed that all males fit into one of three basic somatotypes, *endomorph, ectomorph, or mesomorph* (see Figure 3.1). They contended that youths with a certain physical body shape (somatotype) inherited certain characteristics that made them more prone to certain types of juvenile delinquency:

1  *Endomorph*. Characterized as rotund, soft, and overweight, the endomorph was presumed to be easygoing, gregarious, self-indulgent, and not prone to violence or aggression.
2  *Ectomorph*. The ectomorph had a tall, slender, and fragile body with weaker features and was thought to be nervous, high-strung, more introspective, and prone to be a loner who might engage in vandalism, theft, or other non-violent crimes.
3  *Mesomorph*. Muscular and strong, the mesomorph tended to be less sensitive, far more energetic, and aggressive, consequently, more likely to be involved in violent or aggressive behavior.

Endomorph          Ectomorph          Mesomorph

**Figure 3.1**    Illustration by Marilyn Thompson of Sheldon's Somatotypes.

Today, most scholars reject Gall's, Lombroso's, Sheldon's, and other theories that developed categories of criminal types based on biological or physiological characteristics, but that does not mean the popular notion that criminals are somehow inherently different from non-criminals, or that deviance can be transmitted genetically from one generation to another, no longer persists in some circles. You can probably discern some stereotypes today that may be linked to these long discarded theories that helped lead to the development of the medical model of deviance.

More modern theories of deviance based on biological and physiological causes focus on genetics, hormones, and even metabolism. For example, in 1966, when Richard Speck was convicted of killing eight nursing students in Chicago, it was alleged that he possessed an extra Y chromosome, which may have caused him to be genetically predisposed to be more violent and aggressive than chromosomally "normal" males. Normally, every individual possesses 23 pairs (46) of gene-carrying chromosomes. The sex-determining pair of chromosomes for females is XX and the pair for males is XY. In rare cases, thought to be somewhere around one-tenth of one percent of all males, some men possess an extra Y chromosome, hence XYY. Since both males and females possess the X chromosome, but only males possess the Y, it has been assumed that the Y chromosome accounts for the release of testosterone and the concomitant characteristic for males to be more aggressive and violent than females (Rosenberg *et al.*, 1982). Such an assertion is based on flimsy scientific research at best, but the XYY or so-called "Super Male" theory has been used as a legal defense in murder cases, although no legal precedent has been established in the United States as yet. Although the XYY chromosome theory of deviance is not widely accepted, biologists, geneticists, psychiatrists, criminologists, and a host of other behavioral scientists have spent their entire careers in search of a genetic link to crime causation to little or no avail (Stephenson, 1996). Nevertheless, many researchers today are convinced that genetics, biology, and physiology play an important role in explaining deviant behaviors such as alcoholism, obesity, homosexuality, and others.

The ongoing nature versus nurture debate contributed to the creation of **sociobiology**, *a discipline that combines the scientific approaches of sociology and biology to combine the effects of nature and nurture in attempting to explain human behavior.* Sociobiology essentially declares the nature *versus* nurture debate as obsolete, contending that in order to understand deviance, one must take into account both nature *and* nurture. One sociobiological theory has attempted to link diet to deviant behavior, especially attention deficit disorder and hyperactivity (ADD and ADHD) in children. Some data from studies in the 1980s suggested that poor nutritional habits and diets high in sugar and refined carbohydrates may lead to overstimulation, aggression, juvenile delinquency, and other types of antisocial behavior (Rimland and Larson, 1981; Schoenthaler, 1983), but later research discounted the diet connection, linking the causes of ADHD more closely to familial factors and mothers smoking or drinking during pregnancy (Biederman, 2004). Other studies have attempted to provide sociobiological explanations for various mental disorders including anxiety disorders, panic disorder, agoraphobia, and psychopathology (Baron-Cohen, 1997).

The increased focus on the link between heredity and environment in explaining deviant behavior contributed to the rise of the medical model of deviance. This viewpoint portrayed deviance as being like a disease.

## The medical model of deviance

In the movie *RoboCop* (1987), an elderly gentlemen surmises, "Old Detroit has a cancer … that cancer is crime." That movie character was neither the first nor the last to compare some form of deviant behavior to cancer. As science continued to develop and medicine gained in popularity and prestige, many people began to see aberrant and deviant behavior as being analogous to physical illness or disease. Dr. Lionel VonFrederick Rawlins (2005), President and CEO of the VonFrederick Group proclaimed, "Remember, crime is like cancer: if not treated quickly, swiftly, certainly, and severely, it will get you…. soon!" Similarly, various presidents, governors, mayors, law enforcement officials, and other agents of social control have alluded to crime, juvenile delinquency, violence, drug abuse, drunk driving, compulsive gambling, sexual deviance, and even poverty as "diseases" sweeping our nation.

The key component of the medical model of deviance is viewing deviance as being analogous to an illness or disease. Thus, in order for society to effectively deal with deviant behavior, it is important to first identify and recognize the *symptoms* of deviance. This can lead to an accurate *diagnosis* of the problem, allowing those in charge to make a *prognosis* as to the likelihood of effectively dealing with the deviance. If the prognosis is favorable, then an effective *treatment* strategy can be *prescribed* and implemented, which hopefully will lead to a *cure* for the social ills caused by the deviance in question. Think today how much medical vocabulary is often applied to various types of deviance and deviants.

From a sociological perspective, there are so many myths, fallacies, and problems associated with the medical model of deviance that it would be impossible to discuss them all and it is difficult to even know where to start when identifying them. First and foremost, the medical model of deviance *individualizes* deviant behavior focusing on the deviant rather than the deviance. To summarize all the other flaws of this type of thinking in the most concise way, suffice it to point out that human beings are inherently social and socially interdependent.

In 1998, when Kim Bassinger received a Best Supporting Actress Oscar for her role in *L.A Confidential*, she gushed in her acceptance speech, "I want to thank everybody I have ever met in my entire life" (cited in Callero, 2013:ix). While she may have been guilty of hyperbole, Kim's acknowledgment of the impact of others on her accomplishment reflects an acute awareness of sociological thinking. Whether we are talking about winning an Academy Award, being elected President of the United States, tattooing four-letter words on one's forehead, or committing mass murder, individuals' actions are shaped and influenced by the society in which they live, the culture and subcultures within which they have been socialized, as well as the schools they have attended, the family(ies) in which they were reared, and the various groups to which they have belonged, or from which they have been banished. Perhaps John Donne's (1572–1631) seventeenth century meditative poem summarizes the social imperative of humans best, "No man is an island…"

The medical model of deviance fails to acknowledge the larger social context in which deviance occurs and all of the social aspects of defining deviance that we have covered in the first two chapters of this book. Even more exasperating, is the fact that the medical model of deviance has become so popularly ingrained in the psyche of many Americans that we have moved from merely viewing deviance as being *like* an illness to defining many forms of deviance as actually *being* an illness.

## The medicalization of deviance

A direct outgrowth of the development of the medical model has been the medicalization of deviance. **Medicalization** occurs *when human behaviors, activities, and events that previously were considered to be non-medical, become defined as health or disease related conditions.* For example, for centuries, childbirth was considered to be a natural, if not fairly routine event. It was not until the late nineteenth and early twentieth centuries in the United States with the development of the American Medical Association and the increased emphasis on medical credentials that childbirth became the domain of doctors and hospitals. Previously, most children were born at home, sometimes attended by a midwife, but more often the birthing mother was alone or was aided by another female in the family, or by a nearby neighbor woman. Similarly, death was viewed as a natural part of life and, prior to the twentieth century, most Americans died at home, often in the very same bed in which they had been born.

If life and death have become medicalized, it is no wonder that many other human situations have begun to be regarded as medical conditions, especially those behaviors that could be viewed by some as **pathological**, or *irrational, unreasonable, or "sick."* Consequently, the words *sick* and *deviant*, once thought to be totally unrelated, may become synonymous in some people's minds. For example, when you first read the opening vignette in Chapter 1, you may

How has the medicalization of deviance altered people's views of norm violating behavior? How has it handled society's reactions to deviance? *Source*: Paul Bradbury/Getty Images

have been repulsed and asked yourself, "What kind of 'sick' individual would kill innocent kittens and then horrendously murder another human being?" We often hear mass murderers or others who violate serious norms, mores, and taboos described as being "sick-o's" who should not be allowed to live in a civilized society. Sometimes the euphemism is even expanded to refer to an entire group or even society at large, when people contend, "he comes from a 'sick' family," or "what type of 'sick' society allows people to do such horrible things?"

Media have played a very important role in helping to medicalize various forms of deviant behavior. Popular television programs like *ER, House, Grey's Anatomy, Nurse Jackie,* and others depicted doctors and nurses both medically treating and solving other people's deviance while also suffering from some of their own forms of deviance related to medicine, such as addiction to pain killers and other drugs, not to mention a host of personality and social disorders that contributed to personal and professional problems such as marital infidelity, divorce, depression, and suicide.

Less dramatically, social problems such as alcoholism, drug addiction, mental disorders, sexual deviance, and a host of others, today are defined by members of the medical establishment, and much of the rest of society, literally as diseases. Today, the American Psychiatric Association includes many forms of deviance in its *Diagnostic and Statistical Manual of Mental Disorders*, and most forms of major health insurance will pay for treatment of them if they are diagnosed by certified medical practitioners. We will explore each of these types of deviance in more detail in later chapters of this book, but for now, we will simply indicate that alcoholism, drug addiction, and many of the other forms of deviance that are categorized as illnesses or diseases today, were once thought to be basically behavioral problems or reflection of a lack of control over deviant impulses. The medicalization of deviance will be explored in relation to specific types of deviance in later chapters of this book, especially in Chapter 8 which covers various forms of physical and mental deviance.

Perhaps part of the tendency of the general public to readily accept the medical model and medicalization of deviance is linked to the growing influence of the media and its tendency to sensationalize and individualize the phenomenon of deviance. Perhaps ironically, as the media, especially television and movies, increased their focus on sensational forms of deviant behavior, scientists and the general public began to focus their attention on the media as possible causes of social deviance.

## Blame it on the Media

In the quest to explain why some people deviate from the norms of society while others conform to them, it is inevitable that people look to the media, since it plays such an important role in helping to define deviance. The media also capitalize on the widespread cultural fascination with deviance, by providing vivid images and portrayals of various types of deviance and deviants.

### Print media and deviance

Arguably, one of humankind's major achievements and life-altering inventions was that of Johannes Gutenberg in the mid-fifteenth century when he revolutionized the art of printing by developing a system and a press that used movable type. Not only did Gutenberg's printing press make it possible to create movable type in mass quantities, but it essentially became the forerunner of all print mass media as it provided the technology and mechanism for printing newspapers, magazines, and books. More importantly, the printing press became the catalyst for changing the way people thought and acted (McLuhan and Fiore, 2005). Books were transformed from rare and expensive commodities printed and copied by hand whose ownership and readership was limited to royalty and monks, to relatively inexpensive and plentiful mass produced products that almost everybody could afford to own and read. One of the first, and many would argue the most important mass-produced works to come off Gutenberg's press, were two hundred copies of the two-volume, twelve-hundred page Bible that bore his name. Undoubtedly, some people viewed that book as being deviant in and of itself, while others viewed the Bible as the ultimate source for defining conformity and deviance. If the printing press could produce the "good book" in mass quantities, it also could mass produce what many people would define as "bad" books.

Historians note that pornographic images are as old as humankind, but the invention of the printing press facilitated the mass production and distribution of printed pornographic materials (Hyde, 1964). **Pornography** is usually defined as *explicit materials intended solely for sexual arousal*, but no clear-cut legal or social definition exists. While some people contend that any depiction of nudity or any reference to sex or sexuality is pornographic and deviant, others argue that any material depicting consenting adults, no matter how sexually explicit is harmless and should not be censored. The US Supreme court wrestled with the issue of trying to determine what constitutes pornography or obscenity for decades, eventually deciding that only members of a local community can determine what violates their moral standards. Since almost no community has a unanimously agreed upon moral code, hundreds, if not thousands of battles have been waged over whether certain books, magazines, calendars, or other printed materials are obscene and deviant.

Beyond the argument over whether something is pornographic or obscene, and if the consumption of pornography is deviant in and of itself, is the issue of whether viewing or reading pornography might lead to other more serious types of deviance. For example, many people believe that not only is pornography morally deviant, but it also is degrading, desensitizing and may lead to crimes of violence and aggression against women and children (Taverner, 2011). Debates over pornography and its alleged effects have become even more controversial as other technologies such as television, movies, videos, and the internet have emerged on to the scene.

By the middle of the twentieth century, newspapers had become the main source of news and information for people all around the world. By 1950, approximately one-half of all households in the United States, Canada, and the United Kingdom, subscribed to at least one daily newspaper, and many households subscribed to two or more (Communications Management Inc., 2011). Magazines also enjoyed record numbers of subscribers and were viewed as important sources of news, information, and entertainment. Those numbers began to decline with the advent of television, but like Mark Twain's famous quote, reports of their death were greatly exaggerated. Nevertheless, new forms of media, especially television, movies, and video games swept across the United States and the rest of the world introducing viewers to newer and more technologically sophisticated forms of deviant behavior.

## Television, movies, video games and deviance

When the Pioneer Corporation introduced television sets to America with the slogan, "We bring the revolution home," motion picture mogul Darryl F. Zanuck declared that television would never replace radio or motion pictures because people would soon tire of sitting at home and staring at a plywood box (Edgerton, 2009). Zanuck grossly underestimated the captivating allure of television and the stamina of the American viewing public. By 1950, there were approximately 3.9 million television sets in American homes with just about nine percent of American households having at least one television, and only a decade later that number had grown to just under 46 million television sets with slightly over 87 percent of American homes having at least one set (US Bureau of the Census, 2010). By the beginning of the twenty-first century, 98.2 percent of all American homes had at least one television set with the average homeowner possessing approximately three of the 301 million sets in homes across the nation (US Bureau of the Census, 2010). Despite the growth of the Internet and other forms of social media which cut into television's popularity for entertainment and news, there is no indication that television is on its way to extinction as manufacturers have continually increased the size, picture quality, and capabilities of the medium to adapt to America's technological tastes. Moreover, there is no indication that deviant behavior is any less appealing as weekly television series', made-for-television movies, and so-called reality television all seem eager to capitalize on the viewing public's seemingly insatiable fascination with deviance. Today, television programmers have made programming much more consumer friendly with viewers being able to watch programs on demand, record, watch and re-watch their favorite movies or shows whenever they want, sometimes even determining the plot twists and outcomes through interactive devices. If some consumers are turned off by nudity, profanity, violence, or other forms of deviance, they can carefully avoid or even install electronic devices to block such programming. Conversely, if viewers want even more deviance in their programming, cable and satellite programming will allow them to bring virtually any and every kind of deviance into their household at any time of day or night.

Video games, once only the domain of commercial arcades or bowling alleys became wildly popular during the last couple of decades of the twentieth century. The slow, repetitive, and monotonous two-dimensional simulated tennis game of *Pong* gave way to the more colorful and animated video game of *Pac-Man* and soon almost every home that included a television set and children also possessed a little yellow critter who beeped around the television screen gobbling up different colored pellets or "pac-dots" while trying to avoid being touched by animated ghosts, goblins, and other enemies. Hardly hardcore violence, even early *Pac-Man* had its critics who contended that the character's gobbling up of innocent pellets and gaining the power to "eat" its enemies, or worse, be killed by them, encouraged young players to think of life as adversarial and potentially dangerous, although its defenders claimed the game was one of stealth and pointed out that to win the game, players had to be strategic in avoiding violent confrontations with enemies (Goodman, 1983).

Technology advanced quickly, and video games became increasingly more sophisticated, realistic, and in many cases, violent. By the beginning of the twenty-first century, "gamers" could wield the controls of animated avatars who were potential assassins, military special forces troops, and/or deadly terrorists or counter terrorists, deploying bombs, decapitating enemies, and engaging in almost any other type of violence and mayhem that could be imagined.

Although an age and content rating system similar to that used by the television and movie industry was devised by the Entertainment Software Rating Board (ESRB), the board effectively had no regulating or enforcement power. As with most things in life, unless parents or other adults closely monitor children's activities twenty-four hours per day, seven days per week, they have access to virtually any and everything that is available to any member of the public.

As television, movies, video games, and related media gained in popularity and viewership, however, they transformed from being merely among the many definers and portrayers of social deviance to, in the minds of some, among the major *causes* of deviant behavior. Of particular concern to many critics of television, movies, video games, and other media is the possible link between viewing violence and aggression on a screen and then mimicking or carrying out those or similar deviant behaviors in real life.

## Media violence, aggression, and deviant behavior

A controversial issue in the United States as well as other nations is the possible link between media violence and aggressive or deviant behavior, especially the potential harmful effects media violence may have on children. Social scientific and behavioral research findings on the possible effects of violence in media on television viewers, movie goers, and video gamers are mixed and, due to some of the methodological limitations and biased interpretations of these studies, it is extremely difficult to draw any solid, uncontroverted conclusions from them.

One of the earliest, best known, and oft-cited studies on the possible link between viewing violence on television and aggressive behavior in children are the so-called "Bobo Doll" experiments conducted by Albert Bandura and colleagues in the early 1960s (Bandura *et al.*, 1963; Bandura, 1965). In these studies, after watching television programs that featured violence children repeatedly hit, kicked, and beat an inflatable toy "Bobo" doll in the room. This led Bandura and his colleagues to conclude that children imitated in real life the actions and behaviors they saw on television, hence surmising that watching violent programming on television leads to violent and aggressive behavior among children. Although several subsequent studies have seemingly supported Bandura's findings, others conclude that while exposure to television violence might indeed cause some short-term arousal and have modeling influence, it does not have any long-term detrimental effects (Tan, 1986). Moreover, the point can be made that the "Bobo" doll was a toy which was specifically designed to be hit and kicked (it was an inflatable toy with a clown-like face and body painted on it that was weighted with sand in the bottom so that when punched in the face or upper torso, it would fall backwards and then pop back into an upright position), and that children can readily tell the difference between violence designed for entertainment (especially violence in cartoons) and violence in real-life (Hodge and Tripp, 1986; Jenkins, 2009). Still other researchers contend that media violence may even have a positive or cathartic effect, insisting that viewing violence on television or in the movies or playing violent video games may provide a vicarious outlet for fantasy aggression as opposed to actually engaging in violent or aggressive behaviors in real life (Brown, 1990; Landsburg, 2009).

The question of whether media violence *causes* deviant behavior, *contributes to* deviant behavior, merely *reflects public interest* in deviant behavior, or is *totally unrelated* to deviant behavior will probably remain unanswered with any certainty. What is certain is that millions of youths in the United States and around the globe are exposed to a large amount of violence on television, in the movies, and in the content of video games, and other forms of media every single day. Consequently, deviance and media go hand in hand in today's society and culture.

## The internet and the power of social media

When President Abraham Lincoln was assassinated, it took several days, weeks, and even months for the message to spread across the nation and to other parts of the world. A century later when President John F. Kennedy was shot, the story was on television within a matter minutes and news of his death was spread around the world in only a few hours. In 2001, millions of television viewers watched live as the second plane crashed into the World Trade Centers, and within a matter of minutes people were made aware that America had suffered a terrorist attack. When bombs exploded at the finish line of the 2013 Boston Marathon, members of the crowd immediately posted videos and photos of the event on Facebook as well as tweeted and texted their friends as news spread around the world almost instantaneously. Moreover, private citizens using social media played an important role not only in spreading word about the bombing, but also in identifying potential suspects, and eventually in the pursuit and capture of the alleged bombers. The internet and social media have reduced the timetable for transmitting awareness of deviance and identifying deviants from a period of months, weeks, and days down to nanoseconds.

Just as in the case of more traditional media, however, speed in reporting does not necessarily translate into accuracy of the report. In the case of the Boston Marathon bombing, for example, photos of an innocent person were circulated on the Internet purporting that he was an alleged suspect, and within seconds his photos were circulated around the world via cyberspace and some of the television networks posted the photograph without further investigation into the accuracy of the individual's involvement in the act. Later, the photos were taken down and the networks indicated that his photo had been circulated by mistake. Who knows what social and personal harm came from the erroneous posts? Eventually, however, photos of the two brothers allegedly involved in the plot and bombing were posted, and within only a few minutes, both men had been accurately identified and police were notified of their possible whereabouts. News crews rushed to the scene of a reported shootout between the police and the two bombing suspects, but private citizens with their cell phones scooped the traditional networks by posting videos of the shootout online as it occurred.

Unlike traditional media, good news travels even faster than bad on social networks. According to one researcher, the "if it bleeds" rule that governs traditional media apparently does not apply to social media where people are sharing news with their friends because they seem to be more concerned about how people will react to the news rather than just trying to grab a consumer's attention (Berger, 2013). Consequently, social media may be one of the few media outlets where conformity attracts as much or more attention than deviance.

In Chapter 1, we discussed the role of the media in defining deviance and creating moral entrepreneurship as well as moral panics. In this chapter we see that various forms of media also play a role in explaining the causes of deviance, and in fact, media have been viewed as the cause of some types of deviant behavior, especially violence and aggression among children and youths. Although the social scientific evidence regarding the link between media and violence is mixed, some type of link seems apparent. Whether media are the *cause*, a *contributing factor*, or merely *portrayers and conveyors* of certain types of deviance is uncertain. What is unquestionable, however, is that deviance thrives in the media and the media thrive on deviance.

In Chapter 13 we will examine deviance in the media as we take a look at cyberdeviance including deviance such as hacking, cyberbullying, cyberstalking, cyberporn, and other forms of deviance related to the Internet and social media. Social scientific research on these phenomena has lagged in relation to technological developments making such types of deviance both possible and popular. For now, however, we will continue our focus on deviance causation as we explore sociological explanations for deviance in Chapter 4. First, however, we will take a brief look at the fallacies of popular notions and pseudoscientific explanations for deviance and how they differ from social scientific theories of deviance such as those discussed in Chapter 4.

## Fallacies of Popular Notions and Pseudoscientific Explanations

**Fallacy** is usually defined as *a misconception, a mistaken belief, or an argument based on unsound or illogical reasoning*. This describes virtually all of the popular notions and pseudoscientific explanations for deviance described in this chapter. Often rooted in cultural myth, surrounded by erroneous assumptions, and seemingly supported by anecdotal and inaccurate evidence, as we have pointed out, some of these popular notions have been around for centuries, while others have emerged in more recent decades. Whether old or new, however, none of them is based on solid, systematic, scientific research, and this is what separates them from the social scientific theories about what causes deviance and deviants that we will discuss in Chapter 4. First, as we explored in Chapters 1 and 2, deviance is socially constructed, and therefore deciding what and who is deviant is an inherently social and sociological process. In Chapter 4 we will discuss some of the most prominent sociological theories of deviance, but it is important first to explain what differentiates *theory* from mere speculation, or the fallacious thinking associated with the popular notions and pseudoscientific explanations for deviance.

**Theory** refers to *a set of interrelated propositions or statements that attempt to explain some phenomenon*. Consequently, theories are far more complex than mere guesses or speculation about what causes something to happen. The theory building process generally involves **inductive reasoning**, starting with specific facts and information and putting them together systematically to develop a broader conceptual understanding. Much like detectives, who often piece together numerous small clues and bits of information in order to develop a better understanding of what took place, social scientists develop concepts and form them into propositional statements. Social scientists use observations and other forms of research to link different sociological variables in order to discover meaningful relationships and develop a theory about causation. Once theories have been developed, they can be empirically tested by using the opposite process, **deductive reasoning**, *where a researcher starts with a general theory of what causes a certain type of behavior or activity and then breaks it down into smaller components using various research methods in order to identify meaningful relationships between and among variables*. Theories are systematically developed from empirically derived data. They can be tested and replicated, accepted or rejected, through the use of the scientific method.

In Chapter 4 we will discuss and explore sociological theories that provide general statements that can be systematically and objectively tested for their reliability (consistency) and validity (accuracy) in explaining deviant behavior and the process whereby people become identified as deviant. While there is no single theory that can possibly explain all types of deviant behavior, each of the theories included in Chapter 4 contribute to our understanding of specific types of deviance. By linking these various pieces of the deviance puzzle, we can more thoroughly, systematically, and objectively understand the phenomena that come to be viewed as deviant in society.

## Summary

This chapter began with a discussion of demonology and how at one time much deviant behavior was thought to be the work of witches, demons, and the devil. Although belief in witchcraft, demonic possession, and other supernatural explanations for deviance have waned, some people still believe that deviance can be equated with sin, or at least is directly related to immorality.

During the eighteenth century, belief in supernatural explanations for deviance gave way to scientific explanations and, with the advent of biology and other natural sciences, explanations tended to incorporate biological, physiological, and other pseudo-scientific and scientific theories. The disciplines of sociology, criminology, and sociobiology emerged to focus more on environmental and sociological factors and their link to aberrant or deviant behavior.

As the social and behavioral sciences were still in their infancy, the medical model of deviant behavior became predominant as deviance was likened to a disease or illness. In some cases, deviance went from being defined as *like* an illness, to being defined *as* illness, pathology, or disease. The medical model and the medicalization of deviance persists today as certain types of deviance such as alcoholism, drug abuse, fetishism, and others are viewed as addictions or diseases.

As media technology developed, the media played a more important role in defining and purveying deviance. With the advent of television and various types of social media, the media even came to be identified as a possible cause of some types of deviant behavior, especially those related to violence and aggression. Today the media remain a powerful influence on deviance and are viewed by many as at least partially responsible for encouraging or spreading deviant behavior throughout society.

In Chapter 4, we will explore sociological explanations of deviance. Unlike popular notions and pseudoscientific explanations for deviance, sociological theories are based on systematic and scientific research, facts, data, and information. Those theories dispel many of the myths and fallacies associated with the popular notions and pseudoscientific explanations discussed in this chapter.

## Outcomes Assessment

1  List and explain some of the popular notions used to explain deviance. What are some of the major problems with these popular notions?
2  Trace the evolution of explanations of deviant behavior from demonic possession to the development of positivism. Is there a link between deviance and biological or genetic causes?

3   Explain the medical model and how it led to the medicalization of deviance. Why is the medical model so popular?

4   Explain the popularity of violence in various forms of media and the potential influence of media on violent and aggressive forms of deviance. Also discuss the role of media in defining and reporting deviance.

5   What are some of the fallacies of popular notions and pseudoscientific explanations for deviance? How might sociology help correct some of those public misconceptions?

## Key Terms and Concepts

atavism
criminology
deductive reasoning
demonology
fallacy
free will
inductive reasoning

medicalization
medical model
moral differentiation
pathological
phrenology
pornography
positivism

pseudoscience
science
sociobiology
sociology
theory

# 4

# Sociological Explanations for Deviance

## Student Learning Outcomes

After reading this chapter students will be able to:

1 Define and explain the functionalist perspective on deviance and give some examples of sociological theories of deviance that fit within the functionalist perspective.
2 Define and explain the conflict perspective in sociology and how it views deviant behavior.
3 Define and explain symbolic interaction and the constructionist view of deviance.
4 Discuss and explain the feminist perspective on defining, explaining, sanctioning, and controlling social deviance.
5 Sociologically explain the pervasive influence of the media in contemporary society and its influence on how society perceives deviance and conformity.

*The young couple parked the stroller outside a popular New York City restaurant, made sure the sleeping baby was sound and secure, and then entered the restaurant, told the hostess they needed a table for two, and then proceeded to be seated and give their drink orders to the waiter. Imagine their horror when less than an hour later Annette Sorensen and her husband, Exavier Wardlaw, emerged from the restaurant only to find the stroller and their 14-month-old daughter gone! In panic, they rushed to a couple of nearby police officers and reported that their baby had been kidnapped. The officers, less than sympathetic, informed the couple that their baby had been found abandoned on the street and had been turned over to Child Protective*

*Deviance & Deviants: A Sociological Approach*, First Edition. William E. Thompson and Jennifer C. Gibbs.
© 2017 John Wiley & Sons, Inc. Published 2017 by John Wiley & Sons, Inc.
Companion website: www.wiley.com/go/thompson

*Services. Further, the police proceeded to place Sorensen and Wardlaw under arrest stating that they would most likely be charged with child abandonment and endangerment of a minor child (Ojita, 1997: Thompson, et al., 2016).*

*That night, every major television network news channel in the United States reported that a Danish couple, on vacation to the United States, had recklessly abandoned their infant daughter on a New York City sidewalk. Across the ocean, however, European news agencies reported the story much differently as they recounted that a Danish couple's young child had been seized by the police and turned over to a governmental authority while the couple innocently dined in a nearby restaurant. Within a matter of hours, an international debate erupted over whether the Danish couple had committed a deviant, and possibly criminal, act by abandoning and endangering their infant, or whether American police had overstepped their bounds by seizing a sleeping baby while her parents were dining innocently nearby.*

*How could two accounts of the same incident differ so markedly? Had the Danish couple indeed endangered their child by leaving her unattended for almost an hour on a busy New York City sidewalk where any passerby could kidnap, rape, and murder her? Or, as they claimed, had they merely conformed to the common and pragmatic practice of leaving their sleeping baby outside on a busy sidewalk in broad daylight where any passing adult could attend to her needs if she awoke and cried, while adults dined inside the adjacent restaurant undisturbed by crying children?*

*Eventually a New York judge dropped all charges against the couple and released their daughter back into their custody declaring the whole incident a cultural misunderstanding after Sorenson's attorney produced a videotape confirming that it was common practice in Denmark for adult couples to leave children in strollers parked outside public restaurants while their parents dined inside (Sullivan, 1997). Meanwhile international debate continued over whether it was dangerous and deviant or perfectly sensible and okay to leave an unattended infant on a city sidewalk. Most Americans were shocked by the incident concluding that only a terrible parent would leave an unattended child open to so many risks of terrible things that could happen to her. Conversely, most Europeans, and especially Danish people, wondered what kind of country is the United States, that a sleeping infant would not be perfectly safe sleeping in a stroller on a busy sidewalk?*

This opening vignette illustrates that whether an act is viewed as deviant or conformist depends on a multitude of social and cultural factors. More importantly, it depicts the importance of people's perspectives or viewpoints on norms and the pervasive influence of culture in defining, explaining, and understanding conformity and socially constructing deviance. In Chapter 3 we pointed out the fallacies of popular notions and pseudoscientific explanations for deviance and noted the difference between them and social scientific theories. In this chapter, we look at the major theoretical perspectives in sociology in relation to how they define, analyze, and explain social deviance.

## A Functionalist Perspective on Deviance

When Auguste Comte coined the term sociology to describe the emerging positivistic social scientific discipline that he envisioned studying and explaining society, social groups, and their influence on social life and human behavior, he provided the theoretical foundation for what later became known as the structural functionalist perspective in sociology. This theoretical perspective focuses on the structure of society, especially major social institutions such as government, the economy, family, religion, and education, and how those institutions function interdependently to create and maintain social order. The **functionalist perspective** on deviance provides a **macro-level analysis** that *examines broad social structures and society as a whole.* In doing so, the functionalist perspective tends to focus on social structure, social institutions, social order, social consensus, and social control. From the functionalist perspective, society operates like a large complex piece of machinery, or like a giant organism such as the human body. Herbert Spencer (1889) applied this macro-level approach by developing an **organic analogy** *viewing society as being like a huge organism comprised of interconnected and interdependent parts.* In Spencer's analogy, deviance constituted a form of **social pathology**, *a social problem that potentially threatens the survival of society.* He viewed crime, mental disorders, drug abuse, suicide, and other forms of deviance as social pathologies that needed to be studied and remedied before they spread and grew eventually destroying society. Spencer's organic analogy and concept of social pathology gave rise to at least two major developments in defining and studying social deviance. First, by comparing society to an organism and defining deviance as social pathology, Spencer provided a theoretical foundation for the medical model of deviance discussed in Chapters 1 and 3. Second, Spencer's emphasis on social structure and the dysfunctional aspects of deviance gave rise to what later became known as *structural functionalist theories* of deviance. One of the earliest and best known structural functionalist approaches to deviance can be found in the so-called *strain theories.*

## Strain theories

**Strain theories** *view deviance as a result of the tensions or strain experienced by people because of their position in and relationship to the larger social structure.* Perhaps one of the first and best known strain theories of deviance can be found in Emile Durkheim's (1897/1951) classic study of suicide. Since Durkheim's study on suicide will be dealt with at great length in Chapter 9, Suicide and Self Harm, we will give it only very brief coverage here to illustrate how it focused on social strain as a major factor contributing to suicide rates.

Durkheim's study of suicide, first published in 1897, demonstrated that what appears to be an individualistic and highly personal act – an individual acting in solitary taking his or her own life – is actually a social act. What might seemingly be the domain of psychology, by studying suicide rates instead of individual suicides, Durkheim showed that suicide rates are not randomly distributed among countries, but reflect predictable patterns and trends based on a society's social structure and its influence on **social integration**, *the extent to which people feel that they are a meaningful part of society,* and **social regulation**, *the extent to which society controls or regulates individual behavior.* Based on these two major social factors, Durkheim created four categories of suicide primarily caused by social strain: *altruistic* (too much social integration), *egoistic* (too little social integration), *fatalistic* (too much social regulation), and *anomic* (too little social regulation). These four categories of suicide and more details about Durkheim's landmark study of the phenomenon will be covered in Chapter 9.

Perhaps one of the most important sociological concepts to emerge from Durkheim's suicide study was that of *anomie*. Durkheim coined the term **anomie** to refer to *a state of social strain, normative confusion, or rapid change in norms or social structure which results in people no longer feeling constrained by conventional social norms.* Sometimes defined in introductory sociology books as a state of "normlessness," anomie is much more complex than that. Durkheim would argue that there are always norms in place, consequently, there is no such thing as a state of normlessness. Rather, because of rapid social change or some unforeseen social situation, norms are either confused, temporarily suspended, ambiguous, or no longer enforced, causing people to no longer feel constrained or regulated by them. For example, in times of revolution, war, economic or political upheaval, acts of terrorism, and even natural disasters such as floods, tornadoes, hurricanes, people may commit deviant acts that they would never commit under ordinary circumstances. In the United States, we often see that the aforementioned social situations often simultaneously bring out the very *best* and the very *worst* in people. After the 9/11 attacks on the New York City World Trade Centers, not only first responders, but ordinary citizens rushed to the aid of their fellow human beings offering aid, security, and shelter. At the same time, for some, the terroristic act heightened fear, suspicion, racism, and bigotry accompanied by acts of discrimination and violence. Any time a tornado, hurricane, or flood occurs, the National Guard are called out not only to aid in search and rescue, but to prevent looting and other criminal acts as some people descend on the victims like vultures on prey.

Robert Merton (1938) elaborated on Durkheim's concept of anomie to develop a general structural functionalist theory of conformity and deviance. According to Merton's anomie theory, the primary explanation for conformity or deviance resides in how people respond to their place in the social structure in regard to accepting and pursuing socially accepted goals through culturally approved means. According to Merton, people in a capitalistic society, especially in the United States, are socialized to equate success with the accumulation of material possessions such as nice homes, expensive automobiles, fashionable clothes, fine jewelry, and the high socioeconomic status associated with those things. People are supposed to internalize those goals and then pursue them through culturally approved means such as staying in school, getting a good job, working hard, saving money, and otherwise following established norms deemed to lead to socioeconomic success. This adaptation, Merton identified as conformity. As a result of their place in the social structure, however, not everybody internalizes the same goals or has the opportunity to pursue them equally through culturally acceptable means. For example, what if due to poverty or other circumstances, people see no realistic value in internalizing goals they cannot possibly reach? Or, what if they do internalize those goals, but virtually all culturally approved means for achieving them are unavailable or blocked? This anomic situation, Merton contended, leads to deviant adaptations. Merton developed a typology to describe how categories of people adapt to the social strain they experience in relation to pursuance of societal goals through approved means (see Table 4.1).

The first, and perhaps most common adaptation discussed by Merton is *conformity*. When people accept the socially approved goals and their place in the social structure allows them to pursue them through culturally approved means, even if those means are not easily available to them, they are conforming to norms and generally viewed as conformists. Johnny's parents and society as a whole teach Johnny to want all the success and material things in life that society has to offer. Johnny is fourteen, and his most immediate goal is to be able to get a car when he turns

**Table 4.1**   Merton's Typology of Modes of Adaptive Behavior. (Merton, 1938:676)

| Adaptation | Socially accepted goals | Culturally approved means |
|---|---|---|
| Conformity | Accepts and pursues | Accepts and uses |
| Innovation | Accepts and pursues | Rejects, or cannot pursue Substitutes deviant means |
| Ritualism | Rejects, does not pursue | Appears to accept, but confuses means with goals |
| Retreatism | Rejects, does not pursue | Rejects and does not use |
| Rebellion | Rejects, replaces with deviant goals | Rejects, replaces with deviant means |

sixteen. Johnny stays in school, studies hard, gets two part-time jobs throwing newspapers in the morning before school and mowing lawns on the weekends. Johnny saves a little money and, as a result, when he turns sixteen he has enough money for a down payment on a used automobile – not the car of his dreams, but transportation. By almost all accounts, Johnny is conforming to the norms of society, and even at the young age of sixteen, is a "success."

The second adaptation, *innovation*, involves finding a new alternative route to success, one that may not be culturally approved. In the previous scenario, let's say everything in Johnny's life is the same up to the point where Johnny stays in school. Instead, suppose Johnny is the oldest child in a family with eight children. Johnny's father left the family shortly after the birth of the youngest child, and Johnny's mother who has less than a high school education is working two low-paying jobs to support the family. Johnny at age fourteen is essentially the "man" of the family. Johnny realizes that throwing newspapers and mowing lawns is not going to provide enough income to help support his family, much less provide enough savings to purchase a car at age sixteen. Johnny sees a couple of boys his age in the neighborhood who dress much nicer than he, and at ages 15 and 16, both already drive very nice cars – and one of the boys is not even old enough to have a valid license. Upon inquiry, Johnny learns that these boys ride around on bicycles and "spot" high-end luxury vehicles such as BMWs, Mercedes, Lexus, and others and simply hit a button on a "burner" phone they have been provided and report the location of the vehicle. Each Sunday morning, they ride their bikes to a dumpster behind an abandoned warehouse and pick up a brown paper bag that contains a crisp 100 dollar bill for each vehicle they have spotted and reported along with a new burner phone. Each boy "earns" between five hundred to six hundred dollars per week, for doing virtually nothing. They have never met the person who leaves them the money or a new phone each week, they have not broken any laws, lied to their parents, or even been truant from school, although both boys are considering dropping out of school so that they can cruise the streets more regularly during daytime hours and "earn" even more cash. These boys have discovered an innovative way to achieve what Johnny wants to accomplish, but cannot – at least, not through conventional methods. Of course, by most people's definition, what the boys are doing is deviant, and although temporarily rewarding, may have some long-term negative consequences, especially if the boys "graduate" into higher and more overtly criminal roles in the professional auto theft ring of which they either knowingly or unknowingly are a part.

If Johnny chooses not to adapt innovatively and participate in the deviant activity of spotting cars for theft, he might become dejected and lose faith in his ability to ever achieve the goals society and he have prescribed for him. Yet, Johnny loves his mother and does not want to disappoint her, so even though he now rejects the socially accepted goals, he pretends to pursue them through culturally accepted means by staying in school, throwing the papers, mowing lawns, and putting up the good front, even though all of this is meaningless to him and all he really wants to do is escape it all. Johnny is adapting according to Merton's third type, *ritualism*. Even though he no longer accepts or believes in the goals, he pretends to be pursuing them by adhering to culturally approved means. Ritualism is not reserved for lower class struggling youths like Johnny, however, as many middle class and upper class teenagers often reject the goals, but because of the strain to please parents, or otherwise conform to culturally approved means of behavior, simply "go through the motions." Adults, too, often adopt the ritualistic approach to life sometimes attending church regularly although they no longer believe the dogma, never miss a day of work although they have long since rejected the goals of their employer and absolutely hate their jobs, or stay in meaningless marital relationships, adhering to the "'til death do us part" vow although none of the vows they took now hold any type of meaning for them.

What if Johnny becomes so hapless that he no longer merely rejects the goals, but he also refuses to "play the game?" *Retreatism* occurs when people feel so much strain due to their place in the social structure that they must try to escape it. Johnny might run away from home which could provide at least temporary, or possibly even long-term, escape as might the use of drugs and alcohol. A surefire long-term escape that Johnny might contemplate is suicide. People often quote that suicide is a, "long-term solution to a short-term problem," and in some ways it could be considered the ultimate retreat from social strain.

Merton's final adaptation, *rebellion*, is the one that probably captures most social attention and is the most likely to be readily defined as deviant. If Johnny rejects societal goals, refuses to "play the game," and joins a violent street gang that adheres to a totally different set of goals and pursues them through totally unacceptable means, he is personifying Merton's theory about rebellion.

Keep in mind that Merton is not talking about individual personality types, but modes of adaptation. As illustrated by the examples using Johnny, the same person might adapt in several different ways, either in some type of sequence, or sometimes all at the same time. Merton's theory is sociological, not psychological. He's not talking about individual reactions to social situations, but types of adaptive strategies available to large numbers of people in similar situations because of their place in the social structure. Adaptations available to the wealthy are not always available to the poor, and vice versa. Urban dwellers often have more opportunities to adapt in deviant fashion than do rural people. For example, there is not much use for rural car "spotters" in an area where everybody is related to each other and everyone knows who drives which pick-up. Conversely, urban areas not only provide opportunities for car theft rings, but they also typically become both the generating and collecting places for a wide variety of deviant subcultures.

## Deviant subcultures

Albert Cohen (1955) expanded on Merton's anomie theory of deviance by focusing on the strain and status frustration experienced by lower class boys growing up in neighborhoods where culturally approved means for achieving success are limited. Cohen theorized that as lower class youths internalize the socially approved goals and see others around them from higher socio-economic situations able to accomplish those goals while those same opportunities are not available to them and their efforts are thwarted, they become more and more frustrated until they ultimately reject middle class norms and values altogether replacing them with antithetical norms and values. Hence, much as described by Merton's rebellion adaptation, lower class boys are more likely to join gangs. Unlike Merton, however, who saw most lower class crime and delinquency as a pragmatic and utilitarian adaptation to their place in the social structure, Cohen (1955:25) insisted that much lower class crime and delinquency is "nonutilitarian, malicious, and negativistic."

Picking up on Cohen's theme of status frustration linked to limited opportunities, Richard Cloward and Lloyd Ohlin (1960) added the concept of "differential illegitimate opportunities." They contended that just as lower class juveniles, because of their place in the social structure, have differential "legitimate" opportunities for pursuing socially approved goals, they also have differential "illegitimate" opportunities. They pointed out that when youths find that both their legitimate and illegitimate means for pursuing goals are blocked, their status frustration is compounded, and in some ways they have no choice but to strike out against middle class norms and values, which often leads to striking out against middle class people. They theorized that lower class youths form delinquent subcultures in the form of either "crime-oriented," "conflict-oriented," or "retreatist-oriented" gangs.

Walter Miller (1958) also focused on social structure and social class in explaining deviance, especially crime and delinquency. Miller's research indicated that lower class males have a different set of values or "focal concerns" that focus on trouble, toughness, smartness (street smart, not academic), excitement, fate, and autonomy. He believed that these unique focal concerns came about as a result of social classes being segregated spatially, socially, and economically, and contributed to lower class individuals violating norms and laws created and enforced by middle and upper class entities.

One of the better known theories on deviant subcultures is Wolfgang and Ferracuti's (1967) Subculture of Violence theory which attempted to outline a methodological framework for the empirical examination of violent subcultures. Central to their theory was the hypothesis that higher rates of violence occur among lower class and racially segregated populations because these groups have embraced values and norms that permit, encourage, promote, and reinforce violence. Subsequent researchers have argued that certain geographical areas (e.g., inner cities and rural south) may be examples of how values and norms that promote violence as a way to solve problems or release frustrations encourage deviant behavior. In the south, for example, violence is not only viewed as a way of solving problems (e.g., fighting, capital punishment), but also as a form of entertainment and sport (e.g., gun shows, hunting, football, boxing). Consequently, a subcultural value system develops and is reinforced that encourages various types of violent behavior that may be viewed as deviant by other regions of the country.

While many of the strain and deviant subculture theories focused on crime, delinquency, and violence, they also have applicability to other forms of deviance. For example, Watson (1980) used Miller's theory on lower class focal concerns to explain the development and persistence of outlaw motorcycle clubs, and Thompson (2012) illustrated how those same focal concerns are not limited to the lower class, but could be applied to contemporary motorcyclists' subculture which includes large numbers of middle and upper-middle class riders.

Volumes of research demonstrate that deviants often experience stigma, become social outcasts, and discover that one of the ways to manage their spoiled identities is to congregate with others who share that same fate (see Chapter 2). As we will see in subsequent chapters, nudists tend to form nudist colonies, tattoo parlors tend to locate in certain areas of cities, as do adult bookstores, topless bars, drug paraphernalia stores, and other businesses that cater to certain deviant subcultures. Historically, gays have created enclaves in urban areas that lead to homosocial environments where they can live relatively undisturbed, frequenting gay clubs, going to a gay doctor, gay dentist, and other businesses and professionals without fear of judgment or reprisal.

The formation of deviant subcultures can be quite functional. They offer sociality, camara-derie, protection, identity, unity, and reinforcement for people who have been stigmatized, threatened, and/or exiled by larger society. Conversely, it can be argued that deviant subcultures can also be dysfunctional in that they separate, segregate, isolate, and in some cases may make the deviants within them even more vulnerable to stigma, attacks, and violence from those who wish to persecute them.

## Strengths and weaknesses of the functionalist perspective

One of the strengths of the functionalist perspective on deviance is that it looks at both positive and negative aspects of deviance and how deviance can be both functional and dys-functional. In Chapter 1, we briefly described some of the negative and positive consequences of deviance. Among the negative consequences were: people may be harmed, norms are threatened, social order is threatened, there are huge costs to society, and the concern that violation of one norm may lead to the violation of others. Conversely, some of the positive outcomes of deviance include: norms being reinforced, the promotion of social solidarity, providing a contrast between conformity and deviance, providing a "safety valve" for otherwise conforming individuals, and providing leadership, innovation, and social change. Essentially, this type of analysis of deviance is deeply rooted in the functionalist perspective. If you simply replace the word *negative* with the word *dysfunctional*, you can see that the so-called neg-ative effects of deviance are those consequences of deviance that threaten the overall smooth functioning of society. Functionalists see social deviance as being **dysfunctional** when *it threatens the overall well-being or smooth functioning of society*. In contrast, substitute the word *functional* for positive, and you see that deviance can be **functional** when it *contributes to the overall well-being or smooth functioning of society*, such as reinforcing norms, providing jobs in fields related to social control, or brings about any of the other things cited as potential positive consequences of deviance.

Functionalism takes a consensus view of the norms, meaning that although it acknowledges that not everybody shares the same values, it assumes that norms arise out of consensus about what is right and wrong, good and bad, conformist and deviant. While this macro-level view coincides nicely with the idea of democracy and the value of equality, it may be naïve to the complexity of modern industrial and post-industrial societies like the United States. Take for example Merton's anomie theory. Merton operates from the assumption that there is one set of common socially approved goals that are generally adhered to by *all* members of society. He also assumes that there is one set of universally approved cultural means for achieving those goals. While that perspective might be the case in small homogeneous societies, it hardly reflects the diversity of a complex heterogeneous society like the United States or many European nations. All of the strain theories assume this consensus of norms and sees deviation from them as being problematic and in need of explanation. After all, why would people who share common values and participate in creating norms that reflect those values, then turn around and violate those norms? The subcultural theories address this overall weakness of the functionalist perspective in that it somewhat acknowledges diversity and the fact that certain segments of society may share values and norms that run counter to those of larger society, but it still implies that deviance is unusual if not abnormal, and something with which to be reckoned or controlled.

There are other sociological explanations that disagree with the functionalist perspective on deviance. One such approach is the conflict perspective which also focuses on a macro-level analysis of social structure and its link to deviance and conformity, but acknowledges diversity of values and different vested interests and contends that norms arise out of conflict rather than through consensus.

## The Conflict Perspective and Deviant Behavior

Popular song lyrics of the 1937 George Gershwin song "Let's Call the Whole Thing Off" pointed out that the different pronunciations of "tomaytoes" or "tomahtoes" and "potaytoes" or "potahtoes" were rooted in class differences, not merely regional dialects. While the functionalist perspective focuses mainly on the behaviors that are considered deviant by society, the **conflict perspective** provides *a macro-level analysis that focuses more on the values and origins of norms than on the deviant behaviors or deviants themselves*. Whereas the functionalist perspective views society as an organism, the conflict perspective sees it as an *arena* where various groups with conflicting values and norms compete for dominance and survival.

### The Marxian heritage

The conflict perspective in sociology traces its philosophical roots to the writings of Karl Marx (1867/1967; Marx and Engels 1848/1964). Marx's writings focused on the evils of capitalism and how it created and perpetuated inequality based on social class. Marx basically saw society as divided into two basic social classes: the *bourgeoisie* (capitalist class who owned and controlled the means of production in society) and the *proletariat* (working class who provided the labor to produce things). Marxian philosophy emphasized the differential power experienced by the two classes and the ability of the bourgeoisie (or "haves") to exploit the labor of the proletariat (or "have-nots") in order to maximize their own wealth, power, and prestige while sharing little or none of the profits with the people who actually produced them. Marx believed that as the proletariat became increasingly aware of this exploitation, they would become alienated from their work and ultimately would rise up to overthrow the wealthy and powerful class to replace the capitalistic system with what he viewed as a much more fair and egalitarian communist and socialist one.

Although Marx was not attempting to develop a theory to explain conformity and deviance, many scholars believe he did just that. By looking at the unequal distribution of power and identifying the conflicting interests of the "haves" and "have-nots" in society, it follows that those with the power to create and enforce norms are going do so in such a way as to preserve their vested interests and protect their values. Consequently, from a conflict perspective, those in power can create norms that reflect and reinforce their values coercing those with less power to either conform to those norms, although they are in conflict with their own values and vested interests. Failure to do so results in being defined as deviant and suffering the social, political, and economic sanctions that accompany the deviant status. One of the ways that Marx believed that the state would inflict the will of the elite ruling class on the masses was by creating laws to protect the values and vested interest of the bourgeoisie, thereby criminalizing the actions of the proletariat if they failed to conform to the will of those in power.

## The social reality of crime and delinquency

A number of theorists used the Marxian heritage as part of their framework to explain deviance and conformity. Criminologist Richard Quinney (1970) developed a theory in which he distinguished between what he called the "official reality" and the "social reality" of crime and delinquency. According to Quinney (1970), on the one hand, the "official reality" of crime purports that law violation threatens social order and public safety. Note that this coincides with the functionalist view of deviance. On the other hand, the "social reality" of crime reflects the less visible and more subtle definition that any act that threatens those in power is legally prohibited and legally punished. In short, those in power make and enforce laws that reflect their values and vested interests. The powerless must obey those laws, even though they may be in direct conflict with their values and vested interests, or they will be arrested, fined, imprisoned, or even executed. While it can be that laws that prohibit murder, assault, rape, robbery, burglary, and theft are almost universal and reflect the overall values of most members of society, how those laws get interpreted and apply often favor the wealthy and powerful over the poor and powerless. During the economic recession of 2008, conflict theorists marveled that people convicted of street crimes involving the theft of $100 might receive five years in prison while hedge fund traders and other Wall Street moguls who bilked investors out of millions of dollars were never arrested or punished. Moreover, what about laws that prohibit activities such as loitering, begging, sleeping in public parks, and others that are directly aimed at the poor and powerless, criminalizing activities that, it could be argued, neither harm any person nor damage any property. Perhaps Jeffrey Reiman (2013) sums up the discrepancies in prosecution and penalties for white-collar versus street crimes from a conflict perspective best in his book, *The Rich Get Richer and the Poor Get Prison*. The title pretty much says it all. In a much broader sense for the understanding of deviance, what about laws against homosexual acts, same-sex marriage, public nudity, drug use, or many other forms of deviance that are the subjects of later chapters in this book, some of which clearly seem to be ways that the dominant class can criminalize or at least stigmatize and thereby control the behaviors of those with less power and values that seem to "threaten" those in power.

## Social threat theory

**Social threat theory** *contends that efforts of social control are related to the perceived threat of social deviance to those in power.* Drug laws which are more closely examined in Chapter 7 are a good example of how a perceived threat may be almost totally unrelated to the actual danger posed by a particular behavior. For example, despite the fact that voluminous research indicates that marijuana has much less harmful effects on health or public safety than alcohol, or even tobacco, only a few states have legalized the possession or use of small amounts of marijuana whereas the possession, sale, and use of alcohol and tobacco, while regulated, is legal in all fifty states. Meanwhile, thousands of people are doing time in American prisons for the possession or use of small amounts of marijuana. Distributing and selling the drug brings even stiffer penalties and longer sentences. Numerous writers have pointed out that although both are illegal and may lead to arrest and imprisonment, generally, possession, use, and sale of cocaine (the choice of middle and upper class recreational drug users) bring about less harsh penalties than that of crack, a derivative of exactly the same drug, but in a form that is cheaper and used more by members of the lower class.

Another example of threat theory can be illustrated by *moral panics* which we described in Chapter 1, where the perceived threat of a particular activity far exceeds the actual occurrence or negative consequences of it. For example, in the United States, despite declining crime rates (both violent and property crimes) over the past several decades, rates of incarceration in prisons continue to rise. Although reported violence in public schools in the United States peaked in the 1992–1993 school year and has steadily declined in the decades since, parents are more afraid than ever to send their children to school despite the fact that all data indicate that children are safer in school than they are in their own homes. As a result, school districts continue to hire off-duty or on-duty police officers to patrol their hallways, and after some of the most horrific (but rare) incidences of school violence, some districts in Missouri, Texas, Arkansas, Oklahoma, and other states began allowing and even encouraging their teachers to take basic firearm training and bring guns to school (Eligon, 2013).

Public fears over increases in teenage Satanism, drive-by shootings, child kidnappings, home invasions, teen suicides, drug abuse, mental illness, terrorism, and other forms of deviance have been greatly exaggerated by the media and the general public resulting in allowing those in power to heighten regulation of the behaviors of those who they perceive as threatening the status quo. The social contract that everyone shares by being part of a society necessitates people to sacrifice some of their personal rights and freedoms for the safety and security of themselves and the rest of society. Moral panics and other exaggerated fears of deviance allow those in power to usurp even more social control as people in fear may be willing to sacrifice even more rights and freedoms for what Marx would call the "false consciousness" of perceived security.

## Strengths and weaknesses of the conflict perspective

Strengths of the conflict perspective on deviance include the fact that it takes a macro-level look at deviance and acknowledges the diversity of values that exist and operate in a large, complex, heterogeneous society. Rather than focusing on individual acts or individual deviants, the conflict perspective looks at the overall social structure and the importance of social class and differential power in explaining conformity and deviance. The conflict perspective's main focus is on where the norms come from and how they are created, interpreted, enforced, and sanctioned. In a word, that explanation is *power*. Those in power essentially have the ability to inflict their values and their will on those who do not have power. Conflict theories acknowledge that different races, religions, social classes, and groups have different values and that those various entities create norms that reflect and reinforce their values. Unlike the functionalist approach, however, that assumes these various groups all come to some type of consensus on what the norms of any given society should be, conflict theorists see the process as one of coercion rather than consensus. From the conflict perspective norms arise through competition, exploitation, and coercion more than through negotiation, compromise, and consensus.

Critics of conflict theory contend that it focuses too much on competition and conflict and tends to ignore much of the cooperation and unity that can be found in almost any society regardless of its diversity. While conflict theories shed light on the process of norm creation, they tell us little about why some of those out of power commit deviance while others do not. Conflict theorists contend that those in power dictate the norms and their level of enforcement, and while there may be numerous examples that seem to support that contention, there also are many that do not. For example, conflict theory does little to explain how groups such as MADD (mothers against drunk driving) can organize at the grassroots and make major changes in the creation and enforcement of drinking and driving laws even if they are opposed by large liquor manufacturers and their lobbyists. Or, how despite the fact that those in power deemed it important to pass into federal law DOMA (the defense of marriage act) essentially banning same-sex marriage, public opinion continued to move in the other direction as same-sex marriage became more highly visible, accepted, and legalized in individual states.

Critics of both the functionalist and conflict perspectives contend that these macro-level approaches place too much emphasis on social structure and underestimate the importance of micro-level day to day interaction in defining and responding to conformity and social deviance. Critics also insist that theorists operating from those two viewpoints may be asking the wrong questions. Rather than asking what *causes* deviance and conformity, sociologists operating from the symbolic interaction perspective ask, "what *is* deviance?" and "what *is* conformity?"

## Interactionist Theories and the Constructionist View of Deviance

**Interactionist theories** *view conformity and deviance as flexible and symbolic terms that are defined and redefined through the process of social interaction.* The **symbolic interaction perspective** *views social meaning as arising through the process of social interaction and communication.* Whereas the functionalist and conflict perspectives take a macro-level view of deviance, the interactionist approach uses a **micro-level analysis**, which *focuses on the day to day interactions of individuals and groups in specific social situations.* Functionalists view society as an organism, conflict theorists see it as an arena, and symbolic interactionists compare society to a *stage* where the drama of life is played out on a daily basis. Both functionalism and conflict can be categorized as *structural theories* as they focus on social structure, whereas interactionism is considered a *process theory* in that it focuses on social processes that define, create, and control deviance.

Key to the symbolic interaction approach is the importance of **symbols**, *anything that represents something else.* When most of us think of symbols, things like a country's flag, a crucifix, a Star of David, or other important national or religious symbols may come to mind. And, indeed those are all symbols. Symbols may also include a wide array of hand gestures, sounds, colors, or almost anything else. What makes a symbol meaningful is when it calls out the same meaning in the receiver as was intended by the sender. For example, during a college basketball game you might see a player dribbling the ball down the court holding up his index and middle fingers to indicate to the team that they will be running play number two on offense. If all team members have attended practice, know what they are supposed to do to make play number two work effectively, and then are able to successfully execute their jobs, then holding up the two fingers was a meaningful symbol. Imagine the chaos, however, if the player bringing the ball down the court holds up two fingers indicating "let's run play number two," and one of his teammates thinks he is giving the "V for Victory" sign that held common significant meaning for European and American allies during World War II, while yet another player on the team wonders why his teammate is giving the "peace sign" (also a valid meaning for two fingers held above the head) during an important basketball game. Symbols can mean different things to different people which can threaten the meaning of social interaction, and possibly lead to deviant behavior.

We established in Chapter 2 that deviance is a social status, and quite often becomes a person's *master status.* Every social status is replete with a variety of symbols that represent a person's status to others. We call those symbols *status symbols.* Quite often when we hear the term status symbols we almost immediately think of things like expensive cars, fine jewelry, or designer clothes, and indeed, those are all status symbols. They happen to be symbols of high status. What some people do not realize is that being too poor to own a car, or owning a junker, wearing cheap costume jewelry, and ragged clothes acquired from a charity shop are also status symbols. They just happen to indicate low social status. You may remember that in Chapter 2, we introduced the concept of *stigma symbols,* those things that symbolize deviance or stigma to others such as scars across the wrist that might indicate a suicide attempt, or some physical anomaly that causes a person not to be fully socially accepted by others. Whether something is considered a high status symbol, a low status symbol, or a stigma symbol depends heavily on how things are socially defined and labeled.

As we have alluded with our discussion of symbols which can mean different things to different people, as individuals interact with one another, each one defines the interaction in a way that is meaningful to him or her. In other words, during interaction, each actor creates a **definition of the situation** in which *people create a definition of social reality that is real in its consequences.* If you have ever watched one of the popular television dating shows such as *The Bachelor* or *The Bachelorette*, you have probably viewed scenes where after a date each one talks separately to the camera telling the audience his or her perception of how things went on the date. He might look into the camera and say something like, "I could tell she was really into me by the way she kept smiling and looking away and then looking back and smiling again, and the way she kept reaching out to me and touching me, barely able to keep her hands off of me." Then, we see her talking into the camera as she comments with a look of disgust, "I thought he was ridiculous and could barely keep from laughing in his face ... he was so repulsive, I actually kept physically pushing him away with my hands, but he just kept staring at me and telling me how much he liked me." Were these two people even on the same date? The answer is "yes," and "no." They may have been on the same date, but obviously, each participant has a different definition of the situation. In his mind the date went perfectly and in her view it was an utter disaster. Although often when people interact they come to somewhat of a mutual or shared definition of the situation by communicating with meaningful symbols (language being the most powerful and important symbol of all), sometimes when they interact conflicting definitions of the situation emerge with one person's reality being totally different from another's. Such is the case with defining conformity and deviance. Often, as the functionalist perspective contends, norms arise through a consensus in values with people sharing a fairly common definition of what is permissible and what is not. In contrast, sometimes norms arise out of conflict with one group defining something as right and proper while another views it as wrong and deviant. In those cases, both groups are attempting to label behavior as either conforming or deviant, and in many cases the group with the most power will be the most persuasive.

## Labeling theories

Many people refer to this point of view on conformity and deviance as labeling "theories," while others prefer to call it the labeling view or labeling perspective of conformity and deviance. In other words, some people label this line of thinking as a "theory" of deviance while others label it as more of a "perspective" or viewpoint on conformity and deviance. What is the difference? The difference is in the *label*, the *word*, or the *symbol*. We have already used the word theory numerous times in this book, and defined it in Chapter 3 as *a set of interrelated propositions or statements that attempt to explain some phenomenon*. In science and the social sciences, theories must be based on systematic research and should be testable through empirical scientific investigation. Sociological theories like the ones discussed in this chapter are somewhat more difficult to develop and test than theories in the so-called hard sciences such as biology, chemistry, and physics, since sociological research deals with people interacting in relatively uncontrolled environments as opposed to animals or inanimate objects being manipulated in a controlled laboratory. Nevertheless, social and behavioral scientists adhere to the same scientific method and strive for the same type of methodological rigor as all the other sciences, and the theories developed by them are far more than just opinions or "educated guesses" about human behavior. Based on extensive data gathered through systematic research under different social situations, sociological theories on conformity of deviance have proven to be rigorously developed, rigorously tested and replicated, and although no one theory explains all human behavior, when pieced together these various theories can explain a great deal of what people do and why they do it. In this case, labeling theories are not really trying to explain why people commit deviant acts, but instead are exploring how members of a society determine what constitutes deviant acts. The answer is through defining social situations and then labeling acts and people as either conforming or deviant.

**Labeling theories** *see conformity and deviance as labels applied to certain acts and conformist and deviant as labels assigned to certain people.* If you were to go back and re-read Chapter 2, you would discover that much of that chapter is grounded in the framework of symbolic interaction, illustrating the process of defining situations and people as deviant and then them assuming the deviant status and fulfilling the deviant role. Deviance as a *master status*, *primary* and *secondary* deviance, are all terms and theoretical concepts derived from labeling theories.

Is this young boy more likely to be labeled as "creative" or "deviant?" Sociologically, how significant is the difference between those two labels? *Source*: Locked Illusions Photography/Getty Images

One of the earliest and creative labeling theories of deviance was derived from Howard Becker's (1963) research on jazz musicians and their recreational use of marijuana. We briefly referred to Becker's study in Chapter 2 when we discussed progression through various stages of a *deviant career*. Perhaps Becker's most important contribution from his study of jazz musicians can be found in the title of the book he wrote on the subject, *Outsiders*. Becker (1963:1) explained, "All social groups make rules … and attempt to enforce them … the person who breaks the rule … is labeled an outsider." Becker, and the labeling perspective of deviance that evolved from his research broke the tradition of accepting the label of deviant as a given, and questioned the process whereby that label was assigned or attained. From this viewpoint, deviance is not a quality of an act, but is the consequence of a reaction. In his words, "The deviant is one to whom that label has successfully been applied; deviant behavior is behavior that people so label" (Becker, 1963:9).

From the labeling perspective, one need not violate a norm to be labeled as deviant. For example, a teacher accused of sexually molesting a student might be totally innocent, but the stigma associated with merely being accused may be enough to end his or her career. Similarly, in high profile criminal cases like the O.J. Simpson murder trial or the George Zimmerman and Trayvon Martin case, despite jury verdicts of "Not Guilty," many people apply the deviant label to them nevertheless.

In Chapter 2, we discussed deviance as a master status and we talked about primary and secondary deviance as part of the social process of becoming deviant. Those concepts are derived from the interactionist perspective and are viewed as direct results of the labeling process. Another important result of labeling is what sociologists call the **self-fulfilling prophecy**, in which *saying it's so, makes it so*. In other words, when a person is labeled a certain way, people begin to treat them as if they are what they are labeled, causing the labeled person in many cases to conform to the expectations associated with that label, ultimately legitimizing the label that may or may not have been correctly applied in the first place. For example, if a person is diagnosed as mentally ill, once the label is applied to them by somebody with the power to legitimately do so (a psychiatrist), all of their actions and interactions from that point forward are interpreted within the context of the label (being mentally ill). Denial of the mental illness is almost always listed as one of the symptoms of being mentally ill. Claiming that you have been misdiagnosed, are being mistreated, and being held against your will while being forced to take psychotropic drugs, are all confirmation that you are indeed sick and "need help." If the patient attempts to resist and fights the medical attendants, nurses, or doctors, this is even further proof of mental illness. It is not until a patient admits that they have a problem, which is usually interpreted as the first sign of getting better, and cooperates with their treatment that they have any hope of being diagnosed as "in remission" (note, they are not cured), and have the possibility of being released. Once released, however, the person does not escape the label of mental illness as they now are labeled as "in remission," or an "ex-mental patient," labels that imply that the deviance can and might recur at any time.

In schools, children labeled as "gifted and talented" are often assigned to smaller classes with the best teachers using state-of-the-art equipment as they are challenged to do more difficult coursework that requires higher level thinking. If they struggle, teachers work harder to make sure that the students master the material because, after all, they are gifted and talented students who obviously have the intelligence and skills to do so. The end results are usually a "gifted and talented" student who is mastering work far beyond their age and grade level. Conversely, a student labeled as a "slow learner" is often grouped with other slow learners in a classroom with a teacher who has very low expectations of them, teaches them more slowly, and provides them with below-grade level work hoping that they can experience at least a minimal level of accomplishment. If the students do not learn, that is not unexpected. If they do learn, it will be at a slower pace than "average" students and a much slower and lower level than the "gifted and talented" students. A few years of experiencing the different labels almost guarantee that the labeled children will experience a self-fulfilling prophecy with the gap between the "gifted and talented" students and the "slower" students growing ever wider.

## Social learning theories

**Social learning theories** *contend that much human behavior, including conformity and deviance, is learned through social interaction*. One of the most prominent social learning theories is the theory of *differential association* developed by criminologist Edwin Sutherland and later expanded by Donald Cressey. Differential association theory elaborates on the old adage that, "birds of a feather flock together." In short, **differential association theory** *asserts that people learn values, norms, and behaviors from people with whom they associate and interact*. In nine systematic and testable propositions, differential association theory asserts:

1   Deviance is learned.
2   Deviance is learned through social interaction.
3   The learning of deviance occurs within primary groups.
4   Learning deviance includes learning (a) the techniques of committing deviance, and (b) the motives and rationalizations for committing deviance.
5   Whether people learn to conform or deviate from norms depends on the definitions that are either favorable or unfavorable to the norms.
6   A person becomes deviant because of an excess of definitions favorable to deviance over definitions favorable to conformity.
7   Differential associations vary in frequency, duration, priority, and intensity.
8   Learning deviance involves all the mechanisms of learning any behavior.
9   Although deviance may be an expression of general needs and values, it is not explained by those needs and values, as they also could be met through conformity. A person learns to choose deviance over conformity based upon those with whom he or she associates (Sutherland and Cressey, 1978:80–83).

Ronald Akers (2009) further developed differential association theory with the addition of the importance of **differential reinforcement**, *whether deviant behavior is positively reinforced or negatively sanctioned*. Say a teenage girl shoplifts some expensive cosmetics from a department store and the next day reveals to her three or four best friends how she acquired the make-up. If her friends seem impressed, ask her if she can steal some for them, or teach them how to steal it for themselves, according to differential association and reinforcement, the girl is very likely to repeat her shoplifting in the future. Conversely, if her friends are appalled that their friend stole the cosmetics, and complain that the reason they have to pay so much for expensive make-up is because people like her steal it, and they tell her that they will no longer be her friend if she ever steals again, how likely is she to repeat the behavior? Based on these social learning theories, the girl will either stop her deviant behavior, or find a different set of friends who will respond more positively to her thievery.

**Differential identification theory** *contends that an important variable in social learning is the extent to which a person identifies with a role model*. Whereas differential association, differential reinforcement, and most other social learning theories assert that conformity and deviance are learned through face to face social interaction and communication, differential identification allows that people can learn attitudes, values, beliefs, norms, and behaviors from people they have never even met if they strongly see them as a role model and identify with them (Glaser, 1956). A dimension this adds to social learning theories is that conformity and deviance cannot only be learned and/or reinforced from family members, friends, or other individuals with whom a person interacts, but they also can be learned from afar from role models, real or imaginary, with whom a person may never actually come in contact. This theory gives credence to the powerful influence of media in that young children can learn values and norms from cartoon characters, fictional heroes or antiheroes, professional athletes, musicians, and other celebrities regardless of whether they are real or imaginary, positive or negative influences, intended or unintended role models. This theory provides insights into the potential power of all types of media in terms of socialization and social control.

## Control theories

Control theories are also interactional in nature taking a micro-level look at deviance and assert that most sociological theories on deviance have asked the wrong question. Instead of asking "What causes deviance?," control theorists ask "What causes conformity?" The answer, is social control. Control theorists contend that much of what constitutes deviant behavior, especially relatively minor norm violations, is fun and exciting. In those cases, the appropriate question is not why some people violate norms, but why doesn't everybody do it? Consequently, **control theories** *view deviance as a "normal" response to many social situations and believe that it is conformity that must be explained.*

Gresham Sykes and David Matza (1957) developed **neutralization theory** which *contends that much deviant behavior can be explained by people's ability to rationalize it and thereby neutralize their inhibitions about committing deviance.* They identified five common *techniques of neutralization:*

1 Denial of responsibility.
2 Denial of injury.
3 Denial of a victim.
4 Condemnation of the condemners.
5 Appeal to higher loyalties.

According to neutralization theory if people can deny that the deviance was their fault, or at least contend that nobody was hurt by it, they can more easily rationalize their behavior and neutralize its negative consequences. If somebody was clearly harmed, they still can neutralize the behavior by contending the so-called victim deserved what happened to him or her. It also is common for deviants to condemn the people who are condemning them and often deviants appeal to some higher cause, such as committing the deviance for the good of a group, patriotism or nationalism, or in the name of God, thus claiming that sometimes a less important norm may have to be violated for some higher good, – "you have to break a few eggs to make an omelet." Sykes and Matza primarily developed neutralization theory to help explain crime and delinquency, but you can probably see how these same techniques of neutralization could be used to overcome the power of social control and to rationalize almost any form of deviance.

Walter Reckless (1961) postulated that during childhood socialization, individuals develop *inner containment*, the first barrier against deviance, by learning and internalizing the dominant values and norms of society. For most people, this is enough to cause them to refrain from committing deviance. For others, however, that is not enough. Perhaps as neutralization theory suggests, those with weak inner containment can more easily rationalize and neutralize their deviance. In those cases, Reckless pointed out, society also provides outer containment – parents, teachers, police officers, and other agents of social control who step in to try to insure conformity to norms. Known as **containment theory**, this theory conceptualizes a double line of defense – inner and outer containment – that controls peoples' urges to commit deviance and encourage conformity. Containment also acknowledges the importance of social environment as some social environments have more external agents of social control than others as well as the fact that some environments provide more temptations to deviate and more opportunities to rationalize and neutralize non-conformity.

Travis Hirschi (1969) developed a popular control theory in the form of **social bond theory** which *contends conformity relies on individuals developing a strong bond to society in the form of attachment, commitment, involvement, and belief.* According to this theory, youths who have a strong attachment to parents, peers, school, and other social institutions and are committed to conventional norms are more likely to be involved in conforming groups and activities that help solidify belief in dominant values and norms. This combination of attributes develops a strong social bond between individuals and society, and those with strong social bonds are more likely to conform and less likely to become deviant than those with weaker social bonds.

## Strengths and weaknesses of interactionist theories

A major strength of the interactionist theories of deviance is that they all take a constructionist view of deviance. That is to say, this approach views deviance as socially constructed through the process of social interaction. From this perspective there is no macro-level pervasive rigid social structure that dictates values, norms, and sanctions or that defines conformity and deviance. And, there are no clear-cut definitions for deviance and conformity. Rather, conformity and deviance are socially constructed at the micro-level as people interact and communicate with one another, constructing definitions of the situation that define and redefine values and norms as they go. Over time, these day to day interactions help create cultural traditions and social institutions that help define social reality, so that people do not "wake up in a new world" every day, but nevertheless continue to redefine the meanings and consequences of conformity and deviance through the process of interaction. These theories also emphasize that conformity and deviance are not genetically programmed into people or the result of biological or physiological pathologies, but are the result of socialization and social interaction. Inherently sociological, these theories contend that with whom we interact, how often we interact with them, the nature of our interaction and our relationship, and how people respond to us, are all important explanations for our behaviors whether they are socially defined as conformity or deviant.

A weakness of the interactionist perspective is its lack of acknowledgement of the importance of macro-level phenomena on micro-level behaviors. People are born into a society that consists of social institutions that have to a large extent already defined acceptable and unacceptable behaviors. Although individual actors can and do construct their own social realities by defining and redefining values, norms, and sanctions, social change often comes slowly and individual definitions of the situation that conflict with dominant cultural ideologies often amount to trouble for the dissenter. Critics of the interactionist perspective also assert that while social learning theories help explain how somebody becomes deviant, labeling and neutralization theories focus on how people react to being viewed as deviant with little or no explanation for the behavior that elicited the deviant label that must be neutralized after the fact.

A fourth sociological perspective contends that interactionist theories as well as functionalist and conflict theories all suffer from the same weakness: they are theories postulated by men as a result of research on men, and then are generalized to both men and women.

# A Feminist Perspective on Deviance

The **feminist perspective** *studies, analyzes, and explains conformity and deviance from a gender-focused viewpoint*. This eclectic approach, which is used by both women and men, emphasizes the importance of gender for understanding society and all forms of human behavior (Smith, 1987). Feminist theories incorporate elements of functionalism, conflict, and interactionist theories maintaining that at the macro-level, gender is incorporated into and reflected in the basic social structure of society. Additionally, at the macro-level, feminist theorists point out how traditional sex roles and cultural attitudes regarding gender serve to protect and preserve a status quo of patriarchy in virtually all aspects of society, especially in the institutions of government, economy, family, education, and religion. At the micro-level, feminist theories focus on the powerful influence of sex roles in the ongoing social meanings of gender and the commonly accepted definitions and symbols of masculinity and femininity in everyday face to face social interaction. Feminist scholars are particularly interested in the intersection of race, class, and gender and how these important sociological variables combine to affect people's everyday lives, especially in the social construction of deviance and deviants.

In any society, one of the sure-fire ways to be deemed deviant is to violate the powerful norms that surround sex and gender. In a traditional hunting–gathering society, it is almost always the men and boys who hunt, the women and girls who gather. A woman who hunts or a man who gathers is almost always perceived as deviant and will suffer the social consequences. In advanced industrial and post-industrial societies, despite technological advances and diversity of sex and gender roles, people still tend to have strong opinions about what are considered appropriate and inappropriate behaviors based on a person's sex and the accompanying gender expectations.

In Chapter 1, we introduced the concept of a range of tolerance surrounding norms, and how a certain amount of norm violation is tolerated before we consider a behavior to be deviant to the point of requiring some type of social sanction. That range of tolerance varies greatly on the basis of age, race, sex, and social class. The adage "boys will be boys," has often tolerated norm violating behavior out of boys that would never be tolerated out of girls. Consequently, in many cases gender norms have been far more restrictive for girls and women than for boys and men. This is particularly true in the domain of sexual activities, marital fidelity, and other gender based sex norms. This would apparently mean that as gender norms have become more flexible, and the range of tolerance has increased for females, they would be less likely to be viewed deviant today than in the past. This conclusion, however, may be another sociological example of how things are not necessarily what they seem.

Freda Adler (1975) offered the *liberation hypothesis* as a feminist explanation for why deviance, especially in the forms of crime and delinquency, is increasing among females. According to Adler's **liberation hypothesis**, *deviance is increasing among females because as rigid gender roles become more flexible and more gender equity is achieved, girls and women have more opportunities to participate in deviant activities*. Marcia Millman (1975) contends that pervasive notions in popular culture, especially those espoused by literature, movies, and television have created distorted stereotypes based on gender roles and deviance.

## The Pervasive Influence of the Media

In Chapter 1, we discussed the importance of time, place, situation, and culture in defining deviance and the powerful role played by various forms of media in regard to society members' perceptions of conformity and deviance. Several sociological theories discussed in this chapter acknowledge the pervasive influence of the media not only in the social construction of deviance but also in helping to explain how and why some people become deviant. For example, *social threat theory* contends that the amount and types of social control implemented in any society are directly related to the perceived threat of social deviance. As far as the general public is concerned, their perceptions of threat very often come from the media, often exaggerating certain types of deviance and creating moral panics, while ignoring other forms of norm violating behaviors and activities. In Box 4.1, a former NBC reporter discusses the power of the media, especially television news, in shaping public perceptions about threats to their well-being. We will pursue in greater detail in later chapters of this book, how despite decades of research, facts, and data to the contrary, many people believe that homosexual deviance is far more prevalent than heterosexual deviance, marijuana use is more dangerous than alcohol or tobacco addiction, poor people are crazy while upper class people are just eccentric, school violence is skyrocketing out of control, suicide rates are at all-time highs and increasing exponentially, total strangers are more likely to harm you than family members and friends, and that street crime is more prevalent and costly than white-collar crime. Where do these commonsense notions that amount to nothing more than common nonsense come from? The answer: mostly from the media – especially television and movies.

Perhaps one of the more frustrating and daunting tasks for sociologists in attempting to counter some of the misconceptions about deviance created and perpetuated by the media is how to garner media attention to focus on serious sociological research. Media tend to simplify complex situations and sensationalize deviance, focusing on individual deviants instead of social deviance in ways that belie social scientific research and facts. Because of the pervasive influence of the media in defining deviance and shaping peoples' perceptions of deviance and deviants, sociologists must find ways to use the media to disseminate sociological explanations for deviance as opposed to more gut-level, sensational, knee-jerk reactions to it. In other words, this may be a case where sociologists need to "fight fire with fire" – or perhaps more accurately, fight fiction with facts.

In his Presidential Address to the American Sociological Association, Herbert Gans (1989) lamented the fact that sociologists and our research play a relatively small part in the United States' intellectual life. Gans then went on to suggest several ways that sociologists and sociological research could have more impact on the general public's perceptions and understanding of sociological issues and everyday life. Many of these suggestions involved working with and through various forms of media. For example, Gans expanded upon an earlier article of his in which he urged sociologists to improve relations with print journalists who more often reach out to psychologists or economists to get professional opinions or research findings on social issues because they tend to be more media friendly and more concise and easily understood in the report of their findings than do sociologists who often steep their comments in technical jargon and endless caveats, qualifications, and limitations about generalizability of their findings (Gans, 1988).

**Box 4.1**   In their own words

By Noah Nelson*

Television Journalism 101 taught me at least two truisms: "If it bleeds, it leads," and "If a dog bites a man, it's not news; if a man bites a dog, it is." I never realized just how true those cynical comments were until I became a network correspondent and discovered that even among the most serious news organizations; sensationalism often trumps in-depth investigation, corroboration, and unbiased analysis. The reality of the 24-hour news cycle means that news organizations are under constant pressure to keep up with the never-ending demand for audience enticing content. Many media critics have observed that the once crisp line between entertainment and real news has become blurred.

In this environment the important issues and events of the day are often forced to share air-time with the mundane twists, turns and tweets in the lives of celebrities. And, if something seemingly sensational is involved, all the better. Reputable news organizations now boldly beg, borrow, and attribute their "facts" to blogs and social media gossip channels without blinking. Even with vast collective resources at its command, the US news media repeatedly seems willing to short change the public by giving one or two big stories "24/7" wall-to-wall coverage without actually drilling down to the real meaning of a critical issue or the true root causes of an event.

The biggest pushers of superficiality and blandness are local TV news departments. Overall, gone is the investigative killer instinct that was once the engine that drove the TV news business in the 1970s, 80s and 90s. Gone are the daily news beats to dredge up corruption at city hall, misconduct at the police department, or faulty arithmetic at the local polling place. For the most part, absent is the commitment to spend weeks or months following a juicy lead that might bring down a crooked politician, preacher, or judge. It seems as though the mission of the modern news media is to keep us entertained and avoid being sued by parties made uncomfortable when it does its job.

Does any of this matter? Should we as consumers of news even care? I think the answer to both questions is "yes." To remain a critically thinking society we should constantly check our "news diet" and demand more from those who generate its content. There are solid news organizations out there but today's media marketplace requires that we seek them out. There is still a difference between outfits that hawk celebrity news and act as repeaters of stale facts from those that remember what real news and information really is. Our job is to remember that being tricked and distracted by the "man bites dog story" is not in our best interest, no matter how intriguing that event may be.

---

*Noah Nelson received a bachelor's degree with a major in journalism from East Texas State University and went on to spend approximately thirty years in the news business, sixteen of those years with NBC News.

Popular print media is only one area in which sociological theory is missing. Sociologists generally make poor guests on popular television talk shows, because they refuse to give the short, concise, sensational, and titillating answers that television audiences want and talk show hosts demand. This is not to say that sociologists should "dumb down" their research findings or attempt to be entertainers instead of social scientists, but there is a reason why Dr. Phil has his own popular television show about various forms of deviant behavior that reaches millions of people while most sociologists who study deviance toil away in relative obscurity publishing their research results in formal jargon-laden professional journals most of which will only be read by other sociologists, if even them. Unfortunately, whatever those reasons, sociological explanations for deviance rarely make their way into mainstream media, leaving many people to rely on the popular notions and pseudoscientific explanations we discussed in Chapter 3.

## Summary

When Auguste Comte coined the term sociology to refer to a positivistic approach to the study of society and human behavior, he laid the theoretical foundation for the functionalist perspective on deviance and conformity. One of the first systematic sets of theories on deviance from the functionalist perspective were the strain theories launched by Emile Durkheim's concept of anomie that later translated into Merton's Anomie theory. Functionalists also are very interested in the development of deviant subcultures. Although the functionalist perspective on deviance sheds light on how social structure impacts people's lives and can create social circumstances that may lead to deviant behaviors and subcultures, it relies heavily on the idea of consensus on shared values and norms, ignoring the diversity of values and normative expectations that exist in large heterogeneous societies with diverse populations.

The conflict perspective also tends to take a macro-level approach to deviance looking at social structure and particularly social class, but emphasizes conflict as opposed to consensus when it comes to values and norms. Grounded in the theoretical and philosophical underpinnings of Karl Marx, the conflict perspective focuses on differential power and how groups with power can exploit, dominate, and control those who are less powerful. One of the ways this is done is through creating, defining, and enforcing norms that represent the vested interests of the powerful and ruling class. Conflict theories have been particularly insightful in explaining how criminal laws are created and enforced in such a way as to criminalize those behaviors that threaten the values of the ruling class. While the conflict perspective explains the predominance of interest in street crime over white-collar crime and elite deviance, it somewhat ignores the importance of day to day and face to face interaction and the tenuous nature of power and dominance at the micro-level.

The interactionist perspective on deviance fills the micro-level analytical void left by functionalist and conflict theories. The interactionist approach views conformity and deviance as labels that are applied to various activities and behaviors and conformist and deviant as labels applied to various people for a variety of different reasons. This perspective emphasizes that conformity and deviance are social constructs that have no rigid definitions or criteria. Rather than focusing on social structure or social class, interactionist theories focus on day to day social interaction and how people construct, define, and redefine social reality. Particular emphasis is placed on meaningful symbols and how people symbolically become viewed as deviant or conformist through the process of social interaction.

The feminist perspective on deviance interjects the importance of sex and gender in defining, studying, and explaining conformity and deviance. Social and behavioral scientific theories have been historically dominated by men. Male social scientists studied male behavior and then made generalizations to all people. Feminist sociologists point out the important contributions women can make and have made in sociological research in terms of how they frame research studies, ask research questions, collect and analyze data, and generalize their findings. The feminist perspective can be especially beneficial in studying conformity and deviance as men and women tend to have different values, view the world differently, and define deviance and conformity quite differently.

Finally, the media play a powerful role in explaining deviance and conformity to the general public. Unfortunately, systematic sociological research tends to lack the brevity, simplicity, sensationalism, and individualistic approach to deviance that media consumers demand. With the growth of social media and its pervasive influence on culture and society, sociological explanations for conformity and deviance may be more important and necessary now than ever before.

## Outcomes Assessment

1　Define and explain the functionalist perspective on deviance and give some examples of sociological theories of deviance that fit within the functionalist perspective. What are some of their major strengths and weaknesses?

2　Define and explain the conflict perspective in sociology and how it views deviant behavior. List some important conflict theories and some of their major strengths and weaknesses.

3　Define and explain symbolic interaction and the constructionist view of deviance. How is this view dramatically different from the functionalist and conflict approaches to deviance? What are some of the strengths and weaknesses of the interactionist approach to deviance?

4　Discuss and explain the feminist perspective on defining, explaining, sanctioning, and controlling social deviance.

5　Sociologically explain the pervasive influence of the media in contemporary society and its influence on how society perceives deviance and conformity.

## Key Terms and Concepts

Anomie
containment theory
control theories
differential association theory
differential identification
　theory
differential reinforcement
　theory
dysfunctional
feminist perspective

functional
functionalist perspective
interactionist theories
labeling theories
liberation hypothesis
macro-level analysis
micro-level analysis
neutralization theory
organic analogy
self-fulfilling prophecy

social bond theory
social integration
social learning theories
social pathology
social regulation
social threat theory
strain theories
symbolic interaction
　perspective

# 5

# Deviant Occupations

## Student Learning Outcomes

After reading this chapter students will be able to:

1 Give a brief description and explanation of the sociology of work.
2 Define the concept of *black-collar* occupations and give several examples of occupations that are considered deviant in the United States.
3 Explain how and why occupations might be considered deviant.
4 List examples of illegal occupations and compare them to immoral occupations.
5 Explain the concept of "dirty work."
6 Discuss how deviant occupations are portrayed in the media.
7 Examine two deviant occupations associated with the adult entertainment industry.

*While riding a train from London to Liverpool, one of the authors studied the British gentleman sitting across from him. The man appeared to be in his mid-forties and, despite the temperature hovering around ninety degrees, was attired in a pair of slacks, a long-sleeved dress shirt with a tie, and a plaid tweed sport coat. And although there was not a cloud in the sky, near his side was the ever-present umbrella. The man was reading a newspaper that was folded into a small rectangle, typical of many British railway passengers. Also, typical of many British travelers, despite the fact that they were the only two people in the railway car, the British gentleman never looked up or spoke to his American counterpart. Like many American travelers, the author could not resist speaking to his fellow traveler, so he broke the ice with the innocuous question, "Where you going?" The British man glanced up from his newspaper,*

*Deviance & Deviants: A Sociological Approach*, First Edition. William E. Thompson and Jennifer C. Gibbs.
© 2017 John Wiley & Sons, Inc. Published 2017 by John Wiley & Sons, Inc.
Companion website: www.wiley.com/go/thompson

*briefly sized up the author, who was clad in shorts, t-shirt, and a pair of jogging shoes, and muttered, "Liverpool," as if that should be quite obvious to the "ugly American" who had intruded into his world of silence. Since the train stopped at every station between London and Liverpool, the author did not sense that his question was a stupid one and, undeterred, decided to pursue more conversation, since there was at least another hour of traveling time for the two men. "Where you from?" the author offered as a conversation starter. Again the man glanced up briefly and uttered, "London." Then, he added, "Chelsea, to be precise." Now, we're getting somewhere the author thought, more than a one-word response. "So, what do you do?" he asked, encouraged by the Londoner's newfound talkativeness. This time the man put his paper down, looked at the author somewhat perplexed, and said, "I enjoy reading and riding my bicycle." Now, it was the author's turn to look perplexed. "You do that for a living?" the author queried. "Oh, no, my goodness no," responded the man. "I'm an accountant."*

*Occupation and career are such an important part of most Americans' identities that when asked what they do, they assume that the words "for a living" are implied. Evidently, that is not the case in the United Kingdom where, obviously, at least the man on the train, assumed the words, "for pleasure" were implied in the question. Americans are so obsessed with work, occupation, and career that an entire area of sociology is devoted to the study of the sociology of work.*

## The Sociology of Work

The sociological analysis of the economy, industry, and work was initiated by classical theorists such as Emile Durkheim, Karl Marx, and Max Weber. Durkheim (1893/1964) studied work at the macro-level focusing on the sociological impact of the division of labor in complex industrialized societies as compared to simpler agrarian and pastoral cultures. He was particularly interested in how societies achieve and maintain stability and solidarity when they undergo the process of industrialization. Marx (1848/1964; 1867/1967) also approached the sociology of work from a macro-level perspective, but was much more interested in the experience of the working class as they experienced the transition from cottage industries to industrialization where they experienced disenfranchisement, exploitation, and alienation. Weber (1904–1905/1958; 1947) analyzed work from both a macro-level and micro-level perspective looking not only at how industrialization affected the structure and organization of society, but also how workers' values, attitudes, beliefs, and identities were affected by large-scale economic and social change.

The United States has gone through at least three important distinct economic stages. From its founding up until the mid- to late-nineteenth century, the United States was very much an agrarian nation. The vast majority of all Americans made their living from agriculture, and the few cottage industries and emerging urban industries often centered around agricultural-related activities such as textile manufacturing, food processing, making farm implements, and transportation for taking goods to markets. The industrial revolution indelibly altered the American economy and the world of work by combining three phenomena that had lasting impact on American society and culture: immigration, urbanization, and industrialization. As people moved across geographic and political borders to move into cities where factories were located, the diversity of values, attitudes, beliefs, religions, races, ethnicities, and other factors created unprecedented social and cultural change. Prior to the industrial revolution, the vast majority of

Americans were farmers. After the industrial revolution, the United States not only comprised a large number of butchers, bakers, and candlestick makers, but also factory workers, coal miners, railroad conductors, merchants, bankers, and so many other jobs that the US Bureau of the Census was totally unprepared to classify many of the new occupations. In a relatively short period of time, the United States emerged as one of the wealthiest and most powerful industrial nations in the world. Near the end of the twentieth century, most economists agreed that the United States made another important economic transition, this time moving from an industrial based economy to becoming a post-industrial nation whose economy was primarily based on service occupations. Today, although the United States is still a major manufacturer of automobiles, computers, and other goods, a majority of Americans are employed in the service sector, making their living as accountants, nurses, doctors, lawyers, school teachers, social workers, police officers, fire fighters, journalists, and a host of other non-agricultural, and non-manufacturing occupations.

Throughout all three of these economic periods, occupation played an important role in defining a person's social and personal identity. That probably never has been more the case than in the twentieth and twenty-first centuries. For many years, sociologists divided occupations into two broad categories: white-collar and blue-collar. **White-collar occupations** *generally involve office work, service work, or some other form of non-manual labor*, whereas **blue-collar occupations** *involve manual labor or factory work*. White-collar occupations usually require more education, pay better salaries, are considered more prestigious, and provide fringe benefits such as health insurance as well as pension plans, and are more likely to be considered to be life-long careers as opposed to merely jobs. They also may have a dress code requiring coat, shirt, and tie, hence the euphemism, "white collar" job. Blue-collar jobs tend to require less education, pay lower wages, provide few fringe benefits for workers, and afford them very little prestige. Sociologist Jessie Bernard (1981) created a third classification for work when she coined the term **pink-collar occupations** to describe *occupations dominated by women*, such as airline attendant, clerical work, nursing, and teaching. Although these jobs do not involve manual labor and often require advanced training, they typically do not pay all that well and are not considered very prestigious. Sociologically, it follows that workers engaged in white-collar careers not only view their jobs differently from those involved in blue-collar and pink-collar jobs, but also develop different values, attitudes, and beliefs, not only about work, but also about life in general. Moreover, people in those various lines of work are viewed differently by others.

Beyond outlook on work and life, sociologists who study work contend that occupation and career are also important aspects of a person's personal and social identity. Consequently, the type of work in which a person is engaged is very important to his or her sense of self, and how they are viewed and treated by other members of society. In many countries, and especially in the United States, what a person does for a living helps define that person, and consequently constitutes a master status for most adults.

## Occupation as Master Status

As we pointed out in Chapter 2, in the United States, when you ask almost any adult over the age of twenty-five, "What do you do?," unlike the British gentleman in the opening vignette, he or she most likely will respond by telling you his or her occupation. In the US, to a large extent, one of the most important social identities an adult has is connected to his or her occupation or career (Pavalko, 1988). When two adults meet, often one of their very first questions is "what do you do?" if the other person did not already include that information in his or her introduction, which so often is the case. When two college students meet, often one of the first questions asked is "what is your major?" which is basically the same question, or really translates, "what are you going to do when you get out of school?" Based on the answer to either of those two simple questions, people make a large number of assumptions about an individual, because to a large extent, in the United States, *what you do* defines *who you are* (Smith, 2013).

For many Americans, their occupation constitutes a master status, one that overrides or subsumes the rest of their status set. Consequently, **occupational prestige**, or *the relative ranking of occupations based on people's perceptions of them,* is an important part of a person's social identity. Sociologists have created an occupational prestige scale based on the results of national surveys asking people to rank over 700 occupations and careers. Over the years, the precise rankings have changed a bit, but occupations such as physicians, judges, attorneys, college professors, and scientists, have unwaveringly ranked at or near the top, while garbage collector, janitor, maid, and shoe shiner have consistently ranked at or near the bottom. What do sociologists surmise when analyzing decades of occupational prestige rankings? First, with the exception of a handful of highly skilled blue-collar jobs such as aircraft technician or computer technician, almost all of the prestigious careers in the United States are characterized as white-collar occupations; second, the amount of education required for a particular job is an important determinant of occupational prestige (MacKinnon and Langford, 1994; Rytina, 2000). Although there may be exceptions, generally white-collar occupations rank higher than both blue-collar and pink-collar occupations, and the newly created category of black-collar occupations, to which we now turn, would typically have the least prestige of all.

Since occupation is indeed often a master status, it follows that people who hold prestigious jobs enjoy a certain amount of social and personal respect and stature as a result. Conversely, the result of occupying a low prestige job can be detrimental to a person's social status and feeling of self-worth. Now, take that one step further, and consider the impact of having a **deviant occupation**, *one that is stigmatized either because it may involve illegal, immoral, or simply undesirable activities.* Sociologically, the authors of this book contend that in keeping with the euphemistic collar-color scheme previously discussed, that perhaps we should create yet another category of occupations and euphemistically call that classification **black-collar occupations** referring to *jobs that are considered deviant and stigmatize those who perform them.* Sociologist George Ritzer cited three criteria, any one of which can cause an occupation to be considered deviant:

1   If it is illegal.
2   If it is considered immoral.
3   If it is considered improper (Ritzer and Walczak, 1986).

The first category of what we will now refer to as black-collar occupations, those that are illegal, has been widely studied by sociologists and criminologists and is fairly straightforward. Since we have later chapters that deal specifically with some of these illegal occupations, we will take only a cursory look at that type of occupation in this chapter. The second category, jobs that are considered "immoral" is a bit harder to define since morality, like beauty, is in the eye of the beholder. Nevertheless, occupations such as prostitution, illegal gambling, and dealing illegal drugs may cut across both categories, being both illegal and, in the view of many Americans, also immoral. Recall from Chapter 1, our definition of *moral entrepreneurs*, social reformers and others who are not satisfied with existing rules because they believe that some type of behavior is taking place that should be controlled or eliminated. These individuals and groups often see the aforementioned occupations, whether legal or illegal, as being immoral, sinful, and in some cases, evil, and often launch moral crusades to ban them and stigmatize those associated with them. In this chapter, we will focus on working in the adult entertainment industry as being representative of this category, since the jobs in adult entertainment are legal (in most cases), yet many Americans find them to be morally offensive. The third category is perhaps most interesting, because the occupations and careers in it are considered neither illegal nor immoral, and in fact, often are deemed to be quite necessary. Yet people in those jobs are often stigmatized and considered to be somewhat devalued because they engage in what many people consider to be *dirty work*. In that category, we will focus primarily on morticians and funeral directors who are often stigmatized for their work which involves handling dead bodies, and making a living off death and grief.

## Illegal Occupations

**Illegal occupations** are *jobs that violate criminal laws*. Numerous sociological and criminological studies have been conducted on a wide variety of illegal occupations and it would be nearly impossible and pointless to try to describe or analyze all of them in a chapter on deviant occupations. What is important, however, is being aware of the social and personal consequences associated with being involved in making a living through illegal means. What do being a mafia "hit man," drug trafficker, professional burglar, auto thief, counterfeiter, bookie, racketeer, gun smuggler, or con artist all have in common? For one thing, and perhaps most obvious, all of these occupations carry the risk of being arrested, convicted, and sent to prison. Moreover, people engaged in these occupations, whether arrested or not, experience a certain amount of social stigma. Another common characteristic of these jobs is that the risk associated with them tends to produce a certain amount of curiosity, fascination, and mystique about those who engage in them. We will pursue this fascination factor later in this chapter as we analyze how the media deals with and portrays illegal occupations. Additionally, the risk, potential excitement, and fascination that accompany these occupations may well be part of what attracts people into them (Cockerham, 2006).

Edwin Sutherland (1949) was among the first to systematically study white-collar crime and criminals and we will discuss his research and the concept of *elite deviance* more thoroughly in Chapter 12. Of significance here is that Sutherland broke ground for sociological research on criminal occupations and crimes associated with people's work at a time when very little was known about those phenomena. Sutherland (1949:2) defined **white collar crime** as being "*a crime that is committed by a person of respectability and high social status in the course of his occupation.*" Although Sutherland's definition and intent was fairly clear, it launched a great deal of debate among sociologists and criminologists as to what constituted a white collar crime, and as to whether study of those types of activities fell under the domain of criminologists who up to that point had focused their research and analyses solely on street crimes. Today, there is little controversy as to whether criminologists should study white collar crime, and sociologists clearly contend that whether people commit crimes in the course of their occupations, or not, their occupation is still a very important part of their social and personal identities and often becomes a master status. If indeed a person's occupation is his or her master status, and if any deviant status often becomes a person's master status, then it follows that having a deviant occupation is almost bound to become a person's primary social identity. Although research shows that even illegal occupations differ in prestige with some types of criminal activities being viewed more favorably than others, virtually all criminal occupations are viewed as being less prestigious than non-criminal ones (Matsueda *et al.*, 1992). Nevertheless, sociological research indicates that there are a large number of non-criminal occupations that are viewed as deviant, especially if a substantial segment of the population considers them to be immoral.

## "Immoral" Occupations: Working in the Adult Entertainment Industry

There is no widespread consensus in the United States as to what constitutes morality or immorality. Consequently, there is no consensus on what is or is not an immoral occupation. Whereas illegal occupations involve making a living by breaking laws, **immoral occupations** involve *jobs that violate mores*, the salient norms that have a strong sense of "rightness" and "wrongness" to them. As with almost all forms of deviance, whether an occupation is considered immoral or not is a matter of social definition and social construction. Although morality is often associated with religious beliefs, mores may or may not be connected to religion. Certainly, some individuals and groups, because of their religious beliefs, view certain occupations as immoral and deviant, while other individuals and groups with different religious beliefs may not agree. Meanwhile, still other individuals or groups may define certain occupations as immoral and deviant based on values or ethical codes totally unrelated to religious beliefs. In this chapter we focus on working in the adult entertainment field and two occupations considered by many, but certainly not all, Americans to be immoral: working in the adult film industry and stripping or nude dancing. You may or may not view these occupations as immoral, but may consider some other ways of making a living as being morally questionable. Again, this underscores the social construction of deviance and how individuals and groups with different values define conformity and deviance quite differently.

Chapter 6 deals with sexual deviance and deviant lifestyles, and working in the adult entertainment industry can be considered both of those things, but it seems appropriate to deal with this type of deviance in this chapter since working in the adult entertainment industry constitutes having a deviant and stigmatized occupation. The adult entertainment industry is a somewhat generic term, but basically refers to businesses and jobs which provide sex-related products and is sometimes viewed as synonymous with what some people refer to as the sex industry. Although there are numerous occupations and careers associated with adult entertainment or the sex industry, in this chapter we will focus on the occupations of adult film making and stripping, or topless dancing, because there have been several sociological studies of them, and most people are at least somewhat aware of them, and may hold many preconceived notions about them.

Although legal, this woman's occupation is considered to be deviant by many. What criteria do people use to determine whether or not occupations are deviant? Is it possible to have an occupation that can simultaneously be a status symbol and a stigma symbol? *Source*: Studio10Artur /Shutterstock

## Working in adult films

Perhaps foremost among sex industry jobs that many people view as deviant might be acting in pornographic movies, or what those engaged in the activity prefer to call "adult films." In Chapter 3 we defined pornography as explicit materials intended solely for sexual arousal, but pointed out that the US Supreme Court has basically left definitions of what is pornographic or obscene up to local communities to define based on local standards. Again, this emphasizes how deviance is socially constructed. Nevertheless, whether defined as pornographic, obscene, or merely freedom of expression, making a living by working in the adult film industry is viewed as deviant and stigmatized by a fairly large segment of the US population. In an interview with CNN, Chief Justice of the US Supreme Court, John Roberts, cited a study that indicated there were 4.2 million pornographic websites, some 420 million pages of pornography on the Internet, and approximately 68 million search engine requests for Internet pornography every single day (Balan, 2010). Those numbers do not mean that all the people participating in Internet porn are employed in the sex industry, as much of what appears on the Internet is posted by amateurs who make their living in a wide variety of other jobs and careers.

Pornography and adult entertainment certainly predates the Internet and other forms of social media. As indicated in Chapter 3, pornography may be as old as humankind, as ancient sexually explicit drawings and paintings have been discovered etched on the walls of caves thousands of years ago. As technology evolved, so has pornography as each new media has depicted sexually explicit materials in whatever new format was available. Old grainy black and white 8mm films made the rounds at bachelor parties and fraternity gatherings during the 1950s, but the adult film industry came into its own in the 1960s and 1970s when so-called *hard-core* pornography gained huge audiences in the United States and throughout the rest of the world. One of the first adult film stars to become a "household" name during that time was Linda Boreman, better known as "Linda Lovelace" who starred in the 1972 film *Deep Throat*, which became one of the highest grossing and best-known X-rated films of all time. Adult film star turned author, Lovelace penned two autobiographies in which she promoted pornography as a legitimate enterprise and criticized Americans who stigmatized her and her fellow actors as being prudish and hypocritical. Many Americans agreed, and *Deep Throat* became popular discussion material at country clubs as well as fodder for late night comedians on major television networks. Later, however, Lovelace, dubbed the "Queen of Porn," recanted her support of the adult film industry claiming that she had been forced by her husband, sometimes at gunpoint, to act in *Deep Throat* and other pornographic films, thus bolstering the concerns of millions of other Americans who viewed the adult film industry as deviant, immoral, and potentially dangerous. Boreman became an anti-porn crusader for the remainder of her life characterizing the adult film industry as exploitive, debasing, and degrading (Lovelace and McGrady, 2012).

Despite being stigmatized and viewed as deviant by many members of mainstream society, the adult film industry has survived if not thrived for several decades. Each year, Adult Video News (AVN) holds its version of the academy awards for adult films. Modeled after the Oscars, hundreds of adult film stars, producers, and directors meet annually to acknowledge celebrities in the adult film industry and attempt to give credibility to the profession. Nevertheless, credibility has not been widely forthcoming, as those involved in the adult film industry are largely shunned by the so-called "legitimate" film world, although in one or two isolated instances a performer has successfully made the transition from adult films to Hollywood movies. Traci Lords, for example, began her career in the adult film industry and then, after attending acting school, moved into mainstream films and guest roles on television, although she alleges that her reputation of having been a porn star tainted her legitimate career and limited her offers of legitimate roles (Lords, 2003).

As with any deviant activity there have been numerous attempts to socially control, regulate, censor, and/or abolish adult films. In the case of *People vs Freeman* (1988), the California Supreme Court ruled that adult films were protected under the first amendment as a type of freedom of speech. In that same year, however, the US Congress passed the *Child Protection and Obscenity Enforcement Act* which required all filmmakers to require proof of age of all actors and actresses, and prohibits anybody under the age of 18 from appearing in adult films. The aforementioned Traci Lords may have inadvertently played a role in the enactment of such a law as she purportedly began her adult film career at the age of sixteen. More substantial, however, was the growing concern over child pornography, which with the growth of the Internet had become a multi-million if not multi-billion dollar industry (Gillespie, 2012). Thus while it is virtually impossible to prohibit the production or distribution of adult films in the United States, it is easier to make and prosecute a case that involves child pornography. In the United States, anybody associated with a job that exploits children for sexual purposes is not only considered deviant, but is likely to be charged with a crime, hence making those occupations both categories of illegal and immoral.

In the United Kingdom, the *Criminal Justice and Immigration Act of 2008* included a provision prohibiting what it called extreme pornography, which was defined as anything produced solely or principally for the purpose of sexual arousal which is grossly offensive, disgusting, or otherwise of an obscene character. It included anything that portrayed in an explicit or realistic fashion:

1  An act threatening a person's life.
2  An act which results in serious injury to a person's anus, breasts, or genitals.
3  An act which involves sexual interaction with a human corpse.
4  A person performing a sex act with an animal.

This law was aimed at a variety of deviant sex acts including **necrophilia** *(sex with a human corpse),* **bestiality** *(sex with an animal),* and more specifically at prosecuting anybody associated with the making of a so-called "**snuff film**" *which depicts the actual or staged murder of a human being.* Needless to say, anybody engaged in an occupation that involved any of these activities would be considered deviant by most members of society. Most jobs in the sex industry are far less sensational and morally repulsive than these, however, and are more likely to involve people just trying to make a living, albeit in a way that violates traditional norms, and perhaps mores, of a wide range of individuals and groups. Strippers, nude, semi-nude, and topless dancers are examples of people engaged in a more typical deviant occupation associated with the adult entertainment industry. Since its puritan beginning, there have always been folkways, mores, and norms regarding nudity in the United States. While paintings and statues of nude figures may be considered fine art, various forms of public nudity are often met with less social approval.

## Stripping/nude dancing

Stripping and various forms of nude or partially nude dancing are part of a multi-billion dollar industry in the United States. According to the Association of Club Executives, Americans spent over $14 billion annually in topless clubs in the early part of the twenty-first century (Fairbank, 2003). Almost every state and/or municipality has laws or ordinances that prohibit certain forms of public nudity. In Chapter 6 we will look at the nudist lifestyle as a form of social deviance, but here we are dealing with nudity and partial nudity for entertainment and profit, or more specifically at dancing either nude or partially nude as a deviant occupation.

Officially categorized as *ecdysiasts*, women and men who remove their clothing (strip) for money go by a variety of job titles including strippers, exotic dancers, nude dancers, topless dancers, and adult entertainers but all essentially can trace their "occupational ancestry" to the early burlesque queens. One of the first systematic studies of stripping as a deviant occupation was conducted in the late 1960s by sociologists James Skipper and Charles McCaghy (1970) who analyzed the processes through which women entered the occupation. According to their research, most strippers progress through a career sequence that involves three sociological contingencies:

1  A tendency toward exhibitionistic behavior for gain.
2  An opportunity structure making stripping an accessible occupational alternative.
3  A sudden awareness of the easy economic rewards derived from stripping (Skipper and McCaghy, 1970:391).

Other studies on stripping have focused on the interactions between strippers and customers and what at least one study described as "counterfeit intimacy," where dancers feign sexual interest in customers in order to get more tips (Enck and Preston, 1988:371). More relevant to the topic of this chapter, Thompson and Harred (1992) and Thompson *et al.*, (2003) looked at how topless dancers manage the stigma of being employed in a deviant occupation. According to their research, topless dancers tend to divide their social worlds into those who know about their occupation and those who do not and then utilize many of the same techniques of neutralization and rationalization in order to manage the stigma associated with their work that Sykes and Matza (1957) attributed to male juvenile delinquents. For example, topless dancers almost uniformly use *denial of injury* as a way of neutralizing their deviance, pointing out that nobody is hurt by what they are doing, and that they are simply engaged in harmless entertainment. They also use the technique of *condemnation of the condemners* pointing out the hypocrisy city officials and law enforcement personnel who may officially condemn strip clubs but then frequent them on numerous occasions. Finally, many dancers *appeal to higher loyalties*, indicating that they engage in stripping in order to pay their way through college or support their families (Thompson and Hickey, 1992; Thompson *et al.*, 2003). Box 5.1 illustrates in their own words some of the common techniques used by topless dancers to manage the stigma associated with their occupation.

Far less research has been done on male stripping. Not surprisingly, in keeping with long standing double standards related to sex and gender, the sociological research that has been conducted on male dancers indicates that there may be less stigma attached to the men who remove their clothes for money than for their female counterparts (Montemurro, 2001). Moreover, although there is little or no research on this specific aspect of the occupation, based on those aforementioned double standard gender issues, in the minds of many, it seems that males stripping for money is somehow viewed as less immoral than women doing so.

As with other forms of deviance, stripping and various types of nude dancing have enjoyed widespread media attention. The 1962 movie *Gypsy*, focused loosely on the life and career of one of the most famous strippers of all time: Gypsy Rose Lee. Some of the more notable stripper movies include Jennifer Beals in *Flashdance* (1983), Elizabeth Berkley and Gina Gershon in *Showgirls* (1995), Demi Moore in *Striptease* (1996), Daryl Hannah in *Dancing at the Blue Iguana* (2000), Natalie Portman in *Closer* (2004), and Marisa Tomei in *The Wrestler* (2008). Hollywood has not ignored male stripping, although as with sociological research, less attention has been paid to that phenomenon than its female counterpart with perhaps two of the more notable movies being *The Full Monty* in 1997 and *Magic Mike* (2012) and *Magic Mike XXL* (2015) which featured Matthew McConaughey and Channing Tatum, among others who portrayed male

**Box 5.1    In their own words**

Topless dancers: Managing stigma in a deviant occupation

In the early 1990s, and a decade later shortly after the turn of the twenty-first century, one of the authors was part of a team that interviewed topless dancers in a major metropolitan city in the southwest asking how they managed the stigma associated with their work. It was discovered that in keeping with Goffman's (1963) concept of dividing the social world, most of the dancers had a small circle of friends and/or family who knew what they did for a living, and then the rest of their friends and acquaintances who did not know. For example, in the initial study, one of the dancers indicated,

> I had to tell the woman at day care where I worked because she needed the phone number in case something happened with my daughter. So, I just told her I was a waitress in a club. That way when she calls and they answer the phone with the club's name, she won't think anything. If she asks anybody here what I do, they'll just tell her I wait tables. It's cool (Thompson and Harred, 1993:293).

In the study a decade later, one of the dancers told the interviewers, "My mother knows what I do and is really supportive of me, but if my dad ever found out, he would die – or kill me" (Thompson *et al.*, 2003:560).

In both studies it also was common practice for topless dancers to utilize some of the common techniques of neutralization described by Sykes and Matza (1957) in order to rationalize their deviance and neutralize the stigma associated with it. Most common among them were the techniques of denial of injury, "Why does everybody make such a fuss over tittie dancing? It's not like we're hurting anybody or anything . . ." (Thompson and Harred, 199:299):

> Every day there's people out there murdering, robbing, and raping people. We come in here behind closed doors and shake our tits for guys who pay to see us do it. What possible harm can come from that? (Thompson *et al.*, 2003:562).

Another common technique of neutralization used by the dancers was condemnation of the condemners, where the dancers would point out the hypocrisy associated with those who condemned their occupation. For example, one dancer, exclaimed,

> The mayor's an asshole. He has no idea who we are or what we do. He just wants the publicity of saying he's against these evil clubs. The City Council and the cops think we're just like the prostitutes out on the street. They don't understand that we're decent girls just trying to make a living – and, they seem to forget that this is perfectly legal. Plus, they're a bunch of hypocrites. Half of 'em would probably love to come in here and watch us dance. You should see the cops when they come in. They watch us dance for an hour or two before they bust anybody – and there's usually half a dozen of 'em at a time. How

many cops does it take to write a ticket for lewd dancing to one or two harmless girls? (Thompson *et al.*, 2003:563–564).

One of the final neutralization techniques used by dancers was that of appealing to higher loyalties. For example, one dancer explained,

I have three children. Times are tough and jobs are hard to find – especially if you don't even have a high school diploma. I'm not proud of what I do, but it supports me and my kids. I don't have to ask anybody else for nothing. I don't get food stamps, don't take no welfare – I support me and my kids. If that means I've got to come in here and humiliate myself four or five days a week, so be it. Another thing – with this job I can take off anytime one of my kids is sick, or I can go to their school to see them in a play, or talk to their teacher or whatever. The hours are flexible and the money's good. I do this for my kids.

strippers and disrobed on the big screen. Interestingly, *The Full Monty* was a comedy with stripping seen as humorous as opposed to sexy or immoral, and *Magic Mike* and its sequel were billed as comedy/dramas that portrayed the male strippers more as tragic heroes than deviants.

Not surprisingly, Hollywood film versions of stripping and topless dancing tend to glamorize and sensationalize the occupation as opposed to realistically portraying the mundane day to day hassles of foot problems and backaches, much less the stigma attached to being engaged in what many consider to be a deviant and/or immoral occupation. In the next chapter we will shift our focus from people who are considered deviant because of their occupations to those who are stigmatized as a result of their norm-violating lifestyles, but for now we will turn our attention to occupations that are considered deviant for reasons other than being considered illegal or immoral.

## Black-Collar Occupations: Stigmatized Occupations and "Dirty" Work

Earlier in this chapter the authors coined the term "black-collar" occupations to describe jobs that are legal and sometimes even necessary, but are considered to be deviant by many society members who stigmatize those workers who perform them. Remember that in Chapter 2, we defined stigma as any attribute that discredits an individual from full social acceptance. Generally we associate stigma with physical or mental anomalies, or with some type of specific act that exceeds society's range of tolerance and becomes defined as deviant. A person's occupation can also discredit an individual and cause people to want to avoid interacting with them. In the case of illegal occupations such as those previously mentioned, it may be understandable why parents might be upset to learn that their daughter is dating a mafia family member, drug dealer, car thief, or counterfeiter. As we have noted throughout this book however, a person need not be criminal to be considered deviant, and stigma can be applied to a wide array of people, some of whom have done nothing wrong or violated any norms themselves. For example, imagine the reaction if you announced to your parents that you had just become engaged to Al Capone the third, Jeffrey Dahmer, Jr., or Lizzie Borden's great niece. Although any or all of those individuals might be fine upstanding citizens, have college educations, be employed in highly respectable careers, and have never even received a traffic ticket, their names alone carry a certain amount of stigma. Now, carry that logic further, and imagine introducing your fiancé to your parents with either of the following descriptors: "Mom and Dad, I want you to meet Philip, he's a mortician;" or "I want you to meet Mary, she's the top tip-earner at the all-nude revue out on the turnpike." Although both of those jobs may be legal, and in at least one case might pay a good salary with excellent fringe benefits, and in the other case may generate a lot of non-taxable income and flexible hours, there is a certain amount of stigma attached to both of them.

## Stigma of handling the dead

Historically, in many societies, stigma has been attached to those responsible for caring for the dead, and the job typically was assigned to the lower classes (e.g., the Eta of Japan and the Untouchables in India), and in some cases, those who handled the dead were forbidden from touching the living (Kearl, 1989; Murray, 1969). In the United States, prior to the industrial revolution, there was very little stigma associated with handling the dead as most Americans were born at home, and died at home. Rural people tended to bathe and prepare their loved ones' bodies for burial, and there was little mystery and virtually no stigma associated with the process. Townspeople, however, often turned that job over to an "undertaker ... a special person who would 'undertake' responsibility for the care and burial of the dead" (Amos, 1983:2). Although providing what was considered to be a worthwhile and necessary service, a certain amount of stigma was attached to undertakers because they were viewed as making a profit off of death and grief, and they were, "linked to the American death orientation whereby the industry is the cultural scapegoat for failed immortality" (Kearl, 1989:278). Modern-day morticians and funeral directors are quite aware of negative images and stereotypes associated with their occupation and often develop a wide range of strategies for countering them (Thompson, 1991). Box 5.2 includes excerpts of interviews with morticians and funeral directors who discuss in their own words how they, "handle the stigma of handling the dead."

Earlier in this chapter we examined working in the sex industry where one of the deviant occupations studied was stripping/nude dancing. As different as the occupations of being a mortician or being an exotic dancer may be, you should be able to detect some notable similarities in how people in those two jobs recognize, rationalize, and attempt to neutralize the stigma directed toward them by many members of the general public.

Sociologist Everett Hughes (1958) called many of these stigmatized occupations – jobs that although perfectly legal, and sometimes absolutely necessary to the functioning of society, yet considered undesirable – dirty work, because they involve the type of work that most people in society would rather not perform. Sometimes the so-called dirty work is literally dirty. Street cleaners, butchers, sewer workers, garbage collectors, coal miners, ditch diggers (although that's mostly done now by heavy machinery operators who get a lot less dirty than those who dug ditches by hand), and a host of other jobs might all be categorized as dirty work. These jobs usually require little or no formal education or training, often pay fairly low wages, do not provide a lot of perks or fringe benefits, and are accorded very little prestige either by those who do them or by those who do not. Although these jobs are perfectly legal and in fact necessary for society,

**Box 5.2** In their own words

## Morticians and funeral directors: Handling the stigma of handling the dead

People think we're cold, unfriendly, morbid, and unfeeling. I always make it a point to be just the opposite. Naturally, when I'm dealing with a family I must be reserved and show the proper decorum, but when I am out social, I always try to be very upbeat – very alive. No matter how tired I am, I try not to show it. I try to do everything I can to counter the negative stereotypes people have about us. I keep a hand warmer in my suit pocket, even in the summer. There is no way that anybody is ever going to shake my hand and go away thinking it was cold or clammy feeling. (The words of a 34-year-old licensed embalmer and funeral director who owned and operated a thriving funeral home in a town of approximately 35,000 people in central Kansas – cited in Thompson, 1991:415)

One of the authors of this book conducted a little over two years of ethnographic interviews with 19 morticians and funeral directors in four states: Kansas, Missouri, Oklahoma, and Texas. Most of these morticians and funeral directors were employed in private family-owned businesses that had served their particular communities for several generations, while four of them were employed by branches of large national firms. The funeral homes for which they worked were located in communities ranging from less than 1,000 people to cities with populations over one million. Interviewees included 16 males and 3 females ranging in age from 26 to 64 years. Seventeen of the respondents were white; two were African-American. All of the 19 interviewees acknowledged that the funeral industry was much maligned and stigmatized and were very open about consciously employing techniques to somewhat neutralize the stigma and negative stereotypes associated with their occupation. Here are a few examples, in their own words.

When I am on vacation or in some place where nobody knows me, I rarely tell people what I do for a living. There's just too much baggage that goes with it. When I tell people what I do, they initially seem put off, even repulsed. I have literally had people jerk their hands back during a handshake when somebody introduces me and tells them what I do for a living. If people find out you're in the funeral business, there is almost always one of two extreme reactions: disgust or morbid curiosity. People will either go on and on about how morbid your work is, how they could never do it, and how creepy it must be to work with dead bodies. Or, in a few cases, people will start peppering you with all kinds of questions like, "What's the grossest thing you've ever seen?," "How do you *get all* the vital organs out of the body?," or "Do you get turned on seeing all those naked bodies?" Either way, those are not conversations you want to have. I discovered long ago that the best thing I could say when strangers ask me what I do for a living, is to say that I sell insurance – which is technically true – since I am licensed to sell burial policies. Tell people you are in the insurance business, and they tend to politely walk away as soon as possible, because they figure that you are going to try to sell them insurance (Thompson, 1991:423).

Another mortician, a male in his late forties, indicated:

A lot of people ask us how we can stand to be in this business. They act like we must be strange or something. When I go to conventions and meet with all of the other people there who are just like me, I feel *normal* again (Thompson, 1991:418).

Some of the common ways that morticians and funeral directors handled the stigma of handling the dead, included symbolically redefining their work – "I'm a licensed funeral director and grief counselor, not an undertaker," practicing role distance – "It's what I do, not who I am," emphasizing professionalism – "It took years of training to learn what I do," cloaking themselves in the shroud of service – "Our family has been providing this important service for over four generations," and enjoying socioeconomic status as opposed to occupational prestige – "People may not want to do what I do, but they sure wouldn't mind trading incomes." Almost all of them went to great efforts to shift the emphasis of their work away from handling the dead to providing important and necessary services for the living.

Perhaps one of the most interesting quotes, however, came from a husband and wife, both of whom ran the family business, when they acknowledged that they tended to be somewhat extravagant in their spending from time to time to help assuage some of the negative connotations (stigma) associated with their work, when the wife proclaimed, "Hell, if anybody knows that you can't take it with you, it's us – we figured we might as well enjoy it while we can" (Thompson, 1991:423).

they often are viewed negatively and those who perform them are viewed by many society members as somewhat deviant. The result of being disparaged and/or stigmatized for the type of work they do often leads to social isolation despite the fact that those doing the work tend to view themselves as "good people" doing honorable, if undesirable work (Davis, 1984). These black-collar occupations also sometimes alienate the workers as they feel unappreciated by those for whom they perform the work. In an ethnographic study of dog catchers, for example, Palmer (1978) found that because of the low status of their jobs, and despite the fact that people insisted that stray dogs be picked up by them, dog catchers often felt disparaged and unappreciated, and even devised mechanisms for "getting back" at an unappreciative public. Dirty work and deviant occupations have not gone unnoticed by the media who have seized the opportunity to capitalize on public curiosity and fascination with unusual and extraordinary jobs and those who perform them.

## Deviant Occupations and the Media

For approximately ten years (2003–2012), television spokesperson, Mike Rowe, hosted a one-hour television program each week on the Discovery Channel entitled *Dirty Jobs*. The premise and format of the show revolved around Rowe working alongside people employed in legal, but stigmatized occupations because they involved some of the most difficult, hazardous, challenging, sometimes dangerous, and always dirty jobs available to people. Mike worked as a shark repellent tester, cleaned a home after a sewer back-up, removed road kill, cleaned the cages at a reptile zoo, collected owl vomit, mined coal, worked on engines, retrieved golf balls from the bottom of a lake, and cleaned up pigeon feces to name but a few of his dirty jobs. Regardless of the specific type of work, three common themes permeated each television episode:

1   The jobs were difficult, dirty, and undesirable.
2   The workers took pride in their work, but felt stigmatized by others because of their jobs.
3   Mike Rowe admired these hard workers and wanted viewers to also admire them and to realize that there is nothing wrong with making a living by performing so-called "dirty work."

Some of the work performed on *Dirty Jobs* seemed almost too bizarre to be real, but if a reality show could make truth seem stranger than fiction, then we certainly cannot underestimate the ability of fictional programs to portray deviant occupations in a positive light.

Showtime's multiple Emmy, Golden Globe, and Writers' Guild award winning program *Weeds* enjoyed eight seasons of following the joys, trials, and tribulations of the fictional drug-dealing Botwin family. In that series, Mary-Louise Parker played the role of Nancy Botwin, a young widow whose husband dropped dead of a heart attack at age forty leaving her to raise two young boys in an upper-middle class suburban neighborhood in the mythical town of Agrestic, California. Saddled with a huge mortgage, luxury car payments, and ever-increasing living expenses, while having no college degree or marketable job skills, Nancy turned to dealing pot to her friends, neighbors, and fellow residents, evidently most of whom could not make it through a typical day in the doldrums without getting stoned. Initially, it was easy to not only feel sympathy but also somewhat admire Nancy's innovative entrepreneurial skills as a novice drug dealer and her steadfast adherence to a set of personal ethical norms which forbid her from selling to minors or using the drug herself. Not too far into the series, however, Nancy began to break her own rules as she started supplying a young dealer at the high school, and ultimately bringing first one, and then both of her sons into the illicit business. Nancy's oldest son showed an uncanny skill for grafting, cloning, and cultivating new strains of marijuana, a talent that involved the Botwin family in conflict with a Turkish drug cartel, the Mexican Mafia, and the DEA, along with a host of other criminals and law enforcement officials. Despite the protagonist's penchant for never learning a lesson, even after having several attempts made on Nancy and her family members' lives, as well as a three-year prison sentence for Nancy after she took the rap for her youngest son's commission of murder, viewers could not help but pull for Nancy and the Botwin family to overcome all the unpleasantries and hardships associated with growing and dealing drugs. Although part of the show's appeal may have been its continued pointing out of the hypocrisy and foolishness associated with laws and enforcement attempts at controlling marijuana, Nancy also was involved in trafficking other illegal drugs such as cocaine and heroin, as well as smuggling illegal aliens across the Mexico–US border. It took Nancy being shot in the head and almost dying for her to see the errors of her ways, which ironically led to Nancy and her oldest son pursuing legal careers growing and selling medicinal marijuana. A mixture of comedy and drama, *Weeds'* popularity was testimony that being involved in a deviant and illegal occupation does not necessarily disqualify people from social acceptance. Yet, it also emphasized that deviance, no matter how serious or how trivial, has both minor and potentially very serious consequences.

Other fictional programs have portrayed even more serious forms of deviant occupations in somewhat positive lights. *The Sopranos*, for example, focused on the fictional Italian-American crime boss, Tony Soprano, played by James Gandolfini. Viewers empathized and sympathized with Tony as he tried to balance being a good husband and father with the demands of running a large crime organization. Both reinforcing and exploding many of the common stereotypes associated with the organized crime in the United States, this popular program won multiple Peabody, Emmy, and Golden Globe awards during its six seasons, and then quickly became syndicated, running for several more years, eventually being named in 2013 by the Writers Guild of America as the best-written television series of all time. Viewers seemed more than willing to overlook the Sopranos' involvement in "minor" indiscretions such as drug trafficking, illegal gambling, racketeering, extortion, and murder, in light of the family's endearing qualities and vulnerabilities in dealing with everyday issues related to keeping a marriage together, raising a teenage daughter, and handling the day to day crises of life with which everybody must endure. The Sopranos made being engaged in a deviant/criminal occupation seem not only palatable, but almost admirable in some cases. Yet viewers were also reminded from time to time of the negative consequences associated with such work.

*Boardwalk Empire* aired its pilot episode on HBO in 2009, and made its debut as an HBO series in 2010, thereafter winning several Emmys and other media awards. The main character is based loosely on the real-life political "boss," Enoch Johnson, who informally ruled Atlantic City during the prohibition era. *Boardwalk Empire* episodes involve bootlegging, illegal gambling, prostitution, crooked politics, extortion, murder, and a host of other illegal and deviant activities. Although the characters involved in crime and deviance on *Boardwalk Empire* are hardly admirable, as with any television stars, viewers tend to identify with them and empathize or even sympathize with them and their plights.

Perhaps a more poignant example of glorifying a deviant can be found in the multiple award winning television series *Dexter* which enjoyed a seven-year run on Showtime and one season on CBS. The lead character, Dexter Morgan, was a criminalistics expert for the Miami Police Department who also just happened to be a serial killer who hunted down and murdered criminals who escaped the formal criminal justice system. Although several novels and motion pictures have also centered on the theme of vigilante justice, few have directly portrayed such an antiheroic serial killer as an admirable hero.

Various forms of media have always glorified deviants in some form or fashion and people engaged in deviant and even criminal occupations have been variously portrayed as evil and despicable as well as saintly and admirable. Whether reality television or pure fantasy, media shape people's perceptions of dirty work and deviant occupations and underscore the fact that what people do for a living is very important.

Another category of deviant occupations that the media have been very interested in are jobs in the sex industry. Movies such as *Boogie Nights* and *The Girl Next Door* are but two of the movies that dealt with Hollywood's version of the adult entertainment, or pornography industry. *Risky Business, Taxi Driver, Pretty Woman*, and others have depicted fictional versions of prostitution. While all of those movies may have had elements of truth in their story lines, they were not based on factual information and most certainly not on sociological research. Julianne Moore and Heather Graham are hardly your typical porn stars, and Julia Roberts is not very representative of the typical streetwalker. Nevertheless, all that millions of Americans may know (or think they know) about the adult film industry and prostitution may be based on fictionalized media portrayals. For our purposes, it is far more important to look at sociological research if we want to attempt to understand what it is like to work in the sex industry.

## Summary

The sociology of work indicates that in the United States a person's occupation often becomes their master status, and plays a large role in defining both an individual's personal and social identity. Consequently, if a person is employed in a deviant or stigmatized occupation, it follows that they too will be considered deviant and stigmatized. To supplement the previously established sociological categories of white-collar, blue-collar, and pink-collar occupations, the authors coined the term black-collar occupations to refer to those jobs that are considered deviant and stigmatize the people who perform them.

Some occupations are considered deviant because they involve the commission of crimes. People who deal drugs, are part of organized crime, or otherwise make their living through illegal means are involved in deviant occupations and suffer social consequences as a result. Other occupations are considered deviant because they violate mores or may be considered immoral. Almost anybody who works in or is associated with the adult entertainment industry is considered deviant by mainstream society. This includes writers, directors, producers, distributors, and actors in pornographic films as well as strippers and topless dancers. Still other people are involved in occupations that are perfectly legal, are not considered immoral, but are stigmatized because the type of work involved may be somewhat improper or, more commonly, undesirable. Sociologists coined the term dirty work to refer to those jobs that involve activities that most people do not want to engage in as a way of making a living. For example, hauling garbage, working in sewers, and handling dead bodies as well as a variety of other legal and necessary occupations are often discredited and devalued and lead to those who perform those duties as being stigmatized and viewed as deviant.

All of the occupations included in this chapter illustrate the social nature of deviance as well as the social construction of deviance and deviants. While the law defines illegal occupations, what some people view as immoral, others see as perfectly legitimate and either morally fine or amoral. Dirty work, while viewed as deviant by some and stigmatized by many is more often than not viewed as necessary by almost everybody.

The media are fascinated by deviant and stigmatized occupations and have created a variety of reality and fictional television programs as well as motion pictures that deal with both legal and illegal occupations. Many people's perceptions of deviant occupations are shaped by what they have seen on television or in motion pictures which may or may not be accurate portrayals. Deviant occupations, as with most other aspects of life, are defined by social interaction and are not necessarily what they seem.

## Outcomes Assessment

1   Give a brief description and explanation of the sociology of work.
2   Define black-collar occupation and give several examples of occupations that are considered deviant in the United States.
3   Explain how and why occupation often serves as a master status in the United States.
4   List examples of illegal occupations and compare them to immoral occupations.
5   Explain the concept of "dirty work" and describe why that type of work is considered deviant.
6   Discuss how deviant occupations are portrayed in the media.
7   Discuss two deviant occupations associated with the adult entertainment industry: acting in adult films and stripping/topless dancing.

## Key Terms and Concepts

adult entertainment
bestiality
black-collar occupations
blue-collar occupations
deviant occupation
dirty work

ecdysiasts
extreme pornography
illegal occupations
immoral occupations
necrophilia
occupational prestige

pink-collar occupations
sex industry
snuff film
white-collar crime
white-collar occupations

# 6

# Sexual Deviance and Deviant Lifestyles

**Student Learning Outcomes**

After reading this chapter students will be able to:

1 Explain the differences between sex and gender.
2 Define sexual norms and sexual deviance.
3 Explain specific types of sexual behavior often considered to be deviant including adultery, nudism, transvestitism, transgenderism, and transsexuality.
4 Define homosexuality and homophobia and discuss how laws and attitudes toward homosexuality have changed over time.
5 Define prostitution and discuss specific types of prostitutes and prostitution.
6 Define and give specific examples of phone sex and cybersex.
7 Discuss how the media portray sexual deviance in the United States.

> *What are little boys made of?*
> *Snakes and snails and puppy dogs tails,*
> *That's what little boys are made of.*
> *What are little girls made of?*
> *Sugar and spice, and everything nice,*
> *That's what little girls are made of.*

*Such is the wisdom of Mother Goose, or more probably, English poet, Robert Southey who is largely attributed with first penning those stanzas in the early nineteenth century as part of a longer poem*

*Deviance & Deviants: A Sociological Approach*, First Edition. William E. Thompson and Jennifer C. Gibbs.
© 2017 John Wiley & Sons, Inc. Published 2017 by John Wiley & Sons, Inc.
Companion website: www.wiley.com/go/thompson

*called "What All the World is Made of" (Delamar, 2001:175–177). This well-known nursery rhyme along with catchphrases such as "boys will be boys," and "good girls don't …" when combined with American humorist, Mark Twain's soliloquy: "from the time a woman is a young adolescent up until the time she dies of old age, she is ready for action, and competent … but man is only briefly competent … after fifty his performance is of poor quality, the intervals between are wide, and its satisfactions of no great quality to either party; whereas his great grandmother is as good as new" (Devoto, 1962) serve to introduce the important concepts of sex, gender, and human sexuality.*

## Sex, Gender, and Human Sexuality

Men and women are different. It doesn't take a PhD in sociology or any advanced medical training to know that basic fact. Inherently, the difference is rooted in a person's **sex** – *biological and physiological differences between males and females based on genetics and chromosomes*. Since genes and hormones are invisible to the naked eye, we tend to differentiate males and females based on anatomical differences, as one of the five-year-olds in the movie *Kindergarten Cop* pointed out: males have penises; females have vaginas. As children grow, the differences in males and females become enhanced due to different levels of the hormones estrogen and testosterone. Muscle development, fatty tissue, genitalia, facial hair, vocal cords, and a wide variety of other physiological, biological, and anatomical distinctions become more obvious.

Differences related to gender are far more complicated than those based on sex. Whereas a person's sex is based in genetics and identifiable largely by biological and physiological differences, **gender** *refers to cultural and social understandings about what constitutes masculinity and femininity*. In almost any daycare center, and most certainly on the playgrounds of elementary schools across the United States and around the world, little girls can be seen wearing pink, holding hands, touching each other, whispering in each other's ears, and cuddling baby dolls or stuffed animals in maternal fashion. Little boys can and sometimes do all those same things. More often, however, the boys will be wearing blue, running, hitting, throwing objects, pushing or shoving one another, playing with trucks or guns, and if handed a doll or stuffed animal are more likely to dangle it by one leg, or throw it across the playground as they are to cuddle, love, or kiss it. Although some hardcore geneticists and biologists may insist that these differences are genetically programmed into little girls and boys, even most of them reluctantly agree with almost all social and behavioral scientists who contend that these behavioral differences are primarily the result of social learning through imitation, play, and the process of socialization. As with most nature *versus* nurture debates, most scientific research indicates that these arguments are fruitless, and that most human characteristics are a result of a combination of both nature *and* nurture. Sociologically speaking, sex is a status and gender is a role. In other words, sex determines *who we are*, gender describes *what we do,* or at least tells us what most society members think it is appropriate for us to do or not do based on our sex.

Consequently, when it comes to **human sexuality**, *the wide range of possible ways that people express themselves as sexual beings*, there often is a double standard, with different expectations for males and females. This necessarily leads us to the identification of sexual norms and the concept of sexual deviance. It is important to remember, however, what we learned in Chapter 1 about the social construction of deviance, and the fact that as with other forms of behavior, determining what comprises sexual conformity and what constitutes sexual deviance is a very complex social process. Time, place, situation, and culture are all important variables in defining sexual norms and sexual deviance.

## Sexual Norms and Sexual Deviance

Perhaps no activities in the United States are more socially controlled, or at least attempted to be controlled, than those that are linked to human sexuality. **Sexual norms** are *the multitude of folkways, mores, laws, and taboos that surround and attempt to regulate sexual behavior.* It is impossible to determine when the first sexual norms were created, but because sex is a basic human drive, and because procreation is a fundamental requirement for survival, it is probably safe to assume that some form of sexual norms have probably been around for quite some time. Throughout recorded history, it seems that some members of society have attempted to determine when, where, how, why, and with whom and what it is appropriate for other people to have sex. Whereas some cultures tend to view sex as just another form of natural human behavior, other cultures have tended to surround it with a great deal of mysticism, excitement, and intrigue, while still others have sometimes associated sex with being something forbidden, sinful, and possibly evil. Although sexuality was originally studied individualistically and was assumed to be part of a person's private identity, most social scientists contend that it is an important part of a person's public and social identities (Foucault, 1990).

From the time of the original thirteen colonies, sexual norms, especially mores, have been an integral part of American culture. Many of the sex norms in American society are associated with the Puritan religious movement of the sixteenth and seventeenth centuries, especially English Calvinists, who had strong influence on both religious beliefs and social practices in several of the early colonies. Although the Puritan movement was actually much more about debates over theological differences between Protestants and Catholics, today the term is often somewhat mistakenly associated with prudishness, or anti-sexuality. Clearly, however, whether studying sexual mores and laws of the early colonial period or evaluating the massive number of traditional folkways, religious mores, city ordinances, or state and federal laws aimed at regulating sexual behavior, it probably is safe to conclude that Americans are, and always have been, obsessed with sex.

**Sexual deviance**, or *violating sexual norms* has always exacted both a personal and social toll. A brief reminder of our discussion of stigma in Chapter 2 helps us understand how being labeled as any type of sexual deviant is a powerful stigma that often leads to a spoiled personal and social identity. As is the case with any type of deviance, sexual norms are relative to time, place, situation, and culture. And, as with any type of deviance, social reactions to different forms of sexual deviance vary greatly. While some people contend that anything that transpires sexually between two consenting adults should be nobody else's business, others view even consensual sexual behavior that violates their personal values or society's norms as potentially dangerous. What some people may view as harmless fun or sexual creativity, others may see as perverse and threatening to society. We have already discussed pornography in earlier chapters, so we will forego that topic in this chapter although its link to sexual norms and the varied reactions to it should be quite evident. In this chapter, we will focus on sexual norms related to adultery, mate swapping, nudism, homosexuality, gender roles, prostitution, and cybersex.

Over time, attitudes and norms toward nudity, virginity, premarital and extramarital intercourse, homosexuality, and almost every other type of sexual behavior have changed. During the sixteenth century in Western Europe, for example, it was fashionable for women from common street prostitutes to aristocrats and royalty to wear gowns that fully exposed their breasts (Morris, 2004). Today, not only is it considered deviant for women to expose their breasts, except under highly controlled circumstances, in many cases it is illegal for them to do so and may result in arrest, fines, or possibly even jail time. Although students in a university figure drawing class may be allowed to draw fully nude models, and some of the most famous paintings and sculptures in the world of fine art are of nudes, as we noted in Chapter 5, when either male or female nudity is used for entertainment purposes, or for earning a living, those involved are often highly stigmatized, and typically suffer both personal and social consequences for their actions. Even fine art that features nudity is viewed as deviant by some people. As recently as 2002, US Attorney General, John Ashcroft, ordered that the nude breasts of two 10-foot statues titled *Spirit of Justice* and *Majesty of Law*, be covered with a blue drape before he would hold a televised press conference in front of them in the Great Hall of the US Department of Justice (USA Today, 2002). We will discuss nudism in more detail in a later section of this chapter.

Because of its link to procreation, **heterosexuality**, or *attraction to the opposite sex*, has traditionally been viewed as the dominant normative form of sexual behavior in most cultures. That does not mean that various forms of heterosexuality have not been viewed as deviant. They certainly have been and still are, depending on time, place, situation, culture, and who is involved in the activity and in judging it. As we have already discussed, working in the sex industries either in the form of adult films or in prostitution is highly stigmatized by many people even if it involves heterosexual intercourse and other widely accepted heterosexual behaviors. For centuries, **premarital sex**, or *sexual intercourse prior to marriage*, was not only discouraged, but sometimes even severely punished, but today in the United States, studies reveal that unmarried males and females are more sexually active, become sexually active at earlier ages than ever before, and most young adults expect their spouse to be sexually experienced before they marry (Kost and Henshaw, 2012; Pearson and Wilkinson, 2013). **Adultery**, more often referred to as **extramarital sex**, or *sex outside of marriage*, has been viewed as everything from the norm in ancient Greece and Rome, as well as among royalty and the aristocracies of many countries to a crime punishable by fines, imprisonment, or even death. Although most people in the United States no longer force adulterers to wear the "scarlet letter," cheating on one's spouse is still stigmatized, and exacts a toll in regard to a person's social identity.

## Adultery/Swinging/Mate Swapping/Co-Marital Sex

In Chapter 3, we briefly alluded to Nathaniel Hawthorne's classic book *The Scarlet Letter* in which one of the main characters, a young woman named Hester Prynne, was required to wear a scarlet "A" symbolizing that she had committed adultery. **Adultery**, usually defined as *sex outside of marriage (extramarital sex)*, has long been viewed as deviant behavior in the United States and several other societies. In some cultures adultery is considered a crime and can be punished with fines, imprisonment, or even death. In other countries, adultery is viewed as a violation of mores, and may be sanctioned by gossip, ridicule, shunning, and loss of social status.

In the United States, over time, adultery has been considered a felony, a misdemeanor, a sin, grounds for divorce, and a factor in child custody cases (Lampe, 1987). Yet, despite widespread negative attitudes toward adultery and in some cases, severe penalties for it, Alfred Kinsey and his research associates found that two decades prior to the so-called "sexual revolution," approximately 50 percent of married males and 26 percent of married females admitted they had participated in extramarital sex (Kinsey *et al.*, 1946;1953). More recent studies have put the prevalence of extramarital sex among both men and women somewhere around 26 percent (Atkins *et al.*, 2001). As early social scientific researchers attempted to learn more about the prevalence of adultery, they discovered what initially they termed to be "wife swapping," and later termed as **mate swapping** or **swinging** which involves *couples in a committed relationship (usually marriage) who engage in sexual activities with others as a social or recreational activity.* Swinging may also be called **co-marital sex**, and today, people involved in swinging often simply refer to it as *the lifestyle.*

Swinging can take place in private homes, private clubs, sex clubs, or at public locations such as motels, hotels, or vacation resorts. It is very difficult to assess an accurate number of people who participate in swinging, but estimates by the Kinsey Institute and other researchers range anywhere from approximately 4 million to perhaps as many as 15 million Americans being involved in the lifestyle (ABC, 2005). Adultery has clearly been around for a long time, and research indicates that mate swapping or sharing has as well, but most researchers contend that it became more popularized in the United States during the so-called sexual revolution of the 1960s and 1970s, waned somewhat during the 1980s and 1990s with fears related to HIV and AIDS, and then rebounded in the twenty-first century with many viable subcultures active today (Gould, 1999). Although considered a form of deviant sexual behavior by the majority of Americans, research on co-marital sex indicates that its participants are largely middle class, college-educated, married couples who otherwise live fairly traditional non-deviant lifestyles except for their participation in the lifestyle (Gould, 1999; Bergstrand and Sinski, 2010). Box 6.1 features a member of the lifestyle describing his experiences with mate-swapping or "swinging."

Research indicates that introduction to co-marital sex is often initiated by the male partner, and sometimes entered into by the female partner with a certain amount of apprehensiveness that perhaps her mate is growing tired of her and simply wants the opportunity to have sexual experiences with other women, but once women engage in the activities, the lifestyle often becomes a female-driven phenomenon (Bergstrand and Sinski, 2010). This scenario has not escaped the media who portrayed it in the popular 1969 film *Bob & Carol & Ted & Alice,* and a short-lived television series on CBS set in the 1970s but aired in 2008 entitled *Swingtown.*

As with other forms of deviance, the lifestyle has been greatly affected by the development of newer forms of media, especially the Internet. Hundreds of online magazines, thousands of websites, online chat clubs, formal organizations, discussion boards, and an entire travel industry have emerged to arrange conventions, organizational events, parties, retreats, vacations, and other social events for participants in the lifestyle (Gould, 1999). Like most subcultures, *the lifestyle* practices a certain amount of boundary maintenance, screening potential members, limiting participation in most activities to couples only, and establishing both informal and formal norms that outline what is acceptable and non-acceptable behavior within

**Box 6.1**   In their own words

Swinging and "the lifestyle"

"I CAN DO THIS" were the words that came from my fiancée shortly after we left the house party. After spending the evening at a swingers' club, we were invited to a couple's house with several other couples. We made it clear we were newbies and weren't ready to "play" that night, but we were welcomed to the party nevertheless. We spent the remainder of the evening watching three couples engage in a variety of sexual acts and couplings. Finally, during a break in the action, we left the party and that's when my fiancée made her proclamation. Thus began our experience in "The Lifestyle."

We had our first experience a few weeks later after meeting a couple at the same swingers' club. It was an "off-premises" club, meaning no sex took place at the club. Rather, couples met, danced, chatted and made plans for after-parties at local homes and hotels. Our first experience involved a very experienced couple, who we later found out, prided themselves on searching out newbies and "breaking them in" to the lifestyle. They were attractive, socially adept, and sexually experienced.

My fiancée and I found that our own sexual life was even more exciting as a result of the play in which we engaged with others. Rather than being jealous, we found that it was a turn-on to see our significant other being sexually aroused by other people. We felt it brought us closer together. Other couples expressed the same sentiment. We also found that there were many benefits to being a part of the lifestyle. We developed friendships that lasted for years in some cases. Our sex lives benefitted, but more than that, our social lives were enhanced.

The couples we met comprised teachers, lawyers, business owners, a police officer, and the like. Many were middle class or upper-middle class and well educated as was consistent with the literature on the subject of swinging. The first few months were an extremely exciting time as we became educated on the jargon and norms of the deviant subculture we had joined. Initially, my fiancée maintained that she was only into men, but over time she became interested in women as well. Bisexual behavior among women is strongly encouraged in the lifestyle while bisexual behavior among men is, by and large, taboo.

Our marriage was rich and full and we developed many friendships with couples near and far. My wife underwent something of a transformation, going from a pretty, shy introvert to a confident and desirable woman. The literature on swinging stated that women gained status and men often lost status in the lifestyle and I believe this happened to us as well. The resulting disparity of status, along with the stress of having a child with a serious illness, was more than our marriage could withstand, and after 11 years we divorced. Along with the house and our child, my ex-wife got most of the friends we developed while in the lifestyle.

Upon reflection, it is hard to tell exactly what role the lifestyle played in our divorce, but play a role it did. I learned a lot about myself and this deviant lifestyle, but I am certain it will not be a part of my future. Another thing I have learned is that leaving the lifestyle does not mean leaving behind the stigma. At least two dating relationships ended when I shared information about my past involvement in this deviant lifestyle.

the subculture. Many couples in the lifestyle communicate with others through cyberspace and, much like online dating services, couples often work to create a virtual identity that they believe best represents the impression they want to make on others and they often choose other couples with whom to party based on online correspondence and virtual identities established on the Internet (Griffiths and Frobish, 2013).

Typically uncomfortable with any open or norm-violating forms of human sexuality, agents of social control including local homeowners associations, law enforcement, and city councils have attempted to regulate, control, or eliminate activities associated with the lifestyle. Also, the conservative group, *American Family Association*, monitors television series and movies urging boycotts and protests against any television shows or films that depict anything except traditional heterosexual monogamy. This group also monitors media for any depictions of sexual activities, or even nudity without sexual connotation as going without clothing also violates many cultural norms including mores and laws in the United States. Because of possibilities of fines or other social sanctions, some swingers join other organizations such as "adult only" nudist camps, where their activities may be less likely to attract public scrutiny.

## Naturism/nudism

"If God had intended for us to be naked, we would have been born that way" is a quote often attributed to American humorist Mark Twain, and used as the mantra of many naturists/nudists around the country. Nevertheless, despite the naturalness of nakedness, public nudity is generally considered a form of deviant behavior and virtually every state, county, and municipality in the United States has statutes that regulate the extent of nudity that is allowable, or more precisely, not allowable, by law. As a result, people who believe in naturism, or nudism, a lifestyle based on both private and public nudity, are considered deviant and face much of the stigma and social sanctions that other deviants experience. We have already discussed in Chapter 5 nude and topless dancing as a deviant occupation, and although those activities involve public nudity, when we talk about naturism or nudism, we are describing a totally different thing. Whereas nude and topless dancing is designed to be erotic and sexual, naturists and nudists emphasize the naturalness of going without clothing and make every effort to desexualize their nudity.

Although there are some "adults only" naturist/nudist organizations and functions that may be part of *the lifestyle* previously discussed, most naturist/nudist subcultures are family oriented and focus their attention on carrying out every day routine activities and recreation in the nude as opposed to linking nudity to any type of sexual behaviors. The *American Association for Nude Recreation* (AANR), founded in 1931, is one of the oldest and well-known naturist/nudist organizations in the United States. Once known as the *American Sunbathing Association* (interestingly abbreviated ASA the same as the American Sociological Association), the AANR boasts some 260 chartered resorts and campgrounds across the United States (AANR, 2014.)

The AANR is not only a social organization, but also a political one, and has been active in seeking the repeal of what they view as discriminatory laws against nudists and being an advocate for the acceptance of naturism and nudism. As a result, the organization has established what they call the *Nudists' Bill of Rights* which includes the following assertions:

As law-abiding citizens who are friends of nudism, including many members of the American Association for Nude Recreation, we proudly affirm that we have and are entitled to exercise the following rights. These are self-evident and based on the Constitutions of the United States and Canada, the laws of those countries, and their court rulings.

1   Nudists have the right to hold their values and beliefs.
2   Nudists have the right to petition and be heard by their governments.
3   Nudists have the right to responsibly enjoy nudity within their homes and on private property.
4   Nudists have the right to exercise decision-making in the upbringing of their families in a manner consistent with their beliefs and without interference from others.
5   Nudists have the right to assemble in the nude within appropriate settings.
6   Nudists have the right to decisions about what constitutes acceptable nudity to be made free from considerations of age, gender, marital status, religious beliefs, ethnic origin, or sexual orientation.
7   Nudists have the right to responsibly enjoy being nude within appropriate locations on public lands.
8   Nudists have the right to be free from adverse actions by their employers as a result of their lawful enjoyment of nudity when away from work.
9   Nudists have the right to experience accurate, life-affirming portrayals of the human body in all its stages as depicted in the performing arts, the fine arts, literature, and human history.
10  Nudists have the right to be treated as law-abiding citizens (AANR, 2014).

Once again, the media have played an important role in shaping public attitudes and values toward nudity. It is almost impossible to turn on the television set without seeing a program that features lots of cleavage, peek-a-boo clothing, or pixelated bare breasts, buttocks, and genitalia. Cable television features a number of shows such as *Sons of Anarchy* and others that show naked buttocks as well as simulated sex, while *HBO* and *Showtime* air award winning fictional programs such as *Boardwalk Empire, Californication, Game of Thrones, Hung*, and *True Blood*, all of which feature full frontal nudity and simulated sex acts, as well as reality shows such as *Naked and Afraid, Naked Vegas*, and others that pixelate certain areas while showing others – all of which have pushed the censorial envelope, broadened the range of tolerance, and made various forms of nudity more mainstream. Those same programs feature homosexuality as well as heterosexuality, even further expanding the television envelope's range of tolerance.

## Sex norms and homosexuality

In modern American history, perhaps no attitudes and norms toward sexual behavior have changed more dramatically than those regarding **homosexuality**, *sexual attraction between people of the same sex*. At various times and by various people, in the United States, homosexuality has been considered either taboo, illegal, deviant, unnatural, immoral, a form of mental illness, unhealthy, a deviant choice, a genetic anomaly, or a combination of any and all of those things. Up until 1974, the *American Psychiatric Association* considered homosexuality to be a mental illness and contended that those afflicted with the disease were more prone to other psychopathologies and emotional problems such as anxiety, depression, and tendencies to commit suicide (Bailey, 1999). Today, while some people still may view homosexuality in some or all of those ways, others view homosexuality as simply being different from heterosexuality – no more, or no less deviant. Several states legally acknowledge same-sex marriages, and values, attitudes, beliefs and norms regarding homosexuality vary widely from state to state, family to family, and person to person. As one noted psychologist pointed out, homosexuality became viewed as a mental illness, not through scientific or medical research, but primarily because Freud and others linked it to paranoia and depression; years later, it was miraculously "cured," and determined not to be a mental illness, once again, not by science but by a vote of the American Psychological Association (Hickey, 2013). In keeping with the sociological approach to deviance, the question arises, what other form of "disease" can be created, and then eliminated by popular vote of an organization? As a result of differing attitudes, values, and norms surrounding sexuality, changing laws regarding homosexuality provide some sociological insight into how the phenomenon has been and is regarded in American society.

## Homosexuality and the law

In various parts of the world and at different times throughout history, homosexuality has not only been legal, but has been viewed as conforming behavior in regard to sexual norms and values. In both ancient Greece and Rome, for example, it was common for older men to have sex with adolescent boys, and sexual orientation was not considered to be an important part of a person's social identity (Hubbard, 2003). Among some Plains Indians in North America, high status was granted to homosexual men known as *berdache* who dressed as women and provided sexual favors to male tribal warriors (Williams, 1986). The Etoro of New Guinea not only view homosexuality as acceptable, but as vital for survival. Etoro men believe that semen is a source of men's strength and that males are not born with semen, but must acquire it as young boys by performing oral sex on older men who no longer need it. Consequently, each male has a limited supply of semen that must be replenished from time to time as a result of having sexual intercourse with their wives for procreation (Miller, 2013). In that case, norms support not only heterosexuality and homosexuality, but also **bisexuality**, *sexual attraction to members of both sexes.*

Although acceptability of homosexuality varies throughout the world today, it is still considered to violate sexual norms and values and is both discouraged and socially sanctioned in some parts of the world. The 2014 Winter Olympics held in Sochi, Russia drew attention to Russia's discriminatory laws against lesbians, gays, bisexuals, and transgendered individuals (LGBT) sparking protests and threatened boycotts on the part of many athletes and some countries and urging from the United Nations for the games to promote "social inclusion" (Nichols, 2013). Although there are no explicit laws against homosexuality in Russia, there are laws against openly demonstrating for gay rights and/or distributing what the Russian government perceives as, "propaganda of non-traditional sexual relations" (Nichols, 2013). Although the United States government and US Olympic officials resoundingly criticized Russia's lack of tolerance, Russia is far from the harshest country in dealing with homosexuality. In several Middle Eastern countries including Saudi Arabia, Kuwait, and the United Arab Emirates, people can be fined, jailed, publicly whipped, and even executed simply for being gay (Adomanis, 2013).

The United States has not had a stellar history regarding discrimination against homosexuals either. Although there have been few if any laws making it illegal to *be* a homosexual, there have been many laws in the United States that banned various homosexual activities. Most of these bans came in the form of **sodomy laws** which were *laws passed by individual states banning what was sometimes vaguely referred to as "unnatural sex acts," or in some cases were more explicit in banning oral sex, anal sex, and sex between unmarried couples.* Although sodomy laws could also be applied against heterosexuals, and in some cases even married heterosexual couples, they were clearly aimed at legally prohibiting both consensual and non-consensual sex acts between people of the same sex. Many of these sodomy laws were enacted at the time of statehood, and although most were routinely ignored or very selectively enforced, many remained in effect up until 2003 when the US Supreme Court ruled in the *Lawrence v. Texas* case that private consensual sexual conduct is protected in the due process clause of the US Constitution (Eskridge, 2008).

Some of the most visible changes in laws discriminating against homosexuals can be seen in the number of states that legally recognize same-sex marriages. At the time of this writing, 18 states and the District of Columbia recognized same-sex marriages as legal (see Figure 6.1).

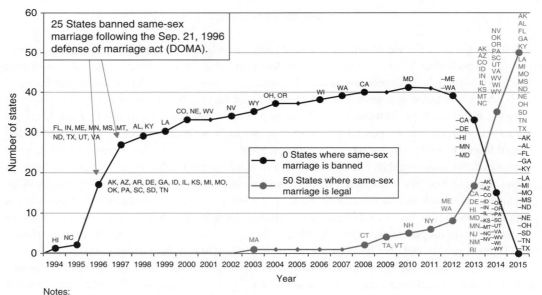

Notes:
- A minus sign before the state indicates that the legal status of gay marriage changed from banned to legal.
- When a state has instituted gay marriage bans multiple times (e.g. by legislative action and then by popular vote), only the most recent ban has been included for each state.
- DC legalized same-sex marriage on Mar. 3, 2010
- California legalized same-sex marriage on May 15, 2008, but banned it on Nov. 4 of the same year.

**Figure 6.1** Timeline of same-sex marriage bans and legalizations by effective date of laws. *Source*: ProCon.org

Conversely, 32 states had some combination of either constitutional bans or state laws prohibiting same-sex marriage, with 25 states having both types of laws, and courts had upheld states' rights that they could not be required to accept same-sex marriages.

Public opinion regarding same-sex marriage changed dramatically during the two decades depicted in Figure 6.1. In the 1990s, public opinion polls showed that almost two-thirds of American adults over the age of 25 opposed same-sex marriage; by the end of 2013, virtually all major polls (i.e., Gallup, Bloomberg, Quinnipiac, Pew, USA Today, ABC, NBC, CBS, CNN) showed that over half of Americans thought that same-sex marriages should be legal (Polling Report.com, 2014). Despite changing attitudes about homosexuality and gay rights, some people still reacted negatively toward people with anything other than heterosexual orientations and identities. Some, to the point of feeling that anything related to homosexuality posed a threat to them, their values, and society.

## Homophobia

Despite the changes in sodomy laws and the movement toward more widespread acceptance of same-sex marriage, many people still consider homosexuality to be a form of deviant behavior, and if not legally prohibited, believe it should be socially condemned. An interview with Reality star, Phil Robertson of *Duck Dynasty*, revealed that he viewed homosexuality as a sin comparable to adultery, bestiality, and drunkenness (Magary, 2014). While many condemned this view, and he was temporarily suspended by the A & E Network, others roundly supported the condemnation of homosexuality. Although younger Americans generally express more tolerant views of homosexuality, Pascoe (2012) discovered that the single most vicious insult one high school boy can sling at another is to say, "Dude you're a fag." Because homosexuality and bisexuality challenge strong norms and some long-held values regarding sexuality, many members of the LGBT community find that their sexual orientations and lifestyles seem threatening to others, resulting in ideological, religious, and even physical attacks against them. This **homophobia,** or *unnatural and unrealistic fear, hatred, and discrimination directed toward homosexuals* provides fuel for political campaigns, religious crusades, and support for maintaining prejudicial and discriminatory laws in the United States and elsewhere. Homophobia may not be universally applied to all types of homosexuality, however. Research suggests that even the most homophobic males may be more tolerant of lesbianism, with some viewing male homosexuality as disgusting while thinking that female homosexuality is "cool" (Pascoe, 2012:55). Unfortunately, in some cases homophobia has also been linked to **hate crimes** which are *crimes against persons or property based on race, ethnicity, religion, or sexual orientation.*

In response to prejudice, discrimination, and homophobia, lesbians, gays, bisexuals, and transgendered individuals often seek out more tolerant environments where their sexual behaviors are more readily accepted. As noted in Chapter 2, it is common for stigmatized individuals to divide their social worlds and often form subcultures where their attitudes, values, and beliefs are shared and accepted. In many major US cities, this has led to the creation of **homosocial environments** that have become *social enclaves containing hotels, bars, restaurants, shops, and other businesses that are owned, operated by, and cater to the LGBT community.* Similarly, certain occupations and professions have traditionally shown more liberal attitudes toward and acceptance of homosexuality and have therefore provided less discrimination and more opportunities for people with different sexual orientations. The fine arts, music, theater, and motion pictures, are but a few examples, which make the media a prominent social catalyst for changing social attitudes toward homosexuality and other differences in social orientation or activities.

## Transvestism, transgenderism, and transsexuality

For several seasons of *Saturday Night Live*, actress Julia Sweeney portrayed an androgynous character named "Pat," who was slightly overweight, wore a loose fitting western-style shirt and jeans and sported a curly hairstyle that could have been appropriate for either a woman or a man. Pat appeared in a number of sketches, the gist of which was various people trying numerous ways to figure out if Pat was a male or a female. **Androgyny**, *the blending of masculine and feminine traits*, is not only used to describe a person who does not fit neatly into either masculine or feminine gender roles, but also refers to non-gender specific objects such as clothing that can be worn by either males or females, or toys that equally appeal to both girls and boys. Androgyny has become more popular in the United States over the past few decades as rigid sex and gender roles have become more flexible, and few Americans now insist that there is such a thing as "men's work" and "women's work" and few if any activities or behaviors are viewed as being appropriate only for women or only for men. Nevertheless, despite the ever changing attitudes toward gender roles, no matter how flexible the range of tolerance, and however socially defined, societal members become somewhat uncomfortable when they cannot distinguish boys from girls or women from men.

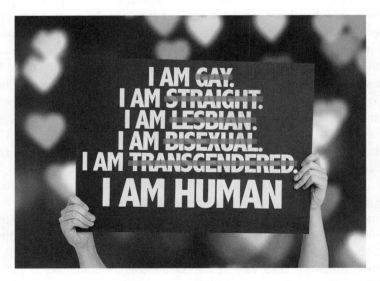

How does this sign signify the struggle for equality faced by those who have been labeled as sexually deviant? *Source*: Gustavo Frazao/Shutterstock

At Mardi Gras or during Halloween or other special occasions, *men might dress as women or women as men* as part of a costume to temporarily appear to be a member of the opposite sex. This temporary **cross-dressing**, usually done for fun or entertainment, is not particularly troublesome for most members of society and is usually not considered deviant unless it is pursued on a regular basis, or is meant to intentionally mislead others during routine social interaction. In those cases, the practice is usually referred to as **transvestism** – *dressing and acting in ways traditionally associated with the opposite sex.* Transvestism can occur among heterosexuals, homosexuals, and bisexuals, and may or may not be associated with **fetishism**, *sexual arousal associated with a specific inanimate object (such as opposite sex clothing).* According to the American Psychiatric Association's *Diagnostic and Statistical Manual of Mental Disorders (DSM)*, if transvestism occurs over a period of six months or more and is associated with sexual arousal, it is considered to be a mental disorder known as *transvestic fetishism* (APA, 2013).

Sometimes, individuals intentionally "bend" their gender roles, a phenomenon that is often referred to in the vernacular as **gender bending**, *actively transgressing prescribed gender roles for a person's sex.* As with transvestism, the gender bender usually dresses in clothing associated with the opposite sex, but beyond simply cross-dressing, the gender bender also acts and behaves like the opposite sex. In these cases, a person is referred to as *transgendered.* There are no clear-cut universally agreed upon definitions for the terms transgender and transsexual, as both refer to people who believe that their gender identities are not in agreement with their biologically assigned sex. **Transgenderism** is somewhat of an "umbrella" term that refers to situations *in which a person's gender identity does not correspond with his or her sex.* Transgenderism is more accurately viewed as a *process* rather than an act, as it involves an individual redefining over time his or her gender identity and gender roles, and taking on the gender identity of the opposite sex. Often transgendered individuals describe themselves as having been a "man trapped in a woman's body" or vice versa, and view their new gender identity as their true gender identity, despite it being in conflict with their assigned biological sex (Teich, 2012). When individuals consciously realign their sex to meet their new gender identity they may make the transition to being a transsexual. **Transsexualism** generally refers to *a person who no longer identifies with his or her biological sex, undergoes counseling and hormone treatments, and sometimes surgery to realign his or her physical appearance to fit the gender identity of the opposite sex.* The *DSM-V* labels transsexual people as having a mental disorder called *Gender Dysphoric*, but most transgendered and transsexual people, along with a growing number of social scientists contend that this is another example of the medicalization of norm violation behavior and labeling it as a mental illness (APA, 2013; Stryker and Whittle, 2006). Supporting the medical view, in 2013, a federal appeals court upheld a lower court ruling that a transsexual inmate in Massachusetts serving a life sentence for murder was entitled to undergo a taxpayer-funded sex change operation, viewing the procedure as a medically necessary treatment.

In some of the movies that have featured transvestism, transgenderism, and transsexualism, a popular theme has centered around a heterosexual male hiring what he thinks is a female prostitute, only to discover that "she" is actually a "he." While this theme may or may not be accurately portrayed in the media – few socially deviant things are – there are both male and female prostitutes, as well as prostitutes who are in various stages of sex or gender transition.

## Prostitution

In one scene of the 1970s comedic sitcom WKRP in Cincinnati, colleagues of one of the more gullible and naïve radio crew members are trying to inform him that his new "girlfriend" who works as an "escort and female companion" is really a prostitute. One of his friends tries to gently break the news by saying, "She's a member of the oldest profession on earth," to which he replies with a look of confusion, "You mean she's a farmer?" There is no historical documentation that prostitution is the oldest profession on earth, but there is plenty of evidence that prostitution has been around for a very long time. It is recorded that bands of prostitutes were hired to accompany ancient Greek and Roman armies across the continent as they waged war in order to help keep up the morale of the troops and to discourage homesickness and desertion (Bauer, 2007).

As with most forms of deviance, prostitution has been both highly condemned and readily accepted, depending upon culture, time, place, and situation. In the United States, especially during westward expansion as male adventurers traversed the vast continent of North America seeking gold, opening new lands, and creating new cities, it was fairly common for saloons and brothels to employ women to entertain the men, and to take their money for the profit of other men who were less adventurous and more entrepreneurial in spirit. As the United States developed, most state legislatures enacted laws making prostitution illegal, and with lingering prurient values, whether legal or illegal, selling sex for money became widely frowned upon and viewed as deviant.

On the surface, prostitution seems relatively easy to define. In general, **prostitution** is *exchanging sexual favors for something of value (usually money) with no emotional involvement.* As with most forms of social behavior, things are not necessarily as they seem, however, and defining prostitution can be quite complicated. For example, if a young man takes a young woman out for a nice dinner and a movie and at the end of the evening she rewards his efforts by having sex with him, has she committed an act of prostitution? Or, if a beautiful or handsome young model or movie star ingratiates her/himself to an older multimillionaire who allows him or her to live a life of luxury and splendor in exchange for companionship and occasional sex, is that a form of prostitution? Hundreds if not thousands of other possible scenarios exist that may be construed as exchanging sexual favors for something of value either with or without emotional attachment. As a result, prostitution tends to be defined more by agents of social control such as legislative bodies and law enforcement personnel more than by the activities or participants involved.

Numerous social scientific studies have been conducted on various forms of prostitution. Most indicate that it is very difficult to measure the extent of prostitution and to determine exactly who or what is involved. *Uniform Crime Reports* indicate that annually in the United States, approximately 50,000 arrests are made for prostitution and commercialized vice (FBI, 2013), but virtually everybody knows that number represents only the proverbial tip of the iceberg. Today, in the United States, prostitution and human trafficking probably involve well over 100,000 people, and around the world the number would be in the millions (Falls, 2013). Figure 6.2 shows the distribution of known human slaves around the world and in the United States. Today, there is far more concern on the part of law enforcement personnel about the crime of human trafficking, selling and buying humans for the purposes of sexual slavery, forced labor, or other illegal purposes, than there is about more traditional forms of prostitution involving consenting adults that many consider to be a "victimless" crime (Marcin, 2012).

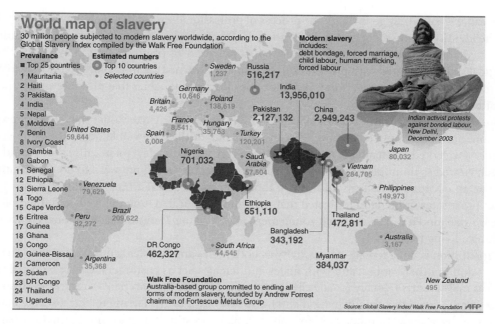

**Figure 6.2** World map of slavery. *Source*: Global Slavery Index / Walk Free Foundation AFP

Early studies of prostitution in the United States indicated that female prostitutes could be categorized into a stratified typology based on physical characteristics, type of work, and amount of money involved. Call girls were at the top of the hierarchy because they tended to be physically attractive, work out of their apartments or hotel rooms, take highly screened clients only by referral, and earn the highest incomes. House girls, or prostitutes who worked in brothels or houses of prostitution, were below the call girls as they were less selective in their clients, had less screening of clients, and often entertained more than one client in a 24-hour time frame. Bar girls were further down the scale as they publicly solicited clients often working hotel or restaurant bars with very little screening of clients. As a result, bar girls were more likely to get arrested, physically assaulted, or bilked out of their fees than house girls and call girls who worked in more controlled environments. At the bottom of the stratification hierarchy is the streetwalker, the most common type of prostitute who publicly solicits clients on street corners, in bus stations, and virtually anywhere they might find an interested customer. Streetwalkers are the most likely prostitutes to be arrested, severely beaten, robbed, or even murdered, as there is basically no screening of clientele and their business is high risk and low reward. Street prostitutes often work for pimps who turn out, or introduce, the new initiate to the world of prostitution, and for a significant cut of his/her take, "protect" him or her from other pimps. Much of street prostitution is a product of deviant street networks that develop in particular areas of cities where there also is drug abuse, street crimes, and a host of other criminal activities (Cohen, 1980).

Nanette Davis (1971; 1993) outlined a three-stage process through which females become prostitutes. First, she found that girls sometimes drift from sexual promiscuity into their first act of exchanging sex for something of monetary value. Then, they undergo a transitional period involving the learning of skills, internalizing the values of prostitution, and learning the role of prostitute. Finally, they go through the process of professionalization in which they actually take on the identity of prostitute and embrace the role. Similarly, research on house girl prostitution indicated that prostitutes typically underwent three areas of training: first, they learned the physical skills associated with prostitution; second, they learned client management (how to get the most money for the least effort); and third, they learned the values that promote and support prostitution (Heyl, 1979).

Some research indicates that not all prostitutes learn or internalize values that support prostitution, but may simply enter into it because it is one of the only viable occupations open to them. As we noted in Chapter 5, many occupations are viewed as deviant because they are either illegal, viewed as immoral, or involve work that most people would not want to do. Prostitution may be an occupation that fits all three of those categories at one time or another. A study of street prostitutes in England indicated that many undereducated, unemployed, and unemployable women (and it can be assumed young men) may turn to prostitution as a rational choice for making a living (Reeve, 2013).

Prostitution is not a female-only activity as both males and females sell sex for money on the streets and in other venues, and both males and females act as customers. Going by monikers such as male escorts (usually female clients), gigolos (usually female clients), rent-boys (usually male clients), hustlers (usually male clients), and "Gay for Pay" (referring to heterosexual males willing to have sex with other men for money), male prostitution shares many characteristics with female prostitution with the exception of more homosexuality involved (Kaye, 2003). Male prostitutes may enter the profession somewhat differently than females. According to one study, males generally pursue one of two paths into prostitution: (1) boys turn to prostitution as a solution to desperate financial and living conditions; or (2) boys turn to prostitution as a sense of adventure selling sexual favors for extra money, sexual excitement, and adventurous lifestyle (Luckenbill, 1985).

If prostitution is indeed one of the oldest professions, it, like other ways of making a living, has not ignored technological developments. Selling sex is no longer solely the domain of the streets, brothels, or other direct contact venues. Today, sex can be bought and sold or found for free in cyberspace. Technology and the advent and accessibility of cyberspace have dramatically altered research strategies on human sexuality and sexual deviance and forever changed the formation and sustenance of sexually deviant communities prompting the need for social scientists to be cognizant of "red light districts on blue screens" (Quinn and Forsyth, 2013:579).

## Phone sex and cybersex

For years, adult magazines have run advertisements for 900-numbers where people could call and have phone sex, simulated sex or sex talk over a telephone, while paying for it on a credit card or having it charged to their phone bill by the minute. As the digital age emerged, however, computers were introduced to the world of human sexuality, and a new term, cybersex, was coined to describe using a computer for flirting, sex-talk, viewing pornography, and other forms of sexual stimulation through cyberspace. Whereas phone sex was primarily limited to an individual calling another person, who they could not see or otherwise interact except through voice, the Internet provides a wide array of pornography sites, chat rooms, blogs, and other venues that feature strip shows, simulated sex, live sex, and virtually any other type of legal or illegal sexual activity imaginable (Meier and Geis, 2006). Today, people seeking more graphic and deviant sexual interaction and hardcore pornography are more likely to go online, whereas telephone sex is more likely to involve sexting – sending out semi-nude or nude photos over mobile phones. Although people of any age can sext, as some scandals with high profile celebrities and politicians have shown, it seems to be most popular with teenagers and young adults who do it as much for fun and entertainment as for sexual gratification (Brown *et al.*, 2009; Lohmann, 2011). Nevertheless, teens and young adults who engage in sexting sometimes learn the harsh social penalties that can be associated with sexual deviance as they may be labeled as delinquent, charged with possessing child pornography, and may be required to register as sex offenders for the rest of their lives (Comartin *et al.*, 2013).

Whatever the form sexual deviance may take, virtually all forms of media have been fascinated with it, and instrumental in shaping people's views and definitions. Adultery, nudity, homosexuality, transvestism, transgenderism, transsexualism, and prostitution have all been themes of popular television programs and motion pictures, and phone sex and cybersex use media as their venue.

## Sexual Deviance and the Media

The media have long been fascinated with sex and sexual deviance, but with the exception of underground pornographic films, human sexuality was only alluded to or hinted at in most major motion pictures and television programs prior to the decade of the 1970s. Even real-life married couple, Lucille Ball and Desi Arnaz, were prohibited from sleeping in the same bed or alluding to any sexual behavior when they portrayed on-screen married couple Lucy and Ricky Ricardo. That is not to say that sex was not an important part of Hollywood and the media, however. Jane Russell, Lauren Bacall, Ingrid Bergman, Ava Gardner, Betty Grable, Rita Hayworth, and a host of other Hollywood stars became famous "pin-up" girls in the 1940s, joined by Elizabeth Taylor, Sophia Loren and others in the 1950s. Newly emerging starlet Marilyn Monroe caused quite a controversy by posing nude for *Playboy* magazine in 1953. These women sex symbols were accompanied by a cadre of "sexy" male "leading men" who included Errol Flynn, Robert Taylor, Humphrey Bogart, Victor Mature, and Rock Hudson, to name but a few. Perhaps no leading man of the 1950s was more revered and admired than 6 feet 5 inch Rock Hudson, the epitome of male sexuality. Hudson appeared in over 60 major motion pictures and his on-screen and off-screen love affairs with leading ladies were well-known and highly documented in the media. What was much less known, however, was that Rock Hudson had been secretly gay his entire adult life. Although close personal friends and a few co-stars later acknowledged that they were aware of Hudson's homosexuality, it was not until 1985 at the age of 59, when he became the one of the first major celebrities to die of an AIDS-related illness, that Rock Hudson's sexual orientation became public knowledge (Hudson and Davidson, 2007).

It is somewhat remarkable that much of the viewing public did not know that Liberace was gay, as he made little effort to disguise his onstage persona decked out in elaborately sequined costumes, high-heeled boots or shoes, and his ever-present crystal candelabra. Yet, it was not until the 2013 release of the HBO movie, *Behind the Candelabra* starring Michael Douglas as

Liberace and Matt Damon as his assistant and star-crossed lover, that millions of Americans' suspicions were finally confirmed.

Television stars also grappled with their sexuality as audiences showed mixed reactions to both heterosexuality and homosexuality on the small screen. As previously mentioned, Lucy and Ricky Ricardo slept in twin beds, as did virtually all married couples on television, if their sleeping habits were portrayed at all. The popular comedy series, *Roseanne*, was one of the first television series to broach the subject of homosexuality in an episode in 1994 entitled "Don't Ask, Don't Tell" when its star, Roseanne Barr visited a gay bar. In that episode, Roseanne's character kissed another woman (played by Mariel Hemingway) on the lips. This episode sparked tremendous controversy, but seemed to break a taboo that would never be revived. Yet, three years later, in the situation comedy, *Ellen*, when the show's popular lead actress, Ellen DeGeneres' character "came out" on national television, public reaction largely indicated that prime time television was not quite ready for homosexuality. For several weeks before the program aired, it was widely discussed in newspapers, magazines, and on television talk-shows as the episode represented both the fictional coming out of television character, Ellen Morgan, and the real-life coming out of television star Ellen DeGeneres. Before the end of that season, the television series was cancelled, with the network executives citing lower ratings as the cause, while Ellen DeGeneres insisted the show was a victim of discrimination and homophobia. Although the public showed mixed reactions, by the year 2000, overt homosexuality became a television mainstay with numerous popular shows including *Will and Grace* and others depicting openly gay characters. These shows went on to garner high ratings, win Emmys and other awards, and set the standard that a character's sexual orientation does not matter. Ellen DeGeneres' career soared. She married fellow Hollywood star, Portia DeRossi, in 2003, began hosting her own daytime talk show which won numerous Emmys and other awards, hosted the Academy Awards several times, and became one of the best known and most beloved celebrities on television.

Just as *Duck Dynasty's* patriarch Phil Robertson's negative comments on homosexuality garnered widespread national attention because of his media notoriety, so too have more tolerant and accepting attitudes toward homosexuality as more and more well-known and highly respected media celebrities have come out, or become open about their previously hidden homosexuality. For decades, because homosexuality (and for that matter, promiscuity, adultery, and almost any form of human sexuality except for procreation) was viewed as deviant, and perhaps even dangerous, high profile celebrities found it necessary to hide their sexual orientations and activities if they were anything but straight-laced, and publicly acceptable.

Motion pictures also acknowledged homosexual themes with movies like *TransAmerica*, *Brokeback Mountain*, *Milk*, *The Kids are All Right*, and several others. These movies won critical acclaim as well as being popular at the box office. Audiences seemingly acknowledged that sexual orientation is only one aspect of a person's being, and perhaps not the most important one, as they became more accepting of what previously had been considered too sexually deviant to be portrayed in mainstream films.

A few areas of human sexuality continued to push the envelope and challenge mainstream norms and values regarding human sexuality and what is or is not deviant. Films such as *Boys Don't Cry, The Crying Game, To Wong Foo Thanks for Everything, Julie Newmar*, and others broached the subjects of transvestitism, transgenderism, and transsexuality, elements of human sexuality previously left largely unexplored by mainstream media. In Chapter 3, we briefly alluded to a popular character, *Geraldine*, portrayed by Flip Wilson who dressed as a sassy African-American woman who regularly proclaimed "the devil made me do it" for regular sketches on his weekly television comedy series. Although 1970s America was not highly tolerant of transvestism, transgenderism, or transsexuality, audiences seemed more than willing to accept Geraldine into their homes on a weekly basis. Perhaps the key was comedy, however, as there was a long tradition in vaudeville and early show business of male comedians portraying female characters. At least two decades before Flip Wilson invented Geraldine, comedians Milton Berle, Jonathan Winters, and others had dressed as female characters much to the delight of their 1950s and 1960s television audiences.

After the so-called "sexual revolution" of the 1960s, television audiences became even more accustomed to and more accepting of cross-dressing and transgendered television characters. In addition to the popular television shows that featured gay characters that we mentioned earlier in this chapter, the small screen became a venue for real-life openly gay characters as well as transvestites, transgendered, and transsexuals. Perhaps best known among these is self-proclaimed Drag Queen, actor, singer, and performer, RuPaul Andre Charles, best known simply as RuPaul. RuPaul hosted a show on VH1 and then created a long-running television series entitled *RuPaul's Drag Race*. One of the contestants on RuPaul's Drag Race was transgendered Carmen Carrera who went on to become a supermodel. Transgendered actor Laverne Cox starred in the popular series, *Orange is the New Black*, and numerous other real-life transgendered individuals garnered success in both television and motion picture roles. One of television's most popular programs, *Dancing with the Stars,* one season partnered with professional dancer, Lacey Schwimmer, male celebrity Chas Bono, who delighted audiences and surprised professional judges with his dancing ability. In 2013 and 2014, the testosterone-driven *FX* series, *Sons of Anarchy*, featured a cross-dressing character named *Venus* that infiltrated the macho world of outlaw motorcycle gangs and fell in love with one of the most violent gang members. This heretofore taboo relationship garnered acceptance, if not approval, by the rest of the motorcycle club.

Motion pictures also reflected more liberal sexual mores as feature-length films began to portray transgendered characters. After a few mostly unsuccessful motion pictures depicted transvestites and transgendered individuals, well-known sex goddess, Raquel Welch, portrayed a transgendered person in the 1970 movie *Myra Breckinridge*. A few years later, Al Pacino starred in the critically acclaimed, *Dog Day Afternoon* (1975), in which his character's lover was a pre-operative transsexual, the presumed motive for Pacino's character robbing a bank in order to pay for the sex change surgery. Another well-known movie, *Dressed to Kill* (1980) featured a transsexual murderer, and in the 1982 classic, *The World According to Garp*, John Lithgow was nominated for an academy award for his portrayal of a transsexual former football player who had become a woman. Actress Felicity Huffman was also nominated for an Oscar for the transsexual role she played in the 2005 movie *Transamerica*. Numerous other films, far too many to mention, featured various transvestite, transgendered, or transsexual characters.

Scholarly research on the impact of media on transgenderism and transsexualism is somewhat sparse, but one study showed that media facilitated transgender and transsexual individuals' identification processes, self-perceptions, and self-actualization (Ringo, 2002). As with most forms of human behavior, whether considered conforming or deviant, media help shape society's definitions of social reality and help determine what is socially acceptable.

Another area of sexual behavior with which the media have been fascinated is prostitution. From hit movies such as *Taxi Driver, Risky Business, Trading Places*, and *Pretty Woman*, to popular television programs including *Deadwood, Game of Thrones, Dollhouse*, and *Mad Men*, prostitution is no stranger to the media. Interestingly, with the exception of a host of documentaries on the subject, rarely is the harsh reality or brutality of the world of prostitution depicted. Further, with a few exceptions, prostitution in movies and on television is generally portrayed as being solely the domain of women, with few male prostitutes seen engaged in the activity. In most media portrayals of prostitutes, the women are extremely attractive, fairly well adjusted, and more often than not, depicted as being relatively satisfied, if not happy with their lives. As we described earlier in this chapter, scholarly research on prostitution reveals quite a different picture.

## Summary

We began this chapter by defining sex and gender and looking at the concept of human sexuality. Perhaps no activity or behavior is surrounded by more norms than human sexuality, and perhaps no area of human behavior is a better example of the social construction of deviance than sexual deviation. Folkways, mores, laws, and taboos tell us what is appropriate, inappropriate, moral, immoral, legal, illegal, and absolutely unthinkable in regard to sexual behavior, but not everybody agrees into which category or categories various forms of sexual activities fit. Pre-marital sex is considered by some to be a sin while being regarded by others as the norm. While some American politicians may be driven out of office in shame for adulterous affairs, others get re-elected, and many Europeans whose leaders openly have both spouses and lovers, wonder why American voters would even care.

Alternative lifestyles that feature either swinging/co-marital sex or public nudity (naturism/ nudism) have been around for quite some time, but are gaining acceptance and becoming more socially recognized in the United States and other countries. Public nudity is widely condemned by many while being viewed as a natural and wholesome lifestyle by others. Again, the media play a role as the limits toward nudity are constantly pushed, and Americans seem much less shocked about the glimpse of bare breasts, buttocks, or even genitalia. Nevertheless, the practice of going about everyday routine activities sans clothing is still considered to be deviant behavior and those people who engage in it are considered deviants by a large segment of the public. The media, especially network television which censors most explicit nudity, uses partial nudity and pixelated nudity to entice more viewers. One can only wonder if the widely popular television show *Dancing with the Stars* would garner nearly as many viewers if the male dancers kept their shirts on and the female dancers were attired in sweat suits.

Homosexuality has been both accepted and severely punished in the United States and around the world, and some people have developed homophobia, or an unnatural fear and hatred of homosexuals and homosexuality. In the United States, values and attitudes toward homosexuality and same-sex marriage have changed dramatically over the past few years and the media have embraced homosexuality and same-sex couples as simply being part of American life.

The media has always been fascinated with sex and with deviance, so it should be no surprise that they are fascinated with sexual deviance. Movies and television programs have focused on virtually every imaginable type of human sexual behavior, and as new media, especially social media and the Internet have developed, they have helped shape American attitudes toward human sexuality as well as transformed how it is carried out in everyday practice. Not too long ago, words like sexting, cybersex, virtual sex, and other types of sexual behaviors were unknown. Today, they are part of the American vocabulary.

As we close this chapter, ask yourself, do you view all of the various types of behaviors discussed in this chapter as being sexually deviant? If not, which ones would you leave out, if you were writing a chapter on the topic? Are there other forms of human sexual behavior that we did not cover in this chapter (or previous chapters) that you think should be included? If you answered no to the first question and/or yes to the third one, you have further confirmed how deviant behavior is socially constructed.

## Outcomes Assessment

1    Explain the differences between sex and gender.
2    Define sexual norms and sexual deviance.
3    Explain specific types of sexual behavior often considered to be deviant including adultery, nudism, transvestitism, transgenderism, and transsexuality.
4    Define homosexuality and homophobia and discuss how laws and attitudes toward homo-sexuality have changed over time.
5    Define prostitution and discuss specific types of prostitutes and prostitution.
6    Define and give specific examples of cybersex.
7    Discuss how the media portrays sexual deviance in the United States.

## Key Terms and Concepts

| | | |
|---|---|---|
| adultery | hate crimes | sex |
| bisexuality | heterosexuality | sexual norms |
| co-marital sex | homophobia | sodomy laws |
| come out | homosexuality | swinging |
| cross-dressing | homosocial environments | the lifestyle |
| cybersex | human sexuality | transgenderism |
| extramarital sex | human trafficking | transvestism |
| fetishism | mate swapping | turn out |
| gender | phone sex | |
| gender bending | premarital sex | |

# 7

# Alcoholism and Other Drug Abuse

**Student Learning Outcomes**

After reading this chapter students will be able to:

1  Define manifest and latent functions and describe the manifest and latent functions of United States legislation prohibiting alcohol and drugs.
2  Identify the differences among various social groups' consumption of alcohol and drugs.
3  Define the stages of alcoholism.
4  Explain how alcoholic can become a master status.
5  Describe the role of the media in promoting alcohol and drugs.
6  Identify the prevalence of substance use on campus.
7  Describe the process of becoming addicted to drugs.

*It started out innocently enough. Out with a group from church, friends pressured her into trying a cigarette. "What's the big deal about this?" she thought to herself. Milkshakes and a smoke became the Monday night routine after the youth group meetings. At a sleepover a few months later, Patty's friend grabbed a beer from her dad's stash and offered Patty one, too. "Why not?" Patty was surprised she enjoyed it – and how easy it was to get into nightclubs at only 17. After graduation, a group of friends was passing around weed. Cigarettes, beer, and liquor weren't as evil as the demons that her parents had warned her they would be, so what could be so bad about pot? She knew she wasn't hooked or anything, but when she started*

*Deviance & Deviants: A Sociological Approach*, First Edition. William E. Thompson and Jennifer C. Gibbs.
© 2017 John Wiley & Sons, Inc. Published 2017 by John Wiley & Sons, Inc.
Companion website: www.wiley.com/go/thompson

*dating Chris – who sold a little on the side – she experimented with everything he offered her. Soon, Patty had tried things she never thought she would, like LSD, just to get high. When Patty's grades slipped, she was placed on academic probation and almost lost the chance to finish college; at the same time, Chris was arrested (again) for DUI (driving under the influence), he lost his driver's license and his parents made him join the military. Patty was afraid her parents would find out what was really going on and, for the first time in a long time, she was worried about her future. At 19, she decided to stop drinking, smoking and doing drugs altogether and changed her circle of friends.*

Alcohol and drug use are accepted – and even expected – in many situations. A champagne toast at midnight on New Year's, drinking wine or smoking tobacco or cannabis during religious ceremonies, and smoking cigars following the birth of a baby are common rituals in American society. We even see the media promoting alcohol and drug use – think, for example, about commercials during sporting events, Jimmy Buffet's classic *Margaritaville* or Toby Keith's song, *Red Solo Cup*, many reality television shows, or the movies *Pineapple Express* (starring Seth Rogen and James Franco) and *Savages* (with Taylor Kitsch and Blake Lively). But, when does this use become "deviant"? In earlier chapters, we mentioned that what is considered deviant largely depends on time and place. Smoking pot alone on a Tuesday morning in a dorm room before class usually is frowned upon, but smoking pot because it was prescribed by a doctor after chemotherapy is considered acceptable by most people. If you see your professor at a local bar on Friday night having a beer, you might say hello and engage in a friendly conversation. On the other hand, if your professor walks into class drinking from a bottle of beer, you might be shocked and wonder how the university makes hiring decisions! On a larger scale like the United States, the social acceptance of drugs and alcohol has changed throughout time and, even today, depends on place and situation. Let's begin this chapter by reviewing when and where alcohol has been considered deviant in America.

## A Brief History of Alcohol in the United States

Alcohol use was popular among America's founders and, for the most part, was not considered deviant. Because water was considered unsafe to drink (and bottled water was not yet invented), alcohol was the preferred, safe and healthy alternative at the time. It helped Colonial Americans make it through the physically difficult work day and, similar to today, was something to enjoy. In fact, Benjamin Franklin said alcohol (particularly wine) was like a gift from a higher power: "Behold the rain which descends from heaven upon our vineyards, there it enters the roots of the vines, to be changed into wine, a constant proof that God loves us, and loves to see us happy" (Isaacson, 2003:374).

However, this was not always the case and not everyone agreed with Franklin. John Adams, another founding father, was concerned about people drinking too much – even though Adams himself drank alcohol. Some religious groups – like the Puritans and Quakers – also discouraged drunkenness, and many members of the early Temperance Movement were against drinking altogether. Local women's groups and other interest groups viewed the overuse of alcohol as a **social problem**, *an undesirable issue (like racism or violence) that has damaging effects on members of a community*. These groups believed drinking too much led to family disorder, domestic

Under what circumstances might alcohol and drug use be considered deviant? Normal? *Source*: © dbimages/Alamy

violence, other crime, poverty, and disease (Bernard, 1991). And, some social groups were thought to have a more difficult time handling their alcohol than others. In particular, Colonial Americans' acceptance of alcohol was divided along racial lines too. Because early Americans disapproved of Native Americans and Blacks drinking, serving anyone belonging to these groups was illegal and Whites could be fined for doing so (Bernard, 1991; Salinger, 2002).

Even in recent history, there has been much debate about alcohol use. Drunkenness was increasingly frowned upon and thought to be related to problems inside the home, and saloons, which allowed gambling and prostitution, added to the concerns surrounding drinking (Duis, 1999; Gunzerath, *et al.*, 2011; Stack, 2000). Interest groups were able to pass laws locally and at the state level to curb alcohol sale and consumption, and eventually the federal government amended the United States Constitution to make the production and sale of alcohol illegal (Hall, 2010). The 18th Amendment, which was ratified in 1919, and the Volstead Act, passed in 1920, began the period known as Prohibition. The publicly stated purpose or **manifest function** – *intended consequences* – behind Prohibition was to reduce the harm associated with drinking.

Prohibition, though, had some **latent functions** or *unintended consequences*. The latter part of Prohibition overlapped with the Great Depression, and many Americans still wanted alcohol; this combination created room for a black market where people could illegally sell alcohol for much more money than when it was legal to do so and the alcohol content was much higher in illegal alcohol, as the government no longer regulated it. Because people involved in the black market could not go to the criminal justice system to resolve disputes, violence was the main form of dispute resolution – and this led to the growth in Prohibition-era gangsters, like Al Capone, Lucky Luciano, and Vito Genovese. Once these organized crime groups had a foothold on illegal enterprises like gambling and prostitution, fighting them became very difficult – even after Prohibition ended.

Gangsters, like Al Capone, were one latent function of prohibition. What might be other latent functions of prohibition and other responses to behavior considered deviant? *Source*: ©INTERFOTO/Alamy

Prohibition ended with another amendment to the US Constitution. The 21st Amendment, passed in 1933, repealed the 18th Amendment and gave control of alcohol regulation back to the states. Even though the sale and consumption of alcohol is legal and regulated by the government, there are many **dry counties** – *those areas where the sale of alcohol is restricted* – in the United States today, and as we can see in Figure 7.1 the bulk of these counties are in the South. The purpose of these dry counties is to curb drinking and related social ills in the area (although people still can travel outside these counties to purchase alcohol and bring it back into the dry counties). But, dry counties have the same amount of driving while intoxicated rates as "wet" counties (Powers and Wilson, 2004; Scalen and Payne, 2011), which suggests that prohibiting alcohol sales does not limit excessive drinking.

## Alcohol Use among Social Groups in the United States

While alcohol use seems to be the same whether people live in wet or dry counties, and most adults – that is, those who are at least 18 years old – have tried alcohol at one point in their lives, drinking does vary by social group. For example, a higher percentage of men than women report trying alcohol (91.2% of men versus 83.7% of women), having alcohol in the past year (74.4% of men versus 66.4% of women) and drinking alcohol in the past month (61.7% of men compared with 50.5% of women; Substance Abuse and Mental Health Services Administration, 2012, Table 2.41B).

Drinking also varies by race and ethnicity – but the social groups who consume the most depends on what kind of alcohol use we are examining. Compared to other social groups, people who identify as non-Hispanic White and people who associate with two or more races have the highest percentage of people who have *tried* alcohol, while the social group with the smallest

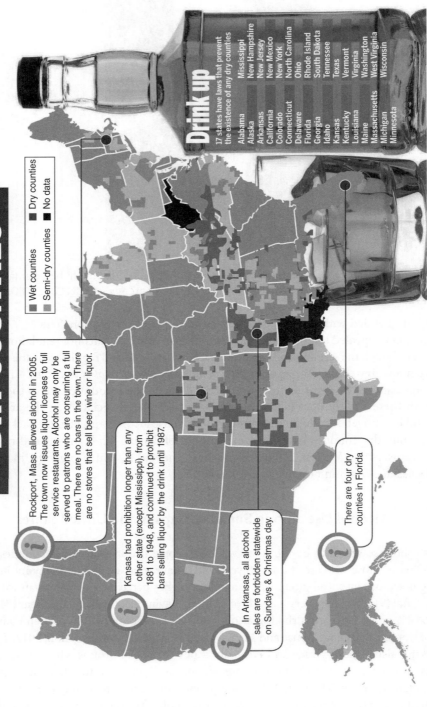

**DRY COUNTIES**

Wet counties
Semi-dry counties
Dry counties
No data

Rockport, Mass. allowed alcohol in 2005. The town now issues liquor licenses to full service restaurants. Alcohol may only be served to patrons who are consuming a full meal. There are no bars in the town. There are no stores that sell beer, wine or liquor.

Kansas had prohibition longer than any other state (except Mississippi), from 1881 to 1948, and continued to prohibit bars selling liquor by the drink until 1987.

In Arkansas, all alcohol sales are forbidden statewide on Sundays & Christmas day.

There are four dry counties in Florida

**Drink up**

17 states have laws that prevent the existence of any dry counties

| | |
|---|---|
| Alabama | Mississippi |
| Alaska | New Hampshire |
| Arkansas | New Jersey |
| California | New Mexico |
| Colorado | New York |
| Connecticut | North Carolina |
| Delaware | Ohio |
| Florida | Rhode Island |
| Georgia | South Dakota |
| Idaho | Tennessee |
| Kansas | Texas |
| Kentucky | Vermont |
| Louisiana | Virginia |
| Maine | Washington |
| Massachusetts | West Virginia |
| Michigan | Wisconsin |
| Minnesota | |

**Figure 7.1** Map of dry counties in the United States. *Source:* Sun Media (Toronto Sun)

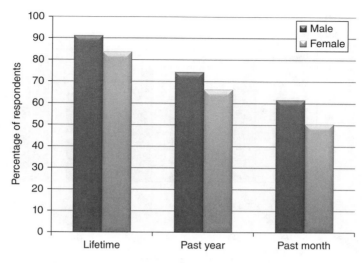

**Figure 7.2** Percentage of people who reported drinking in their lifetime, the past year, and the past month, by gender. *Source*: Adapted from Table 2.41B of the 2011 National Survey on Drug Use and Health (Substance Abuse and Mental Health Services Administration, 2012)

percentage of people who report alcohol use is Asians (Substance Abuse and Mental Health Services Administration, 2012, Table 2.41B). A higher percentage of American Indians or Alaska Natives (11.6%) report *heavy* use – having at least five drinks in a row for five consecutive days in the past month – than any other racial or ethnic group; non-Hispanic Whites (7.1%) were the second largest group and Asians (1.6%) report the smallest percentage of heavy drinkers (Substance Abuse and Mental Health Services Administration, 2012, Table 2.42B).

Another way to compare the drinking differences between groups is to look at **binge drinking** – *having at least five drinks in a row* (Substance Abuse and Mental Health Services Administration, 2012). Younger people – those in their late teens through their early 30s – have the highest amounts of binge drinking in the United States. Men binge drink almost twice as much as women, with 30% of men and 15.8% of women bingeing in the month before being surveyed (Substance Abuse and Mental Health Services Administration, 2012, Table 2.24B). One explanation for the sex differences in binge drinking is the risk of victimization – women are more likely than men to be targets of sexual aggression while drinking (Peralta, 2010). Women also are held to different standards than men. For example, college students reported that women who drink are unattractive and looked upon negatively (Peralta, 2007, 2010).

More Native Americans/Alaskan Natives, non-Hispanic Whites and Hispanics report higher rates of bingeing than non-Hispanic Blacks, African-Americans, or Asians (Substance Abuse and Mental Health Services Administration, 2012, Table 2.24B). Some argue that racism plays a role. One student described why African-American men drink less: "I think the police have something to do with it.... I think for their safety [African-American men] don't do that" (Peralta, 2010:401). Michael, a Black male student, worried about encouraging stereotypes: "I try not to be out there in public view where people can see us. All that does [is] create more stereotypes like, all Black people, all they do is drink and get drunk" (Peralta, 2010:403). Regardless of social group, for some people who suffer from alcoholism, though, heavy alcohol use is difficult to control.

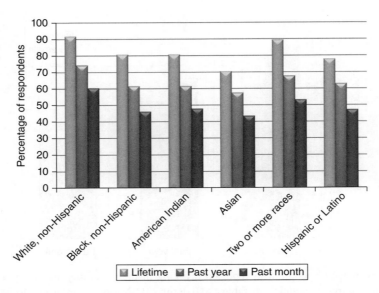

**Figure 7.3**  Percentage of people who reported drinking in their lifetime, the past year, and the past month, by race/ethnicity. *Source*: Adapted from Table 2.41B of the 2011 National Survey on Drug Use and Health (Substance Abuse and Mental Health Services Administration, 2012)

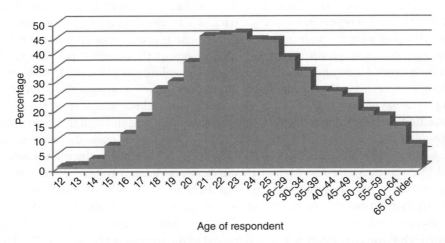

**Figure 7.4**  Percentage of people who reported binge drinking in the past month, by age. *Source*: Adapted from Table 2.16B of the 2011 National Survey on Drug Use and Health (Substance Abuse and Mental Health Services Administration, 2012)

## Becoming an Alcoholic

Because heavy alcohol use has traditionally been viewed as immoral, those who are unable to control their drinking have been stigmatized. **Alcoholism**, also called **alcohol dependence**, is considered *a medical condition involving a craving for alcohol, losing control of drinking, becoming physically dependent on alcohol and experiencing withdrawal symptoms, and increasing tolerance*

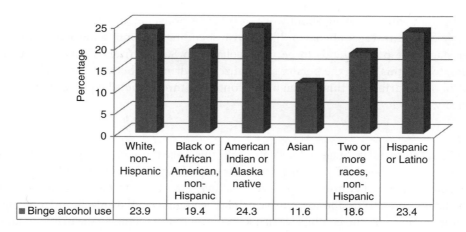

| | White, non-Hispanic | Black or African American, non-Hispanic | American Indian or Alaska native | Asian | Two or more races, non-Hispanic | Hispanic or Latino |
|---|---|---|---|---|---|---|
| ■ Binge alcohol use | 23.9 | 19.4 | 24.3 | 11.6 | 18.6 | 23.4 |

**Figure 7.5** Percentage of people who reported binge drinking in the past month, by race/ethnicity. *Source*: Adapted from Table 2.42B of the 2011 National Survey on Drug Use and Health (Substance Abuse and Mental Health Services Administration, 2012)

*for alcohol so that more and more alcohol is needed to feel the same way* (National Institute on Alcohol Abuse and Alcoholism, n.d.). While alcohol dependence was first considered an addiction or a disease by Dr. Benjamin Rush, a psychiatrist in the 1790s, and the term "alcoholism" was coined by Swedish physician Magnus Huss in 1849 (Gunzerath *et al.*, 2011), the medical model was not applied to heavy alcohol use until the 1950s. Viewing alcohol dependence through a medical lens makes it an illness that can be treated by medical professionals and removes the responsibility for drinking from the drinker (Room, 1983). In that way, the alcoholic is not immoral, but instead is someone with a disease. Following this medical model, becoming an "alcoholic" seems to develop in phases.

## Stages of alcoholism

Yale University professor E.M. Jellinek (1946) conducted one of the earlier studies identifying distinctive phases of alcoholism, which are still used today:

I   the Early or Basic Stage;
II   the Middle or First Intermediate Stage;
III   the Late or Second Intermediate Stage; and
IV   the Very Late/Terminal Stage.

Each phase is characterized by certain behaviors, but not every person who is an alcoholic necessarily experiences all of the behaviors at each stage.

*Stage I*
Early/Basic Stage. Before entering this stage or very early on in this process, the budding alcoholic begins to drink to the point of "blacking out" and sneaks drinks. Here, a compulsion is beginning and the person is losing control of his or her drinking, becoming drunk midweek or

during the day, without caring about work or other responsibilities. Changes in behavior are noticeable, with extravagant behavior like "lavish spending" becoming more common. While in later stages the person tends to become isolated, in Stage I friends may see extroverted behavior, too. In this stage, the person rationalizes the drinking behavior and believes s/he is in control of the drinking; this rationalizing continues throughout the process and increases in intensity.

### Stage II

Middle/First Intermediate Stage. Jellinek also calls this stage the acute compulsive phase. Here, the person goes on "benders" – staying drunk for several days in a row without thinking about his/her commitments. Because compulsive drinking often leads to behavior that is frowned upon by family and friends, the compulsive drinker feels guilty and drinks more to assuage that guilt. Despite this guilt, the compulsive drinker continues to rationalize the drinking and considers him/herself blameless for any misbehavior stemming from the drinking. That means others are to blame, and the compulsive drinker at this stage adopts unreasonable resentments – indicating a further loss of self-control. To regain control, the person tries to change patterns of behavior, like drinking only in particular places or at specific times or only drinking certain types of alcohol to regain control over drinking.

### Stage III

Late/Second Intermediate Stage. Jellinek also calls this the chronic compulsive stage. Friends and family may notice that the compulsive drinker has a hidden stash of alcohol to protect his/her supply. This phase also is marked by anxiety. Alcohol does not seem to give the same relief it did in the past, and compulsive drinkers become fearful or anxious about retribution for their behavior. This fearfulness may result in tremors, which also may be withdrawal symptoms if the compulsive drinker has not consumed alcohol recently. The physical manifestations of the alcohol use may help the drinker realize the rationalizations are not working.

### Stage IV

Very Late/Terminal Stage. At this final phase of the process, the drinker hits rock bottom or reaches his or her "lowest point." During this stage, the drinker is willing to admit to him/herself and perhaps others that drinking is out of control. Here, the person seeks outside help.

Anyone who watched the MTV reality show *Jersey Shore* could see Mike "The Situation" Sorrentino move through these four stages during the show's six seasons. Everyone at the shore house imbibed quite a bit during weekdays, and this drinking often interfered with work at the Shore Store. While we might consider the entire cast of the *Jersey Shore* as being in Stage I, "The Situation" progressed to the other stages, too. Everyone in the house pulled pranks on one another, but Mike seemed to take things too far. In the video confessionals, other housemates complained about Mike's bad behavior, and Nicole "Snooki" Polizzi ended her friendship with Mike after he tried to ruin her relationship with her now-husband, Jionni. Mike consistently shifted the blame away from himself, consistent with Stage II behavior. In later episodes, we see Mike experiencing quite a lot of anxiety, characteristic of Stage III. In the final season of the show, we learn that Mike has stopped drinking altogether, admitting he had a problem with drinking alcohol – Stage IV. While alcohol was not the only substance "The Situation" struggled with, drinking – at least through the camera's eye – seemed to be a recurring theme and perhaps became a master status.

## Alcoholic as a master status

In Chapter 2, we defined master status as *one status that overpowers or supersedes other statuses in a person's status set*. From a sociological perspective, "a person is an 'alcoholic' (or similar label) who is expected to do something about his drinking, whenever the label is attached to him and made to stick" (Mulford, 1977:564). In Box 7.1, "alcoholic" became the master status of the woman convicted of DUI. From her story, we see that she holds several statuses: daughter, friend, student, employee, and more. After her arrest, she reports that her reputation was damaged and even her "closest friends began to judge" her. They no longer saw her primarily as a friend, student, or employee – instead, she became someone who has a problem drinking. Employers, too, view her primarily as an alcoholic, as she is having trouble finding a job.

---

**Box 7.1**   In their own words

### Driving under the influence*

Why did I drive drunk? I was very stressed out. My family was going through a rough period, with my parents getting a divorce, and I had trouble juggling school and work all at the same time. I used alcohol as an outlet to help me to forget my problems instead of dealing with them. That night, I was very intoxicated. I was not thinking clearly. As a result, I was arrested, had to spend a few days in jail, got my license taken away, and forever damaged my reputation. My parents lost faith in me and my closet friends began to judge me. It was the worst decision I have ever made.

After I was arrested, I was ashamed and very mad at myself. I embarrassed myself and my family. I was warned my whole life about the dangers of driving under the influence and I never thought I would do something like this. If I could do it over again, I would not have gotten behind the wheel after drinking. I would have called a friend or my parents to pick me up. What I did was not only legally wrong, but it is against the accepted norms of society. Driving under the influence is scary. It has taken a number of innocent lives and many families have been affected or know someone affected by a drunk driver.

Being arrested for DUI (driving under the influence) really impacted my life. My family and friends were very upset with me and my decisions. I am currently having difficulty finding a job in which I can fully support myself. Lastly, my life has been impacted because not a day goes by that I do not wish that I had handled things differently. I often wonder what could have happened. If I would have injured or even worse, killed someone, I would not have been able to live with myself. I have really been shaken by this and I believe I have changed. I never again want to put myself or others in that situation.

Now I tell people that one should always make sure they have a way of getting home, whether it is through a designated driver or having a friend or family member take you home. Always have a plan and a person you can trust to be there for you because you never know what is going to happen.

After all of this, I learned that drinking is not the solution. Drinking does not reduce stress. It is just a temporary fix. Moreover, drinking it is highly dangerous and even more so when driving is involved. It was not worth it at all. I could have seriously hurt myself or others and I wish I could go back and do it all differently.

---

*Nicole Calhoun conducted this interview.

Before the drinking and driving movement beginning in the 1980s, when police caught people drinking and driving they would follow them home or they would make them leave their car and drive them home. Today, driving under the influence results in an arrest, loss of the driver's license and more. Do you think driving while intoxicated is a social problem?

## Alcohol and the media

You likely have a Facebook or Instagram account, and you probably notice many people posting photos with alcohol – maybe even while they are driving. Though driving while intoxicated is not a good idea, alcohol and social media certainly don't mix! An Oregon teenager was arrested after his Facebook friends notified the police about his updated status on January 1, 2013:

> Drivin drunk … classsic ;) but to whoever's vehicle i hit i am sorry. :P

Jacob Cox-Brown was charged with driving-related misdemeanors (Lopez, 2013).

Alcohol is promoted not only in social media, but other forms of media, too. James Bond fans know that his signature drink is a Vodka Martini, "shaken, not stirred," and the fictional J.R. Ewing popularized "bourbon and branch" to the point that people all around the world were using that phrase to order a shot of bourbon diluted with water. Popular movies almost always have at least one scene in a bar or where one character is drinking alcohol, although alcohol is more prominent in some movies (like *The Hangover* movies or the classic *National Lampoon's Animal House*) than others. In fact, can you think of a movie where all characters avoid drinking alcohol? Even in movies where characters may not be seen consuming alcohol, brand name beer or wine bottles may be seen in the background in what advertisers call strategic "product placement," for which they pay movie producers and directors handsome sums of money. Other forms of media are more subtle when encouraging alcohol use. The next time you watch a sporting event, look at the advertisements. You will notice ads for beer and liquor posted around stadiums, ballparks, and arenas. Some of your friends may tell you that they watch the Superbowl for the commercials – because the beer ads are the most entertaining.

Alcohol is not the only substance featured in the media. A number of other drugs, too, have been prominent in American society throughout its history.

## A Brief History of Drugs in the United States

Similar to alcohol, there was little legislation regulating drugs in Colonial America. In fact, plantation owners grew hemp and tobacco both for their fiber and for their medicinal (and recreational) use. Even legendary war hero and first president, George Washington, grew hemp at Mount Vernon! Opium was a popular medicine recommended by doctors and morphine – made from opium – was used extensively during the Civil War era (Musto, 1999). Hundreds, if not thousands, of wounded Civil War soldiers were sent home with a small leather kit bag containing a needle, syringe, and a few months' supply of morphine sulfate to treat what was called "soldiers' disease" – a combination of chronic pain and opium addiction (Courtright, 2001). Cocaine was used as a treatment for hay fever, considered a cure for opium and alcohol addiction, used by employers to stimulate workers to work longer hours with little food, and was an ingredient in Coca-Cola until 1903 (Musto, 1999). Drug use was prevalent in the early United States and there always were critics, but drug regulation started picking up steam around 1900.

In particular, people were noticing that drugs – especially morphine and opium – could be addictive (White, 1997), and public attitude shifted. In the 1890s, states began passing laws to regulate opiates and other drugs (Musto, 1999; White, 1997). But, these laws varied from state to state, and users could easily cross state lines to purchase drugs where they were legal and bring them back to a state where they were illegal. This led to the passage of the *Harrison Act* of 1914, which was federal legislation requiring a prescription to purchase some narcotics, like cocaine and opiates, and taxing these drugs (MacCoun and Reuter, 2001). Other drugs still could be purchased without a prescription from a drug store – what we would consider "over the counter" medication today (Musto, 1999). While the Harrison Act, or the publicity surrounding it, decreased some drug use (MacCoun and Reuter, 2001), it had some unintended effects. One latent function of the Harrison Act was that it created a black market, which increased the cost of these drugs. For example, before the Harrison Act, addicts could purchase opiates for about three cents a day, while shortly after passage that cost skyrocketed to about $30 a day (White, 1997). Another latent function was the interpretation of the legislation. Supreme Court rulings and law enforcement interpretations of the Act converted the original intent of the law from regulation to *criminalization*. In fact, the Harrison Act set the stage for the creation of the Drug Enforcement Administration (DEA) today. To enforce the taxation part of the law, the Department of Treasury created a Narcotics Division within the Internal Revenue Service (IRS – back then it was called the Bureau of Internal Revenue), which was merged with other agencies in 1930 to form the Bureau of Narcotics and transferred to the authority of the Department of Justice (National Archives, n.d.). The DEA became an official federal agency in 1973 under President Richard Nixon.

In the last 50 years, people have renewed their attention to drugs. The Hippie Movement, in particular, encouraged the recreational use of drugs. (If you are not familiar with the Hippie Movement or hippies, think about Paul Rudd's character in the movie *Our Idiot Brother*.) With the Civil Rights Movement, the Vietnam War, the Women's Movement, and rising crime rates, there was much social unrest in the 1960s, which paved the way for a hippie counterculture to emerge. Hippies promoted an alternative to society, generally encouraging peace and freedom (like "free love" – sex with multiple partners outside the confines of marriage – and freedom from the corruption of government) and criticizing middle-class values. A common element of the hippie scene was drugs – mainly marijuana and LSD. These drugs were thought to connect users with other living things and to bring the mind to another plane; hippies also favored LSD because of the studies conducted by Harvard University psychologist Timothy Leary suggesting psychedelic drugs (which were legal at the time) were the solution to many social problems (Howard, 1969).

Perhaps in response, politicians – including presidents and presidential candidates – weighed in on drug use. President Johnson's Commission on Law Enforcement and Administration of Justice (1967) established the connection between drugs and crime. Shortly afterward, the federal government focused its attention on drugs: President Nixon declared a "war on drugs" – the longest war in American history, as it continues to this day. The DEA and the National Institute on Drug Abuse (NIDA) also were created during the Nixon administration, and government funding was dedicated to drug treatment and law enforcement (White and Gorman, 2000). In the 1980s, First Lady Nancy Reagan launched the familiar "Just Say No" campaign, using the media to encourage everyone to "say no" to drugs. Education programs were introduced into schools – perhaps you took DARE or a similar program when you were in school. The Drug Abuse Resistance Education (DARE) Program was designed to have a police officer come into schools to teach students about illegal drugs and their effects, but these programs had limited effects and some DARE programs actually contributed to increased drug use among DARE participants! Between 1980 and 1989, drug arrests quadrupled and sentencing for drug offenses became tougher; this led to prison overcrowding in the 1990s (White and Gorman, 2000).

Drugs seem to be such a social problem that the government spends quite a lot of money fighting it. The federal government allocates approximately $18 billion every year to drug control and this dollar amount almost doubles when state government spending is included (MacCoun and Reuter, 2001). But, most of the federal budget goes to criminal justice and only about a quarter of the funding focuses on treatment and prevention. Some argue that this may be because drug legislation is aimed at controlling certain ethnic and racial groups.

## Race/ethnicity and drug legislation

As various social groups immigrated to the United States, the drugs they used reached the radar of American citizens – especially when people feared those groups. When drug laws were passed, many were targeted toward minority groups. Of course, no racial or ethnic group is specifically named in any legislation on drugs, but these laws intentionally make recreational pastimes of certain groups illegal (Chin, 2002). For example, people supported making opium illegal because people believed it made the Chinese – whose drug of choice was opium – more likely to have sexual contact with Whites (Chin, 2002; Musto, 1999). Cocaine was outlawed because people believed African-Americans who used cocaine became sexually violent (Chin, 2002; Musto, 1999). And, marijuana – the preferred drug of Chicanos in the Southwest – was thought to lead to violence (Chin, 2002). In fact, marijuana or "reefer" smoking was the theme of the 1936 propaganda movie *Reefer Madness*, a story about high school kids who got high on marijuana at a dealer's apartment; they were instantly hooked and committed several crimes, including an attempted sexual assault, an accidental shooting, and a hit-and-run car accident – all because marijuana drove them "insane."

By passing drug laws, the groups who tend to use that particular drug are more likely to be arrested. With arrest and prosecution comes prison time – but the penalty does not stop there. After prison, the user becomes **disenfranchised**. Specifically, *once someone is convicted of a felony – which many drug crimes are – that person is no longer legally eligible to vote or to receive certain benefits from the government, like student loans* (Chin, 2002). People convicted of felonies who are not U.S. citizens can be deported, and a prior felony can increase the sentence severity of a later felony conviction (Chin, 2002).

The *War on Drugs*, especially, has not affected all drug users equally. African Americans, in particular, are incarcerated more often than other groups. African-Americans account for about 13% of the US population, but this racial group makes up almost 38% of the 2011 prison population (Carson and Sabol, 2012, Appendix Table 6). This may be in part because of drug legislation targeting minority groups. For example, crack cocaine (the rock form of cocaine) is used and distributed more by African Americans, while powder cocaine is used mostly by Whites (Tonry, 1995). However, according to the 1986 *Anti-Drug Abuse Act*, those with 5 g of crack cocaine receive the same mandatory minimum prison sentence, five years, as those with 500 g of powder cocaine. In other words, there is a sentencing ratio of 100:1! This finally changed with the *Fair Sentencing Act* 2010, which reduced the sentencing ratio to 18:1 with the mandatory minimum sentence of five years in prison for those with 28 g of crack cocaine.

What's interesting is that about the same percentage of Whites and Blacks use drugs. Looking at Figure 7.6, we see that about 9% of non-Hispanic Whites have used drugs in the past month and 15% have used illicit drugs in the past year, while 10% of non-Hispanic Blacks have used drugs in the past month and 16% have used in the past year. More Whites (51.1%) have tried illicit drugs at some point in life, while 45.4% of non-Hispanic Blacks have tried illicit drugs. But, a higher percentage of Native Americans report using drugs recently and trying them sometime in their lifetime than either non-Hispanic Whites or Blacks.

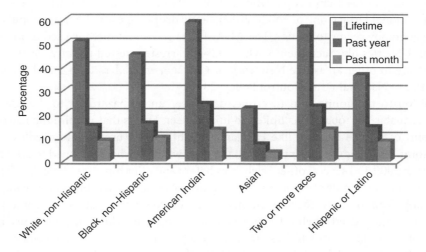

**Figure 7.6**  Percentage of people age 12 and older who reported using illicit drugs, by race/ethnicity. *Source*: Adapted from Table 1.19B of the 2011 National Survey on Drug Use and Health (Substance Abuse and Mental Health Services Administration, 2012)

## Drug-crime connection

Much of the fear driving drug laws is the public perception that there is a connection between drugs and crime. Of course, making drugs illegal generally means that selling or possessing drugs is a crime. But drugs can be related to crime – particularly violent crime – in three ways:

1  The drug might have pharmacological effects, meaning the drug itself may change the user's behavior.
2  Users may commit crimes to pay for drugs.
3  Because drugs are illegal, the criminal justice system cannot be used to resolve disputes so violence is used instead (Goldstein, 1985; Johnson *et al.*, 2000; White and Gorman, 2000).

Some scholars argue that violent crime has gone down in recent years because the drug market has stabilized since the peak of the crack-cocaine epidemic in the 1980s. In other words, drug dealers have established their territories, the demand for crack has declined (and crack users and sellers are the ones most involved in violence) because the younger generation of drug users is afraid of the destruction crack brings and the old generation of crack users is aging (Blumstein and Wallman, 2006, Epilogue). So, there is less violence needed.

Despite this, drugs seem to play a role in many crimes. The Arrestee Drug Abuse Monitoring Program (ADAM), collected through the Office of National Drug Control Policy (ONDCP, 2012), houses information on drug use among men arrested for a crime; about 16–29% of the arrestees were charged with committing a violent crime. ADAM shows that more than 60% of male arrestees tested positive for some drug, most commonly marijuana followed by cocaine; between 13% and 38% tested positive for more than one type of drug at the time of arrest (Office of National Drug Control Policy, 2012). This is known as **polydrug use** – *using more than one drug in a short period of time* (see Altman *et al.*, 1996).

Arrestees who were homeless or unemployed were more likely to have used drugs during the commission of a crime than people who were not homeless and people who were employed (Office of National Drug Control Policy, 2012). Some drugs appear to be more popular in some areas, so geography seems to matter. The ADAM data show that meth is used more frequently in Western US cities like Sacramento, where 43% of arrestees tested positive for the drug, and less frequently in other areas like New York or Chicago, where less than 1% of arrestees used meth (Office of National Drug Control Policy, 2012).

In addition to the connection to crime, drug use can be hazardous to the user's health. Smoking cannabis (or tobacco) is linked to lung cancer. Drugs that require the use of needles (like heroin) can cause diseases like HIV and hepatitis when users share needles. Using too much of some drugs, or overdosing, can kill the user, which is what happened to DJ AM (Adam Goldstein) in 2009 and several other celebrities before and after him (see Table 7.1). The Center for Disease Control and Prevention reports that drug overdosing has been increasing since the 1970s, mainly from opioids, cocaine and heroin, and recently was the second leading cause of unintentional injury death (behind motor vehicle crashes). In addition, drug abuse or misuse accounts for 2.1 million visits to hospital emergency rooms every year (Substance Abuse and Mental Health Services Administration, 2011). So, there is merit to the argument that drug use can be harmful.

**Table 7.1**  Examples of celebrity deaths caused by drugs.

| Celebrity | Date of death | Age | Drug(s) contributing to death |
|---|---|---|---|
| Whitney Houston (singer) | February 11, 2012 | 48 | Cocaine and prescription drugs |
| Amy Winehouse (singer) | July 23, 2011 | 27 | Alcohol |
| Brittany Murphy (actress) | December 20, 2009 | 32 | Multiple drugs |
| Michael Jackson ("King of Pop") | June 25, 2009 | 50 | Propofol (anesthetic) |
| Heath Ledger (actor) | January 28, 2008 | 28 | Prescription painkillers, anti-anxiety drugs and sleeping pills |
| Anna Nicole Smith (Playboy model) | February 8, 2007 | 39 | Chloral hydrate and various benzodiazepines |
| John Belushi (comedian and actor) | March 5, 1982 | 33 | Cocaine and heroin |
| Elvis Presley | August 16, 1977 | 42 | Heart attack from painkillers, tranquilizers and opiates |
| Jimi Hendrix | September 18, 1970 | 27 | Alcohol, barbiturates |
| Judy Garland (Dorothy from the Wizard of Oz) | June 22,1969 | 47 | Barbiturates (sleeping pills) |
| Marilyn Monroe | August 5, 1962 | 36 | Barbiturates |
| Jim Morrison of the Doors (musician) | July 3, 1971 | 27 | Heart attack from heroin overdose |

*Source*: Huffington Post (http://www.huffingtonpost.com/2012/08/26/celebrity-overdoses-deaths-prescription-drugs_n_1831731.html#slide=1439005) and other Internet sources.

## Moral panics and moral entrepreneurs

Another reason for drug legislation is because some interest groups believe that drugs are morally wrong and drug laws were the result of a moral crusade. Remember we talked about moral entrepreneurs and moral crusades in Chapter 1; a moral entrepreneur is a social reformer who is not satisfied with existing rules because s/he believes that some type of behavior – like drug use – is taking place that should be controlled or eliminated. Some people are offended by others' drug use because they think drug use is inherently wrong. In their effort to rid the country of this "evil", these moral entrepreneurs embark on a moral crusade, an effort to identify wrongdoing, inform others of its existence and potentially dire consequences, and establish rules or laws to eliminate the behavior and punish the wrongdoer.

In this moral crusade, moral entrepreneurs often create a moral panic in society – other people become afraid of the drug or drugs being targeted by the moral entrepreneurs. This fear can be created by stereotyping drug use, exaggerating its effects and distorting the facts to fit the arguments of the moral entrepreneurs. The stories are so outrageous that people actually believe them. (This is why your professors talk about critical thinking so much.) Think back to

What motivations might the media have to pass along sensational stories that may not be true?

the propaganda movie, *Reefer Madness*, described earlier in this chapter. As a depressant, would marijuana *really* lead someone to go insane and become violent? LSD use in the 1960s, too, was the focus of a moral panic, likely because LSD and the Hippie Movement challenged middle-class work ethics and morality (Goode, 2008). Perhaps because of this, the public was receptive to unbelievable stories of LSD, like the drug does damage to chromosomes (Goode, 2008).

In the war on drugs, moral entrepreneurs and politicians made many claims about the dangers of drugs that were not based on evidence (Hawdon, 2001). The media, too, play a crucial role in moral crusades, spreading stories the public finds most fascinating – regardless of whether these stories are true (Goode, 2008). Remember the common phrase, "If it bleeds, it leads," that we noted in Chapter 1, referring to the media reporting the most sensational stories. Television, radio, and print media can be very influential in shaping people's opinions – if they weren't, then companies would not spend so much money on advertising. In fact, research has shown that the more television people watch, the more they support spending more money on fighting drugs (Nielsen and Bonn, 2008). The media role in moral crusades has grown in recent years with easier ways to connect person to person. Have you noticed anything on Facebook or YouTube that might constitute a moral crusade?

## Women, drugs, and moral panics

One moral crusade in particular involves women and drug use. In the contemporary war on drugs, pregnant women who used drugs began to be viewed as deviant. Interestingly, in the early 1900s, many white women stayed home with opiates while their husbands went to saloons to drink alcohol – so women were more likely to be addicted to drugs during that time. Before people understood the risks to the fetus, women often drank and smoked tobacco (and used other drugs) during pregnancy – this certainly was not deviant behavior at that time. You may have noticed this portrayed in the television series *Mad Men*, which is set in the 1960s. The attitude toward this behavior changed with the war on drugs.

Fetal Alcohol Syndrome, which leads to low birth weight and other health issues in infants, was not introduced until the 1970s and did not become a widespread concern until over a decade later. In the 1980s and 1990s, women who used illicit drugs, especially, were demonized. Society became concerned with "crack babies" – infants born with the drug in their bodies because the mothers used during pregnancy – and crack babies were seen as a social problem, as people assumed these crack babies would grow up to be criminals. For example, one Georgia newspaper, the Atlanta Journal-Constitution, featured women and crack as a social problem in their week-long series called "Growing Up with Crack" in the fall of 1998. The first story featured a 16-year-old girl called "S", a middle-school dropout (Meyers, 2004). S's mother is addicted to crack and often used drugs in front of S. When S was younger, her mother sold her to a drug dealer for sex. S reported that she "wanted a baby so she could give it the love she never had" (Meyers, 2004:204); S's son is now five months old. Stories like these fueled the fire for a moral panic.

What made this a moral panic was that there was a rush to judgment without solid empirical studies about the long-term effects. Earlier, we established that crack cocaine is associated with inner-city minority groups, while powder cocaine is used primarily by middle to upper class whites. Drug use during pregnancy was criminalized, and women could be charged with child abuse or neglect, have their parental rights revoked, or even imprisoned – and the punitive approach to mothers of crack babies seemed to disproportionately affect women of minority groups.

Remember when we mentioned the latent racism in many of the current drug laws, even though no race was named? Today, there is specific legislation "getting tough" on pregnant women who drink and use drugs. While the law appears to be race-neutral, legislators do not seem to have the same hesitation focusing laws against women.

## Legal and illegal drugs

Despite these drug laws and moral panics, many drugs remain legal – and some illicit drugs are becoming legal. Coffee and energy drinks (like Rockstar, Red Bull, Monster, and AMP) contain caffeine, a legal drug. Tobacco still is legal, although it is very heavily taxed today. Alcohol also is legal – but heavily regulated. These are examples of legal drugs that we may not even consider to be "drugs". Another growing trend is using prescription drugs for non-medical purposes, which now is more common than using illicit drugs – with the exception of marijuana. Marijuana is an interesting drug, as it sits on the fence between legal and illicit. Twenty-four states and Washington, DC have legalized the use of marijuana for medical purposes (like pain management), but the federal government has not. So, the DEA can arrest people for possessing or selling marijuana even for medical purposes – even if it is legal according to state law. Why might the federal government still consider marijuana use deviant? How might state cultures vary in their views on whether marijuana use is deviant?

Today, some states have legalized recreational use of marijuana, too. This creates an issue for some people trying to navigate whether this newly legal behavior is deviant – and where, when, and with whom smoking weed may be considered deviant. Even though marijuana is now legal in some areas and more people consider its use socially acceptable behavior, many people – especially those with security clearances – are uncomfortable being around it (Spencer, 2013). How social etiquette develops in the coming years will be interesting to observe!

## Substance use on campus

Social etiquette surrounding drug use on college campuses is unique. As a college student, you probably know someone who smokes weed or uses prescription drugs to get high, calm down, help focus, lose weight, or for some other reason. Even over-the-counter drugs can be used for a high. In fact, when one of the authors was in college, a nursing student who lived down the hall would "do Tussin" – that is, she would drink an entire bottle of Robitussin to get high. Using "street" drugs, "homework" drugs, and other substances is common on college campuses. In other words, drug use is not limited to shady urban areas. In fact, about 36% of college students have tried at least one illicit drug in the past year; when we exclude marijuana, about 17% of college students have used an illicit drug in the past year (Johnston et al., 2012a).

Illicit drug use among college students peaked in 2001 and has been declining since; however, some drug use has increased while using other drugs has declined in recent years (Johnston et al., 2012a). Smoking tobacco, for example, among college students has decreased from a high of 31% in 1999 to 15% in 2011 (Johnston et al., 2012a). Crack cocaine use decreased since 2007 and crystal meth ("ice") also has declined since 2005 – less than 1% use crack cocaine and only about 0.1% of college students report using crystal meth (Johnston et al., 2012a). On the other hand, non-prescription amphetamine use among college students has increased since 2008, although non-medical use of Ritalin (2.3% of college students use Ritalin) and Adderall (9.8% of college students use Adderall) leveled off in 2009 without any significant change in the past few years (Johnston et al., 2012a). Marijuana use among college students has remained about the same – about one-third of college students smoke marijuana; meth (0.2% of college students use meth) also has remained the same (Johnston et al., 2012a).

Drug selling, too, can be found on college campuses – drug dealers on campus can come from privileged, upper- or middle-class backgrounds. While the media often portray drug sellers as those living in low-income housing and a drug sale as a quick, secretive business exchange, that is not always the case. One college dealer described the buy as much more casual:

You go over their house and you pick up a sack [of marijuana] from them and you feel like, "Oh, I should hang out with them," almost like you had to do them a favor in addition to paying them. There's the unspoken rule that you have to share your first bowl with whoever you are buying it from … It was always like, they ask you a couple of questions about how everything was going … It was almost like they wanted it to be a more personal relationship as opposed to more formal (Mohamed and Fritsvold, 2006:112).

---

### Box 7.2    In their own words

#### Underage drinking*

Like any 20-year-old excited about turning 21, I let my eagerness get the best of me. On July 4th, 2002, just four months before turning 21, I attempted to use a fake ID to get into a bar in Sea Isle City, New Jersey. My friends, all over 21 years of age, were able to go in but I was stopped at the door and quizzed on the details of the ID I gave the bouncer. When I was unable to correctly remember the 'zip code' on the ID, I was turned away. Before I knew it, I was being approached by a police officer and placed in handcuffs. I should also mention that my family and friends were already inside by the time this happened, and they were not aware that I couldn't get in.

The reward for participating was entry to a bar, where my friends and family were hanging out to celebrate the 4th of July weekend. There was obviously alcohol and live music inside to enjoy, as well as socializing. My intention was not to go in there and get drunk, though I understand from the circumstances why someone would perceive that as being the case.

The risk that I would get in trouble with the law for using a fake ID and also for consuming alcohol was something I honestly, at the time, didn't give much thought to. With that obviously comes financial as well as judicial risk, which I guess I accepted by simply ignoring those risks. I think I ignored the risks because I knew that my intentions weren't all that bad, and I thought that laws were in place to punish bad people who do bad things. I learned that some laws are in place to punish good people who make poor decisions.

This was an absolute case of peer pressure. I would not have participated had I not felt a need to get in that bar, at that time, with my friends and family. I would not have randomly attempted to use a fake ID to enter the bar had I not known anyone there. In fact, I had never before possessed or used a fake ID.

I am not a really big drinker. At the time, I was in college and consumed alcohol on a more regular, though not problematic, basis. It was social drinking. My run-in with law enforcement did little, honestly, to alter my drinking habits during that time. It did, however, cure me of ever attempting to use a fake ID again. And truthfully, the entire event was very out-of-character for me, so it was a blessing in disguise that it happened, though it did not seem so at the time.

Obviously after all this happened, I realized the reward was not worth the risk. I should have respected and accepted the fact that I was simply not old enough at the time to join my friends and family in that bar. I had other options, one of which was to meet up with them after. I could have easily killed time doing many other things. It also taught me that you cannot live by the notion that because you're a good person, that it is okay for you to do things that, though minor, are still against the law. Sure, in the long run, it's not a big deal that I tried to use a fake ID, but it's still in defiance of the law.

My family and friends were very understanding of my run-in with the law. I was not judged or criticized. So my dealings with the court were more difficult. I was treated, when I appeared in court several months later, like a common criminal by the judge. I was fined $1,000 and spent $1,500 on a lawyer only to be told I should be ashamed of my actions. Meanwhile, other lawbreakers around me in the courtroom that day had drug and violence-related charges, and were largely given a slap on the wrist. It was a very confusing experience, but a useful lesson for me at the time. Also, on the actual night of the crime, I found the law enforcement officials to be overly aggressive with me despite the fact that I in no way resisted arrest. I was taken away in handcuffs from an area where my family thought I was – and in fact, an extreme panic occurred when I disappeared. I asked the officers to allow me to call my family and friends to let them know I had been arrested, but I was denied that and handcuffed to a bench in the police station.

*Holly Shuter conducted this interview of Scott.
Is binge drinking at college a stage of alcoholism? When might alcohol use become a master status?

## Recreational Drug Use

While college students may use some drugs for specific purposes like improving grades, many drugs are used by people on and off campus for recreational use. Ranking in popularity behind tobacco and alcohol, marijuana is a popular drug among high school students. When asked whether they used marijuana in the past year, slightly more than one-third (36%) of high school seniors reported they had (Johnston *et al.*, 2012b). Even daily marijuana use is relatively rare. Monitoring the Future data, which come from a national survey of students in grades 8, 10, and 12, show that only about 6.5% of high school seniors smoke marijuana daily or almost daily (Johnston *et al.*, 2012b).

About half (49%) of the nation's high school seniors have tried at least one illicit drug in their lifetime, with 40% experimenting with illicit drugs within the past year. This figure, though, includes marijuana – a more commonly used drug. Aside from marijuana, Monitoring the Future data show that 17% of high school seniors have tried illicit drugs such as crack, heroin, cocaine, and narcotics (Johnston *et al.*, 2012b). While most "traditional" drug use among high school students has been decreasing in recent years, some drug use has remained stable (like prescription drugs used without a prescription) or increased (like non-prescription use of Adderall, an amphetamine typically used to treat Attention Deficit Hyperactivity Disorder (ADHD), powder cocaine, crack, meth, and steroids) and new drugs (like synthetic marijuana, created by spraying synthetically-made cannabinoid chemicals on plants, and "bath salts", which contain synthetic cathinones that act like amphetamines) are being introduced (Johnston *et al.*, 2012b). Synthetic marijuana, for example, is a newer drug that is the fourth most popularly used drug among high school students, coming in behind tobacco, alcohol, and marijuana (Johnston *et al.*, 2012b).

Sociologists argue that drug use is not simply taking a drug. How does one know whether to smoke, snort, inject, or eat the drug? There is a process to understanding how to use drugs. Howard Becker (1953) interviewed 50 marijuana users and concluded that people must learn how to properly smoke marijuana in order to achieve a high. One user explained, "Take in a lot of air, you know, and … I don't know how to describe it, you don't smoke it like a cigarette, you draw in a lot of air and get it deep down in your system and then keep it there. Keep it there as long as you can" (Becker, 1953:237). Once marijuana is smoked properly, Becker suggests that people also need to learn to associate the high with the drug; in other words, people must recognize the high. When asked "Did you get high the first time…?", one user responded:

> Yeah, sure. Although, come to think of it, I guess I really didn't. I mean, like that first time it was more or less of a mild drunk. I was happy, I guess, you know what I mean. But I didn't really know I was high, you know what I mean. It was only after the second time I got high that I realized I was high the first time. Then I knew that something different was happening … How did I know? … [T]hey explained to me that that's what it did to you, you had a different sense of time and everything. So I realized that that's what it was. I knew then. Like the first time, I probably felt that way, you know, but I didn't know what's happening (Becker, 1953:238–239).

Finally, users must learn that the high is enjoyable before being able to use marijuana for pleasure. Some people do not like getting high: "… I never did enjoy it at all. I mean it was just nothing that I could enjoy…. I mean I got plenty of reactions, but they were mostly reactions of fear…. I couldn't seem to relax with it, you know. If you can't relax with a thing, you can't enjoy it, I don't think" (Becker, 1953:240). Becker (1953) concludes that people must enjoy the high to continue using marijuana.

Most people stop using drugs recreationally within five years without any intervention or coercion. However, some adults continue using illicit drugs, which can be risky. Not all drugs can be used as purely recreational with the users stopping at any time. Some drugs can be addicting.

## Becoming an Addict

Earlier in this chapter, we defined alcohol dependence as losing control of drinking and we mentioned it is considered a medical condition. The same is true of drug addiction. We often hear drug addiction discussed from the medical perspective, considering drug addiction a

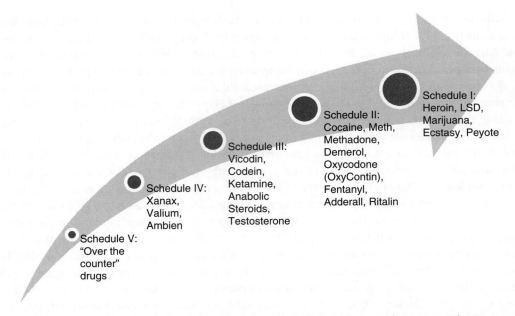

**Figure 7.7**   Types of legal and illegal drugs. *Source*: Adapted from Drug Enforcement Administration (DEA) Drug Schedules, http://www.justice.gov/dea/druginfo/ds.shtml

disease with a biological basis. From this point of view, addiction is something that occurs in the brain. (Some types of drugs have higher potential for addiction, as shown in Figure 7.7.) Psychologists also weigh in on drug addiction. According to the DSM-IV, psychologists consider drug addiction a disorder of compulsive drug-seeking behavior that the user cannot control; in other words, they define addiction as meeting at least three of the following criteria within a 12-month period (American Psychiatric Association, 1994:181–183):

- Tolerance, which means needing more of the substance for a "high" or the same amount of the substance produces much less of the high.
- Withdrawal symptoms when the substance wears off or the substance is taken to avoid withdrawal symptoms.
- More of the substance is used or the substance is used more often than the user initially planned.
- The user is unable to reduce or control his or her use.
- The user invests a lot of time to acquire, use, or recover from the substance.
- Substance use interferes with work or social activities.
- The user continues using the drug even though s/he knows the substance is causing or exacerbating a health issue.

Sociologists look at drug dependence differently. Sociologists might define drug dependence in terms of its social consequences, like neglecting children because a parent is using drugs or spending money for food or rent on drugs instead. Sociologists also look at society's reactions

## Box 7.3 In their own words

### Marijuana User*

My childhood was pretty normal. My parents never fought or anything like that. I was raised Catholic, up until 18 when I didn't have to go to church anymore. My siblings and I had just normal rivalry – just teasing and picking on each other, but we still got along pretty well. Um, we did a lot of volunteer work through the church, mostly because of my Dad. He was big on that sort of thing. I went to prep school after Catholic school so I still had that influence up until I switched to a public high school. I didn't have a "large" group of friends so to speak. Just a small one made of close friends. It's still that way today, I'd say.

How did I start using? Um, boredom mostly. Plus, I pretty much saw everyone doing it up at school. But it started over at Chuck's house. It wasn't the greatest environment, if you know what I mean. Rough home life and all that. I remember it was right after my 18th birthday cause all my friends always made jokes about how I had missed 4/20, which is a pretty big day in the smoking world (laughs).

I used to smoke every single day. I think it was just cause everyone I hung out with at the time did it too, so they were always smoking. But I never had any problem going without it. It's just really weird being in a group when everyone is smoking but you, you know? 'Cause it's like you become some sort of outcast or outsider or something. It's just easier to partake.

Do I prefer smoking in groups or alone? Hmmm, both I guess. I prefer to smoke with friends actually. When I smoke alone I get really paranoid and I start over-thinking things and overanalyzing things. It freaks me out. But if I'm with other people I'm more relaxed cause you can sit and talk to each other and everything. Takes my focus elsewhere.

When I do smoke it's more of a sorta reward for myself, you know? Like if I work hard that day then I allow myself to unwind. But I'm trying to find a better job right now. Like, a good paying one. And I can't get a decent job if I'm always smoking all the time.

I haven't smoked recently. Not at the moment, no. I haven't really decided yet whether I'm gonna continue or not. For one thing, it's really expensive. And I never get anything done when I smoke and I'm trying to go back to school. Not to the same school though. I'm just gonna stay local this time.

When I'm at home I don't really ever smoke just 'cause my parents don't want me to. I have three younger sisters so I have to set some kind of model I suppose, even though they all know I do it. But it's mostly just with friends. The weird thing is I have to smoke in a place that's really clean. 'Cause when I'm high I'll just sit there and think about the dirt and germs and it freaks me out.

Fortunately, I've been lucky enough to not be caught (knocks on wood and laughs). Although there was this one time a security guard at a concert caught us but we didn't get in trouble really, just had to put it out. So I don't think that really counts. And, I don't think I've lost any friends. I mean, not all my friends smoke and not all of them agree but they know that's just who I am. It has affected my family though. It's weird, kinda, cause my one sister Erica and I have bonded over it. It kinda just came out that she smokes too so now we do it together sometimes. And then my sister Maggie really doesn't care, she's indifferent I guess. But my youngest sister, Lucy doesn't trust me at all. She definitely dislikes me because of it. And my mom doesn't approve at all either. My dad doesn't really care though cause he smoked a lot at my age too, so as long as I'm not upsetting my sisters or mom he's cool with it. I guess it's kinda like a "what they can't see can't hurt them" kinda thing or whatever.

---

*Courtney Beyer conducted this interview of Wayne.

Do you consider Wayne's smoking deviant behavior? Is his smoking deviant at some times with some people, but not others? How so?

to people who use drugs frequently. While they acknowledge that some chemicals taken over a long period of time will produce physical withdrawal symptoms when they are removed, sociologists point out that not all drugs are addicting (see, e.g., Becker, 1953).

Despite these differing perspectives, most fields agree that addiction typically occurs in stages (as illustrated in Figure 7.8).

1   First, there is some kind of initiation to the drug (Altman *et al.*, 1996), where the user experiments with drug use. This could occur in a social context, using drugs casually with friends. Drug use with friends reinforces the drug-using behavior.
2   Second, there is an escalation of drug use into heavy, habitual, compulsive use (Altman *et al.*, 1996; Koob and Le Moal, 2005). Heredity, environment, and stress can affect the risk that someone will escalate drug use (Koob and Le Moal, 2005).
3   The third stage is dependence (Altman *et al.*, 1996; Koob and Le Moal, 2005). The user needs the drug to function without withdrawal symptoms.
4   Next, there is a loss of control over drug use (Altman *et al.*, 1996). In particular, stopping use will cause withdrawal symptoms (Koob and Le Moal, 2005). People in this stage are likely to relapse to combat the withdrawal symptoms.
5   The fifth stage is protracted withdrawal (Koob and Le Moal, 2005). Staying away from the drug for a long period of time can make withdrawal symptoms last longer for addicts. Some of these symptoms may include anxiety or depression, difficulty sleeping, and problems focusing. In this stage, relapse also is possible.
6   The last stage is possible recovery (Koob and Le Moal, 2005). Here, the user becomes an ex-addict.

According to the Substance Abuse and Mental Health Services Administration (2012:Table 5.1B), 1.8% of people older than 12 meet the DSM-IV criteria for substance dependence. This may seem like a small amount, but there are about 311 million people in the United States! Indeed, we may initially think this estimate is small because we see drug use and addiction so often portrayed in the media.

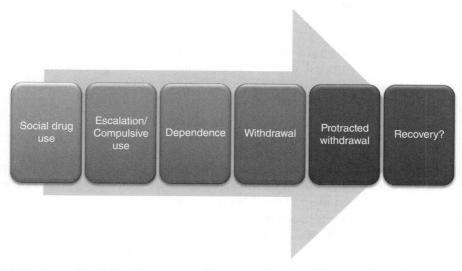

**Figure 7.8**   Stages of drug addiction. *Source*: Adapted from Koob and Le Moal (2005:3)

## Drugs and the Media

Several media examples related to drugs were mentioned throughout this chapter. *The Wire* is one television series, in particular, that shows illicit drugs from several different perspectives, like the dealers, the users, and law enforcement – especially during the first season. While *The Wire* is a fictional story, it is based on observations of the drug–crime connection in Baltimore, Maryland made by former Baltimore Sun newspaper crime reporter David Simon.

The first season focuses on a special unit of police officers trying to collect evidence through a wire tap (hence the title of the show) to take down a drug ring run by Avon Barksdale. The highly organized Barksdale gang is responsible for a large portion of the city's drug trade and frequently uses violence to resolve disputes. In addition to the violence, the drug trade has other casualties like the harm done to drug addicts, like Bubbles (who also informs to the police).

The Barksdale gang and the police are followed throughout the series. In the third season, one story line shows a police major essentially legalizing drugs in one area of the city; Major Howard "Bunny" Colvin instructs his officers to ignore drug law violations in that area, but crack down on any violence there and intensely enforce drug laws in the rest of the district. Drug users flock to this area known as "Hamsterdam", and drug use is seen as safer because health and social service agencies are providing free treatment and free needles, reducing the risk of disease transmission through shared needles. This experiment did not last long, as police supervisors shut it down after learning about it and the major was forced to retire at a lower rank.

*The Wire* offers an interesting look at the dynamics between various actors in the war on drugs. How might the concepts presented in this chapter relate to *The Wire*?

# Summary

Alcohol and drugs always have had a central theme in American society. Over time, as American culture changed, attitudes toward alcohol and drugs began to change. Moral entrepreneurs framed alcohol and drug use as a social problem, but legislation like Prohibition and the war on drugs had many unintended consequences – namely, laws created black markets for prohibited substances and disproportionately affected minority groups. While alcohol and drug use varies by social group, anyone can be at risk for dependence on these substances. Substance dependence typically occurs in stages and can become an individual's master status.

Alcohol and drug use can be harmful, especially considering the relationship between these substances and crime. However, many harmful substances are legal and some substances that are not very harmful remain illegal. One thing is certain – the line between legal and illegal substances is blurring, especially considering the legalization of marijuana in many parts of the country and the abuse of legally prescribed drugs.

The media play a role in how alcohol, drugs, and substance users are viewed. Drug use in particular is considered a problem only in certain areas, yet we found that drug use and selling is prevalent on college campuses and in high schools. Whether alcohol and drugs are considered deviant depends on time and place – and on media representations of these substances.

## Outcomes Assessment

1   Define manifest and latent functions and describe the manifest and latent functions of United States legislation prohibiting alcohol and drugs.
2   Identify the differences among various social groups' consumption of alcohol and drugs.
3   Define the stages of alcoholism.
4   Explain how alcohol can become a master status.
5   Describe the role of the media in promoting alcohol and drugs.
6   Identify the prevalence of substance use on campus.
7   Describe the process of becoming addicted to drugs.

## Key Terms and Concepts

| | | |
|---|---|---|
| alcohol dependence | disenfranchised | manifest function |
| alcoholism | dry counties | polydrug use |
| binge drinking | latent function | social problem |

# 8

# Physical and Mental Deviance

> **Student Learning Outcomes**
>
> After reading this chapter students will be able to:
>
> 1 Describe the role of the media in setting societal norms for the "ideal" body type and the effects this has on physical and mental health.
> 2 Explain why physical disabilities may be defined as deviant.
> 3 Explain the relationship between physical and mental deviance and stigma.
> 4 Identify the various manifestations of physical and mental deviance.
> 5 Compare the sociological view of mental disorders with the medical model.

*Every week after the slaughter, his father – who was a farmer and butcher – would drink a shot of fresh animal blood. He forced Vlad to drink a shot of blood, too, and eat a piece of raw liver because he said Vlad was anemic. As a kid, Vlad did not like it at all! After his first schizophrenic break at the age of 21, while he was in a mental health setting Vlad became exposed to a group of men who claimed to be vampires. Vlad and the other vampires would draw their own blood and drink it, gradually beginning to drink one another's blood. Vlad found it exciting and became sexually aroused every time he drank blood. After a while, Vlad became addicted to it. He started wearing all black, carrying his blood-letting paraphernalia in a black fanny pack and introducing himself as a vampire. And, while he says he never*

*Deviance & Deviants: A Sociological Approach*, First Edition. William E. Thompson and Jennifer C. Gibbs.
© 2017 John Wiley & Sons, Inc. Published 2017 by John Wiley & Sons, Inc.
Companion website: www.wiley.com/go/thompson

*committed a crime, Vlad became fascinated with vampire movies and books – especially those
with cannibalism, cruelty, and criminal themes (Oppawasky, 2010).*

In the opening scenario, Vlad was diagnosed with Renfield's Syndrome – otherwise known as
vampirism. The US media capitalizes on society's fascination with vampires. Before he was
Special Agent Seeley Booth on the television show *Bones*, David Boreanaz played the title
character, a vampire, in the TV show *Angel*, a spinoff of the show *Buffy the Vampire Slayer*.
These earlier shows set the stage for more recent television series like *The Vampire Diaries* and
*True Blood*. Vampires are popular subjects of movies, like the *Twilight* movies, *Bram Stoker's
Dracula*, *Interview with a Vampire* (starring Brad Pitt and Tom Cruise), *Abraham Lincoln:
Vampire Hunter* and *Dark Shadows*. Given the amount of money these movies brought to the
box office, people certainly are fascinated by vampires. However, claiming to be a vampire in
real life may seem weird – or deviant. But in some subcultures in the United States and in other
countries around the world, vampires are not only believed to be real, they are considered
*normal*. In this chapter, we review the sociology of mental deviance. First, we discuss the
sociology of physical deviance and the role of the media.

## Media and the "Ideal" Body

In Chapter 3, we discussed body types (ectomorphs, endomorphs, and mesomorphs) which
were thought to be related to behavior, including deviant behavior. Through commercials, magazines, television shows, advertisements and billboards, movies, and more, the media promote
certain body types for men and especially women – beginning with children. Children's movies
and books tend to encourage thinness by associating this body type with positive attributes and
obesity with negative traits (Herbozo *et al.*, 2004). Movies like *Cinderella*, the *Little Mermaid*,
*Beauty and the Beast*, and *Peter Pan* send such messages about body image (Herbozo *et al.*,
2004). Take Barbie dolls, too. Barbie dolls, originally designed as a marketing tool to sell clothing,
have been a staple of girls' toys for over 50 years – but Barbie's proportions (large bust, thin
waist, long legs, etc.) are extremely rare, as fewer than 1 in 100,000 women are likely to have
Barbie's body shape (Norton *et al.*, 1996). In other words, most girls will *not* grow up to look like
Barbie. Some may interpret Barbie and her media conglomerate (like her magazines, movies,
video games) as sending a message about the "ideal" body type for women – especially considering that her boyfriend, Ken, has body measurements similar to real life men: 1 in 50 men likely
have Ken's body shape (Norton *et al.*, 1996). And this message is received – studies show that
young girls who play with Barbies are more likely to have lower opinions about their bodies and
a desire to be thin like Barbie than young girls who play with other dolls (Dittmar *et al.*, 2006).
These messages about society's standards for beauty continue into adulthood.

Like Barbie dolls encouraging unrealistic body standards for young girls, the media do the
same for adult women. Media body images often are edited. Known as digital retouching, photos
of models or celebrities that are less than perfect, according to the media's standards, are altered.
Jennifer Lawrence, the star of the *Hunger Games* movies who won an Academy Award for best
actress for her role in *Silver Linings Playbook*, reported her surprise about the digital retouching
of her photos for the Dior handbag ad campaign: "That doesn't look like me at all. I love
Photoshop more than anything in the world.... Of course it's Photoshopped.... People don't

look like that" (Stump, 2013). Just as the media affects beliefs of young girls, they have a similar effect on women. When women receive these media images of thinness and attractiveness associated with success, they do the same – often at the expense of their self-worth (Evans, 2003). That is, when women compare themselves to the unrealistic, edited images of "beauty" in the media and the successful stereotypes portrayed by these images, women think less of themselves (Evans, 2003; Groesz *et al.*, 2002).

These media images affect men too. Men are exposed to these media representations of the "ideal" female body type and may have unrealistic expectations about women – especially given the plethora of available images on the Internet. In addition to setting standards for female attractiveness and body type, the media even convey norms for female genitalia. The pubic region of centerfolds in Playboy magazine, for example, became more visible between 1953 and 2007 and promoted hairlessness (e.g., shaved, waxed) over time (Schick *et al.*, 2011). Centerfold models – like models in non-pornographic media – increasingly became thinner and bustier since 1953, too (Schick *et al.*, 2011) – promoting a norm that women need to be unnatural to be sexually attractive.

Not only may men have certain beliefs about what women should look like, but they also may hold themselves to sometimes impractical physical standards. In fact, images of women as sex objects, which sometimes include muscular men, in advertisements affect men's body image and self-esteem (Lavine *et al.*, 1999). Specifically, when men see ads with sexualized portrayals of women and unrealistic images of other men, men become more dissatisfied with their own bodies, believing they are too thin or small and wanting to be larger and more muscular (Lavine *et al.*, 1999). Indeed, the media tell men that they need to be muscular and young-looking to be sexually attractive to women. Think about how many commercials for hair loss you have seen on television!

The media help set norms for society, and sending a message that thinness and attractiveness in women are linked to success and other positive attributes implies something about the opposite – namely, that largeness is deviant among women. You may recall the 2013 controversy about Oscar-nominated television and movie actress Melissa McCarthy, whose weight was tied to a criticism of her performance by movie commentator Rex Reed after the release of her comedy, *Identity Thief*. While there are some notable exceptions to these media messages, like Dove's Campaign for Real Beauty, the media do seem to have an influence on cultural standards for the body and the mind – and media have been linked to both physical and mental health issues (e.g., depression, eating disorders, and steroid use among boys and men).

## Abominations of the Body

The media may have an influence on some physical issues, like body shaping, but not all physical differences can be attributed to the media. While physical disabilities are not influenced by the media, perceptions of people associated with such physical "deviance" can be. In 1963, sociologist Erving Goffman wrote about the perceived stigma associated with abominations of the body, like physical deformities. In Chapter 2, we defined stigma as any attribute that discredits an individual from full social acceptance and a social identity as the way people are perceived by others. Goffman suggested that stigma can spoil a person's social identity. That is, others, who Goffman refers to as "normals," view the stigmatized individual as inferior and treat that person as different. In this section, we first discuss the stigma associated with physical disabilities and then move to something Goffman left out of his early work: obesity and eating disorders.

Do you ever compare yourself to models in advertisements, in magazines, on television and in the movies? Do you think these images are natural or have they been digitally altered? What does this tell us about the "ideal" body type – and do you think this norm is realistic? How do these images make you think about your body, your attractiveness and your success? *Source*: ©ProStockStudio/Shutterstock

## Physical disabilities

Physical disabilities like blindness, deafness, and amputations are accepted in mainstream society more so today than they have been in the past – perhaps because society recognizes that many physical disabilities are beyond a person's control and people are not responsible for them (compared to, say, personal hygiene). The popularity of paralyzed physicist Stephen Hawking (who has his own television show, *Brave New World*, on the Science channel and has made guest appearances on the *Big Bang Theory*), Olympic runner Oscar Pistorius (known as "Blade Runner" because his legs were amputated, and now widely considered deviant because he has been charged with murdering his girlfriend), singers Ray Charles and Stevie Wonder (who are blind), Oscar-winning actress Marlee Matlin (who is deaf), and other celebrities in the media have helped sensitize people to those with physical disabilities. Legislation like the *Americans with Disabilities Act of 1990,* which prevents discrimination against people with physical or mental disabilities, also has reduced inequity against those with physical disabilities. So, why include physical disabilities in a textbook about deviance? We mention them for a few reasons. First, physical disabilities are rare – most people in the general population do not experience them. In other words, the "norm" is the absence of physical disabilities. While this may sound like we are using the statistical definition of deviance here, our second point is that even though society is more and more accepting of them, physical disabilities can carry a stigma – emphasizing the sociological definition of deviance we have been using throughout the text. We already mentioned Erving Goffman's work on the stigma associated with physical disabilities. Third, people who have physical disabilities can group together to form a subculture with unique characteristics. For these reasons, we find it important and interesting to explore these topics.

*Vision and hearing impairment*

As we age, many of us begin having difficulty with our vision and hearing. In fact, some estimates suggest that 14 million Americans age 12 or older have some kind of vision impairment of 20/50 or worse (Vitale *et al.*, 2006), but most nearsightedness or farsightedness can be corrected with glasses, contacts, or laser eye surgery. And, close to one-third of people between the ages of 65 and 74 and almost one-half of those age 75 or older have a hearing loss (National Institute on Deafness and Other Communication Disorders, 2010). Taking advantage of these statistics, shopowners in England played a high-pitched tone (called "the Mosquito") to keep teenage hooligans away from their stores so the older customers could shop – the older patrons could not hear the tone and, consequently, were not bothered by it (Noguchi and Hart, 2006). On the other hand, high school students who are prohibited from using cell phones during classtime use the technology in the form of high-pitched ring tones so they can hear their phones but their older teachers cannot – something we do not recommend in your college courses (Noguchi and Hart, 2006)!

Because diminishing vision and hearing seem to commonly occur with age, you may be wondering why we are discussing these topics in a deviance textbook, asking yourself, isn't this *normal*? Again, we are not implying abnormality, but focus on how people with these disabilities are viewed and treated by others. Some people, though, experience *severe* vision and hearing impairment earlier in life – even from birth. According to the latest data from the National Institute of Health's National Eye Institute, there are over one million cases of blindness in the United States among people age 40 or older. Figure 8.1 breaks down this statistic by age, race, and gender. Notice that the number of cases of blindness increases with age (with the exceptions of younger White males and females). When we take into consideration the cases of blindness among people age 80 and older, the lines on the graph skyrocket: there were 867,000 cases among Whites, 50,000 among Blacks, and 14,000 among Hispanics. Also notice that there are more cases of blindness involving women than men and blindness is more common among Whites than Blacks or Hispanics. However, when we take into account the number of people who identify with a racial group, we see that proportions of blindness are closer among each racial group. That is, about 1% of Whites over

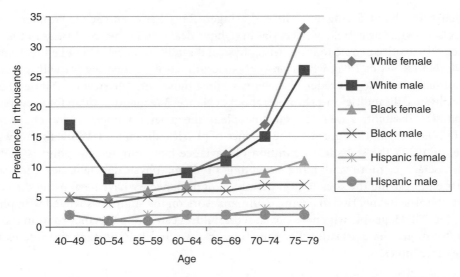

**Figure 8.1** Cases of blindness in the US by age, gender and race/ethnicity, 2010. *Source*: Adapted from the National Institutes of Health, National Eye Institute (http://www.nei.nih.gov/eyedata/blind.asp#3b)

40-years-old and slightly less than 1% of Blacks in the same age group experience blindness, compared with 0.26% of Hispanics over 40 (National Eye Institute, n.d.).

Statistics on hearing loss, though, are less common than on blindness, but of those available, we see that severe hearing loss follows somewhat similar trends. According to the National Institute on Deafness and Other Communication Disorders (2010), about 2 or 3 in 1,000 US children are born deaf or with a hearing loss. Unlike blindness, men are more likely than women to experience hearing loss (National Institute on Deafness and Other Communication Disorders, 2010), and Black Americans are less likely than Whites to lose their hearing as they age (Helzner *et al.*, 2005).

Important to most people with visual or auditory impairments – just like those without such impairments – is that they look and are treated the same as everyone else. Sam, Claudia, and Sue – students who are blind – elaborate:

> SAM:  You just want to look like everybody else, because – let's face it – we ARE just like everybody else, but we can't see.
>
> CLAUDIA:  There's nothing wrong with people knowing you're blind. It's just that, if you behave in a very different way …
>
> SUE:  It's not socially acceptable.

(Kaplan-Myrth, 2000:287)

From their stories, we see that – at least among this group of students – they want to conform to behavioral norms and fit in. However, society may not reciprocate and people may treat those who are blind or deaf differently. For example, those with visual or hearing impairments may have more difficulty being hired than people who do not have these impairments. Employment discrimination is illegal, but people with physical disabilities often have additional hurdles when interviewing for jobs. One visually impaired person described an interview experience: "Many employers are not informed of visual impairment. Employers seem interested [and] then ask, 'How could you or how would you [do the job]?' ... They want to be sure of qualifications – not only of myself, but of all visually impaired persons. They doubt we can do the job. It's an uphill battle" (Leonard, 2002:639).

Some communities of people with physical disabilities form a counterculture, rejecting the "rejectors". These communities view their group as different, but not disabled. For example, Gallaudet University, a private university in Washington, DC for deaf and hearing-impaired students, made headlines in 1988 when students protested against the hiring of another university president who could hear (http://www.gallaudet.edu/x42164.xml). Students insisted that the president of Gallaudet should be deaf, and their movement, known as "Deaf President Now", forced the new president to resign after one week, replaced by the university's first deaf president Dr. I. King Jordan. Almost two decades later, protests resumed in 2006 when Dr. Jordan's successor was, according to many students and faculty, "not deaf enough" to be president because she spoke English, read lips, and learned American Sign Language in her 20s (Majors, 2006). These protests also were successful, leading to the replacement of the president. This symbolized an important shift in the deaf culture: a subculture rejected the notion that they had to change to fit into society, believing that they are not disabled but simply another subculture in America and society should be accepting of them the way they are (Majors, 2006).

## *Amputations*

With media attention to troop withdrawal in Afghanistan and conflicts around the globe, Americans are increasingly exposed to physical injuries like amputations. While we may hear quite a bit about amputations in the news and other media today, this procedure is nothing new. In fact, Hippocrates wrote about the procedure, pointing out that patients would recover from the removal of body parts (Kirkup, 2007:55). Additionally, amputation practices vary across places, cultures, and time. For example, in Muslim cultures, the amputated limb is preserved until the amputee's death so that the amputee can be sent to paradise "whole" (Kirkup, 2007:104).

Although amputation has been practiced for centuries, amputees were not always accepted by society. Early nomadic tribes, for example, may have left behind (or worse, killed!) members who could no longer contribute (Kirkup, 2007). Even today amputation is – and amputees are – frowned upon in some cultures. As recently as 2005, a Pakistani husband refused to allow his wife to have a medically necessary amputation after she was injured in an earthquake, saying he would rather her die than live as an amputee: "I will not permit this. I will let her die than allow cutting her arm. She would not be able to work anyway" (Kirkup, 2007: 97).

Despite some of these examples, acceptance may be tied to the type of amputation experienced. Societies may have been more accepting of accidental amputation that was beyond a person's control or of deliberate amputation because the person overcame a life-threatening experience (Kirkup, 2007). The most stigma seems to be attached to elective amputation, as this type is a person's choice to remove a limb. (We discuss this type in more detail with body modification and scarification in Chapter 10.)

The stigma associated with any type of amputation in American society, however, is eroding. This may be due to the large number of military veterans returning to the US missing limbs. According to the Congressional Research Service, by the end of 2012, more than 1,700 military members survived amputations in Iraq and Afghanistan alone (Fischer, 2013). Resources like the Wounded Warrior Project sponsor events for amputees to help reintegrate them into society and demonstrate that they are just as able – if not more so – than they were before the limb loss. Civilians, too, who have survived limb loss are experiencing greater acceptance. You may recall the viral YouTube video of the woman who built a prosthetic leg using legos.

While acceptance of amputees may be becoming more common, challenges remain for some groups. Of the 1,700 military amputees mentioned in the previous paragraph, about 24 were women (Cater, 2012). At the outset of this chapter, we discussed body image; amputation has a significant effect on how people – especially women – view their bodies. Women who lost limbs during their military service varied in their descriptions of their new body image, ranging from pride to have lost a limb for her country to feelings of being incomplete: "For a while, I was scared to go out in public at all because I was afraid the public would see me as a freak…. It's a struggle. For women, more than men, looking in the mirror and realizing you don't have a limb" (Cater, 2012:1447). Like other forms of physical deviance, how one views body image depends on how she or he copes with limb loss.

**Table 8.1**   Some types of amputations.

| | |
|---|---|
| Accidental | Limb blown off in an explosion or severed during an accident |
| Deliberate | Limb removed to save a person's life because of damage caused by an accident |
| Elective | Voluntary and non-medically necessary |
| Punitive | Limb removal as punishment for some misdeed |
| Ritual | Limb removal according to custom or tribal "magic" |

*Source*: Kirkup (2007)

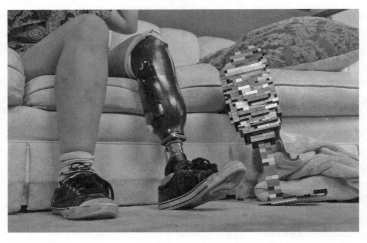

How is this woman managing stigma associated with amputations? What positive role might her viral YouTube video play? *Source*: © Jeff Robertson/Associated Press

## Obesity and eating disorders

Another form of physical deviance that affects body image is obesity. Both in the media through television shows like the *Biggest Loser* and in reality, American society has been sending the message that obesity is a social problem today – so much so that the government has become involved in regulating what people can eat and drink to promote healthier lifestyles. In the fall of 2012, New York City passed legislation prohibiting the sale of super-sized sodas – those larger than 16 ounces. Baltimore imposed a tax on sugary beverages in 2010, and nearby Howard County, Maryland banned their sale altogether on county property. At the federal level, First Lady Michelle Obama has made healthy eating one of her top issues, drawing national media attention when she planted a vegetable garden at the White House. In fact, combating obesity has become such an intense issue that Beyoncé was almost excluded from singing the national anthem at President Obama's second inauguration because she is the spokesperson for Pepsi, which is counter to the First Lady's healthy eating agenda.

Legislators argue that obesity is a public health issue, as obesity can lead to diseases like diabetes, heart disease, and high cholesterol (Mayo Clinic, 2012) – which can cause premature death. In this view, the medical model understands extreme obesity as a physical issue that may be beyond a person's control. On the other hand, many Americans view obesity as a form of deviance because, according to Peralta (2003) it "is looked upon with antipathy because most Americans consider it unsightly and unaesthetic. Obesity is also considered a manifestation of a weak, self-indulgent, or lazy individual" (p. 10). Thus, it is stigmatized. (Interestingly, Goffman (1963) never directly identified obesity as a stigma.) When obesity is stigmatized, it is "a label attached to a person by others" instead of some personal attribute (Cahnman, 1968:293). With stigma comes "the rejection and disgrace that are connected with what is viewed as physical deformity and behavioral aberration" (Cahnman, 1968:293). Accordingly, some members of American society impose sanctions like ridicule to counter this form of deviance. For example, an athlete named Cameron who constantly manages his weight views obesity as laziness:

> The basic equation doesn't change for most people unless you have an illness, right. It's calories in and calories out. If you can't control that simple equation, you deserve to be made fun of. There is so much social support and knowledge now about obesity, that unless a person's genes are screwed up and can't help it, I just think it's fucking laziness. To me, a fat person doesn't care about themselves or what others think of them. And, it [an obese body] says that I don't care about anything in life, because I won't even take the time to control what I eat. How can people respect that and feel sorry for someone who won't work to save their own lives? (Atkinson, 2011:243)

This ridicule is known as **fat shaming**, which is *making a person who is obese feel inadequate*. The view that obesity is a matter of personal responsibility overlooks important sociological factors driving weight gain. Advances in technology have decreased the amount of physical exertion needed for work (Puhl and Heuer, 2010). At the same time, unhealthy high calorie foods have become much less expensive and more easily accessible than healthy, fresh fruits, vegetables and other foods and portion sizes have increased (Peralta, 2003; Puhl and Heuer, 2010).

Some of the stigma associated with larger weight can be divided along cultural lines. Some racial groups have different views on the ideal body type, leading to less ridicule among members of that group. African-American women, for example, often are complimented by their African-American partners for having a larger body size (Beauboeuf-Lafontant, 2003). However, this does not mean that African-American women are immune to other messages about body type or that they avoid measures to control their weight. In other areas of the world, especially where poverty and starvation are prevalent, larger weight is a sign of wealth and status.

On the other extreme, American society also tells people that skinny is beautiful. Earlier in this chapter, we discussed how even young children are exposed to this message about the ideal body type. These perceptions of the ideal body even extend to those who cannot see. Interviews with people who are blind indicate an appearance-based definition of beauty. Kay, for example, reported that women should have, "This super-model 'no fat at all' look – totally skinny" and the ideal body type for men is "Big muscles on show …" (Kaplan-Myrth, 2000:283). When asked how she compared to the ideal body type, Kay responded, "Well, obviously I'd get rid of a lot of the cellulite which I don't particularly want" (Kaplan-Myrth, 2000:283). How does she know she has cellulite? "Well, I just think I do. Because obviously I can't compare myself to anyone else, so I don't know …" (Kaplan-Myrth, 2000:283). Sue explained how people who have visual impairments learn about body type ideals: "You listen to the radio" (Kaplan-Myrth, 2000:283). Perhaps the reach of the media extends further than we may realize!

These pervasive messages about the ideal body type can encourage eating disorders, like anorexia and bulimia. **Anorexia nervosa** is *intentional, purposeful starvation*, and **bulimia** is a *cycle of binge-eating followed by purging through vomiting and or using laxatives* (McLorg and Taub, 1987:177). These eating disorders can become more serious than they sound, leading to death from starvation or suicide. According to the National Institute of Mental Health (n.d.), a little more than one-half of 1% of the US population suffers from anorexia or bulimia, with more women having an eating disorder than men. Eating disorders tend to affect women and men differently. Women tend to starve themselves thin to achieve the feminine ideal, and males count calories to bulk up, exercise, and use drugs in an attempt to achieve a masculine ideal (Atkinson, 2011).

That said, while those who have anorexia or bulimia are overwhelmingly female, obsession with thinness is not limited to women. Men, too, can succumb to eating disorders. **Emaciation** – or *self-starvation leading to an extremely thin and boney body* – among male athletes is more common than one might expect (Atkinson, 2011). Maintaining a certain weight can be learned from coaches or teammates in an effort to do better in the sport. For example, 26-year-old William reports that:

> I had my own ideas about eating, and what worked for me, but I guess you probably should follow the lead of the guys with the most experience with winning. I was shocked at first with how little they ate, but then after some getting used to it, I accepted it. The information about eating for sport I read in books is one thing, but I'd rather place my trust in ground experience … I think it's a major part of being on a team, and accepting the advice of a coach. And, it's a faith thing, really. If the best athletes ate a certain way, or weigh a particular amount, I'll try to emulate that" (Atkinson, 2011:246–247).

**Box 8.1**    In their own words

Bulimia*

A 19-year-old woman shares her experiences with bulimia.

I remember being 14-years-old when I first tried it. I felt numb and worthless for so long, but I never acted on it. Until one night, my boyfriend and I got in a fight and as soon as he left, I made myself throw up. It was like a high. I finally had control. Every time I ate after that, I made myself throw up. I got an adrenal rush whenever I ate because I knew what I'd be doing afterwards. It was my little secret and I liked that. It was my way out to forget about everything and just be in the moment. I also lost several friends throughout those two years and my dad was in an accident where his friend passed away. My world was spinning out of control and food was the only thing I had control over. After several months, I didn't get the high anymore, so I just stopped eating entirely. No one really noticed either since I always had an excuse for why I wasn't hungry.

At first, I thought if I was skinnier then maybe he wouldn't fight with me, or hit me, or cheat on me anymore. So my goal was to lose weight. I was only about 100 pounds, standing at 5' 2" when it all started; so I wasn't anywhere close to fat. I kept losing weight and finally got down to 92 pounds, but he still didn't act any different. He was even harder on me and said I looked gross.

After about two years, I started seeing a therapist in July of 2010 after my dad's accident. I didn't tell my parents what it was for though. It was still a secret. The therapist had me keep a food journal. The very last time I went there, I had not eaten anything for three days, so she tried to get me to eat some goldfish crackers, but I absolutely refused to. That's when she said things were getting too bad and I had to go to intensive treatment. Once my parents found out, they didn't understand why I felt how I did. They wanted to help, but they didn't know what to do. I could tell they watched me so much more closely afterwards and just looked at me differently because they finally knew the reason why I was withering away. In September of 2010, I went into treatment, a specialized intensive outpatient treatment for eating disorders. I was there until December 24th of 2010.

I went back into intensive outpatient treatment towards the end of 2011 for a month. They specialized in behavior disorders, so they didn't know how to handle my problem so I was discharged after a month. This problem will never fully go away, it's a daily struggle. I will always have that little voice in the back of my mind telling me not to eat or that I'm fat, but I've learned to fight it most days. I still have bad days or weeks.

Why do I think that people, generally, are bulimic? Statistic-wise, females are more likely to suffer from eating disorders because they idolize the wrong women. When I was young, my best friend looked up to Britney Spears and wanted to be just like her. All the boys thought she was so hot, so of course girls wanted to get that same attention from the boys. To get that attention, though, girls had to act, dress, and look like her. She was not a modest dresser at all, especially in her music videos. She was young and very in shape, so it was considered all right for her to portray herself off like that.

I think that nowadays people are starting to appreciate the curvy body structure more. No guy wants a girl who has the body of a thirteen year old. It's hard to stay thinner but still have big boobs and a big butt. People in the middle stay in shape because they feel pressure to look good, but most of them have fake boobs, fake hair, face lifts, etc.

In treatment, I was taught that many, if not all, people that appear in magazines or on billboards are not real people. I mean the original base picture is a real person, but they do so many things to manipulate the image so that the end result that we see looks nothing like it did in the beginning. It's amazing that they can Photoshop people to have thicker hair, different face structure, eye color, skin color, smoothness and flawlessness of skin, a smaller waist, and bigger boobs or butt too. The men or women who we are trying to be like aren't even real; it's an unattainable image. Pictures get leaked of stars without make up on and everyone is so shocked that they could even look like that because we expect them to always be dressed up and look perfect since that is how they are always portrayed. In reality, they are people just like us; it takes them hours to look how they have to in front of the cameras. Some of them probably wish they could go out more without being done up and not get criticized for it.

\* Brandon DeLoia conducted this interview.
Do you think men share these views? Why might we hear about eating disorders among women more often than among men?

Male athletes, like 21-year-old Trevor, may view weight control as a sign of devotion to a sport:

If you're body is, well let's just say if it's not lean enough to work [train, compete], you've probably not got enough commitment to stay in the sport for a long time, and people will clock that immediately. It's a dedication symbol to me. When I am in control of how much I have to eat so my body can perform, I control my fate. If you win, it's because you've put in the pain and anguish needed to win. No excuses, no one to blame but me…. (Atkinson, 2011:237).

Both female and male athletes often are associated with other eating disorders to achieve a certain body image. **Anorexia athletic** is *sport-related anorexia nervosa*; that is, this form of deviance occurs in athletes who limit their caloric intake or overexercise with the goal of a particular body image for improved athletic performance (Sudi *et al.*, 2004). At the other extreme is muscle dysmorphia, or bigorexia, which primarily affects male bodybuilders. **Bigorexia**, sometimes called reverse anorexia, is *abnormal eating, often combined with supplements and drug use, to achieve larger muscle mass* (Mosley, 2009). One bodybuilder explains:

Bodybuilding is my life, so I make sacrifices elsewhere. I'm always thinking about the nutritional content of food and how it would affect the way I look, so I can never eat out at restaurants or go to a friend's for dinner because it would mess up my diet. And I spend so much money on stuff like protein-powders and fat-burning pills that I have no money left to go out drinking; to be honest I don't have that many friends anyway. Not enough time for them … I often arrive to work late or leave early because I have to train, and even when I am there my mind is always on my next meal or gym session" (Mosley, 2009:194–195).

Eating disorders can be linked to mental disorders. Finn, a 25-year-old athlete, describes eating with a group of non-athletic friends: "I dunno, when I watch friends eat out at a dinner, it makes me nauseous. Every spoon or fork full of food they shovel in, and, I'm like doing mental calculations in my head [calories]. Crazy, how much people eat and don't need … I try to eat the bare minimum I need to be healthy and excel in sport. This whole thing about eating for enjoyment is full of shit, and it's what gets people into trouble. And, don't even get me started about what it's like to sit at a table and listen to someone saying, 'Is that all you are having? Do you want to die or something?' Like you know what it fucking takes to be a champion!" (Atkinson, 2011:247). What mental disorder do you think is related to an obsession with counting calories and maintaining a certain weight? *Source*: © Bill Gozansky/Alamy

Any extreme can be harmful, so moderation in both exercise and diet seems to be the key to a healthy lifestyle. In addition to body "deviance", sociologists have explored mental disorders as a form of deviance.

## Mental Disorders

Earlier in this chapter, we talked about Erving Goffman's (1963) work on stigma associated with abominations of the body. Goffman identified two other types of stigma, including tribal stigma like race or class and blemishes of individual character like mental illness. In this section, we focus on Goffman's third type of stigma: mental disorders.

Sociologists view mental disorders from a unique perspective. Think back to the first chapter, when we discussed a variety of approaches to understanding deviance. One approach that some sociologists use to understand mental disorders is the social constructionist position. In this view, mental illness is a label for people whose behavior falls outside the range of tolerance. Of course, this varies by place and time. For example, uttering nonsensical statements in a fast food restaurant may lead management to contact police for assistance, while at a religious service such behavior may be considered a sign from a higher power. Twenty years ago we might have thought a man talking to himself while waiting for a bus indicated a mental illness; today, we would probably assume he was talking on a cell phone and, thus, *normal*. Similarly, the Centers for Disease Control (2013) reports that mental disorders among children in the US have been increasing, with up to 20% of children having a diagnosed mental disorder. The most common mental disorder among children is Attention Deficit Hyperactivity Disorder (ADHD), with behavioral or conduct problems coming in second. Sociologists would ask why more children are being labeled with such disorders – especially when the criteria for diagnosing someone with ADHD are broadening with the DSM-V. Is the range of tolerance shrinking for children who can't sit still in class?

Sociologists who adopt the social constructionist perspective also note how the prevalence of mental disorders varies by social group. This implies that power plays a role in the labeling of mental disorders. Consider, for example, that homosexuality was once considered a mental disorder in the American Psychiatric Association's Diagnostic and Statistical Manual of Mental Disorders (DSM); it was removed in 1970s in the seventh printing of the DSM-II and replaced with "Sexual Orientation Disturbance" (Mayes and Horwitz, 2005). Changing – either expanding, tightening, adding, or deleting – definitions of mental disorders has an effect on who receives treatment and which services insurance companies will cover. Realize that members of the APA hold elections and vote (a social process) to determine what is and is not considered a mental illness and included in the Diagnostic and Statistical Manual. Sociologists would argue that those who have power have greater influence over these changing definitions and who profits from changes in services to those with mental disorders.

While the social constructionist perspective contributes to our understanding of mental disorders, this approach has been criticized. Brain scans, DNA testing, and other scientific research indicate a biological basis to many mental disorders, suggesting there might be some relevance to the medical model.


## Mental illness and the medical model

Similar to other illnesses, the medical model views mental disorder as a physical disease to be treated. Just as a broken leg can be fixed with a cast, adherents to the medical model believe mental disorders can be treated with medicine, too. However, opponents of the medical model argue that it is inappropriate for mental illness. While a broken leg may be a broken leg in New York as well as Chicago, the same is not true for mental illnesses. Mental illnesses reveal themselves through their symptoms, which consist of behavior that is considered abnormal or deviant. As we know, deviant behavior varies by place, time, and culture, and, as one opponent of the medical model argued, "Psychiatric knowledge in these matters rests almost entirely on unsystematic clinical impressions and professional lore" (Scheff, 1970:16).

Applying the medical model to mental illness implies an objective, scientific approach to understanding mental illness. Thomas Scheff writes that:

> ... the concepts of mental illness in general ... are not neutral, value-free, scientifically precise terms but, for the most part, the leading edge of an ideology embedded in the historical and cultural present of the white middle class of Western societies. The concept of illness and its associated vocabulary – symptoms, therapies, patients, and physicians – reify and legitimate the prevailing public order at the expense of other possible worlds. The medical model of disease refers to culture-free processes that are independent of the public order ... (Scheff, 1970:15).

Instead of being scientifically-driven, mental illness has become politicized and is now a legal, not truly a medical, concept – at least according to one longstanding opponent, Thomas Szasz (2011). Szasz acknowledges brain diseases, which he classifies as distinct from mental illnesses. Szasz writes that the term mental illness "refers to the judgements of some persons about the (bad) behaviours of other persons" – completely separate from medical science (Szasz, 2011:180).

Opponents of the medical model argue that mental illness should be understood sociologically, through labeling – a perspective we discussed in Chapter 4. In that chapter, we applied labeling theory to understanding mental illness. The label of mental illness is given by a psychiatrist – someone in a position of power. Everything the labeled person does is viewed through the lens of mental illness: protesting the label is interpreted as a symptom of mental illness, confirming the diagnosis.

Despite this debate between those in favor and those opposed, acceptance of the medical model approach to understanding mental disorders appears to be growing in the US. Rates of mental illness have remained steady since the early 1990s, but more and more people are seeking treatment – even though only about half of those seeking treatment actually have a diagnosed disorder (Kessler *et al.*, 2005).

Despite this growing acceptance, some people are hesitant to seek treatment for mental disorders because they are afraid of the stigma and discrimination that might accompany the label of a mental disorder, indicating that sociology still has a role to play in this arena.

## Mysteries of the mind

Stigma seems to be associated with some mental disorders more so than others. People's perceptions of dangerousness play a role in the stigma applied to persons with mental disorders, although demographic factors like race, age, sex, social class, education, and religiosity also matter (Silton *et al.*, 2011). Interestingly, those who are considered dangerous are those affiliated with a lower social class. Society tends to label the poor as "crazy" while the rich are considered "eccentric".

The label of dangerousness attached to some mental disorders can lead the public to fear people with those disorders. This is happening in current events. The phenomenon of mass shootings – like at the movie theater in Aurora, Colorado and at the elementary school in Newtown, Connecticut, both in 2012 – sparked a gun control debate, which quickly led to a focus on restricting gun access from people with mental illnesses. While most people with mental disorders are harmless, the perception of dangerousness remains.

This stigma can affect whether those with a mental disorder seek treatment. One woman diagnosed with schizophrenia explained, "Well I'm too worried about telling people I'm on medication. There are very, very few people that I talk about the [treatment] to ... because it does feel ... well I don't really want to talk about it because I hate it and it's horrible and also I feel there is big stigma attached and if they hear about that they'd think I was really mad" (Dinos *et al.*, 2004:177–178).

Fearing what others may think of a mental illness diagnosis may especially deter those in institutions where it would be considered a weakness, like the military.

---

**Box 8.2**  In their own words

### Diagnosed with bipolar disorder*

I was 27-years-old, working as a legal secretary. I remember all of a sudden not being able to handle work anymore. All of the stress got to me and my husband, he had an affair, and it tore our family apart. I went to the doctor to try to figure out what was wrong with me. That is when I was diagnosed with bipolar disorder and acute manic depression.

I have been in treatment ever since being diagnosed. I guess you could say the treatment has somewhat of a permanent change in my behavior, but not all of them last as long as others. I usually end up relapsing with drugs or alcohol and a different treatment plan has to get changed like my medicine.

I am now 49-years-old and am still taking medicine every day. If I do not take it I become completely unfocused and cannot do anything but lie in bed all day or scream. I wish I could still work. I loved my job. Even if I no longer worked at a law firm, I would like to do something with myself from day to day. Being bipolar makes it hard for me to handle the stress of everyday life, let alone working and dealing with people on a daily basis.

My diagnosis has changed throughout the years as the disorder evolved in me. It's hard to remember the way I used to be other than looking at pictures and trying to reminisce the old times before all of this happened. I get angry easily and resort to bad things to "control" myself.

Other people treat me differently. They talk to me as if I have a mental learning disability which I do not have. They act as if I am inferior to them, when they have no idea how hard this is to deal with. Since my diagnosis, I lost a lot of friends and respect among colleagues. I lost my job and had no motivation to go back to school; I had been working at the law firm on experience only with no degree. Our family fell to poverty and we are still struggling today.

Even my family treats me differently. Sometimes my family gets frustrated with me because I cannot go out to family gatherings for too long before I start to feel the effects taking over my actions and they have to run me home. No one seems to understand what it's like to be me.

I believe I am helping myself at the moment with the actions I choose to do, but find it hard to make rational choices and usually do not realize what I am doing until it is too late. A lot of times something little or irrelevant to someone else becomes a big deal to me. I get into a lot of arguments with my son about having a pack of cigarettes at all times and if he does not cater to that need, my disorder takes over the best of me.

Before being diagnosed the most I ever did was smoke weed with a few friends or my husband and drink alcohol. After my diagnosis, I tried to self-medicate with drugs and alcohol. I have been arrested for assaulting my husband at a time where I was completely dependent on alcohol and illegal drugs. By taking these, I thought it was helping when it was just making things worse. I was found not fit to stand trial and sent to a mental institution for seven months. More commonly I was involved with drugs on a normal day to day basis, including cocaine, crack, weed, and meth. I have been clean for a while now as part of my probation, but occasionally relapse if I get too stressed out. I can't help it. I hate to say this, but I blame the bipolar disorder for the things I engage in. I never did it before, so that seems most explainable to me.

---

\* Angelica Szewczak conducted this interview.
Do you think this woman feels stigmatized? How might stigma contribute to her behavior? What would a social constructionist say about this woman's behavior?

## Mental illness in the military

We have been discussing the importance of stigma in physical and mental deviance throughout this chapter. Here, we have been using our definition from Chapter 2 – referring to stigma as blocking full social acceptance. Stigma, though, is not limited to others' perceptions. **Self-stigma** occurs when an individual *internalizes negative beliefs that others will discriminate against the person with mental illness* and it can be a barrier to seeking help, particularly in the military (Greene-Shortridge *et al.*, 2007). The military thrives on teamwork, as soldiers have to believe that other soldiers will "have their six" – meaning they will watch their backs or help keep them safe from enemy combatants. Any perceived weakness may challenge that belief; soldiers may think others will ostracize them from the team if anyone found out about their mental disorders.

This self-stigma may be diminishing, however, given the media campaign to raise awareness of mental illness in the military. And, a large proportion of military veterans are diagnosed with one or more mental disorders. About one-quarter to one-third of returning military veterans from Iraq and Afghanistan who went to a Department of Veterans Services facility were diagnosed with one or more mental or psychosocial disorder (Seal *et al.*, 2007).

One mental disorder in particular, post-traumatic stress disorder (PTSD), seems to be increasingly more common – or identified and diagnosed more often – in the military today. PTSD is characterized by extreme stress following a traumatic event (like combat) and people with PTSD can experience flashbacks to the traumatic event, difficulty sleeping, and inappropriate expression of emotions like anger; these symptoms make reintegrating into civilian life difficult at best. Among other disorders, PTSD affects those who served in the military, especially in Iraq and Afghanistan, and younger military members and those who were in combat have a greater risk of PTSD than older veterans and military personnel who served in non-combat roles (Seal *et al.*, 2007). With greater attention being paid to mental disorders among military personnel and attempts to reduce the stigma associated with mental illness in the military, more soldiers are seeking help.

---

**Box 8.3    In their own words**

### Alzheimer's and multiple mental illnesses*

I have been diagnosed with bipolar, depression, and Alzheimer's. I take many medications every day but primarily I take two different anti-depressants.

According to my psychologist, I have post traumatic stress disorder. It all started with my abusive childhood. My dad was physically and emotionally abusive to both me and my brothers and sisters. I have always struggled with depression since my childhood and when coupled with the Alzheimer's, it only gets worse and makes the depression even greater.

This affects my family tremendously. My kids have had to learn growing up what my triggers were and be able to sense if I was in a depressed mood. When they sensed that I was in one of my moods, they would leave me alone for awhile until I got better. This was their own way of coping with me and protecting themselves. At times I get angry for no reason and this affects my kids but more specifically my relationship with them. Also at different times in my marriage I have been reminded that my wife would leave me if I did not change because I was not the same person that she married anymore.

At this point, I have a hard time going out in public and wish I could do it and be comfortable with it but I cannot. With the Alzheimer's it is getting much worse and making me paranoid. Also, I wish that I could work and feel like a man because I cannot. At times I feel like a burden on my family and guilty because of how much they take care of me and my inability to provide for them. I wish I did not feel this way.

After the birth of my first granddaughter, I got so depressed that I told my wife you need to take me somewhere because I wanted to kill myself. My family had to get rid of all the guns in the house and checked me into a clinic for a few weeks. This was definitely rock bottom.

Nothing has really changed since my diagnosis, I am still very depressed and never got much relief from it. I have suffered from it for so long that nothing really helps me get out of my funk. The only real thing that helps is my family and spending time with them.

Unfortunately, for the most part I do not deal with it very well especially because of the Alzheimer's. I can see changes in myself and can see that I cannot do the things that I use to do. Mentally, I can feel my abilities slipping which scares me of what it will be like in a few years. The depression gets greater the more I regress.

---

\* Austin Coyle conducted this interview.
Do you think those with more than one mental disorder experience greater stigmatization than those with only one mental disorder?

## Mental Disorders and the Media

Mental disorders have been portrayed very prominently in the media, and when they are, the media play a role in perpetuating stereotypes of mental disorders. A 33-year-old African man explained, "It's just the stigma that's attached to schizophrenia. If it's on the news or TV it's usually because they've brandished a sword on the … street or attacked someone. There's never a story about a schizophrenic who saves life of granny who falls in canal" (Dinos *et al.*, 2004:178).

Several movies, though, show the struggles of those living with mental disorders – like *Silver Linings Playbook*, starring Bradley Cooper (who plays a man with bipolar disorder) and Jennifer Lawrence, *A Beautiful Mind*, starring Russell Crowe (who plays a man suffering from schizophrenia), *Rain Man* (with Tom Cruise's character meeting and eventually caring for his autistic older brother, played by Dustin Hoffman), and *Psycho* (Anthony Perkins' character Norman Bates has a split personality, assuming his dead mother). Perhaps the most famous movie on this topic is the classic, *One Flew Over the Cuckoo's Nest*.

### One flew over the cuckoo's nest

In one of his earlier roles, Jack Nicholson played a character named R.P. McMurphy in the 1975 movie, *One Flew Over the Cuckoo's Nest*. After successfully taking the insanity plea to avoid prison labor, career criminal McMurphy (or "Mac") is sent to a mental institution. Mac quickly becomes a rebellious leader of a group of mental inmates, and, throughout the movie, Mac is at odds with mean Nurse Ratched, who runs the ward. Mac leads a series of shenanigans in a power struggle against Ratched, and, as a result, learns that instead of being released at the end of his criminal sentence, he will remain in the mental institution until Nurse Ratched and the hospital board find him fit to return to society. From there, Mac begins to plan his escape.

The climax of the movie occurs when Mac's girlfriend, Candy, and her friend sneak into the mental institution around Christmas, bringing alcohol to the patients on the ward. The next morning, Nurse Ratched enters the ward to find that one of the patients has had a sexual encounter with Candy, and Ratched berates him to such an extent that he commits suicide – just as Mac was about to escape. An angry Mac returns to the ward and strangles Ratched, who survived only because an orderly hit Mac, knocking him out. Mac is dragged away to be lobotomized. The movie ends with Mac's friend mercifully suffocating him before escaping to Canada.

*One Flew Over the Cuckoo's Nest* portrays life in a mental institution in the 1970s. While most of the patients in the movie were in the institution voluntarily, the movie highlights some negative practices of mental institutions of the past. Today, people with mental disorders are free to live in society without the fear of being committed to a mental institution, as commitments are more difficult now than in the past. What are the benefits of this deinstitutionalization? What might be the drawbacks among people who are not receiving the help they need?

# Summary

This chapter focused on the way that physical and mental deviance varies by social group and society's reaction to these types of deviance. The media send the message that a certain body type – slim for women and muscular for men – is the ideal, and this ideal is necessary for a happy, successful life. This ideal can encourage eating disorders and stigmatization toward those who have physical disabilities, although this is less so than in the past. Just like everyone, those with disabilities like blindness or deafness are concerned with how other members of society treat them – although some social groups are challenged more so than others. This ideal body type also led society – the government in particular – to target obesity as an epidemic.

Similarly, those with mental disorders face stigmatization for the unconventional behavior some disorders create. For this reason, people with mental disorders may be hesitant to have an official diagnosis for fear of being labeled and, consequently, avoid help they may need. Sociologists take note of this, and point out how mental disorders are socially constructed. More often, we are seeing one group in particular portrayed in the media as having mental disorders – the military. Positive attention to raise awareness about mental disorders in the military can reduce some of the self-stigmatization that discourages military personnel from seeking help.

# Outcomes Assessment

1 Describe the role of the media in setting societal norms for the "ideal" body type and the effects this has on physical and mental health.
2 Explain why physical disabilities may be defined as deviant.
3 Explain the relationship between physical and mental deviance and stigma.
4 Identify the various manifestations of physical and mental deviance.
5 Compare the sociological view of mental disorders with the medical model.

## Key Terms and Concepts

Anorexia athletic
Anorexia nervosa
bigorexia

bulimia
emaciation

fat shaming
self-stigma

# 9

# Suicide and Self-Harm

## Student Learning Outcomes

After reading this chapter students will be able to:

1   Define suicide.
2   Explain how suicide is socially constructed.
3   Describe Durkheim's typology of suicide.
4   Identify patterns of suicide in the United States.
5   Define euthanasia and identify the arguments on both sides of the legalization debate.
6   Describe suicide by cop.
7   Explain the history of suicide terrorism and apply Durkheim's typology to suicide terrorism.
8   Describe the relationship between the media and self-harm.

*One month after her boyfriend killed himself, it was reported that 37-year-old country music star Mindy McCready killed his dog and then fatally shot herself on February 17, 2013, leaving behind her six-year-old and ten-month-old sons (Payne and Lavandera, 2013). A few months later, on April 5, evangelical pastor Rick Warren's 27-year-old son, Matthew, apparently committed suicide with a gun. Suicide is not limited to young celebrities; 71-year-old NASCAR driver Dick Trickle killed himself using a gun. If you are unfamiliar with NASCAR, you may have noticed that in a nod to Trickle, Tom Cruise's character in the 1990 movie* Days of Thunder *was Cole Trickle. Other celebrities have attempted suicide: actor Owen Wilson*

*Deviance & Deviants: A Sociological Approach*, First Edition. William E. Thompson and Jennifer C. Gibbs.
© 2017 John Wiley & Sons, Inc. Published 2017 by John Wiley & Sons, Inc.
Companion website: www.wiley.com/go/thompson

*allegedly cut his wrists; actress Halle Berry is reported to have inhaled carbon monoxide; and Teen Mom celebrity Amber Portwood, as well as reality star Jack Osbourne and American Idol Fantasia Barrino, all are alleged to have tried to overdose on drugs. Suicide reaches beyond celebrities – it can affect anyone. In fact there seem to be patterns among various social groups.*

## Defining Suicide

Unlike other forms of deviance, **suicide** seems relatively easy to define: it is *the intentional taking of one's own life* or *"the self-application of lethal violence"* (Manning, 2012:208). While the definition appears simple, understanding suicide is much more complicated. In this book, we have been approaching various types of deviance through a sociological lens. Social constructionists recognize that how a suspicious death is labeled depends on a variety of factors, including pressure from officials to close a case, the family's wishes, and the amount of evidence to make a determination (Pescosolido and Mendelsohn, 1986). Take, for instance, the controversy surrounding the death of actress Brittany Murphy, who was only 32-years-old when she died in 2009. The Los Angeles County Coroner concluded Murphy died of pneumonia – the same illness that killed Murphy's husband, 39-year-old screenwriter Simon Monjak, six months later. Murphy's father later had her hair analyzed by a private lab that concluded she may have been poisoned; the Coroner refused to reopen the case, as testing one strand of hair that likely had been chemically treated over the years did not provide enough evidence to change his opinion (Duke, 2013). While suggestions that Murphy or her husband committed suicide were only rumors, these are suspicious deaths where the label is being questioned – that is, the death classification is open to interpretation and social construction.

You may be wondering what kind of evidence is necessary to classify a sudden death a suicide. The most important piece of information comes from our original definition of suicide – the *intent* of the deceased to end his or her life. One way to understand the state of mind of the decedent is through a suicide note (see Callanan and Davis, 2009). Often, no note is left or no witnesses were present; but there are other ways to make an educated guess about intent, like "how to" guides near the body, other suicide attempts, reports from family members, friends or medical professionals about the decedent, a recent crisis like the end of a relationship, money problems, or loss of another loved one, and how the person died (Timmermans, 2005). Nevertheless, these are only clues to the decedent's state of mind, leaving a lot of room for interpretation in death classification. Sometimes there are parties with vested interests, such as family, law enforcement, and insurance companies, in how the death is categorized.

For example, in an ethnographic study of a medical examiner's office, Timmermans (2005) reports the case of Guy Dubos where the cause of death was changed after pressure from the deceased's family and after other pathologists took another look at the case. Dubos was a White male in his 30s. The investigators found three suicide notes and an empty bottle of antidepressant pills near his body, his girlfriend indicated she and Dubos were fighting about his jealousy, and Dubos recently went bankrupt from his divorce (Timmermans, 2005). However, Dubos' family argued that he would never commit suicide, the suicide notes were actually song lyrics, and Dubos probably died from a combination of diabetes, alcoholism, and other physical and mental health issues. The death originally was classified as "undetermined" and was later changed to "natural causes" upon further review of the case by recently hired pathologists (Timmermans, 2005:320). Beyond this example, studies have confirmed that even experts can disagree about whether a death is a suicide. Focusing on Fulton County, Georgia, deJong and Hanzlick (2000) compared the opinions of the medical examiner investigators, who mostly have a background in law enforcement, with the determination of death by the medical examiners, who are forensic pathologists. The investigators and medical examiners disagreed about the cause of death in slightly more than 12% of the cases (deJong and Hanzlick, 2000).

Indeed, in order to determine whether a suspicious death was intentional, as one scholar pointed out, "The people you really want to talk to are dead" (Wray *et al.*, 2011:517). To work around this important fact, scholars have devised ways to test whether suicide rates are, in fact, social constructions – and some studies suggest they are. For example, we would expect that some groups who stigmatize suicide more than others would have a lower suicide rate than other groups. Early research on suicide indicated that countries with higher proportions of Catholics had lower suicide rates than countries with higher proportions of Protestants; that is, Catholics commit suicide at a lower rate than Protestants (Durkheim, 1897/1951). To test this hypothesis, van Poppel and Day (1996) compared deaths of Catholics and Protestants in the Netherlands from 1905 through 1910, using that time period primarily because the religion of the deceased was reported only during those years. The authors found that Catholics have a higher rate of death than Protestants, but deaths of Catholics are much less likely to be classified as suicide. In other words, had a large proportion of the Catholics who died of "sudden death" or "death from ill-defined or unspecified cause" been Protestant instead, their deaths would have been labeled suicide.

While suicides may be recorded less than they actually occur, most scholars agree that for the most part statistics on suicide are pretty much accurate because the under-reporting of suicides is randomly distributed (see Timmermans, 2005). Before we examine suicide rates among various groups in American society today, we will first review the classical study on suicide: Durkheim's seminal work.

## Durkheim's Classic Study

As we mentioned in Chapter 4, Emile Durkheim, a prolific sociologist, penned the classic study of suicide. In his research, Durkheim ([1897] 1951) used a definition of suicide similar to the one we describe above, "suicide is applied to all cases of death resulting directly or indirectly from a positive or negative act of the victim himself, which he knows will produce this result" (p. 44). His interest in the topic began when his college roommate committed suicide, which, you can imagine, had a profound impact on Durkheim. He was not satisfied with individualistic explanations for this behavior, and he began to explore patterns in suicide.

Specifically, Durkheim took a macro-level approach. That means he looked at information on countries – not individuals, and looked at suicide rates, not individual suicides. He noticed waves of suicide in European countries; that is, the suicide rate remained relatively stable over shorter periods of time, but fluctuated with major changes in society. He explained these patterns through two concepts we introduced in Chapter 4: **social integration**, *the extent to*

**Table 9.1**　Durkheim's typology of suicide.

|  | *Low* | *High* |
|---|---|---|
| Social Integration | **Egoistic suicide** | **Altruistic suicide** |
| Social Regulation | **Anomic suicide** | **Fatalistic suicide** |

*which people feel that they are a meaningful part of society*, and **social regulation**, *the extent to which society controls or regulates individual behavior*. For Durkheim, social integration could be found through religion, family, or other social groups; in well-integrated social groups, suicide was less likely. Durkheim reasoned that the social ties formed in these groups attach people to society, and they provide strength and support during personal crises (Wray *et al.*, 2011). Social regulation also protected against suicide by providing people structure and restraint, offering control over people's desires. According to Durkheim, people need equilibrium in both areas. However, when social integration or social regulation was too high or too low, the risk of suicide increased. Based on this, Durkheim developed four types of suicide: *egoistic, altruistic, anomic,* and *fatalistic*.

## Egoistic suicide

Egoistic suicide is the most common type of suicide, stemming from "excessive individualism" (Durkheim, 1897/1951:209). Excessive individualism blocks social integration. According to Durkheim, when social integration is low, egoistic suicide will be high. The reason is that a well-integrated society has a great deal of control over individuals, and "thus forbids them to dispose willfully of themselves" (Durkheim, 1897/1951:209). Durkheim uses the degree of integration among various religious groups to illustrate this point. Earlier in this chapter, we mentioned that Durkheim found Catholics committed suicide much less often than Protestants. He explained this finding through social integration – the Protestant faith allows more free inquiry and individualistic interpretation of the Bible, while the Catholic faith demands rigid adherence to its teachings and offers little room for individualism. Durkheim further reasoned that because the Protestant church promotes individualism, it is less integrated than the Catholic Church, and this is why he found a greater number of suicides among Protestants than among Catholics. (Recall, though, that other research had the opposite findings.)

Durkheim also used the family as an example, although marriage has a complicated relationship with suicide. Durkheim noted that when people – especially men – marry too young, the risk of suicide increases. However, when men are older than 20 years, marriage can lower the risk of suicide. Recent research suggests that married people commit suicide less often than their unmarried counterparts (Phillips *et al.*, 2010). Durkheim concluded that when people are well integrated into society through the family, the risk of suicide decreases. But, when the bond to society weakens, individuals are free to do what they want. Durkheim (1897/1951) wrote: "The more weakened the groups to which he belongs, the less he depends on them, the more he consequently depends on only himself and recognizes no other rules of conduct than what are founded on his private interests" (p. 209). Another way to look at this is when people cannot

Emile Durkheim.

establish relationships, they cannot integrate into society. We can see examples of this emerging in suicide notes, like one written by a 28-year-old woman:

> You see, what you fail to grasp is that I love you more than any amount of money in [the] world, and everything is secondary when it comes to you, but my love for you doesn't matter one iota to you. So therefore, I have nothing else to look forward to. Loving you was worth living for, without you nothing matters. So that's where it's at (Sanger and Veach, 2008:359).

Finally, Durkheim confirmed his findings by using the political institution as his last example. Events like war and election crises affect suicide. He explains, "great social disturbances and great popular wars rouse collective sentiments, stimulate partisan spirit and patriotism, political and national faith, alike, and concentrating activity toward a single end, at least temporarily cause a stronger integration of society" (Durkheim, 1897/1951:208). And, according to Durkheim, when society is integrated, suicide rates will be low.

## Altruistic suicide

Much less common than egoistic suicide is altruistic suicide. Altruistic suicide is the opposite of egoistic suicide. This type occurs when a person's bond to society is too strong, when it is a duty to commit suicide; the individual is less important than the group. Durkheim offers martyrs and military heroism as examples. In particular, he notes that those likely to commit altruistic suicide are men who are very sick or too old, recent widows (see photo in next page), and loyal servants who recently lost their chief. In these instances, custom dictates that one must commit suicide; social pressure to do so is very high. When a person fails to take his or her own life and fails to fulfill this obligation, the person will be dishonored and even punished.

Widow-burning. Among the seventeenth century Sati in India, widows would lie next to their dead husband and self-immolate, or set themselves on fire, to die with their husbands. Durkheim points out that this custom of suicide is their duty, making this altruistic suicide. What about women who died along with their husbands involuntarily? *Source*: © Lanmas/Alamy

To support his claim, Durkheim pointed to suicide statistics among military forces in various European countries in the late 1800s. In all countries he included (e.g., Austria, United States, Italy, England, France), more suicides occurred among soldiers than among civilians in the same age range. Durkheim (1897/1951) concluded that the army is "a special environment where altruistic suicide is chronic" (p. 228), a place where people commit "what might be called heroic suicide" (p. 240). In groups like the army, the commitment to the social group is more important than each individual, and every member of that group is willing to die for his or her duty – reasoning that extends to suicidal behavior, too.

## Anomic suicide

Social integration is only one social force that, when extreme on one end or the other, can increase the risk for suicide. The other concept that plays a role in suicide, according to Durkheim, is social regulation. Anomic suicide can occur when social regulation is weakened or absent. Recall from Chapter 4 that anomie is *a state of social strain, normative confusion, or rapid change in norms or social structure which results in people no longer feeling constrained by conventional social norms*. So, when social regulation is weak and there is a state of social strain, society no longer is able to control behavior and people are free to commit suicide.

Data suggest that this may be the case for some suicides. Durkheim initially observed that suicide is more prevalent in times of economic crises. In particular, Durkheim noticed that there were more suicides immediately following financial crashes in Vienna and Paris. Recently, researchers found evidence of an increase in suicide – especially among men – during the 2008 recession (Chang *et al.*, 2013). Figure 9.1 shows the trends in suicide rates among racial and sex groups compared with the unemployment rate for the same time period in the US. When unemployment began to rise again in 2008, suicide rates also increased – but only for some groups. Suicide increased for White men and women, but it stayed about the same for Black women and actually decreased among Black men. Interestingly – and absent from Figure 9.1 – the suicide rate among American Indian and Alaskan Native men stayed relatively the same, while women associating with this racial group had a slightly higher suicide rate after 2008 (the rate for women was 4.29 suicides per 100,000 American Indian/Alaskan Native women in 2007 and gradually increased to 5.89 by 2010).

Durkheim (1897/1951) also observed, however, that suicide increased during "fortunate crises", which "abruptly … enhance a country's prosperity" (p. 243). For example, when Germany was unified in 1870 and the country was prosperous, the number of suicides rose, too. And, suicide was lower in poorer countries like Ireland. Recent research indicates that suicide rates are higher among those without a college degree (Phillips *et al.*, 2010); presumably, college graduates earn more and thus are less likely to experience financial strain. Further, the economy was not the only social institution that affected suicide. Marriage rates – or, more specifically, divorce rates – also influence the suicide rate (Phillips *et al.*, 2010).

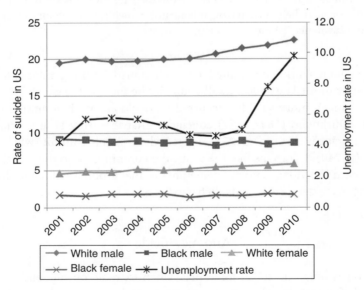

**Figure 9.1**　Trends in US unemployment rate and US suicide rate by race and gender. Do you notice suicide increasing during harsh economic times – in line with Durkheim's theory? Does anomic suicide seem applicable to some social groups more than others? Why might this be so? *Sources*: CDC WISQARS (http://webappa.cdc.gov/sasweb/ncipc/mortrate10_us.html) and Bureau of Labor Statistics (http://data.bls.gov/pdq/). Note that the unemployment rate used is the rate for the month of January of each year, as no annual data were available

From all of this, Durkheim concluded that the crisis itself – whether a financial crisis or crisis of prosperity – affects suicide rates because crises disturb the equilibrium of the collective order. In other words, when there is little social regulation caused by rapid changes in society, people suffer and anomic suicide results.

## Fatalistic suicide

Fatalistic suicide is the opposite of anomic suicide. It occurs when there is too much social regulation, resulting in, "persons with futures pitilessly blocked and passions violently choked by oppressive discipline" (Durkheim, 1897/1951:276, footnote 25). According to Durkheim, fatalistic suicide is rare (so rare that he only discusses it in a footnote!), but we may see it in husbands who are too young, in wives who are unable to have children, or in slaves.

## Criticisms of Durkheim's work

As we described in Chapter 4, Durkheim's work laid the foundation for many sociological concepts we use today. While he contributed a great deal to the study of society and deviance, in particular, Durkheim's work is not without criticism. One critique is that Durkheim's study of suicide commits an **ecological fallacy** (van Poppel and Day, 1996). That is, some accuse Durkheim of *applying macro-level findings to individuals*. Durkheim noticed that areas where Protestants tended to live had the highest suicide rates, areas where Catholics tend to live have lower suicide rates, and areas where Jews lived had the lowest suicide rates. He concluded that the nature of the religion – specifically, the free thinking and greater individualism of Protestants – led to more suicides. In other words, he used information about the religious composition of the district where the decedent lived or died, instead of using the religion of the individuals who died, to draw conclusions about the differences in suicide rates among various religions (see van Poppel and Day, 1996). Making assumptions about individuals based on where they live can lead to faulty conclusions. If we want to explain individual behavior, we must use individual-level predictors. Macro-level information can be used only to explain macro-level outcomes. Had Durkheim had access to such information, his conclusions may have been different (van Poppel and Day, 1996). In fact, almost a century after Durkheim's work was published, researchers who came across similar data to those used by Durkheim – but with more detailed information – avoided the ecological fallacy and had results that contradicted Durkheim's main thesis (van Poppel and Day, 1996).

Another criticism of Durkheim's work is that he did not carefully vet his data sources. Official data – that is, information collected by government agencies – is ripe with issues. Think back to the section on defining suicide at the beginning of this chapter. One major problem with official statistics is defining the phenomenon of interest. Definitions may vary from place to place, making comparisons difficult. How do we know that each place is using the same or a similar definition? Also, politics play a role in suspicious deaths classified as suicides. Durkheim's critics claim that he did not give enough attention to the pros and cons of each data source he used. However, researchers – including Durkheim's critics – continued to use the same data as Durkheim (e.g., Pescosolido and Georgianna, 1989).

## Modern Theories of Suicide

Borrowing from Durkheim and from psychology, Andrew Henry and James Short (1954) developed a theory of suicide. On the psychological end, Henry and Short adapted Sigmund Freud's earlier work, contending that suicidal people tend to internalize their anger instead of directing it outwardly as is basic human nature. And, suicidal people have tough superego demands, originating from internalizing harsh parental demands and expectations on them. Incorporating the frustration–aggression hypothesis (see Dollard *et al.*, 1939), Henry and Short posited that this anger results from frustration, which is where sociological components come into play. According to Henry and Short, the sociological factors driving suicide are Durkheim's inadequate social integration (which they called a weak relational system) and inadequate social regulation (which they called weak external restraint), and the economy. In particular, they observed that suicidal people tend to be unmarried and older and hold higher status (e.g., they tend to be white, male, and have higher income). They further observed that suicides among higher status people were tied to business cycles, positing that in down economic times, higher status people have more to lose than lower status people, experience more frustration, which they direct inward, and commit suicide.

Others have used sociological principles to explain suicide. For example, David Lester (1994), the past President-Elect of the American Association of Suicidology and co-founder of the International Academy of Suicide Research, argued that suicide is learned using the basic principles of learning we outlined in Chapter 4. Similar to the tenets of Henry and Short (1954), Lester agrees that first suicidal people learn from their parents to internalize aggression instead of expressing it outwardly. The behavior is reinforced by the environment, through the media, subcultural norms, modeling suicide by significant others, cultural patterns and more. Importantly, the suicidal person has not learned the dominant cultural norms of life and death. Learned helplessness or a lack of reinforcement may lead to depression, causing thoughts (the stimuli) that might lead to suicide (the response). The suicidal person's expectations about suicide are the reinforcement for engaging in the act.

Each of these theories sounds like plausible explanations. However, theories must be able to explain trends in the patterns of suicide.

## Suicide in the United States

According to the Centers for Disease Control and Prevention (2012), suicide is the 10th leading cause of death in the United States. Drugs and alcohol are part of many suicides – about one-third of suicides involved alcohol, antidepressants were found in the bodies of over 20% of those who committed suicide, and another 20% of suicides involved opiates. But these proportions vary by racial and ethnic group. Firearms are most often used to commit suicide, followed by suffocation and poisoning; however, the method of suicide varies, too, by sex.

## Sex and race differences in suicide

There is a **gender paradox** in suicide: even though *women are more likely than men to have suicidal thoughts and attempt suicide, men are more likely to commit suicide than women* – about 20 men and 5 women for every 100,000 people follow-though with suicide (Centers for Disease Control and Prevention, 2012; Langhinrichsen-Rohling *et al.*, 2009). With 30,277 men and 8,087 women taking their own lives in 2010, Figure 9.2 shows that men commit suicide almost four times as often as women do.

Why might we see such a discrepancy between men and women? Early writers explained it through biological differences between the sexes. For example, when writing about egoistic suicide, Durkheim (1897/1951) explained that women's "… sensibility is rudimentary rather than highly developed. As she lives outside of community existence more than man, she is less penetrated by it; society is less necessary to her because she is less impregnated with sociability. She has few needs in this direction and satisfies them easily…." (p. 215). On the other hand, man, "is a more complex social being, he can maintain his equilibrium only by finding more points of support outside himself, and it is because his moral balance depends on a larger number of conditions that it is more easily disturbed" (Durkheim, 1897/1951:216). In short, Durkheim argued that women reach equilibrium easier than men, which is why women commit suicide less often than men.

Explanations evolved over time, and more recent research shows different sociological correlates for men and women. For example, men and women approach suicide differently. Men are more likely to use active measures, such as firearms, whereas women are more likely to use passive measures, such as pills or poisoning themselves (Centers for Disease Control and Prevention, 2012). This may explain the gender paradox, as firearms are more likely than poisoning to be fatal (Langhinrichsen-Rohling *et al.*, 2009).

In addition to discrepancies in suicide rates between men and women, there are differences in suicide completion among various racial groups. As we might expect, most suicides are committed by Caucasians, as they comprise the biggest proportion of the US population (see Figure 9.3). In fact, 34,690 Whites committed suicide in 2010. Because other racial groups are less prevalent in the US, they make up a smaller percentage of those who died by suicide:

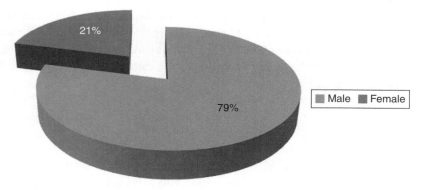

**Figure 9.2**    Percentage of 2010 US suicides by sex. Why might men commit suicide more than women?
*Source*: CDC WISQARS (http://webappa.cdc.gov/sasweb/ncipc/mortrate10_us.html)

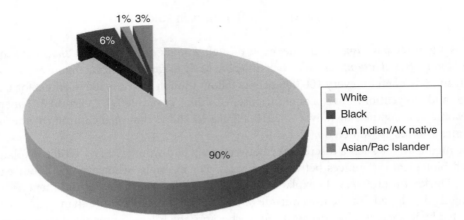

**Figure 9.3** Percentage of 2010 US suicides by race. Using the actual number of suicides tells us one story. How might the racial breakdown of suicide differ when we look at the rate of suicide for each group? *Source*: CDC WISQARS (http://webappa.cdc.gov/sasweb/ncipc/mortrate10_us.html)

2,144 Blacks, 1,061 Asian/Pacific Islanders, and 469 American Indians/Alaskan Natives committed suicide in 2010. Looking at ethnicity, we see that 2,661 Hispanics committed suicide in 2010. However, the story changes when we take into account the population of each racial group to calculate rates.

Whites still dominated suicide commission in 2010: for every 100,000 Whites, almost 14 people commit suicide. American Indians/Alaskan Natives have a high rate of suicide commission too, with about 11 suicides for every 100,000 people. In fact, suicide is the second leading cause of death among this racial group (Centers for Disease Control and Prevention, 2012). For every 100,000 Asians/Pacific Islanders, about six people commit suicide. Blacks, who comprised six percent of those who committed suicide in 2010, have the lowest rate of suicide among these four racial groups, with about five for every 100,000 people. Among Hispanics, the suicide rate is just under six for every 100,000 people.

When we compare men and women of each racial group, we see further differences. For both men and women, the racial group rankings stay the same: Whites have the highest rate of suicide, followed by American Indians/Alaskan Natives, Asian/Pacific Islanders, and Blacks. (The rate for Hispanic men is 9.81 and 2.11 for Hispanic women.) Within each racial group, though, notice the gender differences. The ratio of male suicide rate to female suicide rate is the highest among Blacks, while the male-to-female suicide rate is the lowest among American Indians and Alaskan Natives.

## Age and suicide

Despite the common notion that suicide rates among teens are skyrocketing, looking at Figure 9.5, we see that the suicide rate among adolescents stays below 10 per 100,000 people of that age until age 19, when the suicide rate is 10.4. That said, suicide is more common as age increases until age 22, when the suicide rate is 15 per 100,000 people. The suicide rate dips, but

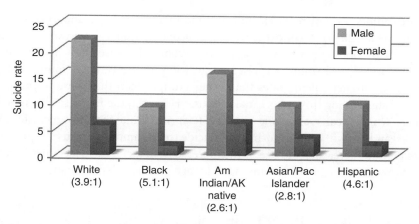

**Figure 9.4** 2010 US suicide rate by race and gender. Note: "Am Indian/AK Native" refers to American Indians and Alaskan Natives. "Asian/Pac Islander" refers to Asians and Pacific Islanders. In parentheses below each racial group is the male-to-female ratio. Notice the similarities and differences between this graph and the graphs in Figures 9.2 and 9.3. When we take into account the number of people in each group, both Black men and Black women commit suicide the least compared with their counterparts in other racial groups. Which set of statistics do you think should be used when discussing suicide trends – raw numbers or information that includes the number of people in each population? *Source*: CDC WISQARS (http://webappa.cdc.gov/sasweb/ncipc/mortrate10_us.html). Note that the age-adjusted (for the year 2000) suicide rate is used.

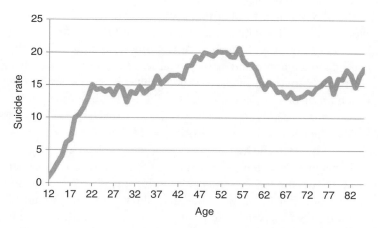

**Figure 9.5** 2010 US suicide rate by age. Notice the trends in this graph. Why might suicide rates dip after middle age, but rise again during age 70 and beyond? *Source*: CDC WISQARS (http://webappa.cdc.gov/sasweb/ncipc/mortrate10_us.html). Note that the age-adjusted (for the year 2000) suicide rate is used.

then continues to increase until the late 40s and early 50s, when it peaks at around 20. It falls after mid-life, and increases again through old age.

During the most recent 10-year period of data available, suicide among adults aged 35–64 increased between 1999 and 2010. A number of explanations have been offered to account for this trend. This could be because suicide prevention tends to focus on youth and the elderly, but largely ignores adults. Recent research indicates the increase may be due to cohort or period effects (Phillips *et al.*, 2010). A **cohort** is *a group of people who share something in common*, like an age range. Baby boomers are an example of a cohort because they were born during a particular time and shared similar experiences growing up. Researchers found that people in this age range had higher suicide rates than other groups when they were younger, so seeing higher suicide rates among this cohort makes sense. However, the increase also may be due to **period effects**, which means *something historical happened* – like the latest recession. Whatever the reason, researchers will be monitoring the suicide trends among various age groups because suicide rates tend to increase in old age. If the increase is, in fact, due to a cohort effect, then we might expect to see a spike in suicide among older age groups as baby boomers age.

## Box 9.1    In their own words

### Effects of suicide on family members*

I've had debilitating stress for nine years now, since the suicide of my father. He did so in my home, while my children were there. I couldn't take it. See, he was a schizophrenic, recently divorced by my mother when she found out he was cheating on her. Being mentally unstable, no one else in my family wanted to care for him. I found it funny that I ended up being the one to take him in, the one that as a child wasn't so golden as my sister was, or anyone else in my family.

I remember that day telling my father that I was going to be out of town for a couple of days and he would have to stay with the kids. He did not like the idea of being left alone, of me not being there. As I told him that I was going food shopping with the kids for the week ahead he looked at me and said, "if you leave me alone, watch what's going to happen". I didn't think anything of it; he was a schizophrenic, scared of anything and everything. When I returned, my eldest daughter, age 11, ran in to find my father hanging by the stairs. She ran out telling me that he was dead, with a smile – I'm guessing that it was an irrational smile because fear was in her eyes. I told her not to kid that way. I tried to pull him up from the straps he had created, but it was too late; he was gone.

I am currently diagnosed with bipolar disorder, which causes irrational stress. On any given day, I can wake up and feel extremely determined, ready to take on God if he came down to test me; hours later I can feel completely alone, and sadness and worthlessness overcomes me, as if I could never accomplish anything. I was able to handle everything prior to my father's death.

I tried a lot of medications to help: Ability, Clonazepam, Depakote, Valium, Zoloft. I tried them all. Some will make me forget the stress I had with never letting go of my father's death. I always felt guilty about that, still do, especially by the fact that I let my children be subjected to seeing that. But like a bad habit, the sadness and depression will only fade for a couple of hours; it couldn't be dropped. I would abuse these drugs to the point where I didn't care how my children viewed me. I stopped working and collected welfare, and every day became a drag. I wanted to vanish and not live anymore.

With the economical strain, I began to sell the prescribed drugs to the neighbor-hood drug addicts and dealers. After some time my doctor switched me from drug to drug, each with a different effect to my emotions. One in particular made me feel the type of rage that no one should ever be subjected to. I became violent towards my family members, threats were made, and verbal abuse was proposed by me to everyone around me. I even vandalized law enforcement patrol cars to the point where I was in combat with officials physically. Here I was a 32-year-old woman making deviant acts a teenager would do. Every day I was hospitalized I grew with more shame, but I couldn't deny what I have now become. A person who is mentally broken. The anger is still there.

---

*Virlen Reyes conducted this interview.
Suicide affects family members, friends, and the community surrounding the decedent. What effects did her father's suicide have on this woman?

## Physician-Assisted Suicide

*Physician-assisted suicide* (PAS), also referred to as **euthanasia**, is a topic of debate in the United States. PAS occurs when a doctor provides patients, typically those dying painfully, with drugs to end their own lives. Some terminally ill patients want to die to avoid suffering. However, physician assistance in doing so violates medical ethics – namely, the Hippocratic Oath to do no harm and preserve life. Outside of the medical profession, some believe people have the "right to die", while others disagree, believing it is a sin or a slippery slope to legalized killings of socially undesirable groups. Public opinion favoring PAS has waxed and waned over the years, but approval has been steadily rising. The General Social Survey shows that the public favors euthanasia ("When a person has a disease that cannot be cured, do you think doctors should be allowed by law to end the patient's life by some painless means if the patient and his family request it?") more than suicide ("Do you think a person has the right to end his or her own life if this person has an incurable disease?"; Duncan and Parmelee, 2006). Public approval of both euthanasia and suicide peaked during the 1990s (70% approval of euthanasia and 62% approval of suicide) and recently has slightly decreased to 1980s levels (Duncan and Parmelee, 2006). In short, the majority of Americans generally approve of one's right to die. In fact, four states have legalized PAS: Montana, Oregon, Vermont, and Washington (ProCon.org, 2013).

The media may have played a role in bringing attention to PAS. Two major figures have emerged over the past few decades, re-igniting the debate. "Doctor Death," Jack Kevorkian, was a Michigan doctor who helped at least 45 people end their own lives during the 1990s (Dowbiggin, 2013). He provided drugs and a contraption he called "Mercitron" so that the patient could administer the drugs him or herself. Kevorkian was tried and acquitted three times, and a fourth indictment resulted in a mistrial. He was eventually convicted of second-degree murder after he publicly killed a 52-year-old man, Thomas Youk, who was suffering from Lou Gehrig's Disease; the death was aired in 1998 on CBS's *60 Minutes* (Dowbiggin, 2013). Kevorkian was sentenced to

"Doctor Death" Jack Kevorkian. PAS supporters claim the practice allows people to die with dignity and alleviates suffering of dying patients. Opponents argue it is akin to murder and it violates medical ethics. Where do you stand on this issue? *Source*: © WENN Ltd/Alamy

10 years in prison. Although he is probably the most popular, Kevorkian was not the first doctor to be tried for a mercy killing. In 1950, Dr. Hermann Sander was indicted – and acquitted – for killing his 59-year-old patient who was dying of cancer (Dowbiggin, 2013). And, the debate over euthanasia did not end with Kevorkian's death in 2011.

Terri Schindler Schiavo, a Florida woman, became a popular figure in the media. In 1990, Schiavo had a heart attack at age 27 and fell into a coma; she remained in a vegetative state, requiring constant care and surviving through feeding tubes (Dowbiggin, 2013). After eight years, her husband sought court approval to have the feeding tube removed, her parents objected, and a public political debate ensued. At one point, the US Congress intervened, but, ultimately, the feeding tube was removed and the courts refused to intervene to reconnect it (Dowbiggin, 2013). Schiavo passed away in 2005.

Both Kevorkian and the Schiavo case galvanized public support on both sides of the issue. While information on how many physician-assisted suicides actually occur in the United States would be impossible to collect, researchers have asked doctors how often they have been accused of PAS. In one sample, more than half of the hospice doctors surveyed said a patient's family or another doctor had viewed his or her actions as murder, and four percent were formally investigated even though they had not intended to accelerate the patient's death (Goldstein *et al.*, 2012). Perhaps for some, a fine line exists between providing medication to alleviate suffering of terminal patients and actively dosing a terminal patient to hasten death. A similar fuzzy boundary exists in another form of suicide: "suicide by cop".

# Suicide-by-Cop

At the outset of the chapter, we described the definitional issues surrounding suicide. One type of suicide that is exceptionally difficult to identify is *law enforcement-forced-assisted suicide*, typically called "**suicide-by-cop**". The main reason for this definitional ambiguity is because the decedent did not physically take his or her own life; instead, the person engaged in dangerous behaviors in the presence of law enforcement, prompting police to respond with deadly force. Typically, when someone directly causes the death of another, the act is called homicide. But, when someone with suicidal intent uses an officer as the "lethal agent", the event can be classified as suicide (Neitzel and Gill, 2011). This characteristic makes suicide-by-cop a unique type of suicide.

Criteria necessary for an officer-involved shooting to be considered suicide-by-cop include:

1  Evidence of the individual's suicidal intent.
2  Evidence that [the decedent] specifically wanted police officers to shoot [him/her].
3  Evidence that [the decedent] possessed a lethal weapon or what appeared to be a lethal weapon.
4  Evidence that [the decedent] intentionally escalated the encounter and provoked officers to shoot (Neitzel and Gill, 2011, p. 1657).
5  Law enforcement officers were required to shoot in the given situation (Neitzel and Gill, 2011:1659).

The last criterion, the legal requirement for the police to take action, is what distinguishes suicide-by-cop from assisted suicide (Neitzel and Gill, 2011). Without that last requirement, the death would be considered a homicide, not a suicide (Neitzel and Gill, 2011). That requirement also is what makes suicide-by-cop an especially dangerous situation for anyone nearby, especially officers. The person must engage in behaviors that threaten the lives of others to provoke the police to take action. An example of a suicide-by-cop incident in New York City is the case of a 43-year-old man. He:

> … had a history of bipolar illness with recent depression and suicidal ideation. A few years prior, he had waved and pointed a pellet gun and knife at people passing by on the street. When police arrived, the decedent told them he wanted to die. Police were able to talk him into dropping the weapons, and he was placed in a psychiatric hospital for 4 months. The decedent had been making suicidal comments in the months preceding his death. He was upset over his medical condition…. He drove to his former work location and threw a rock through his ex-manager's car window. Employees observed him holding a handgun, get back into his car, and drive away. Police were called, and the decedent led them on a high-speed pursuit. The decedent stopped his car, exited the vehicle, and pointed the handgun at police provoking them to fire at him multiple times. Postmortem toxicologic analysis detected no ethanol or drugs of abuse (Neitzel and Gill, 2011:1658).

The case above meets each of the criteria of suicide-by-cop. The man was suicidal and had been for some time. At an earlier encounter, he told police he wanted to die. He had a gun and pointed it at the officers, forcing them to take action.

**Box 9.2** In their own words

Attempted suicide-by-cop

*Officer Lisa was on routine patrol in a small town around 2 am when she noticed a car parked in an empty parking lot.*

As I approached the driver's door and looked through the window, I noticed a man sleeping inside, with a gun on his lap in his left hand. I immediately called for backup – which would be coming from another jurisdiction. But, if he woke up, that would be an especially dangerous situation for me. So, I opened the door and took the gun from him. It was so light weight, I realized it was a fake gun. I called dispatch to tell backup to slow down. As I took the gun I saw a knife on the passenger seat, along with a small cooler containing open alcohol cans and bottles of liquor. I could see something written on the gun, but didn't have time to read it because the guy woke up. He immediately reached down in his lap for the gun but it wasn't there. He reached towards the passenger seat as I was pulling him from the vehicle. Once outside, he started resisting arrest by pulling away, pushing me, and not listening to my commands. At that point, I pulled out my taser and fired. Nothing. One of the taser pins must have hit the zipper of the man's jacket.

He began pulling the wires out and yelling "Shoot me! Kill me!" He then came towards me as I was trying to load another round in the taser. I don't remember whether the man knocked the taser from my hand or I threw it to draw my gun. Either way, I was able to secure the taser in its holster and continued to try to keep my distance from the guy, ordering him to the ground. But he wouldn't listen and kept coming towards me. Even though I was probably legally justified to shoot him and the man was asking me to, I didn't feel I should shoot the guy. So, I put my gun away and pulled out my asp baton.

I gave more commands, but he still wouldn't listen and continued to come towards me. We were all over the parking lot. I hit the guy with the asp baton in the arms and one of the strikes took him to the ground. I got on top to try to handcuff the guy. He was crying, so I thought he was giving up because I broke his collar bone. Once I got on top to handcuff him, though, he pushed me off and the fight was on again. He became more aggressive. He started throwing punches and grabbing for items on my duty belt. I continued to strike him and, at that point, used deadly force by striking him in the head with the baton. The strikes were not stopping him! During the struggle I fell on the ground on my back and the guy was on top of me. I continued to swing the asp baton. The man punched me in the side of the face, ripped my badge off my shirt and tore buttons from my shirt. Just then, he fell off of me. As I looked up, I saw another officer holding a taser.

Luckily, my backup didn't slow down, as I suggested, and another officer arrived just in time as the man and I were fighting on the ground. The other officer thought the situation sounded suspicious, so he decided to check on his fellow officer, even though I called off backup. The backup officer said he saw the man throwing punches and grabbing me.

The entire incident took about six minutes. After it was all over, I discovered that the man had been planning to kill himself that night. He drove drunk all over town in hopes that an officer would try to stop him, he would engage in a high-speed chase to get everyone's adrenaline pumping and commit suicide-by-cop. When that failed, he passed out in the empty parking lot, where I found him. When the man was in custody, my backup officer and I went back to his car. We read the writing on the toy gun, "not cops fault, I wanted to die, good shoot".

How many elements of the suicide-by-cop criteria do you notice in this incident? What effects might suicide-by-cop have on officers?

**Table 9.2**  Comparing suicide-by-cop incidents in movies to reality.

|  | *Movies (%)* | *Reality (%)* |
| --- | --- | --- |
| Previously attempted suicide | 0 | 35 |
| Chronically depressed | 6 | 47 |
| Recently killed someone | 77 | 7 |

*Source*: Stack *et al.* (2012)

The idea of "victim-precipitated" death originated with Marvin Wolfgang in the 1950s. Based on his homicide research in Philadelphia, Wolfgang coined the term "victim-precipitated homicide" to refer to patterns of behavior that make victimization more likely. This concept, though, can be applied to the relatively new concept of suicide-by-cop, as people who are suicidal provoke the police to shoot them (Klinger, 2001). Research generally indicates that those who are more likely to attempt suicide-by-cop are men, Whites, people in their 20s or 30s, and those with a history of suicide attempts (Lord, 2012), although, of course, others also may use the police to end their lives. The media present a different story. Suicide-by-cop incidents are typically glorified in movies, but are unrealistic. Analyzing 16 American movies, researchers found that suicide-by-cop incidents are portrayed as delivering justice to a murderous person (Stack *et al.*, 2012). For example, in the movie *Se7en* (starring Kevin Spacey, Morgan Freeman, and Brad Pitt), Kevin Spacey (a serial killer) provokes Brad Pitt (a police officer) to kill him by having the head of Pitt's wife (played by Gwyneth Paltrow) delivered to him. Table 9.2 highlights the main differences between movies and reality.

As more departments are using less-than-lethal technology like Tasers, future suicide-by-cop incidents may become less successful. For example, one study comparing suicide-by-cop situations that used less-than-lethal technology with those suicide-by-cop incidents that did not use such technology found that the suspect survived in almost half of the former situations, but only about 11% did in the latter incidents (Homant and Kennedy, 2000). The survival rate for other types of suicide is much lower, like in suicide terrorism.

## Suicide Terrorism

Another type of suicide is suicide terrorism. **Terrorism** can be defined as "*the threatened or actual use of illegal force and violence to attain a political, economic, religious or social goal through fear, coercion or intimidation*" (LaFree and Dugan, 2007:184). **Suicide terrorism** is a *terrorist* *attack where the perpetrator is willing to die* to ensure the attack is successful, making it one of the most frightening forms of terrorism. Although the media often refer to this phenomenon as suicide bombing, such attacks can be carried out using any weapon. The perpetrator being present until the actual attack makes suicide terrorism much more destructive than other methods of attack, it signals to the victims that retaliation or deterrence is futile because the perpetrator already is willing to die (what more could the victims do?), and the attack itself sends the message that future attacks are likely because, again, the perpetrator is willing to die – violating norms of violence (Pape, 2005:29).

Suicide terrorism may seem like something new to Americans, but it has been around for centuries. You may have heard of the term, assassin. The Assassins were an extension of a Shia Muslim group called the Ismailis, existing between 1090 and 1275 AD (Burgess, 2003; Gearson, 2002). Their name meant "hashish eater" because of their ritual drug use before a mission (Burgess, 2003). The Assassins attacked in public during the day, and their weapon of choice was a dagger, which meant they had to come into close contact with their victims and signaled their willingness to die (Burgess, 2003).

Drawing from Durkheim's work, political scientist Robert A. Pape (2005) points out that we generally categorize suicide terrorists in the egoistic typology, but many suicide terrorists actually fall into Durkheim's altruistic box. Pape (2005) argues that instead of being overly individualistic and isolated from society, suicide bombers are the opposite – totally enmeshed in the social group for whom they believe they are fighting. They are excessively integrated into society, and they commit suicide terrorism out of a sense of duty.

To support his argument, one of the examples that Pape offers is Al-Qaeda. While Islamists are split on the morality of suicide terrorism, before his death Osama bin Laden and Al-Qaeda's fight against the United States' presence in the region had a great deal of popular support in Middle Eastern countries. Al-Qaeda is embedded into society, sponsoring many social service agencies and providing charity to Muslims around the world. Pape points out that, "Al-Qaeda's discourse on martyrdom emphasizes the altruistic motives and instru-mental value of self-sacrifice to liberate the local community from U.S. occupation" (p. 196). Specifically, Osama bin Laden identified America as an occupying nation focused on destroying Islam, al-Zawahiri (then Al-Qaeda's "second in command") framed Al-Qaeda as freedom fighters against a much stronger enemy and this inferiority required self-sacrifice to minimize casualties and maximize damage, and the self-sacrifice works to coerce the enemy (Pape, 2005:197). According to Pape (2005), then, those who commit suicide terror-ism may not necessarily be suicidal, but are willing to be heroes or martyrs for their community.

# Self-Harm

People who engage in self-harm probably would say that this section does not belong in a chapter on suicide because they are not suicidal (Brown and Kimball, 2013). But the two behaviors have something in common: they are intentionally self-inflicted. Similar to suicidal behaviors, **self-harm** involves "*the intentional harming of one's body in order to reduce* *emotional pain and cope with overwhelming emotions*" (Brown and Kimball, 2013:195). Self-harm can be:

- Cutting
- Burning
- Punching oneself
- Banging one's head
- Pulling one's hair out
- Constantly scratching oneself
- Picking scabs or interfering with wound healing
- Breaking bones (Brown and Kimball, 2013:195)

Self-harm is different from extreme tattooing and self-mutilation, like people who amputate body parts and scarify for beautification and/or other reasons. These topics will be covered in Chapter 10.

Self-harm perhaps is more prevalent than people realize. According to the Centers for Disease Control and Prevention (2012), self-inflicted injuries accounted for 487,700 emergency room visits across the country in 2011. In one study, 15% of the sample of adolescents reported harming themselves (Laye-Gindhu and Schonert-Reichl, 2005), although the proportion of people who engage in self-harm varies by age and gender (Bakken and Gunter, 2012; Barrocas *et al.*, 2012). Self-harm is widespread enough to attract a large audience in cyberspace. There are several social media sites devoted to the topic, with members posting graphic photos, song lyrics, and detailed descriptions of cutting and other harmful behaviors. The popular blogging site, Tumblr, imposed a ban on blogging about self-harm, but an estimated 200,000 bloggers still use language relating to self-harm (Dewey, 2013).

Girls are more likely than boys to deliberately harm themselves (Bakken and Gunter, 2012; Barrocas *et al.*, 2012). There also is a gender difference in the methods of self-harm. Girls tend to engage in cutting, while boys typically hit themselves (Barrocas *et al.*, 2012). And, self-harmful behaviors have been found in children as young as seven years old (Barrocas *et al.*, 2012). Those who engage in self-harm are more likely to have experienced victimization, being bullied, and substance use (Bakken and Gunter, 2012).

People who self-harm see it as a way to deal with overwhelming emotions. One person described it like this: "It's typically something that is more of a way to deal with temporary emotion, it's almost like saying, 'Okay you know, this is just too much for me right now,' almost like 'oh my headache is getting bad, I've gotta take a pill.' That was my pill whenever my emotions got too bad" (Brown and Kimball, 2013:201).

Another person who engaged in cutting behaviors explained:

You just want to match an emotional pain with a physical. And at that moment when you're cutting, it doesn't hurt, but it's something physical to see, to touch. It's tangible. You can see the impurity of the blood … It's matching those two emotions because you can't verbalize or show people how much you're hurting inside, so you do something else to show them (Brown and Kimball, 2013:202)

Many people who engage in self-harm find cyber communities a safe place to share their feelings among supportive people. The Washington Post reported the story of one teenager who used Tumblr to express herself:

> A pretty, articulate high school teenager who loves books and the boy band One Direction, Anouschka nevertheless struggled to fit in at school, where classmates called her fat or left her off their party invite lists. At home, she fights often with her parents and fumbles through sessions with the therapist she has been seeing since her father first noticed the cuts on her arms. Before Tumblr, she could tell no one about her depression – but on her blog, she found a like-minded audience of 1,700.

> "It's just that everyone feels the same. I know they're not going to judge me for self-harming," she said. "It's nice to know that you can tell your story without being judged." (Dewey, 2013)

While social media can serve as a support system, it can also perpetuate the self-harming behaviors by spreading misinformation and convincing people that this form of deviance is, in fact, normal. To help people develop skills necessary to stop this behavior, advocacy groups have pressured social media websites like Tumblr and Facebook to ban content about self-harm. Pinterest also has posted a broad policy banning the promotion of many harmful behaviors:

> You agree not to post User Content that:

> – Creates a risk of harm, loss, physical or mental injury, emotional distress, death, disability, disfigurement, or physical or mental illness to yourself, to any other person, or to any animal ("Pinterest bans content", 2012).

In the meantime, they also have started blogging positive messages with hashtags like #cutting (Dewey, 2013).

---

### Box 9.3   Resources

If you are in crisis or you know someone who is hurting, *please* contact these FREE resources.

| Resource | Phone number | Website |
| --- | --- | --- |
| National Suicide Prevention Lifeline | 1-800-273-8255 | http://www. suicidepreventionlifeline.org/ |
| Contact: From breaking point to turning point | (972) 233-2233 | http://contactcrisisline.org/ |
| Crisis Call Center | 1-800-273-8255 OR Text ANSWER to 839863 | http://crisiscallcenter.org/ crisisservices.html |
| The Trevor Project (for LBGTQQ youth) | 1-866-488-7386 OR Text the word "Trevor" to 1-202-304-1200 | http://www.thetrevorproject.org/ |
| Veterans Crisis Line | 1-800-273-8255 and Press 1 OR Text 838255 | http://veteranscrisisline.net/ |

## Suicide and the Media

Suicide is prevalent in the media. In particular, it is a common theme in music lyrics. Some claim that sad, depressing songs can actually encourage people to take their own lives. In the early 1900s, Bucharest banned from the radio a song – Gloomy Sunday – that was so sad it was linked to 18 suicides (Science Channel, 2012).

> Sunday is gloomy, my hours are slumberless.
> Dearest, the shadows I live with are numberless.
> Little white flowers will never awaken you,
> Not where the black coach of sorrow has taken you.
> Angels have no thought of ever returning you.
> Would they be angry if I thought of joining you?
> Gloomy Sunday (Stack *et al.*, 2007).

Several reports emerged that the song was playing during the suicide attempt or the decedent had the song lyrics nearby at the time of the suicide (Stack *et al.*, 2007).

Suicidal language in music is not limited to the past; it remains a relatively common theme throughout many genres of music today. The song, *Sail*, by AWOLNATION has this verse:

*Maybe I should cry for help | Maybe I should kill myself (myself) | Blame it on my A.D.D. baby.*

Rihanna has a song entitled *Suicide*, with lyrics:

*Loving you is suicide | and it's getting harder everyday. | I'm tryna to keep myself alive | knowing there's a chance it's all too late. | And I'm way past every moment | but I'm still determined to fight | and I know it's taking all my strength | to give emotions alive. | Loving you is suicide.*

Heavy metal songs, like Metallica's *Fade to Black* and Ozzy Osbourne's *Suicide Solution* also focus on suicide and have been linked to actual suicides (Stack *et al.*, 2007).

Music may not necessarily cause a suicide. Instead, people who are depressed and at risk for suicide may be drawn to such sad music. Stack and colleagues explain the role of musical subcultures on suicide:

Through the promotion of cultural symbols and artifacts including concerts, clothing, distinctive hairstyles, and albums, musical subcultures pull like-minded persons together. They provide institutional supports for interaction and the reinforcement of subcultural values and behaviors" (p. 354).

## Summary

Similar to other types of deviance we discuss in this book, suicide is difficult to define and to identify, and classifying a suspicious death as a suicide can be political. Nevertheless, researchers have attempted to study suicide from a sociological perspective. Durkheim explained suicide through social integration and social regulation: risk of suicide is low when there is equilibrium, but suicide risk is high when either social integration or social regulation is excessively low or excessively high. Based on this idea, Durkheim identified four types of suicide: egoistic, altruistic, anomic, and fatalistic.

In the United States, suicide varies by sex, race, and age, with men, Whites, and middle-aged people committing suicide more often than other groups. An ongoing debate involving suicide is the legalization of physician-assisted suicide, with four states allowing it. Those who plan to commit suicide also may attempt suicide-by-cop, compelling police to use deadly force and act as the lethal agent for the suicidal person. On the other side of the spectrum is suicide terrorism; these perpetrators may not even be suicidal, but are willing to be martyrs for their communities – falling into Durkheim's altruistic category. Another group whose members often claim they are not suicidal even though they engage in suicidal behaviors involves people who self-harm. The jury still is out on whether the media – including social media – have a protective effect or increase the risk for self-harm and suicidal behaviors.

## Outcomes Assessment

1  Define suicide.
2  Explain how suicide is socially constructed.
3  Describe Durkheim's typology of suicide.
4  Identify patterns of suicide in the United States.
5  Define euthanasia and identify the arguments on both sides of the legalization debate.
6  Describe suicide by cop.
7  Explain the history of suicide terrorism and apply Durkheim's typology to suicide terrorism.
8  Describe the relationship between the media and self-harm.

## Key Terms and Concepts

altruistic suicide
anomic suicide
cohort
ecological fallacy
egoistic suicide

euthanasia
fatalistic suicide
gender paradox
period effects
self-harm

suicide
suicide-by-cop
suicide terrorism
terrorism

# 10

# Beyond the Range of Tolerance

## *Extreme Deviance*

---

**Student Learning Outcomes**

After reading this chapter students will be able to:

1   Define extreme deviance and list some specific examples.
2   Explain how tattooing and scarification can be considered extreme deviance.
3   Discuss some examples of what may be considered extreme sports.
4   Define survivalism and explain why it is viewed as a form of extreme deviance.
5   Summarize how the media portrays and shapes public perceptions and contributes to the social construction of extreme deviance.

---

*The first tattoo was nothing really. James simply scratched his initials into the skin of his left forearm with an old phonograph needle and dabbed a few drops of India ink into the fresh wound. It wasn't exactly fine art, but James was pleased at how straight he had made the lines and how smooth the curve of the letters appeared. That tattoo, done at age sixteen, was almost imperceptible now, however, as James sports "full-sleeves" on both arms, tattoos up and down both legs, a full back tattoo, over a dozen tattoos on his chest and neck, and two facial tattoos. The tattooing had gotten boring long ago, however. It was the piercing that became more interesting: first, the ears, then the nose, and later multiple piercings of the lips and eyebrows. Piercing both nipples seemed like the logical next step, but it took a lot more courage to pierce the scrotum and head of his penis. James thought he was done at that point, but when he first read about the practice of **penile sub incision**, slicing the penis*

*Deviance & Deviants: A Sociological Approach*, First Edition. William E. Thompson and Jennifer C. Gibbs.
© 2017 John Wiley & Sons, Inc. Published 2017 by John Wiley & Sons, Inc.
Companion website: www.wiley.com/go/thompson

*from the urethra opening down to the base for aesthetic purposes or sexual pleasure,
he knew that he would have to do it – and he finally did. At first the "surgery" was a bit
frightening. He had never used a scalpel before, and although he had injected some lidocaine
a friend had "obtained" for him from a dental supplier, his genitals were not completely
numb when he began the incision. That was part of the thrill, however. The pain, the blood,
the not knowing, the risk of infection – those were all part of why he did things like that.
Only a few people seem to understand the satisfaction that James experiences by tattooing,
scarring, and mutilating his body, but that doesn't matter. James enjoys the pain, but more
importantly, he enjoys the results. People look at him differently. He is unique. James loves
being different.*

As we have discovered to this point, to some extent, being different is sometimes what being
deviant is all about. Also, however, as we have learned over the previous chapters, things are not
necessarily what they seem, and being deviant is much *more* than simply being different. Tattoos,
body modification, scarring, and other forms of risk-taking behavior do not necessarily make a
person deviant. In this chapter we take a look at extreme forms of these behaviors that constitute
what many sociologists call **extreme deviance**, *beliefs, behaviors, and activities that go well
beyond the range of tolerance and often result in serious social sanctions*. It is especially important
in this chapter to be mindful of the important sociological concept, range of tolerance, that we
introduced in Chapter 1 and have applied throughout this book. Many forms of extreme
deviance start with what might be considered just unusual or different, yet generally accepted
behavior, but progresses into what a substantial number of members of society would consider
being beyond the range of tolerance and therefore an extreme violation of acceptable norms. In
this chapter we explore actions and behaviors that in and of themselves may seem to be widely
accepted if performed or practiced in moderation. Emphasizing the social construction of
deviance we will look at *what* constitutes extreme deviance, *who* are some of the people that
engage in it, *how* they do it, and try to pose some explanations for *why* they engage in these
behaviors that many members of society view as being extreme.

## Body Modification and Mutilation

With the abundance of tattoos and piercings sported today by college students, their professors,
and any variety of people in other professions and walks of life, many students might wonder
why these topics are included in a book on deviance. After reading about James, however, you
can see that we are not talking about a simple tattoo or pierced earlobes. What started out as
fairly routine or harmless **body modification** – *any alteration of the body*, escalated into what
many people would consider constituting **body mutilation,** or *extremely bizarre alteration of the
body,* and possibly even frightening and dangerous deviant behavior. In this chapter, we are
talking about extreme behaviors that violate social folkways, if not mores (as well as some laws),
and cause people to be labeled deviant as well as viewed negatively by other members of society
and agents of social control. Also, in addition to norm violation, many activities that comprise
extreme deviance contain an element of risk-taking behavior that could prove dangerous for the
deviant and possibly even for others.

## Extreme tattooing

Nobody is completely certain when humans began tattooing or scarring their bodies, but some of the first written references to body tattoos refer to the practice as being first used and popularized among various ethnic groups in the regions of what is today China and Japan as well as among many of the island cultures of Polynesia, Samoa, Tahiti, and others (DeMello, 2000). In many cultures, tattoos or scarification were and are associated with rites of passage from childhood to adulthood or have other symbolic meanings related to a person's status in his or her society. Around the western world, sailors were among the first to embrace tattoos, seemingly because they traveled to those parts of the world where they were exposed to them. In the United States, tattoos became associated with lower status individuals such as enlisted military personnel, and certain categories of deviants including prostitutes, prison inmates, and members of certain drug subcultures (DeMello, 2000). Despite the loveable cartoon character, *Popeye the Sailor Man* sporting a tattoo of an anchor on his forearm, a poignant scene in the 1982 motion picture, *An Officer and a Gentleman*, depicted Richard Gere's character, the son of an alcoholic Navy Chief being required to cover a tattoo on his upper arm, because it was unacceptable for him to have a visible tattoo as a Naval Aviation Officer candidate. Up until 2003 in the United States, only enlisted personnel and non-commissioned officers in the Navy were allowed to sport visible tattoos, and even after that time, tattoos were generally frowned upon by the upper echelons. In 2006, the US Navy issued a press release spelling out its policies on tattoos, body art, and piercings, making clear that Navy policy, "prohibits any body art deemed prejudicial to good order, discipline and morale or of a nature to bring discredit upon the naval service" (Houlihan, 2006:1). In less bureaucratic language, the message is clear: *no extreme tattoos, body art, or piercings.*

By the 1970s, the American youth subculture began to embrace tattooing, and today, in the United States, and many other parts of the world, tattooing has become somewhat mainstream. Some high school students go with their parents to get "family" tattoos, and college students tattoo everything from sorority and fraternity letters to ancient Chinese symbols on their arms, legs, backs, shoulders, ankles, and buttocks. Popular toy maker, Mattel, even created a controversial tattooed *Barbie* doll, and another toy maker, Fisher Price, made a toy tattoo machine replete with stencils and non-toxic, water-based, temporary "ink" recommended for children ages six and up. Both males and females, young and old, lower and upper classes, seem to have embraced body art to some extent. It is not unusual to walk across a university campus and see multiple "half sleeves" (tattoos from shoulder to elbow), "full sleeves" (tattoos covering the entire arm shoulder to wrist), as well as highly visible tattoos on necks and even occasionally one might spot a facial tattoo, although that is much less common, and may be considered an example of when a tattoo progresses from being "okay" to being "extreme." Although many professional boxers and wrestlers sport highly visible tattoos, heavyweight champion Mike Tyson was one of the first to get a prominent tattoo on his face. The extremeness of this type of tattoo was exemplified by the media when Ed Helm's character (Stu) in the popular 2011 film, *The Hangover Part II*, woke up the morning before his wedding after a drug-induced stupor with the identical facial tattoo as the famous prize fighter. While the facial tattoo might seem less extreme and bizarre on Mike Tyson, who makes a cameo appearance in the movie, it is clearly extreme for Stu's conservative persona as a dentist, and is met with great dissatisfaction from his bride-to-be and her family, especially her ultra-conservative father. This scene, clearly

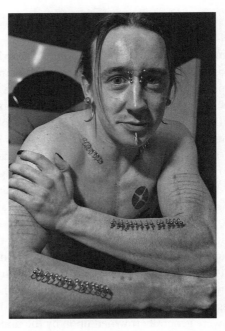

Scarification is considered a sacred ritual in some cultures and deviant behavior in others. What other types of body modifications are considered to be the norm in some cultures and extreme deviance in others? *Source:* © STR News/Reuters

aimed at comic value, nevertheless depicts what we have discussed all along in this book that deviance, and in this case extreme deviance, is socially constructed and defined largely in terms of the act, the actor, and the audience, as well as time, place, and situation.

Some people may consider tattooing as a form of scarification, but **scarification** usually refers to *body modification that involves scratching, cutting, burning, branding, or otherwise permanently scarring the body*. Scarring has been a cultural tradition in many societies for centuries, especially smaller tribal societies, for aesthetic purposes, religious symbols, and to denote important rites of passage from one social status to another (Haviland, *et al.*, 2010).

**Branding** is a popular *form of scarification that usually involves heating a piece of metal and burning the impression into the skin*. Occasionally, an extremely cold object (often cooled by liquid nitrogen) can be used to make a brand, but because of more difficulty in acquiring and handling liquid nitrogen than fire, this method is less commonly used. The results, however, are often the same with a permanent impression (scar) being left on the skin after the burn (or freezing) heals. In the United States, branding has most often been associated with visually proclaiming ownership over livestock, and in earlier times, slaves, but today is more likely to be done for aesthetic purposes or to denote commitment to a particular cause, religion, or organization. Branding, like cutting, can sometimes be erratic or unpredictable, as precise designs are hard to establish since people react differently to cuts and burns, the healing process is somewhat unpredictable, and there are always risks of infection, or other complications.

Cutting of the skin for aesthetic or symbolic purposes is a form of scarification and should not be confused with the type of cutting discussed in Chapter 9 which is done in order to inflict self-harm or pain. In **ritualistic cutting**, *designs may be carved into the face, arms, torso, or legs for cosmetic purposes or to denote social statuses.* In some cases these cuts may be rubbed with ink or some other staining agent, such as juice from plants or berries, and may resemble a tattoo. In other cases, the cuts may be rubbed with dirt, ashes, small pebbles or other objects placed under the skin in order to create a raised effect and more three dimensional design. Generally, when a person gets accidentally cut or if a physician or surgeon intentionally cuts on an individual, every effort is made to prevent or minimize scarring. In contrast when people are cutting themselves for the purpose of scarification, the exact opposite is true as sometimes great pains are taken (literally and figuratively) to exacerbate the healing process in order to build up more scar tissue and make the scarring more pronounced.

## Surgery, implants, and amputation

For some people who are into extreme deviance, tattooing, simple cutting, and scarring is not enough. One of the more extreme ways to modify the body is to perform surgery, implant foreign objects under the skin, or amputate a part of the body. Voluntary plastic surgery for treatment of burns, restorative purposes, reconstruction, or even aesthetic purposes such as facelifts and breast augmentation has been acceptable in western culture for quite some time, and are not considered to be deviant, much less examples of extreme deviance. What we are discussing in this section, however, is a more extreme form of plastic surgery strictly for aesthetic purposes and often for shock value. People sometimes have horns implanted sub dermally on their foreheads, while others practice what they call pearling or beading, where small disks, round discs, or other objects are placed under the skin, sometimes on the arms or legs, and often on the genitals, for decoration. Many African tribes elongate the earlobes, lips, or the neck for cultural purposes, a practice that some young adults in western culture have also undertaken more for shock value than any cultural significance. Other forms of body modification or mutilation can include splitting the tongue (to resemble a snake's tongue), nipple splitting or removal, removal of the labia, eyeball tattooing, scrotal implants, and penile sub incision, which was described earlier in the chapter.

**Amputation**, *the surgical removal of a body part*, is most often considered to be a last resort medical effort to relieve unbearable pain or halt infection in order to save a person's life. Amputation has also been used in some cultures, however, as punishment for certain crimes, as a form of torture, or as a tactic in war or terrorism. Today, in the United States, a segment of the population practices self-amputation, or sometimes pay others to amputate body parts, usually fingers or toes, but sometimes arms or legs, as a form of extreme body modification. Amputation requires a certain amount of knowledge of anatomy and physiology, as well as some medical tools, and carries far more medical risks than some of the previously discussed forms of body modification or mutilation. Whereas self-tattooing or body piercing may carry risks of infection and the possible contraction of hepatitis, licensed tattoo shops today are fairly well regulated and great efforts are taken by reputable tattoo artists to sterilize equipment and prevent any contraction or spread of blood borne pathogens. More risks are involved, however, when some shops offer amputation services to their clients. While states are beginning to pass laws prohibiting tattoo and piercing businesses from amputating body parts, laws regarding self-injury and self-amputation are either non-existent or ambiguous in many states, so the practice is often dealt with more as a form of mental illness than as a crime (Favazza, 1996).

Mental health officials contend that people who want to radically modify their bodies, especially by surgery or amputation, suffer from **BIID**, *body integrity identity disorder*. BIID can include a wide array of practices including some of the surgeries already mentioned, especially, **apotemnophilia** *a strong desire to amputate a healthy limb*. In some states, licensed tattoo parlors not only provide tattooing and body piercing, but are also willing to amputate fingers, toes, or other body parts for an additional charge. As mentioned, many states do not have any laws against self-amputation or voluntary amputation, but lawmakers in those states generally have hurriedly enacted statutes making such amputations illegal, usually citing medical and other public health concerns as the justification for such laws. Nevertheless, the Internet is full of websites that provide step-by-step instructions and even videos showing everything from elongating earlobes to amputating one's own finger, toe, arm, or leg. If you are interested in discovering more forms of body modification and mutilation, you can use any major search engine to explore this aspect of extreme deviance on the Internet. Be forewarned, however, that you may be shocked by what you discover. There is a reason why many of these forms of behavior are considered to be "extreme deviance."

## Suspension

A form of extreme deviance that is perhaps less shocking than modification, mutilation, or amputation, but nevertheless beyond the realm of many people's range of tolerance, or in some cases, even comprehension, is the practice of suspension. **Suspension** involves *suspending a human body in the air from metal hooks placed in various parts of the body*. Acts of suspension may be done in private or at public events such as carnivals, motorcycle rallies, sporting events, or any venue where crowds may gather to witness unusual or nonconforming/deviant activities. As with most acts of body modification or mutilation this activity is not for the squeamish and requires a certain amount of knowledge about anatomy and physiology as well as physics. The number and size of hooks used, the location where they are placed, and the amount of time a person is suspended all require careful calculations based on body height, weight, skin density and texture, and what type of apparatus is used to lift and suspend the body, as well as whether once suspended, the person will remain stationary or swing around in the air (see Box 10.1).

> **Box 10.1**   In their own words
>
> "Hooked" on suspension
>
> One of the authors witnessed several people being suspended at a large motorcycle rally. All of the "performers" were male and appeared to be in their early 20s to mid-30s, and although most of them were relatively small and lean in size, one of them

was approximately six feet tall and weighed well over 250 pounds. It was announced to the audience that this was his first time to be suspended in public and the audience was instructed to provide encouragement, which they did by maintaining complete silence while he was "hooked up" and for several minutes until he was lifted approximately five or six feet in the air, and then the crowd burst into thunderous applause, cheered, whistled, and otherwise showed approval. Another of the people suspended was an obvious veteran of the activity and once lifted approximately twenty feet into the air by a large crane with a block and tackle type apparatus, he began to sway back and forth, and then swung around in large circles almost as if an acrobat. The crowd applauded and cheered loudly and he waved his arms and smiled broadly to show his appreciation. The author spoke with him later and asked a few basic questions about how he got started, why he does it, and the most obvious: does it hurt?

**SUSPENSION ARTIST**\*:    The key is to take your mind off of what is happening to your body. For me, it's a transcendental thing. I mean, it's almost as if I go into a trance. When I first started, I would meditate for thirty minutes or more to get in the proper state of mind before inserting any of the hooks. After a while, I could get into that state of mind in half that time. Now, I can almost go there immediately. It's a mind over matter thing. I simply go to that peaceful place. I hardly even feel the hooks being inserted. To me, being suspended up in the air is a literal high. I can't imagine any better feeling. I feel free. It's like I'm floating in space, yet I'm in total control. I can't really explain it.

**AUTHOR**:    How did you get started doing this? Was it a gradual thing, or did you just jump right into it?

**SUSPENSION ARTIST**:    Well, as you can see (gesturing to his face and body), I've been into tattooing and piercing for quite some time. That's how it started. After I got bored with tattoos, I first had my ear lobes pierced and then the tops of my ears. Next, it was eyelids and nose, and then I did my nipples. I get a strange sensation out of feeling a needle go into my body. It's not like it's erotic or anything, but it's a rush. Then, I met this guy who invited me over to this big garage where guys were inserting huge needles and stainless steel hooks into their chests and backs. I guess one thing kind of led to another. Those guys taught me how to meditate – how to take my mind to another place – and how to not exactly ignore the pain, but to embrace it. I gotta admit that the first few times were a bit dicey. But, once I got the hang of it (he laughed at this) – no pun intended – I really started to dig it. I guess you could say I'm hooked – pun intended. It's a great feeling. I feel really empowered somehow. You should really try it some time.

---

\* The author asked the young man what he called himself and others who suspended themselves from hooks. He thought a minute and said, "Well, we usually just call each other by name, but since I'm a tattoo artist, I guess I also am a suspension artist."

As with most of the other forms of body modification discussed in this chapter, suspension also carries with it a certain amount of health risks. Not only are there risks of infection, but even a tiny miscalculation of weight, pressure, or some other variable could cause a large chunk of flesh to be ripped from the body and lead to a fall from a substantial height that could result in injury or possibly even death. Although people who practice body modification, scarification, and other forms of deviance may cite aesthetic reasons or simply individual choice as their motivation, no doubt, part of the attraction of extreme deviance is the shock value it has on other people who do not participate in it. Another important factor also may involve the risks involved in extreme behavior. Whereas many people avoid risk-taking behavior at all costs, others find taking unnecessary risks provide an adrenaline rush and an exciting break from the monotony of their routine daily activities and lifestyles.

## Edgework, Risk-Taking Behavior, and Extreme Sports

Some psychologists and other behavioral scientists contend that certain people have personality types that predispose them to take unnecessary risks, while other people's personalities cause them to avoid risks as much as possible (Heimer, 1988). Sociologist, James Short (1984), however, pointed out that limiting risk analysis to personality types is a purely psychological approach to what obviously is a sociological phenomenon. For example, even a rudimentary sociological analysis of risk indicates that in any given society at any particular time a certain amount of risk-taking behavior is normative and not only acceptable, but expected. Moreover, it can be argued from a structural functionalist perspective that taking some risks can be not only functional for an individual but also for society, and from an interactionism viewpoint, defining risks and risk-taking is very relative to time, place, situation, and individual. Sociologist, Stephen Lyng (1990, 2005) expanded upon the problem of psychological reductionism in studying risk-taking behavior insisting that more insight could be wrought by using an alternative social psychological framework that conceptualizes the causes of high-risk behavior in terms of more general sociological variables rather than focusing on idiosyncratic motives or personality types. Instead, Lyng (1990:855) introduced the sociological concept of **edgework** as "*negotiating the boundary between chaos and order,*" or skirting the *edge between danger and safety* to describe voluntary participation in high-risk occupations or leisure activities. Borrowing somewhat from the experience and writings of "Gonzo-journalist" Hunter S. Thompson who engaged in a wide variety of risk-taking adventures as the theme for his articles and books, Lyng applied systematic social scientific research skills to describe and analyze edgework from a sociological perspective. Since risk-taking is both a cultural concept and a relative phenomenon, it follows that people who have dangerous occupations such as police officers, fire fighters, or people who work at extreme heights or under extreme conditions, may view dangerous leisure activities as less risky than what they do every day for a living (Douglas, 1992). For example, a motorcycle officer is likely to see riding a motorcycle to and from work or to a biker rally on weekends as a fairly safe activity compared to some of the situations he faces while riding a bike on the job. As a result, a motorcycle officer also may be somewhat reluctant to ride a motorcycle for "fun," since it is what he or she does for work. Instead, motorcycle riding as a leisure activity, which statistics show can be quite dangerous, seems to appeal more to accountants, teachers, lawyers, and other white-collar professionals who perform jobs that most people consider to be relatively safe (Thompson, 2012). In fact, a common characteristic, according to research on edgework, is that people who are most attracted to edgework during their leisure time often have full-time jobs that involve fairly routine, mundane, and physically unchallenging activities (Cockerham, 2006; Lyng, 2005). An example of edgework or risk-taking behavior that has received a considerable amount of sociological attention is participation in what may be categorized as *extreme sports*.

## Extreme sports

Anybody who has ever watched the Olympic games knows that sports enjoy great popularity in most countries around the world, and even a rudimentary knowledge of American culture indicates that sports are a major part of the social and cultural fabric of the United States. Generally, when Americans talk about sports they are referring to athletic competitions such as football, basketball, baseball, soccer (what the rest of the world calls football), tennis, golf, or one of the other many athletic activities available for participation by anyone from the ages of 5 to 105. The fundamentals of many of those sports are taught in elementary school, and most high schools and colleges sponsor teams, and if good enough, there is the potential for a small percentage of people to turn them in to very lucrative careers. In this chapter, however, we are focusing on sports that are considered to be less in the mainstream, and because of the risks and dangers involved, many people may even consider participants as being deviant for being involved in them. We are talking about **extreme sports**, *activities that involve a high level of danger and pose risks of severe injury or death.* Often, but not always, extreme sports involve high speeds, extreme heights, and/or extreme physical exertion. One thing they all have in common is that they are physically challenging and even the simplest mistake could lead to severe injuries or possibly even death. Skydiving, scuba diving, mountain climbing, hang gliding, wing suit flying, ski jumping (and some say downhill skiing), motorcycle jumping or racing (and some contend just motorcycle riding), as well as auto racing can all be considered examples of extreme sports. Some people also refer to these activities as *thrill sports*.

One of the first systematic social scientific studies of an extreme sport was a five-year ethnographic field study of skydivers (Lyng and Snow, 1986). That study concluded that one of the significant motivations for pursuing such a dangerous pastime was the very fact that it was indeed dangerous. The thrill of jumping from a perfectly good airplane while knowing the inherent risks provided an adrenaline rush and a feeling that skydivers rarely experienced in other aspects of their lives. Moreover, there was a sense of satisfaction and accomplishment in knowing that training, practice, and the application of learned skills and techniques allowed them to overcome much of the potential danger involved in such an activity. The exhilaration of feeling on the *edge,* in some cases literally being in a life or death situation, and being able to conquer the fear, meet the challenge, and "come out on top," was a common theme expressed by many of the jumpers. Further research on skydiving and base jumping (parachuting from a fixed object such as a building, tower, or mountain top) utilized what was called an "extended dramatic model" to explain both macro-level social and cultural explanations such as media portrayals, technological developments, and cultural values as well as micro-level interpersonal and intrapersonal influences such as holding a dramatic worldview or cathartic effects to explain interest and participation in high risk activities (Celsi *et al.*, 1993). For those who have never tried it, there may be the misconception that skydivers are fearless, willing to risk their lives every time they jump from a plane with no thoughts, fear, or reservations. Research on skydivers finds just the opposite, however, as even the most seasoned and experienced jumpers typically report feeling a significant degree of anxiousness and fear prior to each jump (Lyng, 1990). So, what allays that fear and provides them with the confidence to go ahead and jump? Again, research indicates that as the jumpers begin final preparation before stepping out of the plane, they tend to go through a mental checklist assuring themselves that the chute is packed correctly, all buckles and straps are in place and secure, and as they recall their training and past successful experiences, the "fear gives way to a sense of exhilaration and omnipotence" (Lyng 1990:860).

Scuba divers often report similar feelings as skydivers in terms of conquering fear, relying on training, and experiencing a sense of accomplishment along with the thrill and exhilaration associated with diving (Brylske, 2012). That feeling of accomplishment leads to an increased sense of self-worth, and can have psychosocial benefits for individuals suffering from lack of self-assurance and self-esteem associated with physical disabilities or other possibly stigmatizing or socially limiting consequences (Carin-Levy and Jones, 2007).

Mountain climbing may represent one of the most exotic and challenging forms of the extreme sports. Although few people actually do it, many people dream of conquering Mt. Everest or some other well-known peak. Little children often play a game where an individual runs up a small hill or climbs up on top of some object and declares himself/herself to be, "King of the Mountain." Challengers may then attempt to scale the same height and "dethrone" the king. The popular 2007 movie *Bucket List* starring Jack Nicholson and Morgan Freeman not only included climbing a mountain as one of the things Freeman's character wanted him and Nicholson's characters to do before they died, but also his desire to be buried at the summit of one of the highest peaks of the Himalayas. Perhaps one of the most oft-quoted motivations for mountain climbing is the purported answer: "Because it's there" when a mountain climber is asked why he/she climbs, and as simple and perhaps trite as that may sound, indeed many mountain climbers do see the mere challenge of a mountain being there as being reason enough to climb it. Richard Mitchell (1983) offers a more sophisticated social psychological explanation, however, as he notes the sense of accomplishment associated with conquering nature, and to some extent gravity, through careful preparation, physical training, and perseverance. Moreover, there is a sense of purity and tranquility experienced at a mountain top that may be like no other, unless one has experienced jumping out of an airplane at ten thousand feet or diving to the bottom of the sea.

The thrill, adrenaline rush, and exhilaration associated with extreme sports are perhaps easier for non-participants to understand than the tranquility or so-called cathartic effect described by many who are involved in such risk-taking behaviors. In an ethnographic study of modern American motorcycling, one of the authors of this text repeatedly heard motorcyclists talk about "being in the zone" (Thompson, 2012:172–174). Every seasoned motorcyclist has experienced the Zen-like qualities and almost out-of-body experience that causes a rider to feel almost as if he or she is floating, hovering above the motorcycle looking down as the bike seems perfectly still while the pavement below flies by at unbelievable speed. Riders must be very careful not to get lulled into a false sense of security or become mesmerized or hypnotized by this feeling as all their senses and their reflexes must remain on full alert looking for objects or debris in the road, oncoming or passing vehicles, wild critters who suddenly dart in front of them, or a myriad of other possible hazards that may arise in a split second.

If motorcycle riding for fun and pleasure is not exciting or thrilling enough, there is a group of riders who call themselves "stunters." They take motorcycling from a leisure-time activity to an extreme sport for sure. Stunters ride specially modified sport bikes, often referred to as "crotch rockets" because of their quickness, maneuverability, and speed. As if riding a motorcycle is not dangerous enough in and of itself, these stunters, as the name implies, perform tricks or stunts on their bikes, sometimes in controlled areas such as parking lots, or at motorcycle shows or rallies, and sometimes on the streets and open highways at daring speeds among traffic. Stunters are usually males in their late teens to late twenties or early thirties, but some females engage in the sport as well, and a few daring riders perform stunts into their fifties or sixties. Probably one of the most famous stunters in American history was Robert Craig "Evel"

This stunter typically draws a few appreciative spectators when he practices his motorcycle stunts in a vacant parking lot as he is in this photo. How do you think people respond, however, when he performs these stunts on a city street where there is other traffic present? *Source*: Authors

Knievel who performed daring motorcycle tricks and jumps from the mid-1960s to the early 1980s including his most famous jump, an unsuccessful attempt to soar over Snake River Canyon in a rocket-powered motorcycle. Knievel, who was inducted into the Motorcycle Hall of Fame in 1999, was entered in the *Guinness Book of World Records* for holding the record of, "most broken bones in a lifetime" (Guinness World Records, 2013).

There is an old adage among motorcyclists that there are *old* riders and there are *bold* riders, but there are no *old bold* riders. Evel Knievel may have been an exception to that adage as was a 54-year-old stunter one of the authors interviewed (see Box 10.2). It is incredible to watch stunters perform tricks on motorcycles that the vast majority of people would have some difficulty just riding, much less performing stunts on them. Most of the riders use 650 cc or 750 cc Japanese bikes with special clutches, remote throttle controls, and other customizations that allow them to control the motorcycle while sitting backwards, standing, or otherwise riding in some unusual position. They usually take a sledge hammer and beat a large indentation in the fuel tank so they can sit or stand on the tank with less chance of sliding off and crashing the bike. Watching stunters is a lot like watching younger children playing on their tricycles or bicycles. It usually starts off somewhat subdued, but as they continue to ride, they continually push their limits, challenge each other, and challenge themselves, taking more and more risks. After each stunter "performs," his or her (stunting is mostly a male phenomenon) peers cheer him/her on, comment on various maneuvers, and give a general critique of the ride. As with other forms of extreme sports, it seems that stunting combines danger with excitement, exhilaration, and a sense of accomplishment.

---

**Box 10.2    In their own words**

"I'm not happy unless I'm in fear for my life"

"Johnny" is a 54-year-old self-described "adrenaline junkie" who started out riding dirt bikes as a child and has ridden street bikes (mostly high-performance sport bikes often referred to as "crotch rockets") ever since. For about the last ten years, he has been a stunter. When the author first interviewed him they had met at a fast food restaurant having been introduced by a mutual friend. The second interview took place in a large parking lot in an industrial area where Jimmy and six of his friends, ranging in age from 19 to 31, were performing stunts on specially customized sports bikes.

**AUTHOR:** So, how does a 54-year-old guy get started doing dangerous stunts on a motorcycle?

**JOHNNY:** (Grinning) Well, I didn't start at age 54. I've been doing it for about ten years now, so I was only about 44 when I got started.

**AUTHOR:** Okay, so, how does a 44-year-old guy get started doing dangerous stunts on a motorcycle?

**JOHNNY:** (Grinning even more) Stupidity, I guess. (Then, being more serious). I started like most riders. When I was a kid, I started out riding dirt bikes popping wheelies, jumping over ditches, going up and down hills, and crashing into rocks, stumps, and whatever else got in the way. After you fall off a motorcycle a couple of dozen times and realize you're still in one piece and can get up and do it all over again, you lose your fear of getting hurt or wrecking the bike. Once I got old enough to ride on the streets I got my license and started riding crotch rockets – the faster the better. I didn't really start doing stunts until about ten years ago, but I was always poppin' wheelies, jumping things, and taking chances I guess from the very beginning. Then, I met some guys that called themselves "stuntas" and I was amazed at the stuff they could do on a bike. I had to try it. One thing led to another, and now it's what I do every chance I get. Rain, shine, hot, cold, you can stunt in any weather.

**AUTHOR:** So, are you one of those guys that I see going down the interstate at a hundred miles an hour riding the center line on one wheel?

**JOHNNY:** (laughs) Well, I have been that guy, yes. But, no, that's not what we do. The guys I ride with do our stunts in parking lots mostly – some place away from traffic where if anybody gets hurt, it's just us. We don't want to put anybody else in danger. We've also put on a couple of shows for some kids' groups.

**AUTHOR:** I've ridden motorcycles for quite some time now, and what you do seems incredibly dangerous. Just how dangerous is it?

**JOHNNY:** It probably looks more dangerous than what it is. I mean it's dangerous at first and when you don't know what you're doing, but we practice, practice, practice. And, we take every precaution we can to make it safe. We wear helmets, neck and back braces, and all the rest of the protective gear. A lot of the stuff we do is pretty routine to us. But, of course, that's when we start to get bored with it, so we always try to push to the next level. If it wasn't dangerous, we probably wouldn't do it. Every stunter I know has broken a few ribs, their collarbone, and suffered a few other injuries here and there, but I only know one or two that were injured severely enough to have to give it up. (Then after a short pause he added) And there was Jeff. He went over the front of the bike, broke his neck, and cracked his skull. He died a few days later.

**AUTHOR:** You're 54, you don't do this professionally, and it's somewhat expensive to maintain the bikes and equipment. What's in this for you? Why do you do it?

**JOHNNY:** I wish I had a dollar for every time I had been asked that question. I would be rich. Most people just don't understand. It's the challenge. It's the rush you get from standing a 500 pound bike on its nose and then putting it back on the back tire and doing a 360. There's no feeling like knowing that one wrong move and you could be on your way to the hospital, but when you do it right, you've done something that very few other people can do. Getting the most out of your bike and out of yourself is a great feeling. I guess that's why I do it. In some ways I guess I'm not happy unless I'm in fear for my life.

There are numerous other examples of extreme sports, but those we have discussed in this chapter, skydiving, scuba diving, as well as motorcycle riding and stunting, serve to illustrate risk-taking leisure activities that may be considered to be deviant by those who do not participate in them and wonder why anybody would enjoy them. It may be more understandable that police officers, fire fighters, or others engaged in dangerous occupations might also be inclined to be involved in risk-taking leisure activities or extreme sports, and indeed some of the participants in extreme sports also have risky or dangerous jobs. Lyng (2005:6), contends however, that extreme sports and other types of edgework and risk-taking appeal most to individuals with very safe and routinized occupations, noting that according to, "the 'weekend warrior' thesis … participants in [risk-taking] activities are seen as seeking a temporary escape from the stultifying conditions of work life and bureaucratic institutions." Regardless of the type of risk-taking behavior engaged in, research consistently indicates that in addition to the excitement and thrill associated with it, participants report a sense of self-realization, self-actualization, and self-determination (Lyng, 1990; 2005).

## Extreme Lifestyles

Some people engage in extreme behaviors not as part of their occupations or as leisure-time activities, but as a fundamental way of life. **Extreme lifestyle** refers to *an unconventional way of living that violates cultural values and norms and is considered deviant and possibly even dangerous by members of mainstream society.* Unlike many forms of deviant behavior which may be intermittent or attributed to one or more values and behaviors that contradict mainstream culture, unconventional lifestyles create deviant identities by choice, and permeate virtually all of a person's life activities, marking them for the social consequences associated with a deviant master status (Bryant and Forsyth, 2012). The people who participate in the extreme sports we discussed in the last section may be considered by some people to have extreme lifestyles, but for the most part, other than the one leisure activity considered extreme in which they are involved, the rest of their lives are fairly normative. There are people, however, who live unconventional and seemingly extreme lifestyles in regard to their everyday ongoing activities. One example is people who live what they usually call a life of *minimalism.*

### Minimalism

Western culture, and particularly the United States, has become a land of excess. Americans pride themselves on being one of the largest countries in the world (albeit there are several other countries with more land mass as well as many others with more population), having one of the largest standing militaries (that may be true depending on how calculated), and being one of the wealthiest nations on earth (again, there are countries wealthier by almost any way of calculating, but the US is probably in the top ten percent of nations in total wealth and wealth per capita). Fast food restaurants offer "biggie" sizes of food and drinks, sports teams are continually building larger stadiums, various buildings vie for the distinction of being the tallest, and there is even an American expression "living large" to describe all the advantages and benefits of having wealth and prosperity. Sociologist Thorsten Veblen (1899) coined the term *conspicuous consumption* in the nineteenth century to describe consumers' desire to express their social standing by acquiring goods and services simply for the purposes of having, displaying, and consuming them. The United States is indeed a materialistic country that embraces and promotes materialistic values and in many ways could be described as a country that thrives on conspicuous consumption. Counter those values with people who live a lifestyle based on **minimalism**, *the practice of living a simple, uncluttered, non-materialistic life.*

At first glance, minimalism may not seem to be deviant, much less extreme deviance, but may sound attractive and admirable as a way of living. Imagine a lifestyle unencumbered by things. A simple hand-made house just large enough to meet your minimal living space needs, only enough material possessions to meet your basic needs – no luxury items, nothing that is not necessary for survival and minimum creature comforts. No worries about mounting bills, cluttered closets, over-filled garage, or any other needless things to get in your way, only the bare minimum necessities in relation to food, clothing, and shelter. Sound appealing? For many it is. For others, while it may sound desirable, living a life of minimalism is beyond their range of tolerance and too extreme for them to maintain. Conversely, contrast that philosophy and lifestyle to the excess materialistic values that are part of most capitalist countries and are deeply ingrained in American culture. Also remember that deviance is not a synonym for bad – it simply means non-conformity. In the words of two of the minimalist movement's main promoters, minimalism is a form of deviant behavior and considered by many to constitute an extreme lifestyle. As one book on minimalism states: "Conformity is the drug with which many people self-medicate" (Milburn and Nicodemus, 2012:1).

One example of minimalism as an extreme lifestyle can be found in the person of Jonathan McGowan of the United Kingdom who has lived the past 30 years by almost exclusively eating road kill (Huffington Post, 2013). Arthur Boyt takes minimalism a step further by not only eating a diet mainly of road kill, but also living in almost total isolation in an area of the United Kingdom known as Bodmin Moor (Banks-Smith, 2008). His small home is hand-built out of mostly scavenged materials, and Arthur, known to many as "the scavenger," insists that it does not bother him at all that others view his lifestyle as extreme and deviant, indicating that he has no desire to conform to society's norms. Both McGowan and Boyt are taxidermists by trade and believe that their knowledge of skinning and preserving animals as well as their concern about people killing animals for pleasure and food led them to retrieving and eating road kill which does not necessitate intentionally killing an animal for food. Although neither consider eating road kill as being particularly deviant, they understand society's apprehension about their unusual eating habits, but attribute their motivation more to environmentalism, conservatism, and concern about animals being needlessly tortured and slaughtered merely for human consumption (Banks-Smith, 2008; Huffington Post, 2013).

A different example of what might be considered extreme deviance, perhaps less potentially nauseating than eating road kill, but still quite deviant from mainstream culture, can be found in Mark Boyle, who decided to live an entire year in capitalist Ireland without money (Boyle, 2010). Boyle, who earned a degree in business, founded the online *Freeconomy Community* which advocates minimalist living with as few manmade and nonorganic materials as possible. His moneyless year gained both positive and negative attention from the media, and inspired others to emulate his minimalist lifestyle. Boyle was so satisfied after one year that he decided to maintain the moneyless minimalist living and has continued that lifestyle up to the time of this writing.

Minimalism and "moneyless" living may seem near impossible in the land of excess known as the United States, but numerous websites, blogs, and other informal and formal organizations advocate and promote the minimalist lifestyle. While there are a multitude of ways to cut back on much of the material excess of what is considered typical American lifestyle, more people in the United States are striving to increase their material wealth and possessions than attempting to minimize them. Nevertheless, despite being regarded as deviant, minimalists insist that being unencumbered with material possessions, and living with less, translates into living a better life and having more (Sherwood, 2014).

Another form of extreme deviance in terms of lifestyle can be found among people in the United States who contend that it does not matter whether you are living a life of extreme excess or minimalism, it all is coming to an end soon. These apocalyptic thinkers go by a variety of names, but are commonly referred to as *survivalists*, or *doomsday preppers*.

## Survivalism and doomsday preppers

**Survivalism** is *a social movement of groups and individuals who are actively preparing for the end of civilization* as we know it. There is no uniform role for survivalists. Some believe that it is only a matter of time before some type of natural disaster strikes such as hurricane, flood, earthquake, or meteor crash that will knock out power and utilities and require people to be able to survive on their own for at least a brief, and perhaps an extended period of time. These survivalists tend to learn emergency first aid, store water and stockpile food, and build shelters that they believe will withstand the storm, flood, or whatever other disaster might be experienced.

Another category of survivalists foresee the possibility of famine, plagues, severe climate change, or other combinations of natural and/or manmade disasters that might bring about dire circumstances for which the vast majority of earth's inhabitants are unprepared. They fear that mutated viruses, contaminated water supplies, and a host of other things that could cause global pandemics could end up killing as much as half or more of the world's populations, with only those in the remotest areas along with those with the most honed foraging and survival skills being able to continue to exist. As events such as the Ebola outbreak of 2014, and other scenarios unfold, many doomsday preppers and other survivalists immediately interpret them as proof that their predictions and lifestyles are valid.

Other survivalists have even gloomier (if that is possible) predictions involving political revolutions, government takeovers, nuclear attacks, or acts of terrorism that will render national, state, and local governments as powerless (or possibly even the source of the attack), believing that it ultimately will come down to every person for himself/herself in an ultimate battle for survival of the fittest. These survivalists not only stockpile food and water, but also weapons and ammunitions. Many have bought acres of land in rural America where they have set booby traps around the perimeter, built underground shelters and caves, and otherwise prepared for the inevitable apocalypse. Books, magazines, websites, and other resources abound providing survival guides for everything from building shelters and purifying water to even "how to" books on "contingency cannibalism" and other more extreme deviant survival techniques (Takada, 1999; Rawles, 2009).

Survivalists are sometimes referred to as *doomsday preppers*, or just *preppers*, as a significant portion of their daily lives is spent in preparation for the gloom and doom of the coming apocalypse. The media has become fascinated with these people with numerous television specials having focused on them and even a weekly television series that is devoted to their extreme lifestyle.

# Extreme Deviance and the Media

Each and every form of extreme deviance covered in this chapter has captured widespread media attention including newspapers, magazines, television, motion pictures, and virtually every aspect of social media. There are at least three or four cable television programs that focus exclusively on tattooing. Spike TV offers a series entitled *Ink Master* in which each season seventeen tattoo artists from across the United States are invited to compete in a series of challenges judged by rock star Dave Navarro and two famous tattoo artists, Oliver Peck and Chris Nunez, with a grand prize of $100,000 in cash and the title of "Ink Master" going to the winner. *Tattoo Nightmares*, also aired on Spike TV, features three well-known tattoo artists, Jasmine Rodriguez, Big Gus, and Tommy Helm, who specialize in covering disastrous tattoo mistakes with beautiful pieces of art. A wide variety of other television series including *Inked, Tattoo Age, Tattoo Highway, LA Ink, Miami Ink, New York Ink*, and others have come and gone, with some leaving their indelible mark on viewing audiences, while others slowly faded away – much like the tattoos about which the programming was focused.

One of the more comical moments in the 2007 movie *Wild Hogs*, takes place when William H. Macy's character (Dudley) sidles up to an outlaw biker in a bar and compliments him on his tattoo asking where he got it. The biker spits back, "San Quentin," to which Macy's character responds by pulling up his sleeve and showing a brand new tattoo of the Apple logo, and says, "Got mine at the mall."

There has been less television and movie interest in scarification, surgery for aesthetic purposes, or voluntary amputation, but a few television documentary-type programs such as *60 Minutes, 20-20, National Geographic*, and *Nova* have aired segments on them. Suspension, on the other hand, has captured the attention of some filmmakers. A 1970 western entitled *A Man Called Horse*, included a scene in which an Englishman underwent a series of physical tests (tortures?) in order to prove his worthiness to a Sioux tribe. In one scene he has huge hooks placed into his chest and he is hoisted several feet off the ground where he must hang in the scorching sun throughout an entire day. Some thirty years later, an action film entitled *Ichi the Killer* (2001), features a gang leader violently torturing a rival gang member by suspending him mid-air with hooks placed in his back, legs, and arms. *Gamer*, a 2009 action film, shows a scene where the main character and his wife run through a club where several people are suspended from the ceiling by large hooks, including a woman who is suspended by large hooks inserted in the skin beneath her breasts. In 2014, independent film maker Uli Hesse released a feature-length documentary on body suspension entitled *Hooked* (Hooked, 2014).

Edgework and risk-taking behaviors, especially extreme sports were made for television. It would be impossible to list all of the television programs and motion pictures that have featured skydiving, scuba diving, mountain climbing, parasailing, NASCAR races, Indy 500 races, motorcycle enduro races, or super motocross. Thrills, spills, and action are often the name of the game for television action movies and documentary films, and extreme sports offer that and more. Perhaps one of the most anticipated media events of all time was the aforementioned attempt by Evel Knievel to jump Snake River Canyon on a rocket powered motorcycle in 1974. Millions of Americans and viewers around the world watched as he prepared and launched his rocket/motorcycle off one side of the mountain only to plunge headlong into the Snake River that lay below. Perhaps the more modern-day equivalent of that event took place in 2012, when daredevil base-jumper Felix Baumgartner attempted a record-breaking high altitude jump from space, some 23 miles above the earth's surface. Millions of mesmerized viewers watched as Baumgartner set the record for high-altitude jump, but failed to break the record for the longest free-fall as he was forced to pull his ripcord and open his parachute sooner than he had planned (Blunt, 2012).

Extreme lifestyles have also enjoyed a lot of media attention. The men who eat only road kill have been featured on several television programs, as have many of those who practice minimalism as a lifestyle. Numerous books abound, and any major search engine reveals dozens if not hundreds of media websites devoted to the phenomena. Perhaps the most popular among extreme lifestyles in the media, however, are the survivalists. The National Geographic channel developed a weekly television series entitled *Doomsday Preppers* that featured individuals, families, and groups as they prepared for almost every conceivable, and even inconceivable end of civilization scenario. These survivalists are caught up in anticipation of numerous fictional motion pictures scenarios depicted in films such as *Mad Max, The Book of Eli, The Day After, Waterworld, The Hunger Games,* and others, as well as popular television series such as *The Walking Dead, Survivors, Jericho,* and *Revolution*. If the media love deviance (and they do), they love extreme deviance even more.

## Summary

We began this chapter by defining extreme deviance and then looking at some examples of body modification and mutilation including extreme tattooing, scarification, surgery, implants, amputation, and suspension of the body by huge stainless steel hooks. That section was followed by a definition of edgework and a look at risk-taking behaviors and extreme sports such as skydiving, scuba diving, motorcycle riding, and motorcycle stunting. Then we looked at two different types of extreme lifestyles considered deviant by most of mainstream society: minimalism and survivalism. Finally, we provided a brief overview of extreme deviance and the media.

What all of the activities introduced and discussed in this chapter have in common is that they not only violate norms (which makes them deviant) but they do so by exceeding society's commonly accepted range of tolerance and becoming what most people consider to be an extreme behavior or activity. Although it may not be against the law to modify and even mutilate one's own body, it certainly is considered to be unconventional and deviant by a large segment of society. Similarly, almost everybody must take some risks in life, but most people go to great lengths to avoid danger as much as possible, therefore finding it almost inconceivable that others intentionally put themselves in harm's way for fun or relaxation. And, as usual, the media portray, embellish, admonish, and encourage any and all of those behaviors, capitalizing on people's fascination with deviance of all kinds. In the next chapter, we turn to another form of deviance that captures media attention and public fascination: street crime and delinquency.

## Outcomes Assessment

1 Define extreme deviance and give some specific examples.
2 Explain how tattooing and scarification can be extreme deviance.
3 Discuss some examples of extreme sports.
4 Define survivalism and explain why it is a form of extreme deviance.
5 Summarize how the media portrays and shapes public perceptions of extreme deviance.

## Key Terms and Concepts

amputation
apotemnophilia
BIID
body modification
body mutilation

branding
edgework
extreme deviance
extreme lifestyle
extreme sports

minimalism
penile sub incision
ritualistic cutting
survivalism
suspension

# 11

# Violence, Street Crime, and Delinquency

---

### Student Learning Outcomes

After reading this chapter students will be able to:

1  Identify sources of crime information.
2  Differentiate between myth and reality regarding crime trends.
3  List "facts" of crime.
4  Describe and evaluate the homicidal triad.
5  Define various violent and property crimes.
6  Identify the elements common to the different definitions of terrorism.
7  Discuss the role of gender and race in criminal offending and victimization.
8  Identify crimes that disproportionately affect women.
9  Explain and list rape myths.
10  Explain the relationship between crime and the media.

---

*As they were crossing the finish line of the 2013 Boston Marathon, runners and the people on the sidelines cheering them on were blown back by two explosions, about 12 seconds apart. Three people – including an eight-year-old boy – died, at least 16 people had limbs amputated and more than 260 people were injured.*

*Authorities began combing through the video footage of the marathon. They saw two suspicious men, one wearing a black baseball cap and another wearing his white hat backward. Both were carrying backpacks, and both left their backpacks in areas where the bombs*

*Deviance & Deviants: A Sociological Approach*, First Edition. William E. Thompson and Jennifer C. Gibbs.
© 2017 John Wiley & Sons, Inc. Published 2017 by John Wiley & Sons, Inc.
Companion website: www.wiley.com/go/thompson

*exploded. The two men were brothers, and authorities learned that the bulky backpacks carried the bombs, homemade in pressure cookers.*

*Three days after this April 15th terrorist attack, the suspects were identified and the man-hunt ensued. The Tsarnaev brothers discovered a Massachusetts Institute of Technology campus police officer, Sean Collier. They fatally shot him in his patrol car then unsuccessfully tried to steal his gun. Afterward, the suspects hijacked a Mercedes SUV, holding the driver hostage for over an hour. The driver was able to escape at a gas station, he called 911, and the information he gave police helped them track the suspects to Watertown, MA. When the police confronted the brothers, a shoot-out ensued. The brothers threw homemade bombs made from pressure cookers and what seemed to be pipe bombs at the police. The older brother was shot, and the police tackled him to handcuff him. Perhaps trying to hit the police and free his brother, the younger suspect escaped in the SUV, but ran over his brother, dragging him with the vehicle about 30 feet. Even though he made it through the police barricade, the suspect did not make it very far. He abandoned the car a short distance away and tried to escape on foot. He was caught later that night by a Watertown resident, who noticed a pool of blood in his boat; a shoot out ensued – covered live on every major television network throughout the world. Authorities apprehended the suspect. After a lengthy trial, Dzhokhar Tsarnaev was sentenced to death on June 24, 2015.*

In Chapter 1, we defined *crime* as a violation of criminal law, and we pointed out that all crime is deviance but not all deviance is crime. In other words, crime is one form of deviance that is codified into law. Most crimes are not as intense as this example. In fact, while the media gives much attention to extreme crimes like terrorism and violent crimes like murder, we will learn in this chapter that these crimes are very rare.

## Measuring Crime in the United States

Even though crime is rare, crime seems to be everywhere. Crime typically is the first story we hear or read in the news, prompting the common phrase, "If it bleeds, it leads." Crime mysteries, reality shows about police and corrections officers dominate television programming. All of this media attention creates a distorted picture of crime in the United States. However, there are a few sources that can describe crime reality. The first source of crime information is collected by the Federal Bureau of Investigation (FBI). The FBI collects *crimes known to the police*, called **official data**. Since the 1930s, the FBI has been compiling annual reports on *Crime in the United States* (referred to as *Uniform Crime Reports* or *UCR*) using official data. These reports focus on eight main crime categories, called "Index Crimes". There are four violent crimes: murder/non-negligent manslaughter, forcible rape, robbery, and aggravated assault; there also are four property crimes: burglary, larceny-theft, motor vehicle theft, and arson. Police departments around the country voluntarily send the FBI the number of incidents occurring in each crime category, using the FBI's definitions of crime because what constitutes a certain crime, like assault, may vary from jurisdiction to jurisdiction. One drawback to this source is that it *only* records crimes known to the police, so *an incident is not included if it does not come to the attention of the police*. In other words, official data ignore the **dark figure of crime**.

To tap into these crimes, another major source of crime information is **victimization data**, which records *how many times people have been on the receiving end of criminal incidents during some time period*, like the last six months. The main source of victimization data is the *National Crime Victimization Survey* (NCVS), collected by the *Bureau of Justice Statistics*. However, victimization data also are imperfect. People may not think an incident fits into the definition, they may be uncomfortable sharing their experiences with an interviewer, they may forget an incident or they may report an incident that occurred outside of the time frame requested. It is also possible that people sometimes report being victimized by a crime that did not occur. For example, a lost, misplaced, or discarded item might be inaccurately reported as stolen even though no theft actually took place. Even though both data sources have drawbacks, we can be confident in crime trends if they both tell the same story. Whenever possible, both sources are used to describe crime covered in this chapter.

## Violence

**Violence** is *the use of force against another person, with the intent to harm*. According to the FBI, violent crimes include murder, forcible rape, robbery, and aggravated assault. Regular viewers of the news might assume that violence is prevalent in society. While this may be true, violent crime has been steadily decreasing since the early 1990s. The FBI reports that the violent crime rate was 747.1 per 100,000 people in 1993; in 20 years, it fell almost by half to 36.79 in 2013. Additionally, violent crimes occur much less often than property crimes. In 2013, about 1.2 million violent crimes were reported to the police throughout the United States, and just under nine million property crimes were recorded. In short, violent crime is rare.

Even though it is rare, it still happens. While violent crime can happen anywhere, it tends to cluster among some social groups and in certain areas. With few exceptions, men are more likely to be both offenders and victims of violent crime. Crime tends to be a young person's game: the **age-crime curve**, depicted in Figure 11.1, illustrates that *criminal offending increases as we age, peaks in the late teens/early twenties, and declines with age*. In other words, for most offenses, younger people tend to commit crime and desist as they "age out" of crime. Crime is much more common in larger cities compared with rural and suburban areas. And, some locations tend to be **hot spots** of crime; that is, a *high concentration of crime occurs at certain locations*. With these "facts" of crime in mind, let's explore a few types of violent crime.

## Murder

If you took an informal survey of your friends, most probably would say that murder in the United States is on the rise. Above, we noted that violent crime is rare. Murder is even rarer, comprising only about one percent of all violent crimes reported to police. And, the murder rate has been *falling* for decades.

Even rarer are two types of murder that captivate the public's fascination: mass murderers and serial killers. Both involve killing multiple people (usually three or more), but the key difference is the time period during which the murders occur. A **mass murder** is the *intentional killing of at*

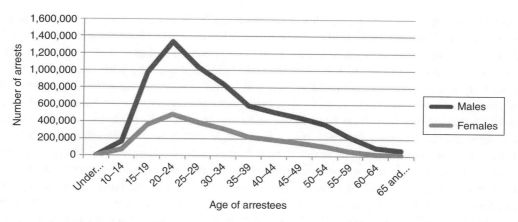

**Figure 11.1**  Age of those arrested for all crimes by gender, 2013. *Source*: FBI's Uniform Crime Reports, 2013 (FBI, 2014)

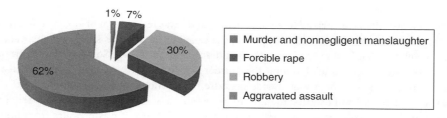

**Figure 11.2**  Proportion of violent crimes in the United States, 2013. *Source*: FBI's Uniform Crime Reports, 2013 (FBI, 2014)

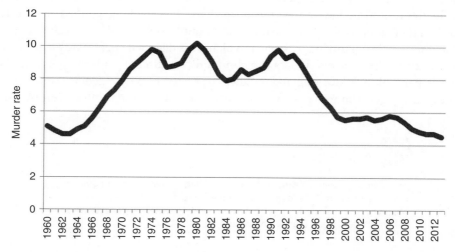

**Figure 11.3**  Trend in murder rate in the United States, 1960–2013. *Source*: FBI's Uniform Crime Reports, 2013 (FBI, 2014)

*least three people during one event*, while a **serial killing** is the *murder of more than three people over a period of time* (Fox and Levin, 2003). *Serial killers are said to have three characteristics in common*, known as the **homicidal triad**: (1) arson; (2) animal abuse; and (3) bedwetting. The homicidal triad is attributed to John MacDonald (1963), although he acknowledged there are other factors, like severe child abuse by parents and "extreme maternal seduction," that play a role in violent behavior. Research suggests that other factors may indicate murderous and other violent behavior; the homicidal triad may not be the best or only predictor of serial killing, leading to many false positives, which means that people with these characteristics may be identified as having violent tendencies when, in fact, they do not. This is only one myth surrounding this type of murder. Another is that serial killing is on the rise. Statistics indicate that murder and most other forms of violence are declining; we would expect that the same is true of types of murder. Some estimates suggest that only one percent of all homicides in the United States can be traced to serial killers (Fox and Levin, 2003). Further, we might expect serial killers to look different from us, like the killers depicted in movies and on television. However, many serial killers seem normal, having jobs, family, and friends and not all are sociopaths (Fox and Levin, 2003). For example, one serial killer interviewed by the FBI had a girlfriend and was in school:

> I had broken up with my girlfriend three days before, and I was feeling a lot of anxiety and pressure. Then the day after this [the murder] happened, she called to say she was sorry and she wanted to see me. Knowing what I'd done and everything, I didn't want to see her. So I stayed away from her for about two weeks … I didn't [commit the murder] just because I was mad at my girlfriend … There was peer pressure; there was outside pressure from school. I had been slacking off in my studies because my girl and I started to have trouble a month or so before this all happened. I felt a combination of things as far as [causing] what actually took place. It was pressure from home to bring up my grades, to get a job, etc. (Ressler *et al.*, 1988/2004:142–143).

Killers often seek notoriety for their actions. In the past, killers such as "Son of Sam" David Berkowitz would contact newspapers to tell their stories. With the advent of social media, those who commit crime have a new forum to share their exploits, confess, ask for forgiveness, explain their actions or otherwise manipulate public opinion. The "Facebook murderer", who killed his wife in Miami in 2013, tried to blame his dead wife before he posted a photo of her dead body. In this new era, killers can communicate directly with the public and do not have to risk parts of their stories being withheld or edited by news agencies concerned about sharing especially gruesome or glorifying details or about copycat crimes (Dewey, 2013).

**Derek Medina**
4 hours ago via mobile

Im going to prison or death sentence for killing my wife love you guys miss you guys takecare Facebook people you will see me in the news" my wife was punching me and I am not going to stand anymore with the abuse so I did what I did I hope u understand me "

This is a Facebook post from Miami's "Facebook Murderer", who also posted a photo of his dead wife. Social media allow killers to bypass reporters and speak directly to the public. What effects do you think this might have on criminal convictions? On copycat murders? *Source*: Dewey (2013)

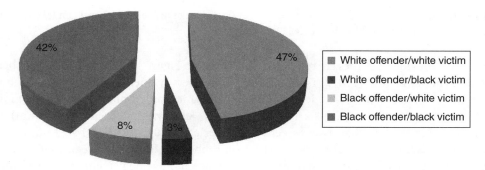

**Figure 11.4**  Homicide offenders and victims by race, 2013. *Source*: FBI's Uniform Crime Reports, 2013 (FBI, 2014)

While serial killers make excellent stories for movies and television shows, again, this type of murderer is rare. Commonly, murder occurs between two people who know one another. Of the 14,196 murders committed in 2013, only 1,281 were between strangers – that's less than 10% (FBI, 2014, Expanded Homicide Data Table 10). Most (61%) murder tends to be a man-on-man crime, meaning that most offenders and most victims are men. According to the FBI, about 26% of murder was male-on-female, with only a small portion of women killing men (7%) and other women (3%). And, murder is intra-racial; that is, Whites typically kill other Whites and Blacks usually kill other Blacks, as depicted in Figure 11.4.

## Robbery

A **robbery** occurs when *an aggravated assault and a larceny-theft occur together* (FBI, 2013). In other words, "Robbery is the completed or attempted theft, directly from a person, of property or cash by force or threat of force, with or without a weapon, and with or without injury" (Bureau of Justice Statistics, 2013). Because this crime involves violence – an assault – robbery is considered a violent crime instead of a property crime. Offenders typically use violence to secure cooperation of the victim. As one robber explained, "It's happened [that some of my victims initially refused to hand over their money, but] you would be surprised how cooperative a person will be once he's been smashed across the face with a 357 Magnum" (Wright and Decker, 1997/2006:163). To convey the threat of violence, robbers might shout, "This is a robbery, don't make it a murder!" (Wright and Decker, 1997/2006:161). What these offenders were trying to convey is that people are easier to control when they are fearful for their safety. By manipulating fear, offenders can better control the situation (Jacobs, 2013). Offenders also seek victims who are fearful, as Tall reports:

> I weren't planning on it, like I got up and said I'm going out to do this. It's just a reaction, I mean it's just something that I felt that … if somebody shows me fear at that particular time, then I'm gonna take advantage of that fear … I was actually asking [the eventual victim] for some change but when he showed me fear, well … I was really wanting change … I wasn't thinking about just grabbing him

outta his car, you know … [But then I thought,] "Why just take his change when I can take his car and get a little bit more?" (Jacobs, 2013:532)

About 30% of violent crimes are robberies (think back to Figure 11.2), with 345,031 robberies reported to police in 2013 (FBI, 2014). Most (42.5%) robbery happens on the street or highway, with some (17%) occurring in residences (FBI, 2014). While bank robbery makes great movies (like the 2010 movie, *The Town*, starring Ben Affleck, Jeremy Renner, and Jon Hamm), it is rare, accounting for less than two percent of robberies in 2013 (FBI, 2014). And, robbery tends to be concentrated in hot spots. Research on robbery in Boston between 1980 and 2008 indicated that half of all commercial robberies took place at only one percent of street segments and intersections, and two-thirds of street robberies occurred at eight percent of the locations studied (Braga *et al.*, 2011).

To threaten violence, most offenders strong arm their victims or use firearms (FBI, 2014). Knives and other weapons are used, but rarely. One offender describes the purpose of using a weapon:

> Robbery itself is an illusion. That's what it's about…. Here is a person that you stick a gun in his face, they've never died, they don't know how it feels, but the illusion of death causes them to do what you want them to do (Wright and Decker, 1997/2006:159).

Despite the threat of violence and weapon use, other factors influence victim injury. For example, robbery victims are more likely to be injured in robberies that occur at night (between 7 pm and 7 am) compared to those happening during the day (between 7 am and 7 pm), and offenders who are under the influence of drugs or alcohol are more likely to be violent toward their victims (Tillyer and Tillyer, 2012). While robberies with more offenders result in victim injury more so than robberies with fewer offenders, robberies with more victims decreased the likelihood of injury to the victims compared with robberies with fewer victims (Tillyer and Tillyer, 2012).

Some research indicates that female robbers are more likely to use violence than male offenders; female victims, on the other hand, were less likely to be injured than male victims (Tillyer and Tillyer, 2012) – perhaps because less violence is used against women as they are seen as passive victims who do not carry weapons and will not resist (Rennison and Melde, 2014). Women offenders also may act as accomplices. Women can lure potential male victims to areas easier to commit a robbery, like enticing a man to leave a nightclub so her male partners can carjack the victim (Jacobs, 2013). Big Mix explains her role in a carjacking:

> I'm hollering and screaming, crying or whatever. I mean it's just hilarious…. You just get a kick out of seeing him [the victim] screaming and hollering and get up…. Yeah, like I'm a victim too, like I don't know what's going on you know (Jacobs, 2013:536).

Women offenders, though, accounted for about 13% of robbers arrested in 2013 (FBI, 2014). Robbery tends to be a crime using dominance and masculinity (see Messerschmidt, 1993) – in other words, a male-oriented crime. For women to commit robbery, they must overcome this hurdle (Rennison and Melde, 2014). Perhaps this is why most robbery tends to be intra-sexual: male robbers tend to rob male victims (about 65% of victims of male offenders are men), while

Women comprise only 13% of those arrested for robbery (FBI, 2013), and they choose women as their victims more often than they choose men as victims. *Source*: © moodboard/Alamy

female robbers tend to rob women (about 62% of victims of female offenders are women; Rennison and Melde, 2014).

In addition to gender differences in robbery, there are differences among various racial groups. Black Americans are more likely to be victims of robbery than Whites or Asian Americans, who have about the same likelihood of robbery victimization (Wu, 2013). And, Black Americans are arrested more often than other racial groups. According to the FBI's Uniform Crime Reports, 56% of those arrested for robbery in 2013 were Black Americans, 42% were White, 1% were Asian or Pacific Islander and 0.7% were American Indian or Alaskan Native. While Black Americans are typically overrepresented in arrest statistics – meaning that a higher percentage of Black Americans are captured by the criminal justice system than are in the population – they are arrested at about the same proportion or are arrested less often than White Americans. The exception is robbery.

## Assault

**Aggravated assault** is "*an unlawful attack by one person upon another for the purpose of inflicting severe or aggravated bodily injury* [and] is usually accompanied by the use of a weapon or by other means likely to produce death or great bodily harm" (FBI, 2013). Present in many movies (think Brad Pitt and Edward Norton's 1999 movie *Fight Club*), television shows, and music themes, aggravated assault is the most common of the FBI's violent Index Crimes, with 724,149 assaults reported to the police in 2013 – a rate of 229.1 per 100,000 people (FBI, 2014). This may sound like a lot, but remember these are spread throughout the United States. A large proportion (43%) of aggravated assaults happen in Southern states; less than one quarter (23%) are reported in the West; and small proportions of aggravated assaults are reported to police in the Midwest (19%) and Northeast (15%; FBI, 2014). And, aggravated assaults are more concentrated in areas with a higher density of bars (Snowden and Pridemore, 2013).

Of the people arrested for aggravated assault in the United States in 2013, 63% were White and 34% were Black; a small percentage was American Indian or Alaskan Native (1.5%) and Asian or Pacific Islander (1.5%). Similar to most other crimes, men are more likely than women to have violent disputes. Women comprise 23% of those arrested for aggravated assault, while most (77%) of the people arrested are men (FBI, 2014). Some people claim that women and girls have become more violent because the **gender gap** – *the difference between men and women* – is closing among violent crimes. However, a closer look at the statistics shows that involvement in violent crime like aggravated assault is decreasing for both men and women. In the 10-year period between 2004 and 2013, arrests for aggravated assaults fell by 16% for men and 4% for women (FBI, 2014). Scholarly research has explained this trend: violent crime is declining, but it is falling faster for men than for women, perhaps because women engage in much less crime than men to begin with (Lauritsen *et al.*, 2009).

Like many crimes, fighting is a young person's game. About half of all persons arrested for aggravated assault are under the age of 30 (FBI, 2014). While those of retirement age sometimes resort to fisticuffs, people over age 65 make up a very small proportion of people arrested for aggravated assault: about 1% of men and less than 1% of women (FBI, 2014). On the other side of the coin, violence among young people, like those still in school, generate a strong societal reaction.

## School violence

One form of assault – and sometimes more serious violence – that has become prominent in the news during the past two decades is school violence. While fights in the school yard likely have existed since the first schools, and traditionally were a rite of passage, perhaps because of the media attention, parents, educators, the criminal justice system, and society in general are focused on safety in schools. Researchers are continuing to report that school violence has many consequences for its victims, like dropping out, and these outcomes vary by racial group (Peguero, 2011).

More severe violence, namely, school shootings, also is not a new phenomenon; a man fatally shot 16 people and wounded 31 more at the University of Texas in 1966. Most people, though, are more familiar with references to the Columbine shooting (in 1999, two students killed 12 of their peers and a teacher at Columbine High School in Colorado). Society was most appalled by the school shooting in Newtown, Connecticut in December 2012 at Sandy

Hook Elementary School, where a gunman killed 20 students and six teachers. Media tend to make the general public think that school violence is on the rise when it actually peaked in the 1992–93 school year (National Center for Education Statistics, 2013). The media also may make school-related deaths seem random and unpredictable. There is some truth to this notion; however, types of school-related deaths vary by social group and location. An analysis of school-related homicides between 1994 and 1999 found that over half of such deaths happened in urban areas characterized by poverty, where the victims and offenders were members of minority racial and ethnic groups (Kaufman *et al.*, 2012). In these incidents, the offenders and the victims tended to be male (78%) and the violence stemmed from gang disputes (Kaufman *et al.*, 2012). In contrast, the school-related homicides in rural areas involved Whites and about half were male-on-female violence (Kaufman *et al.*, 2012). In all, though, school-related deaths are rare. Of all homicides of youth ages 5–18, less than two percent have happened at school over the past two decades (Robers *etal.*, 2013), but the frequency and nature of media reporting has changed during that time (Schildkraut and Muschert, 2014).

With the increased media attention on school shootings, society's reaction to threats of school violence has changed. Earlier in this chapter, we presented a *Facebook* post confessing to a murder; in February 2013, an 18-year-old was arrested for posting what he claims was a sarcastic threat of a school shooting (Malisow, 2014). Photo in next page captures Justin Carter's Facebook threat to "shoot up a kindergarten" (Malisow, 2014). This post resulted in Carter being charged with a terroristic threat, which comes with a possible two to ten year prison sentence, and spending six months in jail where he was sexually assaulted (Malisow, 2014).

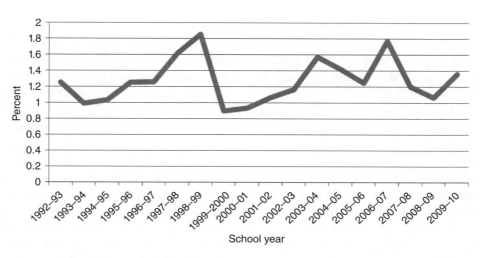

**Figure 11.5**   Percent of homicides of youth ages 5–18 occurring in school, 1992–2010. Of all homicides of youth ages 5–18, less than two percent have happened at school over the past two decades (Robers *et al.*, 2013). What might be driving fear of school shootings in America? *Source*: Robers *et al.* (2013)

How would this Facebook post be interpreted before the Sandy Hook school shooting? How would societal reaction be different – or would it? Do you think the poster would face jail time or would his friends simply ignore it? *Source*: Malisow (2014)

## Child abuse

Harming children was not always considered as serious as it is today. Perhaps your parents or grandparents talk about being chastised at school over a misdeed, having the neighbors scold them on their walk home (uphill in the snow, of course!), and receiving a physical punishment from their parents once home. Today, in many (but not all) states, being "paddled" in school by the principal likely would evoke a public outcry, calling for his or her resignation, and would be considered child abuse.

While it is not listed as a separate crime in the FBI's Uniform Crime Reports Index Crimes, child abuse is considered a serious crime. The Centers for Disease Control and Prevention (2014) writes that **child abuse** encompasses *physical, sexual, or emotional abuse or neglect by a caregiver toward a person under age 18*. Official statistics on child abuse collected by child protective service agencies claim that substantiated cases of child abuse have decreased over the past two decades; however, data collected from hospitals indicate that serious injuries of those under age 18 have increased slightly since 1997 (Leventhal and Gaither, 2012).

Severe physical abuse during childhood is associated with a host of future issues, including those relevant to this chapter – namely, criminal offending and victimization. Of course, this does not mean that everyone who has been victimized during childhood must either offend or continue to be victimized into adulthood. And, some social groups are more likely than others to have contact with child protective service agencies and to have claims of child abuse substantiated, although the relationship is complicated. For example, a study focusing on children in California initially showed that, compared to White children, Black children had twice as much contact with child protective service agencies, child abuse claims substantiated, and placement in foster care (Putnam-Horstein, 2013). However, the opposite was true when controlling for socioeconomic status: White children of lower socioeconomic status were more likely to have contact with child protective service agencies, have child abuse claims substantiated, and be placed in foster care before the age of five than Black children of lower socioeconomic status (Putnam-Horstein, 2013).

Physical violence is not the only form of child abuse. Sexual abuse of children was a prominent headline in the news media for several years, stemming from religious leaders' molestation of children in their care. While girls are more likely than boys to have their claims of sexual abuse substantiated, child sexual abuse has negative effects for children of both sexes – in other words, one sex is not more vulnerable to emotional trauma following such abuse (Maikovich-Fong and Jaffee, 2010). Perpetrators of child sexual abuse typically interpret the abusive behavior as love and claim that the victim wanted the relationship, making excuses for the offending (Lawson, 2003). For example, there are support groups for men who abuse their children. Calling themselves "**fathers' rights groups**", these groups argue that sexual *allegations against fathers are false and the penalty for the "malicious mothers" who make these claims is to give the fathers full custody of the "brainwashed" children; they typically do not advocate paying child support or spending time with children* (Rosen *et al.*, 2009).

Also harmful to victims is when child sexual offenders record the abuse, as photos and videos can be distributed. Child pornography was sold regularly with adult pornography and was legal until Congress passed legislation prohibiting sexual images of children under the age of 18 in 1978; the Supreme Court followed suit a few years later, making the sale of child pornography illegal (Bazelon, 2013). With that, producers and distributors of child pornography dwindled – until the Internet provided a forum for those attracted to child pornography to connect and share materials. One example of child sexual abuse being recorded and distributed is the case of Nicole:

Nicole's parents split up when she was a toddler, and she grew up living with her mother and stepfather and visiting her father, a former policeman, every other weekend … He started showing her child pornography when she was about nine, telling her that it was normal for fathers and daughters to "play games" like in the pictures. Soon after, he started forcing her to perform oral sex and raping her, dressing her in tight clothes and sometimes binding her with ropes. When she turned 12, she told him to stop, but he used threats and intimidation to continue the abuse for about a year. He said that if she told anyone what he'd done, everyone would hate her for letting him. He said that her mother would no longer love her …

When she was 16, Nicole told her mother … what had been going on at her father's house. Her father was arrested for child rape. The police asked Nicole whether he took pictures. She said yes, but that she didn't think he showed them to anyone. A few months later, while her father was out on bail, Nicole was using a computer he gave her ... when she came across a file with a vulgar name that she couldn't open. She showed it to her mother and stepfather, and they brought the computer to the police (Bazelon, 2013).

Facing new charges, Nicole's father fled the country and Nicole appeared on television asking the public for leads. A detective in Toronto, Canada, recognized her as the girl in the videos of a child pornography distribution case and contacted Nicole's local police. The detective told Nicole:

the pictures had been downloaded onto thousands of computers via file-sharing services around the world. They were among the most widely circulated child pornography on the Internet ... For years, investigators in the United States, Canada and Europe had been trying to identify the girl in the images (Bazelon, 2013).

Her appearance on television gave child pornography viewers Nicole's identity, and some began contacting her (Bazelon, 2013). Nicole's story is one example of a larger phenomenon of child sexual abuse. Another form of child sexual abuse is the growing industry of child sex tourism. Typically offered in poorer countries, **child sex tourism** involves *Americans traveling to foreign countries – usually poorer countries like those in Southeast Asia – to purchase children there for the travelers' sexual gratification* (United States Department of Justice, 2010). The media – especially the Internet – have been critical ingredients in the expansion of this industry, showing child sex tourists how to gain access to their victims and where to go, like the places with the least law enforcement (United States Department of Justice, 2010).

Even though violent crimes may seem prevalent because we see them so regularly in the media, property crimes actually occur much more often than violent crimes.

## Property Crimes

**Property crimes** involve *taking others' possessions without the use of force*. Four property crimes are included in the FBI's Index Crimes: burglary, larceny-theft, motor vehicle theft, and arson. While these crimes are infrequently mentioned in the news media, they are much more prevalent than violent crimes, as shown in Figure 11.6. According to the FBI (2014), property crimes cost victims about $16.6 billion in 2013.

Like violent crime, property crime has been declining since the early 1990s, from a rate of 4,660.2 property crimes per 100,000 people in 1994 to 2,730.7 per 100,000 people in 2013 (FBI, 2014). Also similar to violent crime, property crime is disproportionately committed by men, tends to follow the age-crime curve and is concentrated in hot spots – but not to the same degree as violent crime. That is, women are arrested for less than 20% of violent crimes (men are arrested in 80% of violent crimes), but women make up more than 38% of arrests for property crimes (FBI, 2014). The peak of the age-crime curve is earlier; both men and women tend to be arrested for property crime most often during their late teenage years and there are fewer arrests as people age (FBI, 2014).

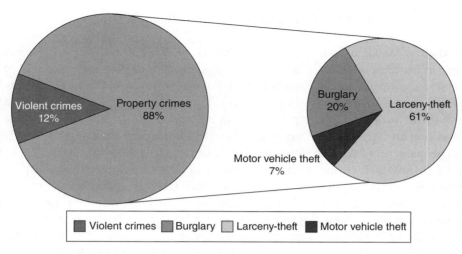

**Figure 11.6**   Percent of crime in the United States, 2013. *Source*: FBI (2014)

## Burglary

Burglary is an interesting crime. Like many jurisdictions, the FBI defines **burglary** as the *"unlawful entry of a structure to commit a felony or theft"*, where a "structure" can be an "apartment, barn, house trailer or houseboat when used as a permanent dwelling, office, railroad car (but not automobile), stable, and vessel (i.e., ship)" (FBI, 2013). Many people think that burglary requires a theft, but that is not necessarily true. For example, if Phil breaks into Jonathan's house and carries out his plan to assault him wearing, say, brass knuckles, Phil's crime may appear in the UCR statistics for burglary – even though Phil did not take anything from Jonathan. Conversely, if Phil used the brass knuckles to take something by force from Jonathan, then that might show up under the violent category of robbery. In general, the distinction between burglary and robbery is that burglaries generally do not involve a confrontation between the perpetrator and the victim, whereas robbery does. Hence, burglary is a crime against property and robbery as described earlier is a crime against person.

Less than a quarter of property crimes are burglaries. Some might be surprised to learn that the majority of burglaries of residences occur during the day rather than at night, while more of the nonresidence (like stores or offices) burglaries happen at night rather than during the day (FBI, 2013). Thinking from the offender's perspective, this makes sense – avoiding capture is easier with fewer people around! Burglars typically describe their motivation as making easy money.

According to FBI (2014) statistics, of the approximately 203,000 burglary arrests in 2013, Whites were most commonly (67.5%) arrested, followed by Blacks (30.4%). American Indian/ Alaskan Natives (1.0%) and Asian/Pacific Islanders (1.2%) made up a small percentage of those arrested for burglary. Men (82.4% of arrests) were arrested for burglary more than five times as often as women (17.6% of arrests). Almost half (45%) of the burglaries in the United States occur in states in the South.

## Larceny-theft, motor vehicle theft, and arson

**Larceny-theft** is *"the unlawful taking, carrying, leading, or riding away of property from the possession or constructive possession of another*. Examples are thefts of bicycles, motor vehicle parts and accessories, shoplifting, pocket-picking, or the stealing of any property or article that is not taken by force and violence or by fraud"* (FBI, 2013). Interestingly, almost one quarter (23.4%) of larceny-thefts involve taking property from an automobile (FBI, 2014). Most (about 70%) property crimes are larcenies. The race of those arrested for larceny-theft mirrors burglary, but the sex of people arrested is much closer together. That is, slightly more than half (57%) of those arrested for larceny-theft are men and just less than half (43%) are women (FBI, 2014).

We mentioned carjacking in our discussion of robbery. Carjacking does involve the taking of a motor vehicle, but offenders do so by confronting the victim and using force. Here, we briefly discuss trends in **motor vehicle theft** – *taking cars or other automobiles without the use of force*. This crime is the least common, comprising only 8% of property crimes (FBI, 2014). The racial distribution of those arrested for motor vehicle theft is the same as that of other property crimes. And, similar to other crimes, most (80%) people arrested for auto theft are men.

---

**Box 11.1    In their own words**

### Auto theft*

Mike was 22-years-old when he was convicted of motor-vehicle theft after stealing his car out of an impound lot.

It all started when I went into a gas station to take a shower because I was homeless. While I was inside my car got towed. I found out where it got towed to and one of my friends worked at that impound lot. He was the person that watched the lot at night and looked out for people who were going to try to break in and take their cars. He let me inside the impound lot so that I could sleep in my car overnight because I had nowhere else to sleep. The next day I drove my car out of the impound lot, which turned out to be illegal because it had been impounded by the police and was being held as criminal evidence. A felony 5 arrest warrant was put out for me and I never knew about it. Six months later I went to visit my mom because I hadn't seen her in about two years. When I got there, there were 10–12 cops and a k-9 unit searching my car. This is when I actually got caught for stealing my car out of the impound lot six months before that.

At the time, I was on drugs so I didn't really have a life. My parents had disowned me because I was on drugs and my son had just been taken away from me. I was really depressed and didn't have anyone in my life. I think I stole my car because I wasn't thinking clearly; I was so depressed and was on drugs. I was working at a Shell gas station but my boss did drugs, too, so I was never sober when I was working.

I have friends that have stolen cars before. I know someone that just went to jail because he stole someone's car while holding them at gunpoint.

I didn't think about the penalties involved at all. I thought, "it's my car; I should have it, screw all of you".

I served three years in county jail. While I was in jail I went into a coma for two weeks because I was de-toxing from being on drugs.

---

\* Rachael Bryslan conducted this interview.
What role, if any, did drugs and alcohol play here? How might drugs and alcohol factor into other crimes, too?

The other Index Crimes listed thus far have been the same since the FBI began collecting these data in the 1930s. The one exception is arson – it was added to the UCR in 1979. **Arson** is, "*any willful or malicious burning or attempting to burn, with or without intent to defraud, a dwelling house, public building, motor vehicle or aircraft, personal property of another*" (FBI, 2013). It is a crime that may span across categories – arson destroys property, but it also may involve force (FBI, 2013). The FBI, though, still includes it as a property crime. That said, arson is a difficult crime to prove, and the collection of arson data varies by law enforcement agency. So, little information is available to track the nature and trend of this crime.

## Terrorism

Because terrorism is intentional violence or the threat of violence, it is a form of crime. We discussed suicide terrorism – a specific type of terrorist attack – in Chapter 9. You may recall that terrorism has a rich history. The earliest known terrorists are the Zealots – a group whose name is the origin for the term, zealot, which means fanatical partisan (Burgess, 2003). The Zealots attacked Romans and Greeks, typically in broad daylight in public, during the first century (Burgess, 2003; Gearson, 2002). The Sicarii, an offshoot religious sect of the Zealots, operated in Palestine between 66–73 AD (Gearson, 2002). The Sicarii are known for attacking people in public during the day, similar to the Zealots, but they used a particular weapon: a sica. A sica is a short sword or dagger, and the Sicarii were known as "dagger men" (Gearson, 2002). Their victims seemed to be selected at random, but they were not – the Sicarii executed people they considered apostate, people who abandoned their religion (Gearson, 2002). They chose these methods of attack to send a message to the public: the state is ineffective; they created a great deal of fear and this led to conflict (Gearson, 2002).

Since that time, terrorism has ebbed and flowed in countries around the world. Our understanding of terrorism, though, is relatively new. One issue with terrorism, though, is its murky definition. Like other forms of deviance, we know terrorism when we see it, but it is difficult to define. In Chapter 9, we defined terrorism as, "*the threatened or actual use of illegal force and violence to attain a political, economic, religious or social goal through fear, coercion or intimidation*" (LaFree and Dugan, 2007:184). Adopting the language from 22 USC section 2656f(d)(2), the National Counterterrorism Center (2009) defines terrorism as, "premeditated, politically motivated violence perpetrated against noncombatant targets by subnational groups or clandestine agents" (p. 1) – the same definition adopted by the United States Department of State. The FBI (n.d.) considers terrorism incidents that:

> Involve violent acts or acts dangerous to human life that violate federal or state law; [and] Appear to be intended (i) to intimidate or coerce a civilian population; (ii) to influence the policy of a government by intimidation or coercion; or (iii) to affect the conduct of a government by mass destruction, assassination, or kidnapping.

According to the FBI, domestic terrorism happens when these incidents occur on US territory, and international terrorism takes place when they occur outside the US. The federal crime of terrorism, defined in 18 USC. section 2332b:

> An offense that [i]s calculated to influence or affect the conduct of government by intimidation or coercion, or to retaliate against government conduct; and [i]s a violation of one of several listed statutes, including § 930(c) (relating to killing or attempted killing during an attack on a federal facility with a dangerous weapon); and § 1114 (relating to killing or attempted killing of officers and employees of the U.S.)." (FBI, n.d.)

These definitions have similarities – like they all include illegal violence or harm and there is some group ideology – but there also are points of disagreement. Because there is little consensus on what terrorism is, scholarly research on terrorism was rare until recently.

Data sources on terrorism have been growing since September 11, 2001. Perhaps the most comprehensive dataset on terrorism is the Global Terrorism Database (GTD), housed at the National Consortium for the Study of Terrorism and Responses to Terrorism (START) at the University of Maryland, College Park. The GTD is an incident level database of terrorist events around the world since 1970. For inclusion in the GTD, an incident must satisfy three criteria:

1 The incident must be intentional – the result of a conscious calculation on the part of a perpetrator.
2 The incident must entail some level of violence (includes property violence).
3 There must be subnational perpetrators (this database does not look at state terrorism, or to phrase it more accurately, it limits itself to acts of non-state terrorism).

In addition, at least two of the following must be present:

1 The act must be aimed at attaining a political, economic, religious, or social goal …
2 There must be evidence of an intention to coerce, intimidate, or convey some other message to a larger audience(s) than the immediate victims …
3 The action must be outside the context of legitimate warfare activities. (National Consortium for the Study of Terrorism and Responses to Terrorism (START), 2012, Codebook p. 5; emphasis removed).

Like most crime, terrorism is more frequently perpetrated by men. However, women also play a role. In fact, compared to other crimes, women make up a larger proportion of terrorist offenders

(Jacques and Taylor, 2009). Some terrorist groups capitalize on recruiting women because women pose particular tactical advantages: (1) because they take on support roles and are more commonly victims, authorities often do not suspect them of terrorist activity; (2) by pretending to be pregnant, they can easily conceal bombs; (3) women who sacrifice themselves receive a great deal of media attention, which terrorist groups can use as a recruitment tool (Bloom, 2005; Cragin and Daly, 2009). Terrorism, though, seems to be uniquely gendered. You probably have heard the promise of some Islamic fundamentalist groups (like Al-Qaeda) of 40 virgins to suicide bombers upon entering the afterlife, while female suicide bombers are referred to as "brides" (Gibbs, 2012). Other crimes tend to focus on women, specifically targeting women as victims.

## Violence Against Women

While men are more frequently victimized than women, the reverse is true for some violent crimes. The victims of crimes like rape, other sexual assault and intimate partner violence are overwhelmingly female – so much so, that the World Health Organization (2013) calls violence against women "a significant public health problem, as well as a fundamental violation of women's human rights" (p. 2). In fact, the World Health Organization (2013) estimates that 35% of women worldwide have experienced these crimes. For this reason, we include this section to detail crimes targeting women.

### Rape and sexual assault

Anyone can be victimized by sexual violence. However, rape and sexual assault more commonly targets women. The National Crime Victimization Survey shows that, of the people who were physically attacked by acquaintances or strangers, the physical attack took the form of sexual violence for 5.3% of women and 0.2% of men; when people were physically attacked by a current or former spouse, boyfriend or girlfriend, the physical attack was sexual violence for 8.2% of women and 0.9% of men (Catalano, 2013). The results of the National Intimate Partner and Sexual Violence Survey, conducted by the Centers for Disease Control and Prevention (Black *et al.*, 2011), estimates that 18.3% of US women (and 1.4% of US men) have been raped, commonly by an intimate partner (51.1%) or an acquaintance (40.8%).

According to some state laws, only women can legally be victims of rape. In fact, until 2013, the FBI's Uniform Crime Report defined forcible rape as, "the carnal knowledge of a female forcibly and against her will" (FBI, 2013). Using this definition, the FBI reports that 79,770 forcible rapes came to the attention of the police in 2013 – a rate of 25.2 rapes per 100,000 women (FBI, 2014). Beginning with the crime data collected in 2013, a new definition was used:

> Penetration, no matter how slight, of the vagina or anus with any body part or object, or oral penetration by a sex organ of another person, without the consent of the victim. Attempts or assaults to commit rape are also included; however, statutory rape and incest are excluded (FBI, 2014).

According to the expanded definition, 53,621 rapes came to the attention of the police, with a rate of 39.8 rapes for every 100,000 people (FBI, 2014).

Recall the criticisms of FBI statistics from the beginning of the chapter. One drawback to using official data is the **dark figure of crime** – that is, *crimes may not come to the attention of the police or make it into official statistics, especially when people do not report crimes.* Sexual crimes against women, in particular, are vastly underreported, with over 60% of rapes and almost three-quarters of other sexual assaults not reported to police (Rennison, 2002:2). For this reason, many people also look at the National Crime Victimization Survey (NCVS) data, mentioned earlier in this chapter. The NCVS has a broader definition than the FBI, including sexual assaults against both women and men ages 12 and older. The NCVS reports 346,830 rape and sexual assaults in 2012, for a rate of 1.3 rapes and sexual assaults per 1,000 people or 130 per 100,000 people (Truman *et al.*, 2013).

## Sexual assault on campus

College students report rape and sexual assault more than any other age group. After 19-year-old Lehigh University student Jeanne Clery was raped and murdered in 1986, Congress passed legislation requiring colleges and universities to make available statistics about crimes on campus – now known as the Clery Act. According to the United States Department of Education's website, where crime information for each college and university can be found, 4,837 forcible and 74 nonforcible sexual offenses were reported to campus authorities in 2012. Like the general population, though, many rapes and sexual assaults go unreported or unacknowledged (that is, the survivor does not identify herself as a victim or does not label the assault as a crime), and these numbers underestimate the amount of rape and sexual assault on campuses in the United States – so much so, that the Obama administration has made college sexual assault a national priority.

Underrepresented groups – like gay, lesbian, bisexual students, and racial/ethnic minority students – and especially women are more likely to be raped and sexually assaulted than their counterparts (Porter and Williams, 2011). Sexual assaults on campus tend to be linked to drinking and drug use, and survivors of these crimes typically experience PTSD symptoms and depression (Hines *et al.*, 2012; Lindquist *et al.*, 2013).

## Rape myths

One reason rape and other sexual assaults may be underreported is the widespread acceptance of rape myths and fear that police and others believe these myths. **Rape myths** are mistaken victim-blaming attitudes that excuse or minimize offenders' behaviors. In other words, they are "*prejudicial, stereotyped, or false beliefs about rape, rape victims, and rapists*" (Burt 1980:217, emphasis added). Some rape myths are:

1  A woman who goes to the home or apartment of a man on their first date implies that she is willing to have sex.
2  One reason that women falsely report a rape is that they frequently have a need to call attention to themselves.

3   Any healthy woman can successfully resist a rapist if she really wants to.
4   When women go around braless or wearing short skirts and tight tops, they are just asking for trouble.
5   In the majority of rapes, the victim is promiscuous or has a bad reputation.
6   If a girl engages in necking or petting and she lets things get out of hand, it is her own fault if her partner forces sex on her.
7   A woman who is stuck-up and thinks she is too good to talk to guys on the street deserves to be taught a lesson.
8   Many women have an unconscious wish to be raped, and may then unconsciously set up a situation in which they are likely to be attacked.
9   If a woman gets drunk at a party and has intercourse with a man she's just met there, she should be considered "fair game" to other males at the party who want to have sex with her, too, whether she wants to or not (Burt, 1980:223).

Victims, too, often hold some of these rape myths. Often, if sexual assaults do not follow a specific "rape script", victims may not acknowledge that the attack was a sexual assault and instead label it an unwanted sexual contact (Cleere and Lynn, 2013). Because many rapes and sexual assaults occur when the victim had been drinking, survivors who adopt rape myths may feel they share part of the blame – even though the only person to blame for sexual assault is the perpetrator.

To demonstrate that these false beliefs apply only to certain crimes like rape, Sanders (1983) surveyed Los Angeles high school students. Half of the students (54% of males and 42% of the females) believed forced sex was justifiable in some circumstances, like if a girl says "yes" but changes her mind or if she has "led on" the boy. Applying these situations to other crimes, like bank robbery, Sanders argued that half of those surveyed also would agree that bank robbery is justified in the same situations. Table 11.1 compares each scenario.

**Table 11.1**   Applying rape myths to other crimes.

| *Rape myths* | *… applied to bank robbery* |
| --- | --- |
| The girl says "yes" then changes her mind | The bank says "yes" to a loan – then changes its mind |
| The girl has "led on" the boy | The bank has led the applicant to believe that he/she will get the loan |
| The girl gets the boy sexually excited | Through advertisement, the bank has gotten the loan applicant excited |
| If they (together) have had sex before | The bank has given the person a loan before |
| If he is turned on | The applicant *really* wants the money |
| If she has slept with other boys | The bank has loaned other people money |
| If she agrees to go to a party where she knows there will be alcohol and other drugs | The loan officer goes to a party where he or she knows drinking and drug use is going on |

Half of those surveyed agreed that forced sex was okay in the circumstances in the left column. Rape myths are false beliefs that are applied to blame the victim for the offender's actions. Why might they be applied only in cases of forced sex and not other crimes? Where do you stand – is forcing sex on someone okay in any of these situations? *Source*: Sanders (1983).

Rape myths are associated with hostility toward women, and they remain prevalent today, more commonly held by men than women (Suarez and Gadalla, 2010). Perhaps because these attitudes are associated with hostility toward women, they might also offer insight into another crime primarily focused on women: intimate partner violence.

## Intimate partner violence

Sometimes called "domestic violence" or "spousal abuse", **intimate partner violence** (IPV) happens *when a spouse or boyfriend/girlfriend uses violence against a spouse or boyfriend/ girlfriend – an intimate partner.* The National Intimate Partner and Sexual Violence Survey estimates that 35.6% of women have survived intimate partner violence (Black *et al.*, 2011). While men can be victims of IPV, too, victimization surveys indicate that only 16% of men claim their intimate partners attacked them, while 84% of women are survivors of IPV (Bureau of Justice Statistics, 2014). According to the National Crime Victimization Survey, women are violently victimized by current or former intimate partners more than three times the rate of men, as shown in Figure 11.7.

The reason for this sex disparity in IPV might be found in its history. While IPV has been prohibited at least since the seventeenth century in New England colonies, laws were rarely enforced to protect the nuclear family (Pleck, 1989). When they were, attention was turned to wives – people wondered what they did to "provoke" a husband's violence (Pleck, 1989). Otherwise, the criminal justice system largely left the resolution of IPV to the family itself, suggesting that IPV was legally permissible. In fact, some courts went as far as regulating when spousal abuse was acceptable. In one case, the Supreme Court of North Carolina refused to punish a husband, agreeing that he was justified in disciplining his wife because he was not malicious and did not cause serious injury. While the incident would have been considered a battery if the

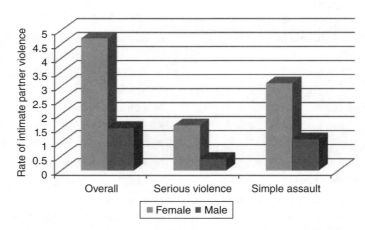

**Figure 11.7** Comparison of the 2011 rate of female and male victims of intimate partner violence per 100,000 people. *Source*: Bureau of Justice Statistics (2013)

**Box 11.2**    In their own words

Intimate partner violence*

*This interview is with a woman whose ex-boyfriend caused or contributed to her harming herself while they were together.*

I self-harmed because he upset me and then he'd get mad at me for doing it which would upset me even more, so it was a never-ending cycle. Whenever I self-harmed, he would purposely squeeze my arm whenever he saw me. As if I didn't already punish myself, he wanted to rub it in my face and cause me even more pain.

I believe my abusive, cheating ex-boyfriend really brought on this problem. He put me down daily, but I tried to shrug it off because he was my first long-term boyfriend. I also lost my virginity to him, so I thought that I had to stay with him. He was a major pothead; I tried to get him to quit so many times and he'd tell me he did, but I'd hear otherwise from other people. I kept forgiving him and giving him more chances. His mom even drug tested him, but didn't punish him. His home environment wasn't structured and his mom was a little crazy. So I know his home life somewhat formed him into the monster he became.

At first, when he started leaving bruises, I just thought it was my fault and I obviously did something wrong to make him that mad. So I had to make it better and never repeat what I did to upset him. It started to become a regular thing, and my anger towards him built up. I didn't tell anyone what was going on, and we put on such a good show in front of people when we were out somewhere together. It got to the point where I started hitting him back once he hit me. I didn't care anymore and I became very aggressive towards him, yet I still stayed with him.

To this day, I cringe at his name. He apologized several times for everything after I broke up with him for good. He thought I might give him another chance, but the people in treatment [for eating disorders] are the ones who helped me stay strong and stand my ground. I guess it was so traumatizing that my mind has blocked out a lot that happened in the two-year relationship. Even with the next few boyfriends after him, I'd flinch if they raised their hand or arm up. It was just instinct. Fortunately, I've learned that not all boys will do that to me.

---

*Brandon DeLoia conducted this interview.
Do crimes and other forms of deviance seem to happen one-at-a-time or co-occur? Why might this be so?

victim was not his wife, the judge ruled, "that the defendant had a right to whip his wife with a switch no larger than his thumb" – prompting what some later referred to as the "rule of thumb" (*State v. A.B. Rhodes* 1868; but see Pleck, 1989). Often, women who were subject to violence at home were revictimized by the criminal justice system:

While it was relatively easy for women victims to bring a complaint to court, it was much harder to ensure that justice would be meted out. In the police court, on occasion, a brawling husband was fined but his wife was sent to jail! Abused wives who fled their homes, and thereby left their children behind, could be charged with desertion. A wife who decided to drop her complaint against an abusive husband could so enrage a police court judge that he would charge her with contempt of court ... (Pleck, 1989:30).

Feminist activists in the 1960s, the Women's Movement, and some highly publicized research and court cases began to change criminal justice responses to IPV in the twentieth century. In 1984, Sherman and Berk published the results of their Minneapolis Domestic Violence Experiment, which found that arrest decreased **recidivism**, or *reoffending*, more so than separation or mediation. This study was highly publicized by media outlets across the country. That, coupled with some high profile lawsuits from IPV victims holding police departments liable for failing to equally protect women (see, e.g., *Thurman v. City of Torrington*, 1984), led police departments in the United States to change their approaches to IPV, and many jurisdictions adopted policies requiring or at least encouraging arrest in these cases. Later research on the effectiveness of arrest in IPV incidents had mixed results – arrest seems to "work" best when offenders have a stake in conformity and something to lose, like a job or reputation (Sherman *et al.*, 1992). Around the same time, the Violence Against Women Act (VAWA), the short name for Title IV of the Omnibus Crime Control Act (Pub. L. 103–322), was signed into law by President Clinton in 1994. VAWA established the Office on Violence Against Women and funding to combat IPV. Since 1994, the rate of serious IPV has declined for both women and men (Catalano, 2013).

## Crime and the Media: The CSI Effect

On television crime dramas like CSI: Crime Scene Investigation, crimes are investigated and solved in less than 60 minutes with remarkable scientific precision. There is little ambiguity,

---

**Box 11.3**   Resources for survivors of violence

If you have been a victim/survivor of violence, here are some resources that may help. We encourage you to contact some of them or your local women's shelter.

| Resource | Website/telephone |
| --- | --- |
| Rape, Abuse, and Incest National Network (RAINN) | http://www.rainn.org/1-800-656-HOPE |
| The National Domestic Violence Hotline | http://www.thehotline.org/1-800-799-SAFE (7233) |
| National Online Resource Center on Violence Against Women | http://www.vawnet.org/ |

results are always certain and sophisticated tests – required in every criminal incident portrayed on TV – are performed and returned by the crime lab almost immediately.

In reality, few crimes require such sophisticated tests or crime lab involvement; when they do, investigators may need to wait months or even years for results because of backlogs at the crime labs and limited resources. In fact, one forensic scientist estimates that 40% of the science presented in CSI does not exist, and the way that most of the "real" science is portrayed is fictionalized, not occurring in reality (Cole and Dioso, 2005).

The public, though, may not understand that, and this translates into jury decisions. In this **CSI effect**, as it is called, *because of crime dramas like CSI, jurors expect definitive scientific proof and, at the same time, are more critical of the forensic evidence presented to them.* Prosecutors argue the bar has been raised, as juries will only convict when they have forensic evidence and have high expectations for the scientific evidence prosecutors offer.

On the other side of the coin, defense attorneys argue that shows like CSI make their jobs more difficult because juries are more likely to believe any forensic evidence presented in court, believing it to be infallible like that portrayed on television. Still a third effect of television crime dramas like CSI is the increase in interest in forensic studies and criminal justice programs in colleges and universities.

While the evidence about whether a CSI effect truly exists is mixed (Schweitzer and Saks, 2007; Shelton *et al.*, 2006), one thing is clear: television crime dramas certainly have had an influence on American understanding of crime.

# Summary

Most people learn about crime through the media or from friends, which leads to many misconceptions about the nature and prevalence of crime in the United States. In this chapter, we reviewed two primary sources of crime information: official crime statistics and victimization surveys, like the National Crime Victimization Survey, to have a better sense of crime. Violent crimes – like murder, forcible rape, robbery, and aggravated assault – are rare, despite what we see on television or other media outlets. Both violent crimes and property crimes, which are much more common than violent crimes, have been steadily declining since the 1990s. Crimes share many traits – like they are committed by men more often than women, younger people are more involved in crime than older people, and crimes are concentrated in larger, urban areas and hot spots. Society's attitudes toward crimes focused against children – like school violence and child abuse – have changed in recent years and greater attention is focused on these issues. In the United States, terrorism has come to the forefront, but terrorism happens relatively infrequently compared to other crimes in the US and compared to terrorism in other countries. What some call terrorism inside the home – violence against women – is far more likely to occur. Even though these crimes – like rape, sexual assault, and intimate partner violence – now receive a response from the criminal justice system similar to other crimes, myths about the crime, the victim and the offender are prevalent in the US. It seems that the media has had an influence on society's perceptions about crime and the criminal justice system.

## Outcomes Assessment

1   Identify sources of crime information.
2   Differentiate between myth and reality regarding crime trends.
3   List "facts" of crime.
4   Describe and evaluate the homicidal triad.
5   Define various violent and property crimes.
6   Identify the elements common to the different definitions of terrorism.
7   Discuss the role of gender and race in criminal offending and victimization.
8   Identify crimes that disproportionately affect women.
9   Explain and list rape myths.
10  Explain the relationship between crime and the media.

## Key Terms and Concepts

age-crime curve
aggravated assault
arson
burglary
child abuse
child sex tourism
csi effect
dark figure of crime
fathers' rights groups

gender gap
homicidal triad
hot spots
intimate partner
     violence (IPV)
larceny-theft
mass murder
motor vehicle theft
official data

property crimes
rape myths
recidivism
robbery
serial killing
terrorism
victimization data
violence

# 12

# Corporate Crime and Elite Deviance

---

**Student Learning Outcomes**

After reading this chapter students will be able to:

1  Define, compare, and contrast white-collar and corporate crimes.
2  Argue whether white-collar and corporate crimes are, indeed, crimes.
3  Identify Edelhertz's typology.
4  Describe the varieties of political corruption.
5  Explain the "Dirty Harry" problem and other forms of police misconduct.
6  Describe the role of the media in elite deviance.

---

*In the early 1970s, Ford Motor Company developed its Pinto, a popular and inexpensive two-door car available as a coupe, hatchback, or station wagon. During production, they learned that the Pinto had a faulty gas tank, but because they were trying to compete with foreign automakers, company president Lee Iacocca was in a rush to produce the car at a low cost and production moved forward – without fixing the problem. Once the Pinto was on the road, more than 500 people died and many were injured as a result of the gas tank exploding during rear-end collisions. A memo was circulated around the company, comparing the costs of recalling the cars with the faulty gas tanks with the costs of lawsuits by the families of people killed in crashes. Ford decided that it was less expensive to pay death settlements than to spend $137 million to fix the faulty gas tank. In 1979, Ford was the first US corporation to*

*Deviance & Deviants: A Sociological Approach*, First Edition. William E. Thompson and Jennifer C. Gibbs.
© 2017 John Wiley & Sons, Inc. Published 2017 by John Wiley & Sons, Inc.
Companion website: www.wiley.com/go/thompson

*be indicted and tried on criminal charges. After a three-month trial and a 25-hour jury deliberation, the company was acquitted of reckless homicide charges (Sherefkin, 2003).*

> *Four decades later, Toyota Motor Corporation learned that its cars had a faulty accelerator – the car would suddenly accelerate, even when drivers would try to brake. This led to several fatal accidents, increasing in 2002 in Toyota cars that used a "drive-by-wire" system. Initially, Toyota resisted the National Highway Traffic Safety Administration's (NHTSA) recommendation to recall or fix the cars. In 2009, Toyota claimed the problem was due to the floor mat, and issued a recall for that – still denying that there was a defect with the cars. However, the problems persisted. In 2010, Toyota acknowledged a sticky accelerator pedal, and issued a recall for that. These recalls, though, did not stop the wrongful death lawsuits or the criminal justice system. Similar to the Ford Pinto case, Toyota was charged criminally, but at the federal level for the way (and the delay) the company disclosed the problems with the cars; the US Department of Justice launched a four-year criminal probe of the company. In March 2014, Toyota reached a $1.2 billion settlement with the Department of Justice – the largest penalty for a car manufacturer in US history.*

Are the cases of Ford and Toyota crimes or are they just shrewd business practices? When most people think about crime, they think about the crimes mentioned in the previous chapter – street crimes, like murder, rape, robbery, assault, burglary, and theft. Rarely will corporate crime be the first considered. This may be because people are not afraid of corporate crimes like they are of violent street crimes, there is a lot of distance between the offenders and the victims so the victims may not realize they have been victimized by the offender, the offenders and the general public do not consider the offenders "criminals", and the offenders are usually upstanding, respectable people in society. However, white-collar and corporate deviance cause much more harm and affect many more people than street crimes do. Street crimes cost victims about $15 billion and taxpayers pay around $180 billion to fund police, courts, and correctional services (McCollister *et al.*, 2010); about 10% of households experience property or violent crime victimization (Truman andand Langton, 2014). Compare this to white-collar and corporate deviance: white-collar crime alone costs the American public between $300 and $600 billion dollars every year, victimizing about one in four households (Huff *et al.*, 2010). These types of deviance, along with other elite deviance like political and police corruption, are the focus of this chapter.

## White-Collar Crime

The term, white-collar *crime*, suggests that this form of deviance is a violation of criminal law. However, as we alluded in Chapter 5, there is much debate about what constitutes white-collar crime. With most forms of deviance we have discussed in this book, we may not be able to define it, but we know it when we see it. With white-collar and corporate crime, this may not necessarily be true. Like the Ford Pinto and the Toyota faulty accelerator cases presented at the outset of this chapter, we wonder whether these cases can be considered criminal or whether they were rational business practices in the pursuit of profit, with some collateral damage along the way. You may be familiar with Michael Douglas's Gordon Gecko character in both *Wall Street* films – the original

Wall Street in 1987 pushing Gecko's philosophy, "Greed is good", and the sequel released in 2010 beginning when Gecko is released from prison. In the original movie, Charlie Sheen plays Bud Fox, who is a stockbroker mentored by Gecko, one of his clients. Fox gives Gecko insider information about an airline his father works for, and Gecko asks Fox for more. Over the next year, we see Fox breaking into corporate offices, posing as a cleaner and stalking businesspeople for more insider information; Fox (and Gecko) make quite a lot of money using this information that has not been made public to trade stocks. Fox is promoted at work to a corner office, he moves into a penthouse and lives a wealthy lifestyle. By the end of the movie, Fox and Gecko turn on one another after Fox learns of Gecko's plans to liquidate the company Fox's father works for; the authorities are involved, and both men go to prison. The sequel begins with Gecko's release from prison and attempts to reconnect with his estranged daughter (Carey Mulligan) through her stockbroker boyfriend, Jake (played by Shia Lebouf). Gecko begins mentoring Jake who later gives Gecko the money from his daughter's trust account. Gecko steals it instead of investing it, becoming a billionaire again. The movie ends on a happy note with Gecko returning the money, everyone reconciled, and Gecko attending his grandson's first birthday party. The Gordon Gecko character in both movies uses any means necessary – legal or otherwise – to make money for himself. This is an example of white-collar crime.

## Defining white-collar crime

Edwin Sutherland, the criminologist who coined the term "white-collar crime", was one of the first scholars to bring attention to this form of deviance. In Chapter 5, we presented his definition of white-collar crime, "a crime that is committed by a person of respectability and high social status in the course of his occupation" (Sutherland, 1949:2). Sutherland used this definition in his 1949 book, which presented his research on white-collar crime and a new theory, Differential Association, to explain this and other crimes. Sutherland took 70 companies that were on both the 1929 and 1938 lists of the Top 200 Businesses. He found that each of these 70 companies had some kind of civil, criminal, or administrative decision against the corporation, and of the 980 guilty findings only 16% were from criminal court while 37% were administrative decisions. Sutherland also found that corporate deviance is very pervasive, as most companies were "habitual offenders" having four or more offenses and companies were more often recidivists than desisters.

Sutherland's work also was the impetus for a debate about what white-collar crime is and whether it falls under the domain of criminologists. Sutherland adopted a broad definition, considering white-collar deviance and violations of civil law and administrative policies in his concept of white-collar crime. Paul Tappan, a lawyer-sociologist, disagreed with this and took a legalistic approach to white-collar crime. For Tappan (1947), a crime strictly is an intentional violation of criminal law and behaviors that violate civil laws or administrative policies do not fall under the definition of white-collar crime. When this definition is expanded, according to Tappan, the risk is labeling as criminal those who have not been convicted of a crime in a court of law. From Sutherland's (1945) point of view, white-collar crime is socially injurious and is a violation of some law or policy – even if it is not necessarily against criminal law. Therefore, all of these behaviors are fair game for study, especially those that do not result in criminal conviction, as white-collar crimes are difficult to prosecute.

Edwin Sutherland defined white-collar crime as "a crime that is committed by a person of respectability and high social status in the course of **his** occupation" (Sutherland, 1949:2, emphasis added) – a definition which seems to exclude women. However, women have been convicted of white-collar crime. In 2003, Martha Stewart was charged with insider trading as a result of selling her stock of ImClone in 2001 after receiving a tip that the stock was going to fall – before that information became public. She was convicted in 2004 of perjury and obstruction of justice, and spent five months in prison. Do you think Sutherland, if he was writing today, would consider Martha Stewart a white-collar criminal? What would Paul Tappan say? *Source*: © ZUMA Press Inc/Alamy

Since the Sutherland–Tappan debate, others have weighed in, expanding the domain of what is considered white-collar crime. Under the rubric of white-collar crime, scholars have written about occupational crime, finance crime, enterprise crime, and avocational crime, among others (Friedrichs, 2002). Some writers forego a specific definition and instead use a typology to identify white-collar crimes. One of the most popular typologies is one developed by Edelhertz (1970), who considers white-collar crime to be, "an illegal act or series of illegal acts committed by nonphysical means and by concealment or guile, to obtain money or property, to avoid the payment or loss of money or property, or to obtain business or personal advantage" (p. 3, emphasis removed). The **Edelhertz typology** (1970:19–20, 73–75) divided white-collar crime into four types:

1  *Personal crimes*, which are those illegal actions that serve to benefit the individual in nonbusiness contexts (e.g., cheating on income taxes, bankruptcy fraud, insurance fraud, welfare fraud).
2  *Abuses of trust*, which are crimes that occur in legal businesses or government, but that violate an employee's loyalty to his (or her) company or client (e.g., commercial bribery, embezzlement, stealing office supplies or expense account frauds, securities fraud through insider trading).
3  *Business crimes*, which are those actions that occur in the context of regular business operations to advance the corporation but that violate the law (e.g., tax violations, antitrust

violations, food and drug violations, publishing false financial statements, deceptive advertising) – this is what we refer to as corporate crime, a topic discussed later in this chapter.

4 *Con games*, which occur when the white-collar crime is the business (e.g., medical fraud, home improvement schemes, personal improvement schemes like diploma mills or correspondence schools, Ponzi schemes).

Perhaps the biggest con game in history is a fairly recent one – the Bernie Madoff Ponzi scheme. A **Ponzi scheme**, "is one in which *victims are promised large interest or profit returns on their investments, but are in fact paid out of the capital investments of subsequent victims*" (Edelhertz, 1970:24, footnote 2). Madoff took billions of dollars from investors. When those investors asked for their money, Madoff paid them with money from other investors. He was able to keep the scam going for years until he confessed to his sons – who alerted authorities – in 2008. Earlier, we mentioned there is a great distance between white-collar criminals and their victims, which is one reason why people may not recognize white-collar crime as a crime. With the Bernie Madoff scandal, many people lost their retirements – something that can be directly attributed to the collapse of the Ponzi scheme. Indirectly, the Madoff scandal may even affect you – those who invested with Madoff and who were ready to retire had to continue working because they could not afford to retire; this means that their jobs are still filled instead of opening up for young employees just out of college … like you! Madoff pleaded guilty to several federal crimes and was sentenced in 2009 to 150 years in prison.

Bernie Madoff. *Source:* © Tribune Content Agency, LLC. All Rights Reserved. Reprinted with permission

## Measuring white-collar crimes

The extent of Ponzi schemes and other types of white-collar crime are difficult to know. Unlike street crimes described in the last chapter, there are no official data sources like the FBI's Uniform Crime Reports for white-collar or corporate crime. Much of the research on these crimes has relied on sensational cases that have come to the attention of authorities and that are picked up by the media. That said, the FBI attempts to measure some of the extent of white-collar crime. Introducing yet another definition, the FBI defines white-collar crime as:

> those illegal acts which are characterized by deceit, concealment, or violation of trust and which are not dependent upon the application or threat of physical force or violence. Individuals and organizations commit these acts to obtain money, property, or services; to avoid the payment or loss of money or services; or to secure personal or business advantage (Barnett, n.d.:1).

With this definition in mind, the FBI recommends the use of some Part II offenses listed in the UCR, drawing additional details about these offenses through the National Incident Based Reporting System (NIBRS), to measure white-collar crime. Specifically, the FBI suggests using forgery and counterfeiting, fraud (in five categories: false pretenses/swindle/confidence games, credit card/ATM fraud, impersonation, welfare fraud, and wire fraud), embezzlement, bribery, and bad checks (Barnett, n.d.). Of the more than 3.7 million crimes against property, only nine percent are crimes that could be considered white-collar crimes: fraud offenses (seven percent), counterfeiting and forgery (two percent), embezzlement (less than one percent), and bribery (less than one percent). In 2012, the number of these crimes totaled 354,074, with 389,671 people victimized (FBI, 2013).

These statistics, though, should be considered only a crude measure. These are only some of the crimes that make up what we consider white-collar crime. Also, remember our discussion about official statistics in Chapter 11 – these are crimes brought to the attention of the police.

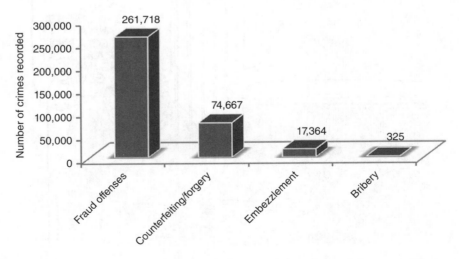

**Figure 12.1**   Crimes reported to the police, 2012. *Source*: FBI (2013)

While there are no annual, government-sponsored victimization surveys like the National Crime Victimization Survey for white-collar or corporate crime, there is one source of white-collar crime victimization information: the National White-collar Crime Center (NW3C) surveys households every five years. During the summer of 2010, the NW3C conducted a telephone (and cell phone) survey of over 2,500 random households about their experiences with white-collar crimes in the past year. They asked specifically about (1) "mortgage fraud"; (2) "credit card fraud"; (3) "identity theft"; (4) "unnecessary home or auto repairs"; (5) "price misrepresentation"; and (6) "losses occurring due to false stockbroker information, fraudulent business ventures, and Internet scams" (Huff *et al.*, 2010:8). Someone in almost one-quarter of the households surveyed was victimized by at least one of these white-collar crimes, with credit card fraud, price misrepresentation, and unnecessary repairs occurring most often. But just over half of these respondents reported their victimization to the police (Huff *et al.*, 2010).

Because many people do not realize they have been victimized, and for other reasons, more white-collar crime victimizations occur than appear in surveys like this and even more are unknown to the police – and we do not know this dark figure of crime. That said, these data and studies like that done by Edwin Sutherland give us a window into the nature and extent of white-collar crime.

Studies of white-collar crime certainly are helpful to understanding this form of deviance. However, while Sutherland's work was groundbreaking at the time, it had some drawbacks. In particular, Sutherland's definition – like the definitions of many to follow him – is offender-based, focusing on the individual; Sutherland's work seemed to concentrate on the employee who victimizes the employer for personal financial gain. Missing from this work is the corporate actor.

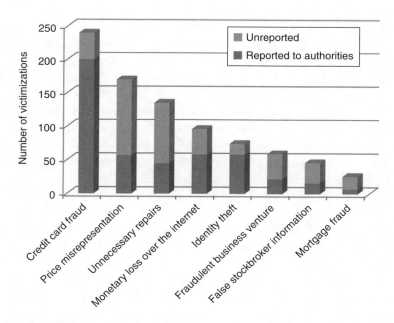

**Figure 12.2**   Number of white collar crime victimizations unreported and reported to authorities, 2010.
*Source*: 2010 National Public Survey on White Collar Crime (Huff *et al.*, 2010)

## Box 12.1    In their own words

### Compilation of interviews with Bernie Sanders

"Nothing that I say should be taken as an excuse for my behaviour.... I take full responsibility for what I did. I was aware of what I was doing" (Gelles and Tett, 2011).

"You have to understand my history" (Gelles and Tett, 2011). "I had a father who was very successful in business. He invented the punching-bag stand. The Joe Palooka punching-bag stand" (Fishman, 2011). [But his business failed.] "I watched my father go bankrupt" (Gelles and Tett, 2011). "You see a father whom you idolize all of a sudden lose everything, and you're frightened about something like that happening" (Fishman, 2011).

"I started with $500 in capital … I was very driven" (Gelles and Tett, 2011). "It was always a business where you had to have an edge, and the little guy never got a break. The institutions controlled everything. I realized from a very early stage that the market is a whole rigged job. There's no chance that investors have in this market" (Fishman, 2011). "… I was always outside the club, the club being the New York Stock Exchange and white shoe firms. They fought me every step of the way" (Gelles and Tett, 2011).

"Put yourself in my place. Your whole career you are outside the 'club' but then suddenly you have all the big banks – Deutsche Bank, Credit Suisse – all their chairmen, knocking on your door and asking, 'Can you do this for me?' … [I was] under a lot of pressure – a lot. And I was embarrassed. It was the first time in my life that something hadn't worked. I was just dumb. Dumb! Starting in the early 1990s there were no trades. It was just paper. But let me tell you. It looked real" (Gelles and Tett, 2011).

"… I had all of these major banks … It is a head trip … It feeds your ego. All of a sudden, these banks which wouldn't give you the time of day, they're willing to give you a billion dollars … It was just that I thought it was a temporary thing, and all of a sudden, everybody is … [s]aying, 'Listen, if you can do this stuff for us, we'll be your clients forever.' Look, these banks and these funds had to know there were problems. I wouldn't give them any facts, like how much volume I was doing. I was not willing to have them come up and do the due diligence that they wanted. I absolutely refused to do it. I said, 'You don't like it, take your money out,' which of course they never did" (Fishman, 2011).

"Look, I tried to give moneys back to my individual clients when I realized it was impossible to get myself out. I tried to return funds to my friends, moneys to the smaller clients. They wouldn't take it back … Everybody said, 'No, you can't do that. You can't send me my money back. I've been a friend of yours, or a client, for years' … I couldn't tell them I would have been doing them a favor. I couldn't. I mean, could I have insisted? Yes…. I did block it out of my mind. I had no choice" (Fishman, 2011).

"They were all told by me, 'Don't invest any more money than you could afford to lose. This is the stock market. There's always stuff that can happen. Brokerage firms can fail. I could go crazy and do something stupid. If you want a [safe thing], put your money in government bonds. So everybody understood this. Everyone was greedy. I just went along. It's not an excuse" (Fishman, 2011).

"It's not like I ever considered myself a bad person. I made a horrible mistake and I'm sorry…. I don't believe I'm a bad person. I did a lot of good for people. I made huge sums of money for some people" (Lee, 2014). "How could I have done this? I was making a lot of money. I didn't need the money. We made a very nice living" (Fishman, 2011). "It wasn't to buy yachts or homes. I had that from the beginning from legitimate money I made" (Lee, 2014). "I didn't need the investment-advisory business. I took it on and got myself involved in it, but if you think I woke up one morning and said, 'Well, listen, I need to be able to buy a boat and a plane, and this is what I'm going to do,' that's wrong. I had more than enough money to support my lifestyle and my family's lifestyle. I allowed myself to be talked into something, and that's my fault. I thought I could extricate myself after a short period of time. But I just couldn't" (Fishman, 2011).

"It was a nightmare for me. It was only a nightmare for me. It's horrible. When I say nightmare, imagine carrying this secret. Look, imagine going home every night not being able to tell your wife, living with this ax over your head, not telling your sons, my brother, seeing them every day in the business and not being able to confide in them…. Look, even the regulators felt sorry for me … The first day I came [to prison], they said, 'How did you live with this? Not being able to tell anybody?' … I definitely have obsessive-compulsive tendencies" (Fishman, 2011).

"I hold myself responsible for [my 46-year-old son, Mark's] suicide. My grandchildren are without their father. That's probably the worst…. The thing that was important to me was family, but that's all gone. That's more punishment than being incarcerated" (Lee, 2014).

## Corporate Crime

The main difference between white-collar and corporate crime is who benefits from this deviance. You may have gathered that in white-collar crimes, the crimes serve the employee. With corporate crime, on the other hand, the crimes are committed for the advancement of the corporation. You may have seen *The Rainmaker*, starring Matt Damon (released in 1997), or the 2000 movie *Erin Brockovich*, with Julia Roberts in the title role – both movies portray corporate crime. In *The Rainmaker*, Matt Damon plays a young lawyer, taking on a health insurance company that refused to pay for a bone marrow transplant that would have saved a 22-year-old leukemia patient's life. Damon's character files a bad faith lawsuit on behalf of the patient's parents for punitive damages for their son's death; in the end, they win the lawsuit, but the insurance company declares bankruptcy to avoid paying the plaintiffs or any other class action lawsuit. In a similar story based on real events, the movie *Erin Brockovich* tells the story of a single mother who takes a secretarial job at a law firm and ends up investigating multi-billion dollar utilities company, Pacific Gas and Electric's, illegal toxic dumping in the nearby town of Hinckley for 30 years. Many residents became chronically sick, and the firm employing Brockovich launched a class action lawsuit resulting in a 1996 settlement of $333 million dollars to 600 Hinckley residents (Brockovich, n.d.).

Bad faith insurance and toxic dumping are only two examples of **corporate crime** – "*conduct of a corporation, or of employees acting on behalf of a corporation, which is proscribed and punishable by law*" (Braithwaite, 1984:6, emphasis added). Notice the differences between white-collar crime and corporate crime. First, and perhaps most important, the goal of corporate crime is to benefit the corporation – not the individual's personal agenda. Second, this definition of corporate crime recognizes both the corporation and individuals within the corporation. In the previous section, we talked about crimes of individuals. But, can corporations commit crime? What are corporations? Frank Pearce (1993) listed several elements of corporations, writing that corporations:

1   … are legal registered entities.
2   … engage in legitimate activities.
3   … are a "juridic person", meaning they have responsibility.
4   … have a goal of maximizing profit.
5   … have stockholders, shareholders, and stakeholders who invest and profit from the company.
6   … are global entities, making the ability to control their behavior difficult.

The debate over whether corporate crime is crime or just greedy business practices is even more pronounced than for white-collar crime – mainly because determining intent and figuring out who is responsible for corporate crime is challenging at best. The nature of the organization itself shields the offenders, offering protection in the corporate hierarchy (Shapiro, 1980). Offenders can defer responsibility for corporate crime, arguing that they were just doing what they were told. The corporation also increases the distance between the offender and the victim (Shapiro, 1980). The distance can be physical, social, or in time. For example, in the Erin Brockovich story described earlier, the utilities company was improperly dumping toxic waste, which was slowly leaking into the ground water, but years passed before residents started becoming ill. With street crimes, especially violent street crimes, there is some physical contact between the victims and offenders; there is no such contact with corporate crimes. Employees within a corporation often may be in a higher social class than their victims, which affects the type and amount of resources each party has to deal with the offense. Years may pass before victims realize that, (1) they have been victimized; and, (2) that the corporation was the offender. This temporal distance makes connecting the crime to the corporation and proving intent difficult at best.

For these reasons and similar to white-collar crime, measuring the extent of corporate crime is problematic. The FBI publishes reports on Financial Institution Fraud and Failure (the most recent is from 2006–2007), Financial Crimes, and Mortgage Fraud. The bulk of the information contained in these reports, though, are of cases pending, which tells us more about regulatory agency and law enforcement behavior instead of corporate crime – especially considering that federal agencies vary in their use of deferred prosecution or non-prosecution agreements with corporations. Street crime information is mixed in with corporate crimes, and who benefited from the crime – the individual or the corporation – is unknown. Academic studies of corporate crime use varying definitions, different time periods, limited crimes, and a variety of types of corporations or organizations, so there is a wide range in estimates of the amount of corporate crime. In short, we simply do not know how prevalent corporate crime is.

# Political Corruption

White-collar and corporate crimes typically are classified differently from street crimes because white-collar and corporate criminal offenders have to be in a professional position to have the opportunity to commit these crimes. Similarly, political corruption is committed by those in positions of power. Using this position of power for personal gain can be tempting, and political corruption certainly is nothing new. In 1887, Lord Acton famously wrote, "Power tends to corrupt and absolute power corrupts absolutely" (Dalberg-Acton, 1887/1907). Thinking of this axiom, one scholar cleverly pointed out that any definition of political corruption assumes non-corrupt politics (Heywood, 1997). Adopting this assumption, Heywood (1997) classified **political corruption** as those, "*activities which take place either wholly within the public sphere or at the interface between the public and private spheres – such as when politicians ... use their privileged access to resources (in whatever form) illegitimately to benefit themselves ...*" (p. 421, emphasis added). Political corruption does not encompass activities that happen in private businesses nor is it financial corruption – these would be considered white-collar or corporate crimes (Heywood, 1997). And, while police are public servants and have the potential to engage in political corruption, police misconduct is detailed in the next section – it is not considered political corruption here.

Of course, political corruption, like beauty, is in the eye of the beholder. Activities that one person deems corruption is considered "just politics" by another (Peters and Welch, 1978). Figure 12.3 highlights this continuum of political corruption. For example, when a politician is acting as a private citizen, actions are less corrupt than when the politician is acting in his or her public role. If the end result of the politician's actions is to benefit constituents, the actions are less corrupt than when the actions benefit nonconstituents or the politician himself or herself.

Some actions, like bribery and other abuses of power, clearly fall within the realm of political corruption. **Bribery** usually consists of *a payment to coerce someone in a position of power to overlook his or her duties* (Lowenstein, 1985). Bribery is much more common in developing countries, but the media rarely cover bribery occurring in the United States. One exception is the case of Former Virginia Governor Robert McDonnell and his wife, Maureen, who were indicted in 2014 for using the governor's position to profit themselves. The diet supplement company, Star Scientific, Inc., gave the McDonnells and their family cash gifts, loans, a Rolex watch, vacations, shopping sprees, and more in exchange for help promoting the company, including using the governor's mansion for receptions and connecting the company with other government officials who could help Star Scientific (Robertson, 2014).

Other political bribery cases received media attention around the same time. When then-senator Barack Obama resigned his seat to become the President of the United States, the governor of Illinois, Rod Blagojevich, tried to personally profit by appointing Obama's successor to the US Senate. During a US Department of Justice investigation, Blagojevich was recorded during a telephone call saying, "I'm going to keep this Senate option for me a real possibility, you know, and therefore I can drive a hard bargain. You hear what I'm saying. And if I don't get what I want and I'm not satisfied with it, then I'll just take the Senate seat myself.... [the Senate seat] is a fucking valuable thing, you just don't give it away for nothing"

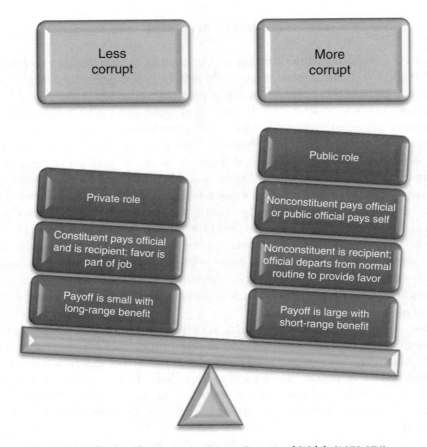

**Figure 12.3** Continuum of political corruption. *Source*: Peters and Welch (1978:976)

(*USA v. Blagojevich and Harris*, 2008:56). In exchange for the Senate seat, Blagojevich asked for several things, including an ambassadorship, his own appointments to Secretary of Health and Human Services or to the Secretary of Energy, or heading a private organization – positions that pay a substantial salary (*USA v. Blagojevich and Harris*, 2008:57–58). "I've got this thing and it's fucking golden, and, uh, uh, I'm just not giving it up for fuckin' nothing. I'm not gonna do it. And, and I can always use it. I can parachute me there" (*USA v. Blagojevich and Harris*, 2008:59). Blagojevich's wife, Patti, frequently proclaimed her husband's innocence during her stint as a contestant on the reality television show, *I'm a Celebrity, Get Me out of Here*, in the summer of 2009, after a judge barred Blagojevich himself from appearing on the show.

The former governor's political corruption was not limited to soliciting bribery. Among other crimes, Blagojevich also was convicted of extortion, a crime similar to bribery. In the context of political corruption, **extortion** occurs when *others give money or property to a political official because that official threatened the person*; the criminal complaint charged Blagojevich with "intending to be influenced and rewarded in connection with business and transactions of the

The classic example of political corruption in the United States is "Watergate". The Watergate building was part of a Washington, DC office complex where the Democratic Party's National Committee office was located. In June 1972, burglars broke in, bugging the telephones and photographing documents, among other things. Then-president Richard Nixon tried to cover up his involvement, but investigators found the political corruption of his administration extended far beyond the Watergate incident. Nixon resigned from office two years later, making Vice President Gerald Ford his replacement. *Source*: © David Hume Kennerly/Getty Images

State of Illinois involving a thing of value of $5,000 or more" (*USA v. Blagojevich and Harris,* 2008). Among his many crimes, he pressured the owners of the *Chicago Tribune* to fire employees of the newspaper who criticized him and, if they didn't, he would derail a deal between the *Tribune*'s owner and the Illinois Finance Authority involving Wrigley Field (*USA v. Blagojevich and Harris*, 2008). Ultimately, the governor was impeached, removed from office and sentenced to 14 years in prison.

Similar to both bribery and extortion, **graft** is *abusing political office for personal profit*. Some describe examples of "**honest graft**", where people can *use positions of power – legally – to become personally wealthy* (Kroft, 2012). Earlier in this chapter, you probably noticed a picture of Martha Stewart, who was accused of insider trading. What happens when politicians use their position to trade stocks for their personal benefit? In November 2011, the television program, *60 Minutes*, documented the stock portfolios of several US Congresspersons – on both sides of the aisle – who held stocks for companies affected by legislation on which they voted. Is this considered political corruption? At the time the *60 Minutes* program aired, there was no law against insider trading among legislators; one was proposed, but only six Congresspersons co-sponsored it and only a few people appeared for the hearing (Kroft, 2012). The Congresspersons featured in the program denied using non-public information they learned through their position – and voting to benefit their stock portfolios – claiming that their stockbrokers handle their trades and they often are unaware of them (Kroft, 2012). However, there is evidence that many politicians made quite a lot of money making stock trades just before the global financial meltdown of 2008 – something politicians, but not the public, knew was about to happen and profited while the American public suffered (Kroft, 2012). Since the airing of the program, the STOCK Act (Stop Trading on Congressional Knowledge Act, Pub.L. 112–105, S. 2038, 126 Stat. 291) was passed by Congress and signed into law by President Barack Obama on April 4, 2012. Initially, the **STOCK Act** *prohibited insider trading among Congresspersons and executive branch members, expanded financial disclosures and made politicians' trading more easily searchable by the public* (Keith, 2013). Congress amended the STOCK Act one year later, and President Obama signed legislation that narrowed the amount of information released to the public (Keith, 2013).

Another questionable practice is a new industry using something called **political intelligence**. After leaving Capitol Hill, *politicians and staff members return to gather information that has not yet been made public to sell to Wall Street* (Kroft, 2012). Having this information before it is released to the public is highly profitable.

These examples may give the impression that the United States is a corrupt country. Comparatively, though, the United States is among the least corrupt nations in the world, ranking 19 of 177 countries on Transparency International's Corruption Perceptions Index. And, while it is true that corruption is prevalent in today's society, the government is much less corrupt today than it was in earlier times. One aspect of government corruption that has been reduced is police misconduct.

**Table 12.1**  Most and least corrupt nations.

|  | Rank | Country |
| --- | --- | --- |
| Least corrupt | 1 (tie) | Denmark and New Zealand |
|  | 3 (tie) | Finland and Sweden |
|  | 5 | Norway |
|  | 19 | **United States** |
|  | 173 | South Sudan |
|  | 174 | Sudan |
| Most corrupt | 175 (tie) | Afghanistan, North Korea, and Somalia |

*Source*: Transparency International's Corruption Perceptions Index, 2013.

## Police Misconduct

Some consider police misconduct a part of political corruption. Historically, the police have been deeply tied to politics. Law enforcement positions were sources of patronage jobs for local politicians, who would use them to reward people for their support. **Nepotism** and **cronyism** also occurred, as police *jobs were offered to politicians' family members and friends*. These people often were not the best employees, and the process of hiring was unfair. In the late nineteenth century, the **civil service** system was adopted, requiring testing of applicants and *hiring the best qualified candidates for the job*. The civil service system reduced political favoritism in policing.

Despite hiring police officers based on merit instead of political connections, police across the United States often are accused of misconduct. **Police misconduct** occurs when *police use their authority inappropriately*. Police have authority to use their discretion in a variety of situations, like whether to stop or frisk a suspect, whether to report or investigate a crime, whether to make an arrest, what enforcement strategies to use, and the type and amount of force to use. Accordingly, police misconduct can range from serious abuses of physical or deadly force to drinking while working.

Some behaviors clearly fall into the realm of misconduct, like when police officers commit crimes. In the spring of 2014, a former police captain with the Bethany Police Department near Oklahoma City, Oklahoma, was charged with larceny for stealing prescription drugs from the department's evidence room (Monahan, 2014). Around the same time, a former K9 officer with the Concord Police Department near San Francisco, California, was charged with burglary and elder abuse for using his status to enter homes and steal senior citizens' prescription medications (CBS San Francisco, 2014). In 2013, a New York City Police Officer was accused of conspiring to kidnap and kill women, illegally using a government database to find more information about potential victims, after his wife found violent websites on his computer's browser history; FBI investigators found much more, including a file for, "Abducting and Cooking Kimberly: A Blueprint" (Hays and Neumeister, 2013). These are extreme – and rare! – examples of police misconduct.

However, like much human behavior, there is much gray area in policing and the profession is wrought with ethical dilemmas. Police often are faced with the worst of humanity and interact with victims and offenders on what may be the worst day of their lives. This may affect officers, who may stretch the law, leading to **noble cause corruption** or the **"Dirty Harry" problem**: *Do good ends justify unethical means?* San Francisco Police Inspector Harry Callahan – "Dirty Harry" – was a character played by Clint Eastwood in a series of movies during the 1970s. Some quotes from those movies are popularly cited like, "Go ahead, make my day". During the series, Dirty Harry often violated department rules and constitutional rights to catch suspects.

In the late 1990s, one of the largest police misconduct cases was exposed at the Los Angeles Police Department's (LAPD) Rampart Division. The Community Resources Against Street Hoodlums (or CRASH) anti-gang unit of the Rampart Division began with a noble goal: to remove violent gang members from the streets of Los Angeles. The CRASH unit was given much leeway and told to make arrests by any means necessary. Police ethics seemed to erode from there; officers were accused of planting evidence and framing suspects. Officers in the Rampart Division went even further when they started using deadly force against suspects, stealing drugs so they could profit from the sales, and robbing banks. The television show,

*The Shield*, was loosely based on the Rampart Division of the LAPD. On air from 2002 through 2008, *The Shield* starred Michael Chiklis as Vic Mackey, a detective with an anti-gang unit in the LAPD who tries to reduce crime in his district – disregarding the rules – while also personally profiting. In the end, over 70 officers affiliated with the CRASH unit were accused of misconduct, and some were sentenced to prison.

## Elite Deviance and the Media

The media play a crucial role in elite deviance. There is no database of these crimes, so researchers often depend on cases that receive media attention to learn more about the nature and extent of this form of deviance. The media also affects public perception of the severity and pervasiveness of elite deviance. By focusing on street crimes, the media can distort the true nature of crime, leading people to believe that violent crimes happen much more frequently and are more dangerous than white-collar and corporate crimes. (We learned in Chapter 11 and in this chapter that the opposite is true.) In fact, some studies suggest that the media shape whether the public considers elite deviance "crime".

Since the 1980s, though, there has been a movement against white-collar and corporate crime, and the media have begun to reflect this increased interest (Wright *et al.*, 1995). However, studies indicate that the amount of coverage of elite scandals is influenced by the political ideology of the news agency, and news coverage tends to focus on the sentencing and punishment of elite crimes (Benediktsson, 2010).

## Summary

Because "crimes in the streets" like those discussed in the last chapter are predominantly covered by the media, the public often forgets about "crimes in the suites", like white-collar and corporate crimes and political corruption. However, these crimes may be more prevalent and they are more costly and harmful to society than street crimes. Unfortunately, there is no annual national data source like the FBI's Uniform Crime Reports, so we know very little compared to what we know about street crimes. Nevertheless, we can understand part of these crimes by studying incidents brought to the attention of the media, which play an important role in defining elite deviance and crime.

## Outcomes Assessment

1   Define, compare, and contrast white-collar and corporate crimes.
2   Argue whether white-collar and corporate crimes are, indeed, crimes.
3   Identify Edelhertz's typology.
4   Describe the varieties of political corruption.
5   Explain the "Dirty Harry" problem and other forms of police misconduct.
6   Describe the role of the media in elite deviance.

## Key Terms and Concepts

bribery
civil service
corporate crime
cronyism
"Dirty Harry" problem
Edelhertz typology

extortion
graft
honest graft
nepotism
noble cause corruption
police misconduct

political corruption
Ponzi scheme
political intelligence
STOCK Act

# 13

# Cyberdeviance

## Student Learning Outcomes

After reading this chapter, students will be able to:

1 Define cyberdeviance.
2 Identify the deviant uses of technology.
3 Distinguish between the four categories of cyberdeviance in Wall's typology.
4 Explain the various forms of hacking.
5 Describe cyberwarfare.
6 Describe the various forms and motivations of cyberbullying and compare and contrast cyberbullying with cyberaggression.
7 Explain cyberstalking.
8 Identify the role of the media in cyberdeviance.

*Dharun Ravi was known for experimenting with technology, especially webcams. In high school, he tried to connect a webcam with a coil gun as a science project. He also wrote a program directing webcams to intermittently take pictures and automatically post them to a website. While he was able to convince some of his friends to install this program by telling them its purpose was something else entirely, most of them knew Ravi's intentions were less than honorable when the webcam light on their computers indicated the webcams were actively recording them (Parker, 2012). Ravi's cyberdeviance continued to college.*

*Deviance & Deviants: A Sociological Approach*, First Edition. William E. Thompson and Jennifer C. Gibbs.
© 2017 John Wiley & Sons, Inc. Published 2017 by John Wiley & Sons, Inc.
Companion website: www.wiley.com/go/thompson

*In September 2010, 18-year-old Rutgers freshman Tyler Clementi asked Ravi, his roommate, for privacy during Clementi's date with another man. Unbeknownst to both men, their intimate interactions were being livestreamed by Ravi's webcam through iChat – a computer program like Skype where people can videochat with one another. Ravi and another freshman, Molly Wei, watched the two men kiss from Wei's room. After watching the encounter, Ravi posted about Clementi on his Twitter feed: "Roommate asked for the room till midnight. I went into molly's room and turned on my webcam. I saw him making out with a dude. Yay" (Parker, 2012). In fact, Ravi bragged on Twitter that he would be setting up a "viewing party" during Clementi's next date. He invited several people, sending them instructions on how to access the video over iChat (Parker, 2012).*

*Clementi discovered the invasion of privacy by reading Ravi's tweets. He unplugged Ravi's power strip to be sure that his webcam was off, reported Ravi to authorities at Rutgers and requested a new roommate. Two days later, though, he traveled to New York City, where he jumped off of the George Washington Bridge – a 200-foot fall (Parker, 2012). Just before committing suicide, Clementi posted a status update on Facebook, "Jumping off the gw bridge sorry" (Parker, 2012). After a criminal trial, Ravi was convicted of bias intimidation – a type of hate crime – and invasion of privacy and spent 30 days in jail, along with a $10,000 fine, 3,000 hours of community service and 3 years of probation (Heyboer, 2012). He ultimately served 20 days in jail (Heyboer, 2012).*

Technology has introduced a host of tools we can use for work, play, and socializing. But, this also has introduced new opportunities for deviance, especially because the Internet has no boundaries. **Cyberdeviance** – a term created mainly by the media – *is harmful behavior or otherwise deviant activities that are "somehow related to a computer"* (Wall, 2001:2, emphasis added). While the harmfulness of deviant uses of technology can range from one extreme like the Rutgers case, deviant uses of technology can be as innocuous as guessing someone's password.

Indeed, cyberdeviance, "signifies a range of activities and has considerable currency" (Wall, 2001:3). The Internet creates new opportunities for deviance in that it provides a new forum for existing forms of deviance (like accessing pornography online) and creates new forms of deviance (like illegally downloading music; Wall, 2001). Wall identified four types of harmful activity on the Internet:

1   "'(Cyber)-trespass', or hacking/cracking, is the unauthorized crossing of the boundaries of computer systems into spaces where rights of ownership or title have already been established" (Wall, 2001:3).

2   "'(Cyber)-deception/thefts' describes the different types of acquisitive harm that can take place within cyberspace. At one level lie the more traditional patterns of theft, such as the fraudulent use of credit cards and (cyber)-cash, and ... potential for the raiding of on-line bank accounts ..." (Wall, 2001:4).

3   "'(Cyber)-pornography/obscenity', as the term suggests, is the publication or trading of sexually expressive materials within cyberspace." (Wall, 2001:6). Cyberporn is an interesting form of cyberdeviance because pornography itself is legal, but cyberpornography generated a moral panic in the 1990s – largely because children under the age of 18 can

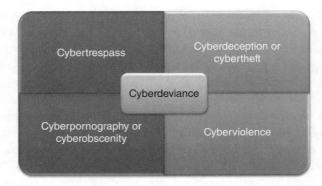

**Figure 13.1**   Wall's typology. What other types of cyberdeviance can you think of? Do any fall within these categories? *Source*: Wall (2001)

easily access sexually explicit material online (Holt *et al.*, 2012; Wall, 2001). We discussed pornography in Chapter 5.

4   "'(Cyber)-violence' describes the violent impact of the cyberactivities of another upon an individual or a social or political grouping. Whilst such activities do not have to have a direct physical manifestation, the victim nevertheless feels the violence of the act and can bear long-term psychological scars as a consequence" (Wall, 2001:6). Cyberviolence can range from hate speech to cyberstalking (Wall, 2001).

These and other opportunities exist for deviant behavior online. We begin by elaborating on some of the types of deviance identified in **Wall's typology**: hacking and online piracy.

## Hacking and Online Piracy

Hacking falls into the first category of Wall's typology because it is a form of cyber-trespassing. Within this category, there are two types of cyber-trespassers: (1) **hackers**, who *have principles like believing all information should be freely accessible to the public*; and (2) **crackers**, who *have no such principles and may simply be anti-establishment* (Wall, 2001:4). Both types of cyber-trespassing involve using computers and technology to infiltrate other computers and, what's becoming common, smartphones without permission (Holt *et al.*, 2012). While this type of cyberdeviance can be as "innocent" as trying to guess someone else's passwords, it also can cause significant damage when hackers gain access to financial accounts and steal another's identity (Holt *et al.*, 2012).

On one end of the spectrum is **white collar delinquency**, which consists of *computer crimes committed by juvenile offenders* (Pontell and Rosoff, 2009). The term is not new; prominent sociologists were talking about it in the 1960s, referring to the delinquency of middle and upper class juveniles (Matza and Sykes, 1961). With the advancements in technology, though, the term has new meaning as juvenile online offending has become more sophisticated. Pontell and Rosoff (2009) write that, "what once were regarded as seemingly harmless acts and pranks by computer hackers have evolved into major economic crimes and acts of terrorism …"

May be you guys heard of Credit Reports . Now what I will say is little tricky , hope you will get it easil
credit report like

http://www.truecredit.com
http://www.annualcreditreport.com/
http://www.creditreport.com/

these sites are for example only , you can search for more on google . Now get your self registered at
put all the info , they will ask you trick questions . Normally all 3 of them will ask you same question .
any good screen capture software .

Obviously you don't know the answers of the questions they will ask , so here we begin . Go to the firs
After that take a screen shot of screen to remember what answers u gave . After that click Submit but
verified then it means its done . You don't need to do anything else with other credit report websites .
website and go the 2nd one . Here questions are almost same . Check the screen shot of last website t
and then put diffrent answers after that take the screen shot again and click submit . Wait and see wh
then its done , otherwise do the same procedure again with the 3rd one . The third one will work 100

This is an online bulletin board post from a hacker explaining to other potential hackers how to access others' personal information from credit report bureaus – information that can later be used to steal another's identity and fraudulently open credit accounts. How harmful do you think is this behavior – more or less harmful than other forms of deviance, like street crimes? *Source*: Sullivan (2012)

(p. 147) – different from traditional youthful offending. And, this is more than just hacking. White collar delinquency is more than a simple nuisance; crimes like denial of service attacks and large-scale piracy – even if they are committed by juveniles – can have major financial consequences (Pontell and Rosoff, 2009).

Just as harmful – or even more so – is hacking that is done by organized criminal groups. International organized crime groups (like those in Eastern Europe, China, and Africa) rely on cybercrime to generate funding to support their organization. Consequently, they hack into computers to access the latest technology to use in their cybercrimes (Kearney, 2014). In fact, a recent report of an investigation by the California Attorney General found that California companies were the target of 17% of hacking by international organized crime groups in 2012 (Kearney, 2014).

Also harmful are hackers who do not profit from cyberattacks. An example is the loosely organized Anonymous movement. There is no leader, and members of the movement have done considerable damage. In response to the prosecution of Bradley (now Chelsea) Manning, a US Army intelligence officer who released classified documents to the public through WikiLeaks, Anonymous launched "Operation Payback". This was an attack against Paypal and credit card companies, as well as some government websites, because these companies would not route donations to WikiLeaks (Shone *et al.*, 2014).

## System trespassing

Bypassing companies' cybersecurity systems is fairly prevalent in the United States. Of 168 wealthiest US companies, 162 – over 96%! – had computers that had been accessed by hackers (Menn, 2012). This **system trespassing** is *hacking for profit*. In a heist designed for the new millennium, the first ATM hacking occurred in May 2013. For seven months, hackers targeted prepaid debit cards. Once they eliminated the withdrawal limits, they reprogrammed gift cards and went from ATM to ATM, withdrawing tens of millions of dollars from ATMs around the world, including Manhattan (Goldfarb, 2013). This scheme did not affect consumers, but it cost banks a great deal. Another example of system trespassing is cyberespionage for profit. Hackers in China, Russia, Israel, and France steal trade secrets from companies in the United States and around the globe (Nakashima, 2013).

Malware and advice on hacking techniques are becoming increasingly prevalent across the Internet. So much so, that companies are starting to "hack back". Companies are using techniques where they delay the hacker by making the hacker believe he or she has gained access to sensitive files that turn out to be impossible to download or they allow hackers to download files that contain a sort of tracer to identify the hacker's machines (Menn, 2012). This "**active defense**" or "**strike back**" **technology** is *retaliatory action by companies against hackers* (Menn, 2012). Beyond this, some companies are going on the offensive. For example, Facebook identified the Russian hackers who were responsible for the Koobface software, which spammed users of social networks (Richmond, 2012). The Koobface gang made about $2 million from social media users who clicked on an invitation to watch a "funny" or "sexy" video (Menn, 2012; Richmond, 2012). A message would appear to update the Flash software; users would be redirected to a site that would instead install the Koobface software on the unsuspecting users' computers (Richmond, 2012). The Koobface gang profited by selling to infected users official-looking fake anti-virus software and they were paid by advertisers when the clicks from users' web searches were delivered to marketers (Richmond, 2012).


## Cyberpiracy

Cyberpiracy falls into the second category of Wall's typology: online theft. **Cyberpiracy** is *using computer technology to copy "digital goods that include software, documents, audio (including music and voice), and video for any reason other than to back up without explicit permission with intent to deny compensation to the copyright holder"* (Higgins *et al.*, 2012:412). Cyberpiracy involves using the Internet to take a computer program or digital code created by another or taking virtual products like music (Wall, 2001). Cyberpiracy also can involve counterfeiting products like designer labels (Wall, 2001). Cyberpiracy – especially sharing music and videos – is most common among young adults (Holt *et al.*, 2012). While this does not sound as harmful as other forms of online piracy like counterfeiting products, sharing music and videos in violation of copyright costs the entertainment industry billions of dollars each year (Higgins *et al.*, 2012). This may not seem like a big deal, but those lost dollars cannot be taxed, which means that society loses out on tax revenue (Higgins *et al.*, 2012).

One of the more popular music sharing websites was Napster, operating from 1999 through 2001. Napster was a unique website that cataloged dispersed websites where people had uploaded songs and music albums to share. Through Napster, people could search for artists or music and search results would link the searcher to the music sites, where the searcher could download the music for free. One major problem with Napster was that it violated copyright law – people were sharing mp3 files of music without compensating the artists or record companies. After being sued in federal court, the company was forced to shut down – but not before other file-sharing websites emerged around the Internet.

## Cyberwarfare

Technology always has advanced military training and operations, but the introduction of the Internet has allowed a new form of warfare: cyberwarfare. Also referred to as "**netcentric**" **warfare** by the Pentagon, **cyberwarfare,** "*involves the actions by a nation-state or international organization to attack and attempt to damage another nation's computers or information networks through, for example, computer viruses or denial-of-service attacks*" (RAND Corporation, n.d., emphasis added). In other words, it is politically-motivated hacking of a country by another country's government. In 2010, the United States and Israel were accused of launching Stuxnet, infecting the computer system in Iran's uranium enrichment facility and triggering the malfunction of its centrifuges (Finkle, 2012). By the time Iranian authorities found the virus, the nuclear program had suffered a setback. The attack, though, prompted Iran to focus more of its efforts in building its own cyberarmy (Windrem, 2013).

Countries like Iran, Israel, Palestine, Sudan, and Syria seem to be the most targeted by cyberwarfare, as cybersecurity firms identify the most infected computers in these countries (Finkle, 2012). On the other side, the United States, Russia, and China are in a cyberarms race to develop cyberweapons capable of damaging an enemy's infrastructure, with the United Kingdom, Germany, Israel, and Taiwan falling just behind (Windrem, 2013). These cyberweapons can be computer viruses, worms, or Trojan horses and their delivery can be quite deceptive. One technique used to attack the government and military is called spearfishing. Similar to phishing, **spearfishing** is more targeted, *trying to elicit sensitive information from key personnel by sending official-looking email messages with attachments that look legitimate but actually launch spyware programs.* These emails seem to come from coworkers, friends, or key contacts. Considering that almost everything is computerized in the new millennium, spearfishing or any cyberweapon that can bypass security has the potential to shut down electricity, water, heat, transportation, and more (Windrem, 2013).

Cyberwarfare is a unique military strategy in that it makes response from the target country very challenging. Like other forms of cybertrespassing, this new military strategy is difficult to detect. Governments can mask their identities or launch attacks using foreign servers (Manson, 2011). Even if the source of the attack is uncovered, the government can simply claim they had no knowledge of the attack, blaming "hacktivists" – a technique used by China and Russia – and avoiding repercussions (Manson, 2011). Ultimately, unless clear evidence can be found, there can be no retaliation.

## Cyberbullying

While childhood and adolescent bullying traditionally has been seen as a rite of passage, parents, educators, and even the criminal justice system have begun viewing bullying as a serious form of deviance, as you may have guessed from the Rutgers case at the opening of this chapter. This may be due to advancements in technology providing bullies a new forum: the Internet. Called "cyberbullying", this online harassment falls into the cyberviolence category of Wall's typology. **Cyberbullying** is "*repeated, unwanted, hurtful, harassing, and/or threatening interaction through electronic communication media*" (Rafferty and Vander Ven, 2014:364, emphasis added). This is different from **cyberaggression** or online aggression, which is the same thing except the *behavior is not repeated* (Rafferty and Vander Ven, 2014).

Similar to offline bullying (that is, in real life), cyberbullying can include name calling: "stupid," "ugly," "dorky," "boring," "gay," "lesbian," "whore," "slut," "fatass," "pig," "whale," "loser," and more (Mishna *et al.*, 2009). However, while only those within earshot would witness an offline bullying incident, with cyberbullying malicious messages can be broadcast on social networking sites which can be accessed by the public 24 hours a day (Holt *et al.*, 2012). Cyberbullying also can involve rejection of the victim, but different from offline bullying, a new form of rejection is available online: blocking. One victim elaborated on this: "I get sick of my friends rejecting me. Whenever I'm on msn, I try talking to people and they block me" (Mishna *et al.*, 2009:111).

Cyberaggression can affect anyone, and offline, adolescents with little prominence tend to be the victims of the most frequent and severe bullying. However, research indicates that teenagers who are more popular are more likely to be targets of cyberbullying – probably because they

At the beginning of this chapter, we summarized the case of the Rutgers student who violated his roommate's privacy and tweeted about it, leading to Tyler Clementi's suicide. Could this case be classified as cyberbullying? What about cyberaggression? *Source*: © MBI/Alamy

have a larger online and offline social network and more opportunities exist for victimization (Badaly *et al.*, 2013).

Research indicates that cyberbullying and cyberaggression are driven by three main motivations: (1) cybersanctioning; (2) power struggles; and (3) entertainment (Rafferty and Vander Ven, 2014). Cybersanctioning involves attempts to modify someone else's behavior usually through name-calling. One woman described being on the receiving end of cyberbullying from her boyfriend's former girlfriend:

> A girl was upset that I was dating her ex-boyfriend. She would harass me with text messages telling me I was a bad friend and a slut. Then, she turned to Facebook and started posting between her and her friend bad things about me and said my boyfriend was cheating. This went on for a good six months (Rafferty and Vander Ven, 2014:369).

The second motivation for cyberbullying is power struggles, which are "attempt[s] to hurt, humiliate, or influence the behavior of another individual in order to gain or regain access to some valued resource" like boyfriends or girlfriends or even winning video games (Rafferty and Vander Ven, 2014:370–371). One woman recounted the story of how her ex engaged in a power struggle to force her back into the relationship:

> I was in an abusive relationship and when I tried to cut off all ties with him, he began contacting me in any form possible. First it was calling and texting. I blocked his number, then he began finding more numbers to call and text me through. After blocking 5 of his numbers he began threatening me through Facebook messages (Rafferty and Vander Ven, 2014:371–372).

The third motivation for cyberbullying is entertainment, or "trolling". **Trolling** is "*the attempt to hurt, humiliate, annoy, or provoke in order to elicit an emotional response for one's own enjoyment*" (Rafferty and Vander Ven, 2014:372, emphasis added). Like cybersanctioning, trolling involves insults and name-calling, but cyberbullies who troll tend to strive for anonymity. Additionally, there is no benefit to the cyberbully who trolls, like there is with cybersanctioning (behavior modification is the desired outcome) or power struggles (where access to some resource is the goal). One woman described her friend's experience with a cyberbully trolling:

> My friend has a Tumblr and there was some guy following her. He started telling her she was a boring teenager and that her blog should be more exciting and [she] replies with "no it's mine, I'll post what I want." He then started calling her all the vulgar names and telling her she was ugly and boring and only an object to men, etc. (Raffety and Vander Ven, 2014:373).

While some of these examples involved male perpetrators, girls and popular teens are more likely to be cyberaggressive themselves. In fact, engaging in cyberaggression can increase popularity of girls (but decrease popularity for boys). It seems that aggression and dominance can elevate social standing among adolescents because they do not seem to be related to how well a teen is liked by her peers (Badaly *et al.*, 2013).

**Box 13.1**    In their own words

## Confessions of a cyberbully*

To me, cyberbullying takes place using electronic technology, which includes using computers, cell phones, or social networks to communicate a message of some sort. I have participated in cyberbullying. I would use social networks such as Facebook or Twitter to post nasty pictures or messages on others' blogs. I would spread rumors about others through social networks. It was a quick and easy way for me to humiliate the victim. Also a large amount of networkers could witness them being humiliated.

My friends would tell me in "private" that I need to be careful of what I post on Facebook and Twitter because they felt that many of my comments on the sites were "disrespectful". I would make cruel comments about other girls' photos on Facebook. My friends would honestly tell me that I was cyberbullying others. A couple of my friends would approach me, to try to convince me that what I was doing was wrong.

The girls I was victimizing attended the same high school as me. I did not see them at school on a regular basis. But when I did run into them, I would not have the nerve to humiliate them in person, so I would rely on social networks to do so. The girls that I chose to bully used to be in my circle of friends.

I was actually surprised to discover that the victims of cyberbullies know their perpetrators. I believed that many cyberbullies used fake names when they harassed their victims because I thought they had a fear of getting caught. But many perpetrators use their true identities when engaging in cyberharassment.

My computer acted as a mask. It was so easy for me to log into Facebook, without even giving it much thought, to post a cruel comment to another. I guess I felt as if I had an "alter ego" because I would pretend to be someone else on a social network site. Since my true identity was concealed, I felt less negative emotions when posting something cruel. As long as the victim did not find out who I truly was, it gave me an adrenaline rush to know that I had some sort of control over them. I would have described the experience as making others miserable because I was miserable with myself. If I had felt insecure that day I wanted to make others feel the same. If I brought my victims down in a negative way, my ego was boosted.

My peers were engaging in the activity and seemed to be getting excitement from it, so I decided to join in with them. I would feed off of my peers' negative comments; it was almost as if we were all in competition to see who could say the most hurtful comments. I feel that others engage in cyberbullying because they use the Internet to form a false identity to become someone they are not. Once the false identity is formed, a perpetrator feels they are free to say whatever they please. A perpetrator is less likely to censor cruel comments because they believe their false identity will not be revealed to their victims.

Thinking back, I believe that cyberbullying could lead to serious crime. It has been reported in the news or media that children, teens, and adults that have been cyberbullied have turned to self-harm to cope with the emotional and psychological stress it can bring.

Some victims may develop anxiety, depression, or post-traumatic stress disorder. Others have tried to self-medicate to reduce the symptoms that they have. In extreme cases, the victim may try to commit suicide or overdose on medication because they feel, by doing so, it will put them out of their misery. Victims of cyberbullying are more likely to commit suicide, which is considered a serious crime.

Now, I believe there should be harsher punishments for people who engage in cyber-bullying. As I was engaging in cyberbullying I was not aware of the consequences. I became aware of the consequences when the police and my school authorities got involved. I was charged with cyberharassment and had to attend court. States should enact strict punishments so cyberharassment does not lead the victims to harm them-selves or others. Cyberbullying should be taken seriously.

---

\* Odelia Wilson conducted this interview.

Despite social standing, cyberbullying is just as harmful as offline bullying. Victims report feeling depressed and lonely (Mishna *et al.*, 2009). One victim described cyberbullying experiences:

i don't no [sic] if i fully healed from the last incidence [sic]. i can't take this now. I can't make it go away. I can't get the words, the voices out of my head. Those hurtful words keep coming back and killing me every time. I don't no [sic] how much longer i can take it. I'm cracking and i don't no [sic] how many more words will make me shatter into a million pieces. As I'm writing this I'm crying (Mishna *et al.*, 2009:111).

## Cyberstalking

In Chapter 11, we discussed intimate partner violence. When this happens online, it falls into the fourth category of Wall's typology: cyberviolence. One form of cyberviolence is **cyberstalking**, "*the persistent tracking and harassment of an individual by another … and the sending of obscene messages or even death threats*" (Wall, 2001:6, emphasis added). In other words, cyberstalking is, "repeated pursuit of an individual using electronic or Internet-capable devices" (Reyns *et al.*, 2012:1). The tracking, harassment, and pursuit are repeated, persistent, and unwanted, typically with, "coercive or intimidating wording or sexual overtones" (Reyns *et al.*, 2012:1). These electronic communications can include repeatedly sending unwanted emails, text or video messages, and instant messages and can occur through email, on blogs, in chat rooms, on Facebook or other social networking websites, or other websites (Reyns *et al.*, 2012; Wall, 2001).

Some studies suggest that more than 40% of college-age people – more likely to be women than men – have been victims of cyberstalking and about 20% have been offenders – who are more likely to be men than women (Reyns *et al.*, 2012). While cyberstalking, by definition, happens online, it is related to real life behavior. Harassing behavior online tends to occur with harassing behavior in person – at least in the context of intimate partner violence (Zweig *et al.*, 2013).

In Chapter 6 we briefly discussed the popular trend of *sexting*, sending and receiving electronic messages (like texts) or photos about intimate behavior, usually via cell phones. Often, people engaging in sexting believe the explicit sexual or nude photos they send will be kept private by the recipient. However, this often is not the case and these photos can be distributed on social networking websites, like Facebook. What follows is social shaming of the victims, who are usually women or girls and negatively called "web cam whores" (Mishna *et al.*, 2009).

Social websites like Facebook host an array of personal information (e.g., name with a photo, address, telephone number, email address) easily accessible to potential cyberstalkers. Even if a person protects her or his personal information, offenders may find home addresses, telephone numbers, what school the victim attends, and more through something as simple as a username or a friend who is less vigilant about guarding personal data (Mishna *et al.*, 2009). One teenage victim of cyberstalking wrote, "my friend was stupid and gave him my address on msn ... now I'm scared cause I know about creepy people ... and this predator knows where I live" (Mishna *et al.*, 2009:111).

## Cyberdeviance and the Media

The various forms of cyberdeviance reviewed in this chapter describe the range encompassing this form of deviance. Electronic media also can be used to commit other crimes, like sexual abuse of children. You may have gathered from Chapter 11 that the Internet can be used to connect predators with potential victims. However, media also can be used to combat such crimes. From 2006 through 2008, NBC's Dateline produced a reality television show called *To Catch a Predator*. Dateline partnered with an organization called Perverted Justice, whose employees posed as underage girls interested in sexual relations with older men. The "girl" would tell the men that her parents were away for the weekend; when the men would arrive at the house, after a brief interaction with a young-looking actress, the television show host Chris Hansen would walk out. Hansen would interview the would-be pedophile, publicly shaming him, before letting him leave through the front door, where police would be waiting to arrest him.

Filmed in various cities around the United States, Dateline exposed over 300 men. However, several cases were thrown out by the district attorney in at least one city because the evidence obtained against these suspected child molesters was considered tainted by the police department's relationship with the television show (Ross and Walter, 2007).

## Summary

The advent of the Internet and other technology has led to new types of deviance, new opportunities for deviance, and new platforms to engage in deviant behavior. This new deviance, called cyberdeviance, involves harmful or other deviant activities somehow related to a computer and it encompasses a vast array of behaviors. Hacking (or cracking) can cause little harm when it takes the form of guessing someone else's passwords, but it can be financially devastating when hackers steal identities or engage in system trespassing – hacking for profit. Cyberpiracy, too, has the potential to drive up costs to produce music and other forms of entertainment, suppress artists' motivation to create, and deprive society of tax revenue that would have been collected from legitimate purchases of the illegally downloaded material.

The Internet also is being used for more dangerous operations, like cyberwarfare. The United States is only one country in a cyberarms race to engage with enemies in the new millennium. While the Internet has allowed intercountry hostilities to move online, it also has offered a platform for more personal aggression, like cyberbullying and cyberaggression. In extreme cases, cyberbullying can push the victim to suicide. Cyberstalking, too, is a form of cyberviolence that can have devastating consequences for its victims.

Like other forms of deviance discussed throughout the textbook, the media play an important role in cyberdeviance. The Internet, in particular, allows hackers access to banks, government information, and business trade secrets, and social media sites to connect cyberbullies and cyberstalkers with their victims. Considering the opportunities available with the new technology, this chapter only touched on some of the forms of cyberdeviance. As technology advances, so do opportunities for cyberdeviance.

## Outcomes Assessment

1  Define cyberdeviance.
2  Identify the deviant uses of technology.
3  Distinguish between the four categories of cyberdeviance in Wall's typology.
4  Explain the various forms of hacking.
5  Describe cyberwarfare.
6  Describe the various forms and motivations of cyberbullying and compare and contrast cyberbullying with cyberaggression.
7  Explain cyberstalking.
8  Identify the role of the media in cyberdeviance.

## Key Terms and Concepts

active defense technology
crackers
cyberaggression
cyberbullying
cyberdeviance
cyberpiracy

cyberstalking
cyberwarfare
hackers
netcentric warfare
spearfishing
strike back technology

system trespassing
trolling
Wall's typology
white collar delinquency

# 14

# Deviance, Deviants, and Social Control

---

### Student Learning Outcomes

After reading this chapter, students will be able to:

1  Differentiate between informal and formal social control.
2  Explain the various types of informal social control.
3  Briefly describe the history of the police.
4  Identify the roles of the courtroom workgroup members.
5  Differentiate between the various forms of corrections.
6  Describe the relationship between the media and public opinion.

---

*On February 26, 2012, 17-year-old Trayvon Martin walked to a 7-Eleven store from his father's house in Sanford, Florida, where he was visiting while serving a 10-day suspension from school after drug residue was found in his backpack. Martin bought a pack of Skittles and an Arizona iced tea and headed back to his father's house in a gated community. It was then that George Zimmerman, a 29-year-old neighborhood watch captain who was patrolling the area in his SUV, noticed him. Zimmerman called 911. According to the transcript, Zimmerman told the dispatcher:*

*Hey we've had some break-ins in my neighborhood, and there's a real suspicious guy … This guy looks like he's up to no good or he's on drugs or something. It's raining, and he's just walking around looking about.*

*Deviance & Deviants: A Sociological Approach*, First Edition. William E. Thompson and Jennifer C. Gibbs.
© 2017 John Wiley & Sons, Inc. Published 2017 by John Wiley & Sons, Inc.
Companion website: www.wiley.com/go/thompson

DISPATCHER:  *OK, and this guy is he white, black, or Hispanic?*

ZIMMERMAN:  *He looks black.*

DISPATCHER:  *Did you see what he was wearing?*

ZIMMERMAN:  *Yeah. A dark hoodie, like a grey hoodie, and either jeans or sweatpants and white tennis shoes …*

DISPATCHER:  *OK, he's just walking around the area …*

ZIMMERMAN:  *… looking at the houses.*

DISPATCHER:  *OK …*

ZIMMERMAN:  *Now he's just staring at me … Now he's coming towards me. He's got his hand in his waistband. And he's a black male.*

DISPATCHER:  *How old would you say he looks?*

ZIMMERMAN:  *He's got button on his shirt, late teens … Something's wrong with him. Yup, he's coming to check me out, he's got something in his hands. I don't know what his deal is.*

DISPATCHER:  *Just let me know if he does anything ok*

ZIMMERMAN:  *How long until you get an officer over here?*

DISPATCHER:  *Yeah we've got someone on the way, just let me know if this guy does anything else.*

ZIMMERMAN:  *Okay. These assholes, they always get away. When you come to the clubhouse you come straight in and make a left. Actually you would go past the clubhouse … Shit he's running.*

DISPATCHER:  *He's running? Which way is he running?*

ZIMMERMAN:  *Down towards the other entrance to the neighborhood …*

DISPATCHER:  *Are you following him?*

ZIMMERMAN:  *Yeah*

DISPATCHER:  *Ok, we don't need you to do that.*

ZIMMERMAN:  *Ok (City of Sanford, Florida, 2012)*

*The call ended with Zimmerman giving the dispatcher his contact information and address and agreeing to meet the police when they called him upon their arrival in the neighborhood. At that point, Zimmerman had lost sight of Martin.*

*About five minutes before the police arrived in the neighborhood, Martin was talking on his cell phone with his girlfriend. He told her that Zimmerman was following him, and she told him to run. He pulled his hoodie over his head and rushed to find his father's house. During this phone conversation, the 16-year-old girl said she heard Martin ask, "What, are you following me for?" and Zimmerman responded, "What are you doing here?" (Weinstein, 2012). She said she knew the confrontation became physical when she heard Martin's headset fall and the line went dead (Weinstein, 2012). Neighborhood residents reported to police that they heard a fight, someone scream, and a gunshot. By the time police caught up with Zimmerman, Martin lay dead in the grass. According to the police, Zimmerman admitted to shooting Martin in self-defense and had injuries supporting this claim – namely, he had a bloody nose and the back of his head was bleeding (CNN Library, 2014). Medical records from the day after the shooting document that Zimmerman had a broken nose, two black eyes and the back of his head was cut (CNN Library, 2014). He was questioned by police and released.*

*Immediately, there was a public outcry against Zimmerman for racially profiling Martin, the Sanford Police Department for failing to charge Zimmerman, and the Stand Your Ground*

How does the social construction of each actor play a role in the culmination of the Trayvon Martin tragedy? How does it inform the social reaction? Was Trayvon Martin engaging in deviance? Was George Zimmerman? *Source*: © Paul Davey/Alamy

*law. In 2005, Florida passed a self-defense law called "Stand Your Ground", which allowed gun-owning citizens to respond with lethal force instead of retreat when they think they are faced with a deadly threat. The law did not, however, permit people to pursue and confront others or vigilantism – which seems to be what happened in the Martin tragedy.*

*Ultimately, Zimmerman did not invoke the Stand Your Ground law in his defense, using only a self-defense claim, and was acquitted by a jury of six women in July 2013.*

This case is a tragic example of both informal and formal social control. We began our discussion of social control in Chapter 1, when we described sanctions – ways of enforcing norms. Sanctions are reactions to behavior in an attempt to exert social control. **Social control** consists of, "*all of the processes by which people define and respond to deviant behavior*" (Black, 1984:xi, emphasis added). In other words, it is, "the capacity of a society to regulate itself according to desired principles and values" (Janowitz, 1975:82). Social control is different from personal control in that personal control is a person's capacity to manage him or herself toward individual goals while at the same time attempting to avoid disruption to others (Janowitz, 1975). Social control can be **formal**, *involving the criminal justice system or other official government agencies*, or **informal**, involving everyone else, like you, *using unofficial sanctions to enforce norms*.

## Informal Social Control

You may not realize that you are an informal agent of social control. Everyone can exert social pressure to coerce others to change their behavior – even through something as simple as gossiping about someone or teasing a friend. In the previous chapter, we described cybersanctioning. In the new millennium, people apply informal social control through social media as well as face to face. Gossip, ridicule and shame are some types of informal social control that can take form online or in person.

## Gossip, ridicule, and shame

Practically everyone gossips. Any of the "Real Housewives" programs and the popularity of tabloid magazines are testament to that. **Gossip** is more than just idle talk, it is, "*small talk with social purpose*" (Fine and Rosnow, 1978:162, emphasis added). Notice in this definition of gossip that there is no value judgment; in other words, gossip can be positive or negative. While gossip can be *entertaining*, it also provides *information* and wields considerable *influence* (Fine and Rosnow, 1978). Gossip helps to socialize new members of society by passing along information about norms. Gossip is influential, too, in that it has some effect on attitude change. What do you think of a celebrity after hearing about his or her life on TMZ?

Different from gossip, **ridicule** is *mocking or teasing directed at individuals*. Like gossip, ridicule has the power to change behavior or attitudes. Because no one wants to be rejected when others laugh at him or her and retaliation sends the message that the ridicule target can't take a joke, ridicule is a form of "jeer pressure" (Janes and Olson, 2000). Fear of being ridiculed by others is a strong motivator to conform (Janes and Olson, 2000).

**Shame** is an *emotional feeling similar to guilt or embarrassment*, and this can be used as a method of social control. The process of shaming is different from stigmatization, which labels the person as a wrongdoer; instead, shame labels the actions as wrong but accepts the deviant back into society. This approach to deviance is widespread in Japanese culture, which is based on duty and obligation (McCrann, n.d.). In this type of culture, what others think plays a larger role in one's behavior and how someone perceives him or herself (McCrann, n.d.). So, if others are suspicious or if someone does not meet his or her obligations, that person is shamed (McCrann, n.d.). Shame is relevant in American culture, too, but not as much as in Japan. For example, students often report that disappointing parents or loved ones is much worse than making them angry. Shaming can be used to reintegrate those who violate social norms back into the community, and countries like the US and Australia are adopting some of these Japanese principles of social control. In practice, restorative justice conferences bring all parties involved to the table to determine a way that the community can be restored to what it was before the deviance. A restorative justice conference may be used if, for instance, a boy playing baseball outside hits the ball through a neighbor's window. Instead of calling the police, the neighbor may agree to meet with the boy and his parents, along with any other community members and a neutral body, to explain the damage done and how it impacted him. They might agree to having the boy mow the neighbor's lawn all summer to pay for the damaged window. In this way, all harm has been fixed.

While all of these methods of informal social control can be done face to face, more commonly online forums like social media are used to gossip about people, and ridicule and shame them in an effort to change deviants' behaviors. In Chapter 13, we mentioned cybersanctioning as a possible motivator for cyberbullying. We defined **cybersanctioning** as *attempts to modify someone else's behavior usually through name-calling* (Rafferty and Vander Ven, 2014). Using this definition, cybersanctioning can be a form of online informal social control. Cybersanctioning reprimands others' deviant behavior and shames them for their deviance (Rafferty and Vander Ven, 2014). Internet shaming is a popular trend. Instagram, Facebook posts, and even entire websites are dedicated to embarrassing people (and pets) for deviant behavior. One woman described using Facebook status updates to cybersanction another woman for her promiscuous behavior:

> This girl kept hooking up with literally 15 guys while she had a boyfriend and she was hooking up with other girls' boyfriends. So me and my friends would make our status about how we liked being home wreckers etc. We never said her name but she knew we were talking about her because nobody else acted that way with guys (Rafferty and Vander Ven, 2014:370).

## Ostracism

In extreme situations, deviants may be *excluded from the social group*, or **ostracized**. Ostracism can be as extreme as exile from an area or as relatively minor as the "silent treatment" after an argument. On social media sites like Facebook, someone may be ostracized when others "block" that person. And, ostracism is not limited to civilians. Research indicates that police officers who break the police code of silence (that is, do not "rat" on another officer) risk being made an

Shaming is popular around the Internet. Do you think shaming through this medium is effective at encouraging conformity? *Source*: Jane Taylor

outcast. One officer described this ostracism as peer retaliation, "Nobody wants to be around a cop that [sic] is gonna talk about what's done on the streets … and I guarantee you that this officer is sooner or later gonna get zeroed out" (Cancino and Enriquez, 2004:330). Another officer elaborated, "He's pretty much usually alone all the time, eats by himself, because you don't wanna do anything around him, because you know he will tell or report on you" (Cancino and Enriquez, 2004:331). The fear of being alone on the streets – the fear of being ostracized by fellow officers – is enough to make officers conform (Cancino and Enriquez, 2004).

In the corporate world, the board of directors may attempt to make changes in an organization to meet the demands of shareholders, and these changes often are in the best interest of the company instead of the personal gain of the corporate executive officer (CEO). Despite public relations campaigns and glossy annual reports to shareholders, CEOs continue to receive high bonuses and many perks. One reason for this is that they exert informal social control to pressure the board of directors to conform to their norms. CEOs can do this through social distancing, a form of informal ostracism where CEOs can exclude the members of the board from work and social interactions (Westphal and Khanna, 2003). Members of the board of directors who experience this social distancing report being "treated like the enemy"; one described being left out of a business meeting: "After we fired the CEO I got the cold shoulder from [colleagues at another board] … I didn't get invited to an important meeting" (Westphal and Khanna, 2003:387). Because of this informal ostracism, members of the board are hesitant to impose any future restrictions on CEOs: "I haven't been involved in any action like that since and eventually my [relations with other directors] returned to normal" (Westphal and Khanna, 2003:391).

Techniques of informal social control like gossip, ridicule, and ostracism often work hand in hand with formal social control. For example, people might gossip after learning about an acquaintance's arrest. When asked, "Which is worse: Being arrested by the police or having to tell your parents or spouse that you had contact with the police?", students overwhelmingly report they would rather be arrested than tell parents or a spouse about a negative interaction with the police.

## Formal Social Control

In contrast to informal social control, formal social control is administered by officials in society, usually members of government agencies. Formal social control is purposive, intentional and "supported by the will of society" (Ross, 1896:519). This type of social control involves official agencies created for the specific purpose of promoting the social interest.

The primary formal social control mechanism is the criminal justice system. The criminal justice system begins with contact with law enforcement agencies, who are tasked with enforcing codified norms to maintain social order. After an arrest, norm violators have the opportunity to defend themselves in court. If found guilty of the norm violation, though, the offender is moved under the supervision of the corrections component of the criminal justice system.

Typically when we talk about formal social control, we are referring to the criminal justice system. However, there are some organized groups of citizens who work closely with the criminal justice system specifically for the purpose of social control. One such group is neighborhood watch groups.

**Table 14.1** Comparing Informal and Formal Social Control.

| Informal Social Control | Formal Social Control |
| --- | --- |
| Can be casual or incidental | Purposive; intentionally created |
| Informal | Has designated agencies that are formally constituted |
| May serve social interest or personal interest | Serve social interest |
| No supervision | Constant supervision from above |
| Incident of association | Necessary social function |
| Reaction to informal and formal norm violations | Reaction to violations of formal norms only |
| Examples: gossip, shame, cybersanctions | Examples: citation, arrest, prosecution |

*Source*: Adapted from Ross (1896:519).

## Neighborhood watch and vigilantism

**Neighborhood watch programs** became popular in the United States during the 1980s in an attempt to stimulate informal social control efforts of neighborhoods. While not all neighborhood watch programs are the same, the general idea is to *involve citizens in crime prevention efforts in their own neighborhoods* (Garofalo and McLeod, 1989). In other words, "The idea is to induce people to exercise some degree of social control in their environments where they live. A willingness of people to enforce standards of behavior in their own neighborhoods is seen as a key element in the prevention of crime and disorder" (Garofalo and McLeod, 1989:327).

The structure and organization of neighborhood watch programs varies. In many neighborhoods, residents simply agree to keep an eye on other residents' property. Some neighborhoods send newsletters to residents or hold regular meetings focused on residents' concerns. In other neighborhoods, residents organize patrols of their neighborhoods. For example, groups of residents and sometimes a representative from the local police department walk around the neighborhoods, looking for suspicious activity. Members of the neighborhood watch group are supposed to be unarmed and they contact the police for assistance if anything in the neighborhood seems out of place. At the opening of this chapter, we reviewed the fatal shooting of Trayvon Martin by neighborhood watch volunteer, George Zimmerman. Zimmerman's actions violated the code of the watch in that he left his vehicle to engage another citizen. The role of neighborhood watch volunteers is simply to watch or observe happenings in the neighborhood and alert the police about anything suspicious.

When community members *bypass the police and take criminal matters into their own hands*, they are known as **vigilantes**. Vigilantes do not have legal authority to arrest law violators, but they act as if they are the police and seek justice (or revenge) for crimes. With this definition in mind, would you consider George Zimmerman a vigilante?

More formal watch programs can take the form of urban patrols. One example is the *Guardian Angels* in large cities like New York City and San Diego. Formed by Curtis Sliwa in New York City in 1979, the **Guardian Angels** are *an international, nonprofit citizen group dedicated to safety*. Their primary service, on which the organization was founded, is safety patrols from

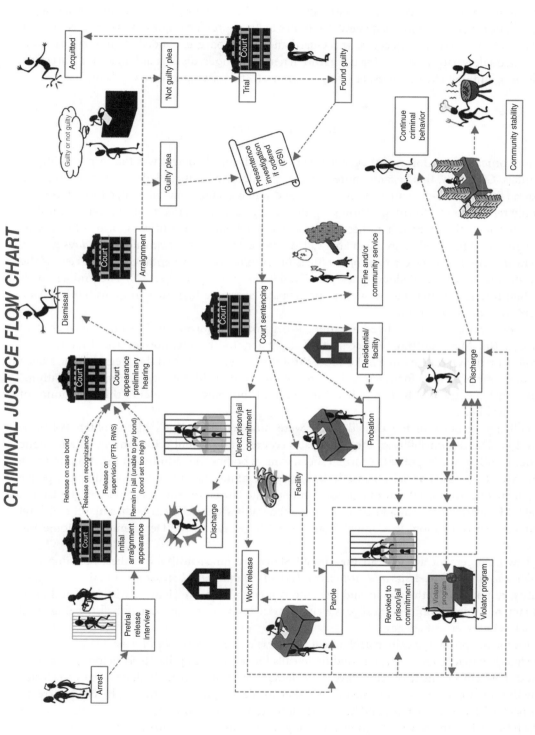

# CRIMINAL JUSTICE FLOW CHART

Arrest

Pretrial release interview

Initial arraignment appearance

Court

Release on case bond

Release on recognizance

Release on supervision (PTR, RWS)

Remain in jail (unable to pay bond) (bond set too high)

Court appearance preliminary hearing

Court

Arraignment

Court

Dismissal

Discharge

'Guilty plea

'Not guilty plea

Guilty or not guilty

Acquitted

Trial

Court

Found guilty

Presentence investigation if ordered (PSI)

Court sentencing

Court

Fine and/or community service

Residential/ facility

Direct prison/jail commitment

Facility

Probation

Work release

Parole

Revoked to prison/jail commitment

Violator program

Violator program

Discharge

Continue criminal behavior

Community stability

How effective do you think this form of social control is in encouraging people to conform? *Source:* Chris Thompson, IA Department of Correction, Canyon County dusk to dawn by unarmed citizens wearing berets and clothing with the Guardian Angel logo. The Guardian Angels have made news headlines by their presence riding subways in New York City. Over the past few decades, the Guardian Angels have expanded their services from unarmed safety patrols to cleaning up graffiti in neighborhoods, disaster aid (like after Hurricane Katrina), and first aid and internet safety programs (http://www.guardianangels.org).

## Law enforcement

Before official law enforcement agencies were formed, social control was the responsibility of families. Gradually, this became more organized under the Mutual Pledge System in England around 900 AD – the precursor to neighborhood watch groups. Mutual Pledge formalized this family responsibility, forming **tithings** – *groups of ten families* – tasked with bringing to justice anyone within the group of families who violated social norms. *Ten tithings* formed **hundreds**, and groups of hundreds were in an area called a **shire**, which is the *equivalent of today's county*. A **shire reeve** *oversaw the groups of hundreds in his shire*; today, we know the shire reeve as the sheriff (say "shire reeve" aloud quickly and you'll hear the word "sheriff"). The problem with mutual pledge was that few wanted to participate; everyone had other responsibilities. And, there was little supervision.

After a variety of short-lived attempts at organizing informal and formal social control efforts, the **Metropolitan Police Act** of 1829 led to the creation of the first trained, professional civil police force in London. Sir Robert Peel established the Metropolitan Police around nine principles focused on crime prevention and positive police-community relations. You may have heard of British police referred to as "bobbies" or "peelers"; this is in honor of Sir Robert Peel.

Policing agencies in the United States were modeled after Peel's Metropolitan Police in London. The responsibility of the police is to control and prevent crime and maintain public order. In other words, police are formal social control bodies who administer sanctions to those who violate codified social norms. Today, there are more than 12,500 local municipal police departments, over 3,000 sheriff's offices, and 50 state law enforcement agencies in the United States (Reaves, 2011) – in addition to several federal law enforcement bodies like the Federal Bureau of Investigation, the United States Secret Service, and the Department of Homeland Security.

Law enforcement agencies in the United States are **quasi-military** bodies, meaning they *follow the military courtesies and customs and adopt a military rank structure*. But, they are a civil entity, responsible to the public, and law enforcement officers are civilians with legal authority. In fact, most police officers must pass a civil service test as one requirement before being hired by a law enforcement agency.

Municipal police typically patrol a **beat**, which is *a small geographical area that can be effectively supervised by an officer*, responding to calls for service and proactively helping citizens in need. Law enforcement officers have considerable discretion in their duties and can decide whether to stop or question someone, whether to file a report of a crime, whether to arrest a suspect, whether to use force and how much force to use, and more. Police officers also exercise discretion when investigating crime, including what tools to use to further their investigations.

More often, police departments are taking advantage of the Internet and social media to enforce the law and improve public confidence in their services.

While many police departments encourage citizens to follow them on Twitter and Facebook, and may even have a presence on YouTube to post videos of wanted suspects or give citizens a peek at departmental training, law enforcement agencies use social media sites in investigations, too. Officers can use social media for clues about crime and disorder in a jurisdiction. For example, Facebook status updates and posting photos and videos of illegal behavior provide evidence that can be used in investigations – like the status update of the "Facebook Murderer" in Chapter 11.

Police departments also may use the Internet as a public relations tool to increase confidence in police officers and perceptions of police effectiveness, especially among social groups who have negative views of police. African-Americans, for example, are more likely than other racial groups to hold negative views of police (Dowler, 2003).

## Courts and corrections

Once police make an arrest, the case moves to the criminal court system. The purpose of the court system is to seek justice, balancing society's need for order and the rights of the norm violator. There are three players in the **courtroom workgroup**: *the prosecutor, the defense attorney, and the judge.* The prosecutor is the lawyer responsible for seeking justice for society, while the defense attorney ensures the offender receives a fair trial and is protected from overzealous social control. The judge falls in the middle; the judge is a neutral body making decisions about the trial process and ultimately the appropriate sentence if the offender is found guilty. Most cases are resolved rather quickly through **plea bargaining**, where *an offender makes a deal with the prosecutor for a lesser charge or shorter sentence in return for a guilty plea.*

Once an offender pleads guilty or is found guilty by a jury, he or she is sentenced to the supervision of a corrections agency. There are a variety of agencies responsible for norm violators, like prisons, jails, probation agencies, and parole agencies. For longer than the last decade, the total number of offenders incarcerated in prisons or community corrections (probation and parole) has hovered around seven million people and has been steadily decreasing since 2007 (Glaze and Herberman, 2013).

Depending on the severity of the offense and the offender's history of contact with the criminal justice system, the supervision can be as light as **probation**, where *the offender can live in the community with periodic checks by a probation officer, but will revisit the judge for a harsher sentence if a new crime is committed during the term of probation.* For offenders who committed an offense deemed more serious and who have a longer criminal history, the sentence might be years in **prison** – *a correctional facility housing those convicted to more than one year of confinement.* In 2012 in the United States, 609,800 offenders were sentenced to prison for either parole violation or new court commitments, over half (53%) for violent offenses (Carson and Golinelli, 2013). This may seem like a lot of people, but this was the lowest number of prison admissions since 1999 (Carson and Golinelli, 2013). And, the bulk of those sent to prison are men: in 2011, over 351,000 men were sentenced to prison on a new court commitment and 184,513 returned to prison for violating parole, while only about 47,000 women were

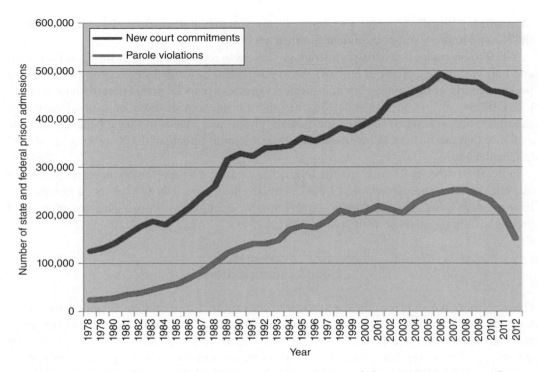

**Figure 14.1** Number of state and federal prison admissions by type of admission, 1978–2012. Reflecting on Chapter 11 and what you now know about street crime and delinquency, what do you think accounts for this trend in prison admissions? *Source*: Carson and Golinelli (2013)

sentenced for a new court commitment and just under 16,000 violated parole (Carson and Golinelli, 2013). Most offenders who were sent to state prison in 2011 on a new court commitment were Black (156,661), while about 146,000 were White and about 70,000 were Hispanic (Carson and Golinelli, 2013). There was a similar pattern for parole violators, with 83,342 Black offenders, 68,784 White offenders and 37,078 Hispanic offenders returning to prison on a parole violation (Carson and Golinelli, 2013).

Although both prisons and jails house offenders, **jails** are for *short-term confinement of less than one year*. Jails often are managed by the county sheriff. After a convicted offender has served his or her prison sentence, he or she may be released on parole. Similar to probation, offenders on **parole** may *live in the community with frequent visits with the parole officer, but if the offender commits a new offense or violates the rule of parole, a judge may order the offender to return to prison*. For offenders who have never had legitimate work, the thought of parole can be intimidating, as explained by one inmate:

> Every time I got close to paroling, I ended up doing something to get me more time. And I'd get really, really close to … I'll be doing good, and doing what I got to do, and they start talking about we are going to send you home, I'd mess up. And I continued to do that … I've never cashed a check, I've never collected a paycheck, I've never held a real job, I've never had my driver's license, I've never even balanced a paycheck (Suto, 2007, as cited in Frank and Aguirre, 2013:41).

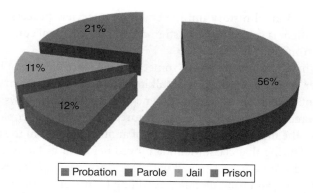

**Figure 14.2** Correctional supervision in the United States, 2012. Notice that the majority of those supervised by correctional agencies are on probation and parole instead of confined to jails and prisons. Why might this be so? *Source*: Glaze and Herberman (2013)

Any form of correctional supervision is unpleasant for convicted offenders, but confinement in prisons or jails can have several negative outcomes for offenders. One inmate describes his depression for feeling like he failed his son:

> Sometimes I get to the point when it doesn't matter to me if I'm alive or not. And I hate getting in that spot because it's really hard that I know; I don't know what to do ... my son just told me that he is mad at me because I'm back here again. It seems that I just can't do anything right (sobs) ... It wasn't getting better, you know. It kept getting bigger and bigger and bigger, like the snowball effect, you know ... I was hopeless about the whole situation. And my life was hopeless and useless (Suto, 2007, as cited in Frank and Aguirre, 2013:40–41).

Sometimes the corrections component can be skipped altogether. For some forms of deviance, specialized courts exist. Specialized courts have been created for drug offenses, domestic violence, mental health and, recently, offenders who are veterans. The idea behind such problem-solving courts is to rehabilitate offenders through a structured court program involving various social service agencies. If the offender completes the programs, the reward typically is having the charges dropped. With the charges dropped, there is little, if any, stigma attached to the deviant.

## Social Control and Stigma

In Chapter 2, we defined stigma as *any attribute that discredits an individual from full social acceptance* (Goffman, 1963). Informal methods of social control like gossip, ridicule, and ostracism can send a message to society that the deviant is discreditable or already discredited, which can lead to more gossip and ridicule. Contact with the criminal justice system stigmatizes a person, sometimes for life. You may have noticed on a recent job application a box to check whether the applicant has been convicted of a crime – although with the "Ban the Box" movement, more places are enacting legislation prohibiting government and other employers from asking about a criminal history until later in the interview process. The reason for this "Ban the Box" movement is so that persons stigmatized by a criminal conviction are not immediately disqualified from a job at the outset.

Despite trying to hide past indiscretions, sometimes deviance is "outed". In the middle of the spring 2014 semester, one of the authors was walking into a classroom when she was approached by one of her students, Melinda, who handed her a cell phone with a news website open on its screen. She shared a recent news article, which featured mug shots of people arrested in a prostitution sting. One of the mug shots was a picture of another student in the class, who regularly sat next to Melinda. During that class, Melinda moved her chair as far away as she could from the other student, and she no longer talked with him during group discussions. Word spread among the other students, and soon no one was willing to interact with him. He was ostracized from the group, stigmatized because of his contact with the criminal justice system.

Informal deviance can invoke similar social reactions. In Chapter 5, we talked about deviant occupations, like those in the adult entertainment industry, and the stigma that adult entertainers often face. That stigma can follow a person throughout life. Few people have successfully transitioned from pornography to mainstream Hollywood productions. Finding a creative way to account for employment time spent in pornography on a resume or job application can be difficult and hiding experience in pornography because of the stigma can become problematic later, when employers and coworkers inevitably discover the truth. Many of the women involved in pornography retire to become stay-at-home mothers and wives. Documentary director Bryce Wagoner describes the continuing stigma of *Life after Porn*:

> We found the men stayed in the business as long as they could and were mostly OK with it … Every woman we spoke to—apart from Amber Lynn, who's still going strong – had to reboot [her life] at 30 and start over in some small town … We found many stories where people tried to move on only for their neighbors to find out that they once made a bunch of dirty movies. One guy couldn't coach his son's Little League team anymore. One woman lost her real-estate job … John Leslie [a male porn star for 30 years] lives up in Mill Valley, near San Francisco, which is a really nice area. He's an artist, a chef, a very cultured guy. His wife is a therapist. A serious professional. But some neighbors found out about his past and they wouldn't let him babysit (Macaulay, 2010).

Societal reactions to people who were associated with the "immoral occupation" of pornography vary, but the majority of the cases in Wagoner's description suggest that former adult entertainers are ostracized from mainstream employment and social circles throughout life.

## Media and Public Opinion

Recall from Chapter 11 that contact with police tends to vary by sex and race. The public's attitudes toward the police can depend on that contact with police, but most people rarely interact with police. People do, however, interact quite a bit with mass media – through their television sets, newspapers, Facebook, and other Internet sites. Shows like CSI (we talked about the CSI Effect in Chapter 11) and other media portrayals of crime and the criminal justice system can have an effect on the public's attitudes toward the criminal justice system.

When one of the authors was enrolled in a criminal justice course and studying constitutional law, a family member balked when learning that the Miranda warnings (derived from the Supreme Court case *Miranda v. Arizona*, 1966) must be read before custodial interrogation, not necessarily upon arrest. (That means that police must warn people of their constitutional rights when the person is no longer free to leave – in custody – and before the person is questioned – interrogated.) Despite being shown the case summary in two constitutional law books, his opinion would not change: "I don't care what your books say. Police always have to give the Miranda warnings before they arrest someone. If they didn't, then why would police tell everyone they 'have the right to remain silent' before they arrest them on every television show?!" Many people, including students studying deviance and social control, are swayed by the mass media. As a result of the many television crime shows, almost every American over the age of five can cite the Miranda warning from memory.

Even though crime has been steadily decreasing since the 1990s and violent crime is uncommon, as we learned in Chapter 11, many people still believe it is increasing and society has never been more violent – even though this is not the case. This might be so because of people's exposure to crime through the lens of the media. As we noted in earlier chapters, with the media, "If it bleeds, it leads", which means that more shocking stories are told first to grab people's attention. The more people watch a television station, the higher its ratings. Similarly, ads on the Internet pay the host site based on traffic to that site or per the number of "clicks" on the advertisement – the more people who visit the host site, the more chances the ad has of being "clicked".

Research shows the media influence people's perceptions of crime and criminal justice. The more crime drama people watch on television, the more fearful of crime they become (Dowler, 2003). Perhaps this is because crime is presented in stereotypical ways that often do not reflect reality. For example, victims – usually women – are often portrayed as innocent and virtuous, while offenders are violent, evil, and always engaged in crime. The reality is that the line between victims and offenders typically is blurred. And, offenders are no different than anyone else – people who engage in crime have families, often hold jobs, and make decisions like the rest of society. Female offenders, for example, sometimes drop their kids off at daycare before committing a crime.

Presenting crime in stereotypical ways can have a detrimental impact on the criminal justice system. People who buy into these stereotypes presented by the media may adopt more punitive attitudes toward law violators. In many cases, pressuring the government for harsher punishments can cause more harm than the crime itself. Reality television, like court shows, can contribute to a punitive attitude among viewers.

## Judge Judy

One television channel is devoted entirely to the court process. Shows on Court TV present sensationalized cases, like murder, sex crimes, and kidnapping. While these crimes do happen, we learned in Chapter 11 that they are rare. In addition to Court TV, regular broadcast stations have half- or full-hour blocks dedicated to "reality" shows about the court process. Shows like the People's Court, Judge Alex, Judge Joe Brown, Judge Mathis, and Divorce Court portray civil (not criminal) small claims court cases where one person sues another. In most cases, the motivation to have the case heard in front of these television judges is money, as both parties receive some compensation (usually around $250, according to Shugart, 2006) for appearing on the television show. These shows:

> ... typically feature two small-claims litigation cases in each half-hour episode. As the lead-in reminds viewers each time, defendants and plaintiffs are "real people" who have agreed to have their cases heard in the court at hand and broadcast to the nation, absent of legal representation. Furthermore, we are informed dramatically, all rulings are final. As the parties file into the court-room prior to each case, an announcer identifies them and briefly summarizes the particulars of the case. Once the subjects take their respective positions, the case commences, observed by an audience that fills the benches of the small courtroom. Following the conclusion of the case, the announcer usually meets briefly with at least one but typically both of the subjects outside of the courtroom to gauge their reactions to the judge's ruling (Shugart, 2006:82).

None of the judges on these "reality" shows, though, is a member of the judiciary while appearing on these "syndi-courts".

One of the first of these court shows (modeled after Judge Wapner's People's Court television show) is particularly popular, due in part to the "no nonsense" approach by the judge: Judge Judy Sheindlin. First broadcast in 1996, Judge Judy is well known for her stern chastisement of the defendant and anyone else who she deems disrespectful in the courtroom, including the plaintiff. A former Manhattan family court judge, Judge Judy frequently mentions her background and her Jewish heritage in her decision-making process. For several years, Judge Judy has been ranked in the top 10 syndicated television programs, at one point outpacing both Oprah Winfrey and Jerry Springer (Asimow, 1999; Shugart, 2006).

Similar to other programs in the judge show genre, Judge Judy reinforces cultural stereotypes. People appearing on these shows tend to be working class. Judge Judy focuses her attention on their moral lapses, often reprimanding them for their life choices and failure to be fiscally responsible. In one episode, even though she ruled in favor of the plaintiff, she chastised the woman for her moral choices:

> However, you don't escape without a tongue-lashing. If you're being stupid, don't expect me to be sympathetic. You don't give a boyfriend a credit card – ever, no way, nothing! You don't give anybody a credit card, especially somebody that you are not related to by blood or marriage or committed to by virtue of an engagement – even then it's dumb and stupid – so you don't get any awards for brains (CBS, May 29, 2002, as cited in Kohm, 2006:713).

Also like other court reality shows, viewers are encouraged to call the television show and vote for a verdict, although viewers' opinions likely do not affect the outcome of the case. The Judge Judy show has its own website, where viewers can play games to test their legal knowledge, connect with Judge Judy products like her best-selling self-help books, and learn more about the show. Judge Judy even has a smartphone app, where fans can vote from their phones, among other activities. Given this pervasiveness, what influence might a television judge like Judge Judy have on public attitudes toward courts and sentencing?

# Summary

People use a variety of social control mechanisms to encourage others to conform to norms. A disapproving glare, spreading rumors about another, teasing with the purpose of changing another's behavior, and the "silent treatment" are examples of informal social control. Formal social control, on the other hand, is administered by a government agency like the criminal justice system.

The criminal justice system is designed to hold offenders responsible for crimes they commit. It consists of three main components: police, courts, and corrections agencies. Police are responsible for investigating crimes and apprehending offenders. Courts serve as a neutral body to arbitrate between the victim (in criminal matters, the victim is usually the state, representing society at large) and the offender. Corrections agencies are responsible for supervising offenders who have been convicted (that is, found guilty) of crimes.

The media play a large role in social control and people's perceptions of social control mechanisms. Gossip, ridicule, and public shaming are easily communicated via the Internet through cybersanctioning. Criminal justice agencies can use the Internet and other forms of mass media to communicate information, to investigate crimes, and as a public relations resource. Television programming, especially syndi-court or reality court television shows, can have another effect on the criminal justice system, reinforcing the stereotypes about crime and justice.

# Outcomes Assessment

1  Differentiate between informal and formal social control.
2  Explain the various types of informal social control.
3  Briefly describe the history of the police.
4  Identify the roles of the courtroom workgroup members.
5  Differentiate between the various forms of corrections.
6  Describe the relationship between the media and public opinion.

# Key Terms and Concepts

| | | |
|---|---|---|
| courtroom workgroup | neighborhood watch | ridicule |
| cybersanctioning | programs | shame |
| formal social control | ostracism | shire |
| gossip | parole | shire reeve |
| Guardian Angels | plea bargaining | social control |
| hundreds | police beat | tithings |
| informal social control | prison | vigilante |
| jail | probation | |
| Metropolitan Police Act | quasi-military | |

# References

AANR (2014) American Association for Nude Recreation, www.aanr.com (accessed 10 January 2014).

ABC News (2005) The 'Lifestyle' – real-life wife swaps, ABC 20/20, Mar 18.

Adomanis, M. (2013) Barack Obama's surprising lack of patience for Russia's anti-gay laws. *Forbes* (Aug 9) http://www.forbes.com/sites/markadomanis/2013/08/09/barack-obamas-surpsrising-lack-of-patience-for-russias-anti-gay-laws/(accessed 31 Dec, 2013).

Akers, R. (2009) *Social Learning and Social Structure: A General Theory of Crime and Deviance*, Transaction, New York.

Alexander, A. and Hanson, J. (2013) *Taking Sides: Clashing Views in Mass Media and Society* 12th edn, McGraw-Hill, New York.

Altman, J., Everitt, B.J., Glautier, S., Markou, A., Nutt, D., Oretti, R., Phillips, G.D. and Robbins, T.W. (1996) The biological, social and clinical bases of drug addiction: commentary and debate. *Psychopharmacology*, 135 (4), 285–245.

American Psychiatric Association (1994) Diagnostic and Statistical Manual of Mental Disorders: DSM-IV. American Psychiatric Association, Washington DC.

Amos, E.P. (1983) *Kansas Funeral Profession Through the Years*. Kansas Funeral Directors' Association, Topeka.

APA (2013) *Diagnostic and Statistical Manual of Mental Disorders*, 5th edn, American Psychiatric Association, Arlington, VA.

Asimow, M. (1999) Justice with an Attitude: Judge Judy and the Daytime Television Bench. *The Judges' Journal*, 38, 24–47.

Atkins, D.C., Baucom, D. H. and Jacobson, N. S. (2001) Understanding Infidelity: Correlates in a National Random Sample. *Journal of Family Psychology*, 15 (4), 735–749.

Atkinson, M. (2011) Male athletes and the cult(ure) of thinness in sport. *Deviant Behavior*, 32, 224–256.

Badaly, D., Kelly, B.M., Schwartz, D. and Dabney-Lieras, K.(2013) Longitudinal associations of electronic aggression and victimization with social standing during adolescence. *Journal of Youth and Adolescence*, 42 (6), 891–904.

*Deviance & Deviants: A Sociological Approach*, First Edition. William E. Thompson and Jennifer C. Gibbs.
© 2017 John Wiley & Sons, Inc. Published 2017 by John Wiley & Sons, Inc.
Companion website: www.wiley.com/go/thompson

Bailey, J.M. (1999) Homosexuality and Mental Illness. *JAMA Psychiatry*, 56 (10), 883–884.

Bakken, N. W. and Gunter, W.D. (2012) Self-cutting and suicidal ideation among adolescents: Gender differences in the causes and correlates of self-injury. *Deviant Behavior*, 33 (5), 339–356.

Balan, M. (2010) CNN Highlights Pornography's Destructive Effects on Society? *NewsBusters*, http://newsbusters.org/blogs/matthew-balan/2010/07/28/cnn-highlights (accessed 23 October, 2013).

Bandura, A.J. (1965) Influence of Models' Reinforcement Contingencies on the Acquisition of Imitative Responses. *Journal of Personality and Social Psychology*, 1, 589–595.

Bandura, A.J., Ross, J.D. and Ross, S. (1963) Imitation of film-mediated aggressive models. *Journal of Abnormal and Social Psychology*, 66, 3–11.

Banks-Smith, N. (2008) Last night's TV: Wonderland: The man who eats badgers, *The Guardian* (Jan 23).

Barnett, C. (n.d.) *The measurement of white-collar crime using Uniform Crime Reporting* (UCR) data. US Department of Justice, Federal Bureau of Investigation, Criminal Justice Information Services (CJIS) Division, Washington, DC, http://www.fbi.gov/stats-services/about-us/cjis/ucr/nibrs/nibrs_wcc.pdf (accessed Feb 25, 2016).

Baron-Cohen, S. (ed.) (1997) *The Maladapted Mind:Classic Readings in Evolutionary Psychopathology*. Psychology Press, East Sussex, UK.

Barrocas, A.L., Hankin, B.L., Young, J.F. and Abela, J.R.Z. (2012) Rates of nonsuicidal self-injury in youth: age, sex, and behavioral methods in a community sample. *Pediatrics*, 130 (1), 39–45.

Bauer, S.W. (2007) *The History of the Ancient World: From the Earliest Accounts to the Fall of Rome*. W.W. Norton, New York.

Bazelon, E. (2013) The price of a stolen childhood. *The New York Times Magazine*. www.nytimes.com (accessed January 24, 2013).

Beauboeuf-Lafontant, T. (2003) Strong and large black women? Exploring relationships between deviant womanhood and weight. *Gender & Society*, 17 (1), 111–121.

Becker, H.S. (1953) Becoming a marihuana user. *American Journal of Sociology*, 59 (3), 235–242.

Becker, H. (1963) *The Outsiders: Studies in the Sociology of Deviance*. The Free Press, New York.

Benediktsson, M.O. (2010) The deviant organization and the bad apple CEO: Ideology and accountability in the media coverage of corporate scandals. *Social Forces*, 88 (5), 2189–2216.

Berger, J. (2013) *Contagious: Why Things Catch On*. Simon & Schuster, New York.

Berger, P. (1963) *Invitation to Sociology: A Humanistic Perspective*. Anchor Doubleday, Garden City, NY.

Bergstrand, C.R. and Sinski, J.B. (2010) *Swinging in America: Love, Sex, and Marriage in the 21st Century*. Praeger, Santa Barbara, CA.

Bernard, J. (1991) From fasting to abstinence: The origins of the American temperance movement, in *Drinking: Behavior and Belief in Modern History* (eds S. Barrows and R. Room), University of California Press, Los Angeles, CA, (pp. 337–353).

Biederman, J. (2005) Attention-Deficit/Hyperactivity Disorder: A Selective overview. *Biological Psychiatry*, 57 (11), 1215–1220. DOI: 10.1016/j.biopsych.2004.10.020.

Black, D. (ed.) (1984) *Towards a General Theory of Social Control*. Academic Press, Inc., Orlando, FL.

Black, M.C., Basile, K.C., Breiding, M.J. *et al.* (2011) *The National Intimate Partner and Sexual Violence Survey (NISVS): 2010 Summary Report*. National Center for Injury Prevention and Control, Centers for Disease Control and Prevention, Atlanta, GA.

Bloom, M. (2005) Mother. Daughter. Sister. Bomber. *Bulletin of the Atomic Scientists*, 61 (6), 54–62.

Blumstein, Al. and Wallman, J. (eds) (2006) *The Crime Drop in America*. Cambridge University Press, New York.

Blunt, T. (2012) Breaking News – Man Parachutes From Edge of Space. *The FW*: (Oct 14) http://thefw.com/breaking-news-man-parachutes-from-edge-of-space/(accessed Feb 28 2014).

Boyle, M. (2010) *The Moneyless Man: A Year of Freeconomic Living*. Oneworld Publications, Oxford, England.

Braga, A.A., Hureau, D.M. and Papachristos, A.V. (2011) The relevance of micro places to citywide robbery trends: A longitudinal analysis of robbery incidents at street corners and block faces in Boston. *Journal of Research in Crime and Delinquency*, 48 (1), 7–32.

Braithwaite, J. (1984) *Corporate Crime in the Pharmaceutical Industry*. Routledge and Kegan Paul, London.

Brockovich, E.(n.d.) *My story*. http://www.brockovich.com/my-story/(accessed March 13, 2014).

Brown, T.B. and Kimball, T. (2013) Cutting to live: a phenomenology of self-harm. *Journal of Marital and Family Therapy*, 39 (2), 195–208.

Brunker, M. (2013) Dorner died of self-inflicted gunshot wound to the head, authorities say. *NBC News*. (16 February) http://usnews.nbcnews.com/_news/2013/02/15/16978359- dorner- died- of- self- inflicted- gunshot- wound- to- the- head- authorities- say (accessed February 16, 2013).

Bryant, C.D. and Forsyth, C.J. (2012) The complexity of deviant lifestyles. *Deviant Behavior*, 33 (7), 525–549.

Brylske, A. (2012) *The Complete Diver: The History, Science and Practice of Scuba Diving*. Dive Training LLC, Kansas City.

Brody, P. (2013) *Son of Sam: A Biography of David Berkowitz*. Bookcaps, Anaheim, CA.

Brothwell, D.R. (1963) *Digging up Bones; the Excavation, Treatment and Study of Human Skeletal Remains*. British Museum (Natural History), London.

Brown, H.N. (1990) Can Violent Films Help Troubled Teens? *Dallas Morning News*, (March 11), p.4C.

Brown, J., Keller, S. and Stern, S. (2009) Sex, Sexuality, Sexting, and Sexed: Adolescents and the Media. *The Prevention Researcher*, 16 (4),12–16.

Bureau of Justice Statistics (2013) *Robbery*, (Oct 23) http://www.bjs.gov/index.cfm?ty=tp&tid=313 (accessed Feb 28, 2014).

Bureau of Justice Statistics (2014) *Number of violent victimizations by victim-offender relationship and sex, 2008–2012*. Generated using the NCVS Victimization Analysis Tool at www.bjs.gov

Burgess, M. (2003) *A brief history of terrorism*. Center for Defense Information (CDI), Washington, DC.

Burt, M.R. (1980) Cultural myths and supports for rape. *Journal of Personality and Social Psychology*, 38, 217–230.

Cahnman, W.J. (1968) The stigma of obesity. *The Sociological Quarterly*, 9 (3), 283–299.

Callanan, V.J. and Davis, M.S. (2009) A comparison of suicide note writers with suicides who did not leave notes. *Suicide & Life-Threatening Behavior*, 39 (5), 558–568.

Callero, P.L. (2013) *The Myth of Individualism: How Social Forces Shape Our Lives* (2nd edn), Rowman and Littlefield, Lanham, MD.

Cancino, J.M. and Enriquez, R. (2004) A qualitative analysis of officer peer retaliation. *Policing: An International Journal of Police Strategies & Management*, 27 (3), 320–340.

Carin-Levy, G. and Jones, D. (2007) Psychosocial Aspects of Scuba Diving for People with Physical Disabilities: An Occupational Science Perspective. *Canadian Journal of Occupational Therapy*, 74 (February), 6–14.

Carlson, K.B. (2012) Luka Rocco Magnotta manhunt ends with whimper in Berlin. *National Post* (Tues June 5).

Carson, E.A. and Golinelli, D. (2013) *Prisoners in 2012: Trends in Admissions and Releases, 1991–2012*. US Department of Justice, Office of Justice Programs, Bureau of Justice Statistics, Washington, DC. http://www.bjs.gov/content/pub/pdf/p12tar9112.pdf (accessed April 13, 2014).

Carson, E.A. and Sabol, W.J. (2012) *Prisoners in 2011*. US Department of Justice, Office of Justice Programs, Bureau of Justice Statistics, Washington, DC. http://bjs.ojp.usdoj.gov/content/pub/pdf/p11.pdf (accessed April 13, 2014).

Catalano, S. (2013) *Intimate partner violence: attributes of victimization, 1993–2011*. US Department of Justice, Office of Justice Programs, Bureau of Justice Statistics, Washington, DC, http://www.bjs.gov/index.cfm?ty=pbdetail&iid=4801

Cater, J.K. (2012) Traumatic amputation: Psychosocial adjustment of six Army women to loss of one or more limbs. *Journal of Rehabilitation Research and Development*, 49 (10), 1443–1456.

Cavan, R.S. (1964) The concepts of tolerance and contraculture as applied to delinquency. *Sociological Quarterly*, 2 (Spring), 243–258.

Celsi, R.L., Rose, R.L. and Leigh, T.W. (1993) An exploration of high-risk leisure consumption through skydiving. *Journal of Consumer Research*, 20 (1), 1–23.

Centers for Disease Control and Prevention, National Center for Injury Prevention and Control (2005) *Web-based Injury Statistics Query and Reporting System (WISQARS)*. www.cdc.gov/ncipc/wisqars (accessed Dec 30, 2013).

Centers for Disease Control and Prevention, National Center for Injury Prevention and Control (2012) *Suicide: Facts at a glance*. http://stacks.cdc.gov/view/cdc/21865 (accessed Dec 30, 2013).

Centers for Disease Control and Prevention (2013) Mental health surveillance among children – United States, 2005–2011. *Morbidity and Mortality Weekly Report*, (May 17), 62 (Suppl 2), 1–35.

Centers for Disease Control and Prevention (2014) *Child maltreatment prevention* (Jan 23), http://www. cdc.gov/violenceprevention/childmaltreatment/ (accessed March 3, 2014).

Chang, S.-S., Stuckler, D. Yip, P. and Gunnell, D. (2013) Impact of 2008 global economic crisis on suicide: time trend study in 54 countries. *BMJ*, 347, f5239. DOI: 10.1136/bmj.f5239.

Chin, G.J. (2002) Race, the war on drugs, and the collateral consequences of criminal conviction. *The Journal of Gender, Race & Justice*, 6, 253–275.

City of Sanford, Florida.,(2012) Transcript of George Zimmerman's call to the police, Feb 26. *Mother Jones*. http://www.motherjones.com/documents/326700-full-transcript-zimmerman (accessed March 31, 2014).

Cleere, C. and Lynn, S.J. (2013) Acknowledged versus unacknowledged sexual assault among college women. *Journal of Interpersonal Violence*, 28 (12), 2593–2611.

Cloward, R.A. and Ohlin, L.E. (1960) *Delinquency and Opportunity*. The Free Press, New York.

CNN Library (2014) Trayvon Martin shooting fast facts (Feb 22). *CNN.com*. http://www.cnn. com/2013/06/05/us/trayvon-martin-shooting-fast-facts/ (accessed March 31, 2014).

Cockerham, W.C. (2006) *Society of Risk-Takers: Living Life on the Edge*. Worth, New York.

Cohen, A. (1955) *Delinquent Boys: The Culture of the Gang*. The Free Press, New York.

Cohen, B. (1980) *Deviant Street Networks: Prostitution in New York City*. Lexington Books, New York.

Cohen, S. (2011) *Folk Devils and Moral Panics*. Routledge, New York.

Cole, S. and Dioso, R. (2005) Law and the lab: Do tv shows really affect how juries vote? Let's look at the evidence. *The Wall Street Journal* (May 13) http://truthinjustice.org/law-lab.htm (accessed March 10, 2014).

Coleman, J.W. (2006) *The Criminal Elite*, 6th edn, Worth, New York.

Collins, G. and Adleman, A. (2011) *Breaking the Cycle: Free Yourself from Sex Addiction, Porn Obsession and Shame*. New Harbinger, Oakland, CA.

Comartin, E., Kernsmith, R. and Kernsmith, P. (2013) Sexting and Sex Offender Registration: Do Age, Gender, and Sexual Orientation Matter? *Deviant Behavior*, 34 (1), 38–52.

Communications Management Inc. (2011) *Sixty Years of Daily Newspaper Circulation Trends: Canada, United States, United Kingdom*. Communications Management Inc. (May 6) http://media-cmi.com/downloads/Sixty_Years_Daily_Newspaper_Circulation_Trends_050611.pdf

Connor, T. (2013) Hunt on for ex-LAPD officer suspected in revenge slayings. *NBC News* (Feb 7). http://usnews.nbcnews.com/_news/2013/02/07/16884539- hunt- on- for- ex- lapd- officer- suspected- in- revenge- slayings (accessed Feb 7, 2013).

Cooley, C.H. (1902) *Human Nature and the Social Order*. Scribner's, New York.

Courtright, D.T. (2001) *Dark Paradise: A History of Opiate Addiction in America*. Harvard University Press. Cambridge, MA.

*References*

Cragin, K. and Daly, S.A. (2009) *Women as Terrorists: Mothers, Recruiters, and Martyrs.* ABC-CLIO, Santa Barbara, CA.

Cromwell, P. and Olson, J.N. (2004) The reasoning burglar: Motives and decision-making strategies, in *In their own words: Criminals on crime,* 4th edn (ed P. Cromwell), Roxbury Publishing, Los Angeles, CA, pp. 42–56.

Dalberg-Acton, J.E. (1887,1907) Letter to Bishop Mandell Creighton, April 5, 1887, in *John Emerich Edward Dalberg, Lord Acton, Historical Essays and Studies,* (eds J.N. Figgis and R.V. Laurence), Macmillan, London. http://oll.libertyfund.org/index.php?option=com_content&task=view&id=1407& Itemid=283 (accessed March 17, 2014).

Davis, D.S. (1984) Good people doing dirty work: A study of social isolation. *Symbolic Interaction,* 7 (Fall), 233–247.

Davis, N.J. (1971) Becoming a Prostitute. *Studies in the Sociology of Sex,* 297–322.

Davis, N.J. (1993) *Prostitution: An International Handbook on Trends, Problems, and Policies.* Greenwood Press, Westport, CT.

DeJong, J. and Hanzlick, R. (2000) Level of agreement between opinions of medical examiner investigators and forensic pathologist medical examiners regarding the manner of death. *The American Journal of Forensic Medicine and Pathology,* 21 (1), 11–20.

deKay, J. and Huffaker, S. (1985) *The World's Greatest Left-Handers.* M. Evans and Company Inc., New York.

DeMello, M. (2000) *Bodies of Inscription: a Cultural History of the Modern Tattoo Community,* Duke University Press, Durham NC.

Devoto, B. (1962) *Mark Twain Letters from the Earth.* Fawcett, New York.

Dewey, C. (2013) Self-harm blogs pose problems and opportunities. *The Washington Post* (Sep 9) http://www.washingtonpost.com/national/health-science/ (accessed Sep 9, 2013).

Dewey, C. (2013) Why we should fear Miami's 'Facebook murderer'. *The Washington Post,* (Aug 11) www.washingtonpost.com/national/ (accessed Aug 11, 2013).

Dinos, S., Stevens, S. Serfaty, M. *et al.* (2004) Stigma: the feelings and experiences of 46 people with mental illness: Qualitative study. *British Journal of Psychiatry,* 184, 176–181.

Dittmar, H., Halliwell, E. and Ive, S. (2006) Does Barbie make girls want to be thin? The effect of experimental exposure to images of dolls on the body image of 5- to 8-year-old girls. *Developmental Psychology,* 42 (2), 283–292.

Dollard, J., Miller, N.E., Doob, L.W. *et al.* (1939) Frustration and aggression. Yale University Press, New Haven, CT.

Dowbiggin, I. (2013) From Sander to Schiavo: Morality, partisan politics, and America's culture war over euthanasia, 1950–2010. *The Journal of Policy History,* 25 (1), 12–41.

Dowler, K. (2003) Media consumption and public attitudes toward crime and justice: The relationship between fear of crime, punitive attitudes, and perceived police effectiveness. *Journal of Criminal Justice and Popular Culture,* 10 (2), 109–126.

Duis, P. (1999) *Saloon: Public Drinking in Chicago and Boston, 1880–1920.* University of Illinois Press, Champaign, IL.

Duke, A. (2013) Brittany Murphy poison report 'ridiculous,' expert says. CNN, (Nov 20). http://www.cnn.com/2013/11/19/showbiz/brittany-murphy-death/ (accessed Nov 21, 2013).

Duncan, O.D. and Parmelee, L.F. (2006) Trends in public approval of euthanasia and suicide in the US, 1947–2003. *Journal of Medical Ethics,* 32, 266–272.

Durkheim, E. (1951) *Suicide: A Study in Sociology.* Translated by J.A. Spaulding and G. Simpson. The Free Press, New York.

Douglas, M. (1992) *Risk and Blame: Essays in Cultural Theory.* Routledge, London.

Durkheim, E. (1893, 1964) *The Division of Labor in Society.* Free Press, Glencoe, IL.

Durkheim, E. (1897, 1951) *Suicide: A Study in Sociology*. Translated by J.A. Spaulding and G. Simpson, ed. G. Simpson. The Free Press, New York.

Durkheim, E. (1938) *Rules of the Sociological Method*. Translated by S.A. Solovay and J.H. Mueller, ed G.E.G. Catlin. Free Press, Glencoe, IL.

Dworkin, S.L. and Wachs, F.L. (2009) *Body Panic: Gender, Health, and the Selling of Fitness*. New York University Press, New York.

Edelhertz, H. (1970) *The Nature, Impact and Prosecution of White Collar Crime*. US Department of Justice, Office of Justice Programs, National Institute of Justice. Washington, DC.

Edgerton, G. (2009) *The Columbia History of American Television*. Columbia University Press New York.

Edwards-Levy, A. (2012) Bill Clinton's speech the highlight of Democratic convention: Poll. *The Huffington Post* (Sep 10).

Elamar, G.T. (2001) *Mother Goose: From Nursery to Literature*. Backinprint.com edition, iUniverse.com, Authors Guild, Lincoln, NE.

Eligon, J. (2013) A Missouri school trains its teachers to carry guns, and most parents approve. *The New York Times* (April 14) p. A10.

Enck, G.E. and Preston, J.D. (1988) Counterfeit intimacy: A dramaturgical analysis of an erotic performance. *Deviant Behavior*, 9, 369–381.

Eskridge Jr., W.N. (2008) *Dishonorable Passions: Sodomy Laws in America, 1861–2003*. Kindle Edition. Viking, New York.

Evans, P.C. (2003) If only I were thin like her, maybe I could be happy like her: The self-implications of associating a thin female ideal with life success. *Psychology of Women Quarterly*, 27, 209–214.

Fairbank, K. (2003) Dancing for Dollars. *Dallas Morning News* (Feb 22) p. 2F,3F.

Falls, A. (2013) *Human Trafficking: A Global Perspective of Modern Day Human Trafficking and Sex Slavery*. Kindle Edition, Amazon Digital Services.

Favazza, A. (1996) *Bodies Under Siege: Self-Mutilation and Body Modification in Culture and Psychiatry*. Johns Hopkins University Press, Baltimore.

FBI (n.d.) *Famous cases and criminals:Al Capone*. http://www.fbi.gov/about-us/history/famous-cases/al-capone (accessed Apr 14, 2014).

FBI (2013) Crime in the United States 2012. *Uniform Crime Reports*, Table 43.

FBI (2013) 2012 National Incident-Based Reporting System. US Department of Justice, Federal Bureau of Investigation, Criminal Justice Information Services Division, Washington, DC. http://www.fbi.gov/about-us/cjis/ucr/nibrs/2012

Federal Bureau of Investigation. (n.d.) Definitions of Terrorism in the US Code. United States Department of Justice, Federal Bureau of Investigation, Washington, DC. http://www.fbi.gov/about-us/investigate/terrorism/terrorism-definition (accessed Feb 28, 2014).

Federal Bureau of Investigation (2013) Crime in the United States, 2012. United States Department of Justice, Federal Bureau of Investigation, Washington, DC. https://www.fbi.gov/about-us/cjis/ucr/crime-in-the-u.s/2012/crime-in-the-u.s.-2012 (accessed Jan 22, 2014).

Federal Bureau of Investigation (2014) Crime in the United States, 2013. United States Department of Justice, Federal Bureau of Investigation, Washington, DC. http://www.fbi.gov/about-us/cjis/ucr/crime-in-the-u.s/2013/crime-in-the-u.s.-2013 (accessed Nov 25, 2014).

Felson, M. and Boba, R. (2010) *Crime and everyday life*, 4th edn Sage, Los Angeles.

Fine, G.A. and Rosnow, R.L. (1978) Gossip, gossipers, gossiping. *Personality and Social Psychology Bulletin*, 4 (1), 161–168.

Finkle, J. (2012) Powerful "flame" cyber weapon found in Middle East. *NBC News* (May 29) http://www.msnbc.msn.com/id/47590214/ns/technology_and_science-security/t/powerful-flame-cyber-weapon-found-middle-east/ (accessed May 28, 2012).

Fischer, H. (2013) *US military casualty statistics:Operation New Dawn, Operation Iraqi Freedom, and Operation Enduring Freedom.* Congressional Research Service, Washington, DC.

Fishman, S. (2011) The Madoff Tapes. *New York Magazine* (February 27), http://nymag.com/news/features/berniemadoff-2011-3/index8.html (accessed May 2, 2014).

Foucalt, M. (1990) *The History of Sexuality, Vol. 1.* Translated by R. Hurley. Vintage Books, New York.

Fox, J.A. and Levin, J. (2003) Serial murder: popular myths and empirical realities, in *Critical Issues in Crime and Justice,* 2nd edn (ed. A.R. Roberts), pp. 51–61.

Frank, L. and Aguirre, R.T. P. (2013) Suicide within United States jails: A qualitative interpretive meta-synthesis. *Journal of Sociology & Social Welfare,* XL (3), 31–52.

Friedrichs, D.O. (2002) Occupational crime, occupational deviance, and workplace crime: Sorting out the difference. *Criminal Justice,* 2 (3), 243–256.

Gallup Historical Data (2012) *Historical Presidential Approval Ratings.* US Politics, About.com http://uspolitics.about.com/od/polls/l/bl_historical_approval.htm

Galveston, A.P. (2007) Devil Made Dad Hurt Baby, His Wife Says. *Dallas Morning News* (21 May) p.3A.

Garofalo, J. and McLeod, M. (1989) The structure and operations of Neighborhood Watch Programs in the United States. *Crime & Delinquency,* 35 (3), 326–344.

Gearson, J. (2002) The nature of modern terrorism. *The Political Quarterly,* 73 (s1), 7–24.

Gelles, D. and Tett, G. (2011) From behind bars, Madoff spins his story. *Financial Times* (April 8), http://www.ft.com/cms/s/2/a29d2b4a-60b7-11e0-a182-00144feab49a.html (accessed May 2, 2014).

Gibbs, J. (2012) Gender and terrorism (box insert), in *International Handbook of Crime and Gender Studies.* (eds. C.M. Renzetti, S.L. Miller and A.R. Gover), Routledge, Abingdon.

Gillespie, A.A. (2012) *Child Pornography: Law and Policy.* Routledge, New York.

Glaze, L.E. and Herberman, E.J. (2013) *Correctional Populations in the United States, 2012.* US Department of Justice, Office of Justice Programs, Bureau of Justice Statistics., Washington, DC, http://www.bjs.gov/content/pub/pdf/cpus12.pdf (accessed April 13, 2014).

Goffman, E. (1961) *Encounters: Two Studies in the Sociology of Interaction.* Bobbs-Merrill, Indianapolis.

Goffman, E. (1963) *Stigma: Notes on the Management of Spoiled Identity.* Prentice-Hall, Englewood Cliffs, NJ.

Goldfarb, Z.A. (2013) ATM thieves conducted massive cyberattack. *The Washington Post* (May 9), http://www.washingtonpost.com/business/economy/atm-thieves-conducted-massive-cyberattack/2013/05/09/0c3c3a1c-b8ec-11e2-92f3-f291801936b8_story.html (accessed May 9, 2013).

Goldman, R. (2012) Carjacker Whose Chase Ends with Suicide on Live TV. *ABC World News,* Sep 29.

Goldstein, N.E., Cohen, L.M., Arnold, R.M. *et al.*(2012) Prevalence of formal accusations of murder and euthanasia against physicians. *Journal of Palliative Medicine,* 15 (3), 334–339.

Goldstein, P.J. (1985) The drug/violence nexus: A tripartite conceptual framework. *Journal of Drug Issues,* 15, 493–506.

Golijan, R. (2012) Pinterest bans content encouraging self-harm or self-abuse, (Mar 24), http://sys06-public.nbcnews.com/today/money/pinterest-bans-content-encouraging-self-harm-or-self-abuse-543796 (accessed Mar 24, 2012).

Goode, E. (2008) Moral panics and disproportionality: the case of LSD use in the sixties. *Deviant Behavior,* 29, 533–543.

Goodman, D. (1983) Pac-Mania: Examination of handheld tabletop, home computer, and home video game versions of Pac-Man. *Creative Computing Video and Arcade Games Vol. I* (Spring), 122.

Gould, T. (1999) *The Lifestyle: A Look at the Erotic Rites of Swingers,* Kindle Edition. Vintage, Canada.

Greene-Shortridge, T.M., Britt, T.W., and Castro, C.A. (2007) The stigma of mental health problems in the military. *Military Medicine,* 172 (2), 157–161.

Griffiths, H. and Frobish, T.S. (2013) Virtual deviance: Swinging and swapping in an on-line network. *Deviant Behavior,* 34 (11), 875–894.

Groesz, L.M., Levine, M.P. and Murnen, S.K. (2002) The effect of experimental presentation of thin media images on body satisfaction: A meta-analytic review. *International Journal of Eating Disorders*, 31 (1), 1–16.

Guiness World Records (2013) *Guinness World Records 2014*. Guinness World Records, New York.

Gunzerath, L., Hewitt, B.G., Li, T.-K. and Warren, K.R. (2011) Alcohol research: Past, present, and future. *Annals of the New York Academy of Sciences*, 1216, 1–23.

Hall, W. (2010) What are the policy lessons of National Alcohol Prohibition in the United States, 1920–1933? *Addiction*, 105, 1164–1173.

Haviland, W.A., Prins, H.E.L., McBride, B. and Walrath, D. (2010) *Cultural Anthropology: The Human Challenge*, 13th edn. Wadsworth/Cengage, Belmont, CA.

Hawdon, J.E. (2001) The role of presidential rhetoric in the creation of a moral panic: Reagan, Bush, and the War on Drugs. *Deviant Behavior*, 22, 419–445.

Hays, T. and Neumeister, L. (2013) NYC cop said he was 'dying to taste some girl meat,' FBI agent testifies. *NBC News* (Feb 27). http://usnews.nbcnews.com/_news/2013/02/27/17116231-nyc-cop-said-he-was-dying-to-taste-some-girl-meat-fbi-agent-testifies (accessed February 27, 2013).

Heimer, C.A. (1988) Social structure, psychology and the estimation of risk. *Annual Review of Sociology*, 14, 491–519.

Helzner, E.P., Cauley, J.A., Pratt, S.R. *et al.* (2005) Race and sex differences in age-related hearing loss: the health, aging, and body composition study. *Journal of the American Geriatric Society*, 53 (12), 2119–27.

Henry, A.F. and Short, J.F. (1954) *Suicide and Homicide*. The Free Press, New York.

Herbozo, S., Tantleff-Dunn, S., Gokee-Larose, J. and Thompson, J.K. (2004) Beauty and thinness messages in children's media: A content analysis. *Eating Disorders*, 12, 21–34.

Heyboer, K. (2012) Tyler Clementi's family plans no legal action over Rutgers webcam spying case. *NJ.com* (Oct 4) http://www.nj.com/news/index.ssf/2012/10/rutgers_webcam_spying_suicide.html (accessed March 28, 2014).

Heyl, B.S. (1974) *The Madam as Entrepreneur: Career Management in House Prostitution*. Transaction Books, New Brunswick, NJ.

Heywood, P. (1997) Political corruption: Problems and perspectives. *Political Studies*, XLV, 417–435.

Hickey, P. (2011) Homosexuality: The mental illness that went away. *Behaviorism and Mental Health: An Alternative on Mental Disorders*. http://www.behaviorismandmentalhealth.com/2011/10/08/homosexuality-the-mental-illness-that-went-away/ (accessed Jan 1, 2014).

Higgins, G.E., Marcum, C.D., Freiburger, T.L. and Ricketts, M.L. (2012) Examining the role of peer influence and self-control on downloading behavior. *Deviant Behavior*, 33 (5), 412–423.

Hines, D.A., Armstrong, J.L., Palm Reed, K. and Cameron, A.Y. (2012) Gender differences in sexual assault victimization among college students. *Violence and Victims*, 27 (6), 922–940.

Hitchens, C. (2012) *Mortality*. Twelve, New York.

Hodge, R. and Tripp, D. (1986) *Children and Television: A Semiotic Approach*. Polity Press, Cambridge, UK.

Holt, T.J., Bossler, A.M. and May, D.C. (2012) Low self-control, deviant peer associations, and juvenile cyberdeviance. *American Journal of Criminal Justice*, 37 (3), 378–395.

Homant, R.J. and Kennedy, D.B. (2000) Effectiveness of less than lethal force in suicide-by-cop incidents. *Police Quarterly*, 3 (2), 153–171.

Hooked (2014) *Hooked, The Movie*. www.hookedmovie.com (accessed Feb 28, 2014).

Hostetler, J. (1993) *Amish Society*, 4th edn. Johns Hopkins University Press, Baltimore.

Houlihan, B. (2006) Navy spells out policy on tattoos, body art, piercings. *America's Navy*. Story Number NNS060421-15, release date 4/21/2006.

Howard, J.R. (1969) The flowering of the Hippie Movement. *Annals of the American Academy of Political and Social Science*, 382, 43–55.

*References*

Hubbard, T.K. (2003) *Homosexuality in Greece and Rome: A Sourcebook of Basic Documents*. University of California Press, Berkeley.

Hudson, R. and Davidson, S. (2007) *Rock Hudson: His Story*. Carroll & Graf (Avalon), New York.

Huff, R., Desilets, C. and Kane, J. (2010) *The 2010 National Public Survey on White Collar Crime*. National White Collar Crime Center, Fairmont, WV.

Huffington Post (2013) Jonathan McGowan, 44-Year-Old UK Man, Lives Off Roadkill for 30 Years. *Huffington Post*, (first posted Oct 17, 2011, updated Mar 28, 2013), (accessed Feb 25, 2014).

Hughes, E.C. (1958) *Men and their Work*. Free Press, Glencoe, IL.

Humphreys, L. (1970) *Tearoom Trade: Impersonal Sex in Public Places*. Aldine, New York.

Hyde, H.M. (1964) *A History of Pornography*. Heinemann, Portsmouth, NH.

Isaacson, W. (2003) *Benjamin Franklin: An American Life*. Simon and Schuster, New York.

Jacobs, B. (2013) The manipulation of fear in carjacking. *Journal of Contemporary Ethnography*, 42 (5), 523–544.

Jacques, K. and Taylor, P.J. (2009) Female terrorism: a review. *Terrorism and Political Violence*, 21 (3), 499–515.

Janes, L.M. and Olson, J.M. (2000) Jeer pressure: the behavioral effects of observing ridicule of others. *Personality and Social Psychology Bulletin*, 26 (4), 474–485.

Janowitz, M. (1975) Sociological theory and social control. *American Journal of Sociology*, 81(1), 82–108.

Jellinek, E.M. (1946) Phases in the drinking history of alcoholics: Analysis of a survey conducted by the Official Organ of Alcoholics Anonymous. *Quarterly Journal of Studies on Alcohol*, 7, 1–88.

Jenkins, H. (2009) The problem of media violence is exaggerated, in *Media Violence: Opposing Viewpoints*, (ed. D.M. Haugen), Greenhaven Press, Chicago, pp. 37–48.

Johnson, B.D., Golub, A. and Dunlap, E. (2000) The rise and decline of hard drugs, drug markets, and violence in inner-city New York, in *The Crime Drop in America*, (eds A. Blumstein and J.Wallman), Cambridge University Press, Cambridge, UK, pp. 164–206.

Johnston, L.D., O'Malley, P.M., Bachman, J.G. and Schulenberg, J.E. (2012a) Monitoring the future national survey results on drug use, 1975–2011: *Volume II, College students and adults ages 19–50*. Institute for Social Research, The University of Michigan, Ann Arbor. http://www.monitoringthefuture.org// pubs/monographs/mtf-vol2_2011.pdf (accessed Jan 27, 2013).

Johnston, L.D., O'Malley, P.M., Bachman, J.G. and Schulenberg, J.E. (2012b) The rise in teen marijuana use stalls, synthetic marijuana use levels, and use of 'bath salts' is very low. University of Michigan News Service, Dec 19, Ann Arbor, MI. www.monitoringthefuture.org (accessed Jan 24, 2013).

Kaplan-Myrth, N. (2000) Alice without a looking glass: Blind people and body image. *Anthropology & Medicine*, 7 (3), 277–299.

Karlsen, C.F. (1998) *The Devil in the Shape of a Woman: Witchcraft in Colonial New England*. W.W. Norton and Co., New York.

Kaufman, J.M., Hall, J.E. and Zagura, M. (2012) Sex, race/ethnicity, and context in school-associated student homicides. *Journal of Interpersonal Violence*, 27 (12), 2373–2390.

Kaye, K. (2003) Male prostitution in the twentieth century: Pseudohomosexuals, hoodlum homosexuals, and exploited teens. *Journal of Homosexuality*, 46 (1,2), 1–77.

Kearl, M.C. (1989) *Endings: A Sociology of Death and Dying*. Oxford University Press, New York.

Kearney, L. (2014) Kamala Harris calls California a major target for cyber criminals. *Huffington Post* (March 20), http://www.huffingtonpost.com/2014/03/20/california-cyber-criminals_n_5003842. html (accessed Mar 20, 2014).

Keith, T. (2013) How Congress quietly overhauled its insider-trading law. *NPR* (April 16), http://www.npr. org/blogs/itsallpolitics/2013/04/16/177496734/how-congress-quietly-overhauled-its-insider-trading-law (accessed Mar 17, 2014).

Kerbel, M.R. (2000) *If it Bleeds, It Leads: An Anatomy of Television News*. Basic Books, New York.

Kessler, R.C., Demler, O., Frank, R.G. *et al.* (2005) US prevalence and treatment of mental disorders: 1990–2003. *The New England Journal of Medicine*, 352 (24), 2515–2523.

Kinsey, A.C., Pomeroy, W.B. and Martin, C.E. (1946) *Sexual Behavior in the Human Male*. Indiana University Press, Bloomington, IN.

Kinsey, A.C., Pomeroy, W.B., Martin, C.E. and Gebhard, P. (1953) *Sexual Behavior in the Human Female*. Indiana University Press, Bloomington, IN.

Kirkup, J. (2007) *A History of Limb Amputation*. Springer, London.

Klinger, D.A. (2001) Suicidal intent in victim-precipitated homicide: Insights from the study of "suicide-by-cop". *Homicide Studies*, 5 (3), 206–226.

Kohm, S.A. (2006) The people's law versus Judge Judy justice: Two models of law in American reality-based courtroom TV. *Law & Society Review*, 40 (3), 693–728.

Koob, G.F. and Le Moal, M. (2005) *Neurobiology of Addiction*. Elsevier, London.

Kost, K. and Henshaw, S. (2012) *US Teenage Pregnancies, Births and Abortions, 2008: National Trends by Age, Race and Ethnicity*. Guttmacher Institute, New York.

Kroft, S. (2012) Congress: Trading stock on inside information? *60 Minutes* (June 11) Aired on Nov 13, 2011. http://www.cbsnews.com/news/congress-trading-stock-on-inside-information/(accessed Mar 17, 2014).

LaFree, G. and Dugan, L. (2007) Introducing the Global Terrorism Database. *Terrorism and Political Violence*, 19 (2), 181–204.

Lampe, P.A. (1987) *Adultery in the United States: Close Encounters of the Sixth or Seventh Kind*. Prometheus Books, New York.

Landsburg, S.E. (2009) The internet reduces violent behavior, in *Media Violence: Opposing Viewpoints*, (ed. D.M. Haugen) Greenhaven Press, Chicago, pp. 189–194.

Langhinrichsen-Rohling, J., Friend, J. and Powell, A. (2009) Adolescent suicide, gender, and culture: a rate and risk factor analysis. *Aggression and Violent Behavior*, 14, 402–414.

Lauritsen, J.L., Heimer, K. and Lynch, J.P. (2009) Trends in the gender gap in violent offending: New evidence from the National Crime Victimization Survey. *Criminology*, 47 (2), 361–399.

Lavine, H., Sweeney, D. and Wagner, S.H. (1999) Depicting women as sex objects in television advertising: Effects on body dissatisfaction. *Personality and Social Psychology Bulletin*, 25 (8), 1049–1058.

Lawson, L. (2003) Isolation, gratification, justification: Offenders' explanations of child molesting. *Issues in Mental Health Nursing*, 24, 695–705.

Laye-Gindhu, A. and Schonert-Reichl, K.A. (2005) Nonsuicidal self-harm among community adolescents: understanding the "whats" and "whys" of self-harm. *Journal of Youth and Adolescence*, 34 (5), 447–457.

Lee, M.J. (2014) Bernie Madoff speaks: Politics, remorse and Wall Street. *Politico* (March 20) http://dyn.politico.com/printstory.cfm?uuid=0E9EDA7B-EF01-4034-80BB-C3CDC6A0F9F6 (accessed May 2, 2014).

Lemert, E.M. (1951) *Social Pathology: A Systematic Approach to the Theory of Sociopathic Behavior*. McGraw-Hill, New York.

Lemert, E.M. (1982) Issues in the study of deviance, in *The Sociology of Deviance* (eds M.M. Rosenberg, R.A. Stebbin and A.Turowetz), St. Martin's Press, New York, pp. 233–257.

Leonard, R. (2002) Predictors of job-seeking behavior among persons with visual impairments. *Journal of Visual Impairment & Blindness*, September 2002, 635–644.

Lester, D. (1994) A comparison of 15 theories of suicide. *Suicide and Life-Threatening Behavior*, 24 (1), 80–88.

Leventhal, J.M. and Gaither, J.R. (2012) Incidence of serious injuries due to physical abuse in the United States: 1997 to 2009. *Pediatrics*, 130 (5), 847–852.

Liazos, A. (1972) The poverty of the sociology of deviance: Nuts, sluts, and perverts. *Social Problems*, 20 (Summer), 103–120.

Lindquist, C.H., Barrick, K., Krebs, C. *et al.* (2013) The context and consequences of sexual assault among undergraduate women at Historically Black Colleges and Universities (HBCUs). *Journal of Interpersonal Violence*, 28 (12), 2437–2461.

Lohmann, R.C. (2011) Sexting teens. *Psychology Today*, Mar 30, http://www.psychologytoday.com/blog/teen-angst/201103/sexting teens (accessed Jan 9, 2014).

Lombroso, C. (1911) *Crime, Its Causes, and Remedies*. Translated by H.P. Horton. Little, Brown, Boston.

Lopez, C. (2013) Oregon teen arrested after posting 'drivin drunk' Facebook status. *ABC News* (Jan 4). http://abcnews.go.com/blogs/headlines/2013/01/oregon-teen-arrested-after-posting-drivin-drunk-facebook-status/ (accessed Jan 5, 2013).

Lord, V.B. (2012) Factors influencing subjects' observed level of suicide by cop intent. *Criminal Justice and Behavior*, 39 (12), 1633–1646.

Lords, T.E. (2003) *Traci Lords: Underneath It All*. Harper Entertainment, New York.

Lovelace, L. and McGrady, M. (2012) *Out of Bondage*. Lyle Stuart, Secaucus, NJ.

Lowenstein, D.H. (1985) Political bribery and the intermediate theory of politics. *UCLA Law Review*, 32, 784–851.

Lowney, K.S. (1995) Satanism as oppositional youth subculture. *Journal of Contemporary Ethnography*, 23 (January), 453–484.

Lowney, K.S. (2003) Television talk shows construct morality, in *Social Problems: Constructionist Readings*, (eds J.Best and D.R. Loseke), Aldine de Gruyter, New York, pp. 66–73.

Luckenbill, D.F. (1985) Entering male Prostitution. *Journal of Contemporary Ethnography*, 14 (2), 131–153.

Lyng, S. (1990) Edgework: A social psychological analysis of voluntary risk raking. *American Journal of Sociology*, 95 (January), 851–886.

Lyng, S. (2005) *Edgework: The Sociology of Risk-Taking*. Routledge Taylor and Francis, New York.

Lyng, S.G. and Snow, D.A. (1986) Vocabularies of motive and high risk behavior: The case of skydiving, in *Advances in Group Processes, Vol 3*, (ed. E.J. Lawler.), JAL, Greenwich, CT, pp. 157–179.

MacCoun, R.J. and Reuter, P. (2001) *Drug War Heresies: Learning from other Vices, Times,& Places*. Cambridge University Press, New York.

MacDonald, J.M. (1963) The threat to kill. *American Journal of Psychiatry*, 120 (2), 125–130.

MacKinnon, N.J. and Langford, T. (1994) The meaning of occupational scores: A social psychological analysis and interpretation. *Sociological Quarterly*, 35 (2), 215–245.

Magary, D. (2014) What the duck? *GQ*, (January), http://www.gq.com/entertainment/television/201401/duck-dynasty-phil-robertson (accessed Dec 31, 2013).

Magnay, D. (2012) Canadian dismemberment suspect arrested in Germany. *CNN* (June 4) http://edition.cnn.com/2012/06/04/world/americas/canada-body-parts-investigation/

Majors, D. (2006) Gallaudet battle hits core issues of deaf life in America. *Pittsburgh Post-Gazette* (Oct 29), http://www.post-gazette.com/stories/news/us/gallaudet-battle-hits-core-issues-of-deaf-life-in-america-456837/ (accessed Feb 26, 2013).

Malisow, C. (2014) A young man's violent threat on Facebook lands him in jail, and limbo. *Houston Press* (Feb 12), http://www.houstonpress.com/2014-02-13/news/justin-carter-facebook/full/ (accessed Feb 14, 2014).

Manning, J. (2012) Suicide as social control. *Sociological Forum*, 27 (1), 207–227.

Manson III, G.P. (2011) Cyberwar: The United States and China prepare for the next generation of conflict. *Comparative Strategy*, 30 (2), 121–133.

Marcin, S. (2012) Prostitution and Human Trafficking: A Paradigm Shift. Law Enforcement Bulletin. Federal Bureau of Investigation. http://www.fbi.gov/stats-services/publications/law-enforcement-bulletin/2013/March/prostitution-and-human-trafficking (accessed Jan 9, 2014).

Marley, D.J. (2007) *Pat Robertson: An American Life*. Rowman & Littlefield, Lanham, MD.

Marx, K. and Engels, F. (1848, 1964) *The Communist Manifesto*. Translated by S.Moore, (ed. J. Katz), Washington Square Press, New York.

Marx, K. (1867, 1967) *Capital*, (ed. F. Engels) International Publishers, New York.

Matseuda, RL., Gartner, R., Piliavin, I. and Polakowski, M. (1992) The Prestige of criminal and conventional occupations: A subcultural model of criminal activity. *American Sociological Review*, 57 (December), 752–770.

Matthews, W. (2012) *World Religions*, 12th edn, Wadsworth, Belmont, CA.

Matza, D. and Sykes, G.M. (1961) Juvenile delinquency and subterranean values. *American Sociological Review*, 26 (5), 712–719.

Mayes, R. and Horwitz, A.V. (2005) DSM-III and the revolution in the classification of mental illness. *Journal of the History of the Behavioral Sciences*, 41 (3), 249–267.

Mayo Clinic (2012) *Obesity: Complications*, Aug 3, http://www.mayoclinic.com/health/obesity/DS00314/DSECTION=complications (accessed Mar 4, 2013).

McCollister, K.E., French, M.T. and Fang, H. (2010) The cost of crime to society: New crime-specific estimates for policy and program evaluation. *Drug and Alcohol Dependence*, 108(1–2), 98–109.

McCrann, T. (n.d.) Most honorable son: Shame, honor, and duty. *PBS.org*. http://www.pbs.org/mosthonorableson/shame.html (accessed Apr 4, 2014).

McLorg, P.A. and Taub, D.E. (1987) Anorexia nervosa and bulimia: The development of deviant identities. *Deviant Behavior*, 8, 177–189.

McLuhan, M. and Fiore, Q. (2005) *The Medium is the Message: An Inventory of Effects*. Gingko Press, Berkeley, CA.

Meier, R.F. and Geis, G. (2006) *Criminal Justice and Moral Issues*. Roxbury, Los Angeles.

Menn, J. (2012) Hacked companies fight back with controversial steps. *MSNBC* (June 17), http://www.msnbc.msn.com/id/47849023/ns/technology_and_science-security/ (accessed June 17, 2012).

Merton, R.K. (1938) Social structure and anomie. *American Sociological Review*, 3, 672–682.

Messerschmidt, J.W. (1993) *Masculinities and Crime*. Rowman & Littlefield, Lanham, MD.

Meyers, M. (2004) Crack mothers in the news: A narrative of paternalistic racism. *Journal of Communication Inquiry*, 28 (3), 194–216.

Milburn, J.F. and Nicodemus, R. (2012) *Minimalism: Live a Meaningful Life*. Asymetrical Press, Dayton, OH.

Miller, B. (2013) *Cultural Anthropology*, 7th edn, Pearson, Boston.

Miller, W.B. (1958) Lower class culture as a generating milieu of gang delinquency. *Journal of Social Issues*, 14 (3), 5–19.

Mishna, F., McLuckie, A. and Saini, M. (2009) Real-world dangers in an online reality: A qualitative study examining online relationships and cyber abuse. *Social Work Research*, 33 (2), 107–118.

Mitchell, R.G. (1983) *Mountain Experience: The Psychology and Sociology of Adventure*. University of Chicago Press, Chicago.

Mohamed, A.R. and Fritsvold, E. (2006) Damn, it feels good to be a gangsta: The social organization of the illicit drug trade servicing a private college campus. *Deviant Behavior*, 27, 97–125.

Montemurro, B. (2001) Strippers and screamers: The emergence of social control in a noninstitutionalized setting. *Journal of Contemporary Ethnography*, 30 (3), 275–304.

Morris, D. (2004) *The Naked Woman: A Study of the Female Body*. Thomas Dunne Books, New York.

Mosley, P.E. (2009) Bigorexia: Bodybuilding and muscle dysmorphia. *European Eating Disorders Review*, 17 (3), 191–198.

Murray, M.A. (1969) *The Splendor that was Egypt* (rev. edn). Praeger, New York.

Musto, D.F. (1999) *The American Disease: Origins of Narcotic Control* (3rd edn), Oxford University Press, New York.

Nakashima, E. (2013) US said to be target of massive cyber-espionage campaign. *The Washington Post* (Feb10),https://www.washingtonpost.com/world/national-security/us-said-to-be-target-of-massive-cyber-espionage-campaign/2013/02/10/7b4687d8-6fc1-11e2-aa58-243de81040ba_story.html (accessed Feb 10, 2013).

National Archives (n.d.) Records of the Drug Enforcement Administration [DEA]. http://www.archives.gov/research/guide-fed-records/groups/170.html (accessed Jan11, 2013).

National Center for Education Statistics (2013) *Indicators of School Crime and Safety:2012 (NCES 2013–036)*. US Department of Education.

National Consortium for the Study of Terrorism and Responses to Terrorism (START) (2012) Global Terrorism Database (data file), http://www.start.umd.edu/gtd

National Counterterrorism Center (2009) 2008 Report on Terrorism. Office of the Director of National Intelligence, National Counterterrorism Center, Washington, DC. http://www.fbi.gov/stats-services/publications/terror_08.pdf

National Highway Traffic Safety Administration (2012) 2011 Motor Vehicle Crashes: Overview. *Traffic Safety Facts: Research Note*. DOT HS 811 701. US Department of Transportation, National Highway Traffic Safety Administration, Washington, DC, http://www-nrd.nhtsa.dot.gov/Pubs/811701.pdf

National Institute on Alcohol Abuse and Alcoholism. (n.d.) Alcohol use disorders. National Institutes of Health, National Institute on Alcohol Abuse and Alcoholism, Bethesda, MD. http://www.niaaa.nih.gov/alcohol-health/overview-alcohol-consumption/alcohol-use-disorders (accessed Jan 5, 2013).

National Institute on Deafness and Other Communication Disorders (2010) *Quick statistics* June 16 (updated). National Institute on Deafness and Other Communication Disorders, http://www.nidcd.nih.gov/health/statistics/Pages/quick.aspx (accessed July 20, 2013).

National Institute of Mental Health (n.d.) *Eating disorders among adults – anorexia nervosa*. National Institute of Mental Health, Rockville, MD, http://www.nimh.nih.gov/statistics/ (accessed Oct 2, 2013).

Neitzel, A.R. and Gill, J.R. (2011) Death certification of "suicide by cop". *Journal of Forensic Sciences*, 56 (6), 1657–1660.

Nichols, M. (2013) Russia's gay rights storm prompts U.N. to urge for "social inclusion" during 2014 Olympics. *Reuters News Service* (Nov 6, 2013), http://www.huffingtonpost.com/2013/11/06/russia-gay-inclusion-olympics_n_4227997.html (accessed Dec 31, 2013).

Nielsen, A.L. and Bonn, S. (2008) Media exposure and attitudes toward drug addiction spending, 1975–2004. *Deviant Behavior*, 29, 726–752.

Nimmo, D. (1978) *Political Communication and Public Opinion in America*. Goodyear, Santa Monica, CA.

Noguchi, Y. and Hart, K. (2006) Teens find a ring tone in a high-pitched repellent. *The Washington Post* (June 14), http://www.washingtonpost.com/wp-dyn/content/article/2006/06/13/AR2006061301557.html (accessed July 20, 2013).

Norton, K.I., Olds, T.S., Olive, S. and Dank, S. (1996) Ken and Barbie at life size. *Sex Roles*, 34 (3/4), 287–294.

Office of National Drug Control Policy (2012) 2011 annual report, Arrestee Drug Abuse Monitoring Program II. Executive Office of the President, Office of National Drug Control Policy, Washington, DC, http://www.whitehouse.gov//sites/default/files/email-files/adam_ii_2011_annual_rpt_web_version_corrected.pdf (accessed Jan 24, 2013).

Ojita, M. (1997) They're not in Denmark anymore. *The New York Times* (May 18) p.D2.

Olson, S. (2011) *Exorcism Now: The Ritual, Use, and History of the Roman Ritual*, (2nd ed), Metatron Press, Galway, NY.

Oppawasky, J. (2010) Vampirism. *Annals of the American Psychotherapy Association*, Winter, 58–63.

Palmer, C.E. (1978) Dog Catchers: A Descriptive Study. *Qualitative Sociology*, 1 (May), 79–107.

Pape, R.A. (2005) *Dying to Win: The Strategic Logic of Suicide Terrorism*. Random House Trade Paperbacks, New York.

Paperluss, M. (2012) Egypt Bill: Husbands can have sex with dead wives. *Newser*, Apr 27.

Parker, I. (2012) The story of a suicide: Two college roommates, a webcam, and a tragedy. *The New Yorker* (Feb 6), http://www.newyorker.com/reporting/2012/02/06/120206fa_fact_parker?currentPage=all (accessed Mar 28, 2014).

Pascoe, C.J. (2012) *Dude You're a Fag: Maculinity and Sexuality in High School*. University of California Press, Berkeley.

Pavalko, R. (1988) *Sociology of Occupations and Professions*. F.E. Peacock, Itasca, IL.

Payne, E. and Lavandera, E. (2013) Country star Mindy McCready dead at 37 of apparent suicide. *CNN Entertainment* (Feb19), http://www.cnn.com/2013/02/18/showbiz/mindy-mccready-death/ (accessed Jan 12, 2014).

Pearce, F. (1993) Corporate rationality as corporate crime. *Studies in Political Economy*, 40, 135–162.

Pearson, J. and Wilkinson, L. (2013) Adolescent sexual experiences. *International Handbook on the Demography of Sexuality*, 5, 167–193.

Peguero, A.A. (2011) Violence, schools, and dropping out: Racial and ethnic disparities in the educational consequence of student victimization. *Journal of Interpersonal Violence*, 26 (18), 3753–3772.

Peralta, R.L. (2003) Thinking sociologically about sources of obesity in the United States. *Gender Issues*, 2 (3), 5–16.

Peralta, R.L. (2007) College alcohol use and the embodiment of hegemonic masculinity among European American men. *Sex Roles*, 56, 741–756.

Peralta, R.L. (2010) Raced and gendered reactions to the deviance of drunkenness: A sociological analysis of race and gender disparities in alcohol use. *Contemporary Drug Problems*, 37, 381–415.

Perez-Pena, R. (2012) Studies find more students cheating, with high achievers no exception. *The New York Times* (Sep 7), p.A14.

Pescosolido, B.A. and Georgianna, S. (1989) Durkheim, suicide, and religion: Toward a network theory of suicide. *American Sociological Review*, 54 (1), 33–48.

Pescosolido, B.A. and Mendelsohn, R. (1986) Social causation or social construction of suicide? An investigation into the social organization of official rates. *American Sociological Review*, 51 (1), 80–100.

Peters, J.G. and Welch, S. (1978) Political corruption in America: A search for definitions and a theory, or if political corruption is the mainstream of American politics why is it not in the mainstream of American politics research? *The American Political Science Review*, 72 (3), 974–984.

Phillips, J.A., Robin, A.V., Nugent, C.N. and Idler, E.L. (2010) Understanding recent changes in suicide rates among the middle-aged: Period or cohort effects? *Public Health Reports*, 125 (5), 680–688.

Pleck E. (1989) Criminal approaches to family violence, 1640–1980. *Crime and Justice*, 11, 19–57.

Polling Report.com (2014) *Same-Sex Marriage and Gay Rights*. http://www.pollingreport.com/civil.htm (accessed Jan 1, 2014).

Pontell, H.N. and Rosoff, S.M. (2009) White-collar delinquency. *Crime, Law and Social Change*, 51, 147–162.

Porter, J. and Williams, L.M. (2011) Intimate violence among underrepresented groups on a college campus. *Journal of Interpersonal Violence*, 26 (16), 3210–3224.

Powers, E.L. and Wilson, J.K. (2004) Access denied: The relationship between alcohol prohibition and driving under the influence. *Sociological Inquiry*, 74 (3), 318–337.

Powers, M. (1991) Decay from within: The inevitable doom of the American saloon, in *Drinking: Behavior and Belief in Modern History*, (eds S. Barrows and R. Room), University of California Press, Los Angeles, CA, pp. 112–131.

President's Commission on Law Enforcement and Administration of Justice (1967) *The Challenge of Crime in a Free Society*, Washington, DC.

ProCon.org (2013) State-by-State Guide to Physician-Assisted Suicide, Dec 13, http://euthanasia.procon.org/view.resource.php?resourceID=000132 (accessed Jan 3, 2014).

Puhl, R.M. and Heuer, C.A. (2010) Obesity stigma: Important considerations for public health. *American Journal of Public Health*, 100 (6), 1019–1028.

Quinn, J.F. and Forsyth, C.J. (2013) Red light districts on blue screens: A typology for understanding the evolution of deviant communities on the Internet. *Deviant Behavior*, 34 (7), 579–585.

Quinney, R. (1970) *The Social Reality of Crime*. Little, Brown, Boston.

Rafferty, R. and Vander Ven, T. (2014) I hate everything about you: A qualitative examination of cyberbullying and on-line aggression in a college sample. *Deviant Behavior*, 35 (5), 364–377.

RAND Corporation. (n.d.) *Cyber Warfare*. http://www.rand.org/topics/cyber-warfare.html (accessed Mar 24, 2014).

Rand, M.R. (2009) *National Crime Victimization Survey: Criminal Victimization, 2008*. US Dept of Justice, Bureau of Justice Statistics, Washington, DC.

Rawles, J.W. (2009) *How to Survive the End of the World as We Know It: Tactics, Techniques, and Technologies for Uncertain Times*. Plume, Penguin Group, New York.

Rawlins, L.V. (2005) *Theories of Crime Causation*. http://www.vonfrederick.com/pubs/Theories%20of%20Crime%20Causation.pdf

Real, M. (1977) *Mass-Mediated Culture*. Prentice-Hall, Englewood Cliffs, NJ.

Reaves, B.A. (2011) *Census of state and local law enforcement agencies, 2008*. US Department of Justice, Office of Justice Programs, Bureau of Justice Statistics. http://www.bjs.gov/content/pub/pdf/csllea08.pdf (accessed Apr 9, 2014).

Reeve, K. (2013) The morality of the 'immoral': The case of homeless drug-using prostitutes. *Deviant Behavior*, 34 (10), 824–840.

Reid, S.T. (2011) *Crime and Criminology*, 13th edn, Oxford University Press, Oxford.

Reiman, J. (2013) *The Rich Get Richer and the Poor Get Prison*, 10th edn, Pearson, Boston.

Rennison, C.M. (2002) *Rape and Sexual Assault: Reporting to Police and Medical Attention, 1991–2000*. US Dept of Justice, Bureau of Justice Statistics, Washington, DC.

Rennison, C.M. and Melde, C. (2014) Gender and robbery: A national test. *Deviant Behavior*, 35 (4), 275–296.

Ressler, R.K., Burgess, A.W. and Douglas, J.E. (1988, 2006) Serial killers: Antecedent behaviors and the act of murder, in *In Their Own Words: Criminals on Crime*, 4th edn, (ed. P. Cromwell), Roxbury Publishing, Los Angeles, CA, pp. 142–149.

Reyns, B.W., Henson, B.and Fisher, B.S. (2012) Stalking in the twilight zone: Extent of cyberstalking victimization and offending among college students. *Deviant Behavior*, 33 (1), 1–25.

Richmond, R. (2012) Web gang operating in the open. *The New York Times* (Jan 16) http://www.nytimes.com/2012/01/17/technology/koobface-gang-that-used-facebook-to-spread-worm-operates-in-the-open.html?pagewanted=all (accessed Mar 28, 2014).

Rimland, B. and Larson, G.E. (1981) Nutritional and ecological approaches to the reduction of criminality, delinquency, and violence. *Journal of Applied Nutrition*, 33 (2), 39–52.

Ringo, P. (2002) Media roles in female-to-male transsexual and transgender identity formation. *International Journal of Transgenderism*, 6 (3), 1–17.

Ritzer, G.H. and Walczak, D. (1986) *Working: Conflict and Change*, 3rd edn, Prentice-Hall, Englewood Cliffs, NJ.

Roach, M.K. (2004) *The Salem Witch Trials: A Day-by-Day Chronicle of a Community Under Siege*. Taylor Trade Publishing, Lanham, MD.

Robertson, G. (2014) Former Virginia governor pleads not guilty to bribery charges. *Chicago Tribune* (Jan 24) http://articles.chicagotribune.com/2014-01-24/news/sns-rt-us-usa-virginia-mcdonnell-20140121_1_indictment-chief-executive-jonnie-williams-bribery (accessed Mar 19, 2014).

Robers, S., Kemp, J., Truman, J. and Snyder, T.D. (2013) *Indicators of School Crime and Safety, 2012.* (NCES 2013-036/NCJ 241446). National Center for Education Statistics, US Department of Education and Bureau of Justice Statistics, Office of Justice Programs, US Department of Justice, Washington, DC, http://bjs.ojp.usdoj.gov

Romano, E., Voas, R.B. and Lacey, J.C. (2010) *Alcohol and Highway Safety: Special Report on Race/Ethnicity and Impaired Driving.* National Highway Traffic Safety Administration, Washington, DC.

Rosen, L.N., Dragiewicz, M. and Gibbs, J.C. (2009) Fathers' rights groups: Demographic correlates and impact on custody policy and women's safety. *Violence Against Women*, 15 (5), 513–531.

Rosenberg, M.M., Stebbins, R.A. and Turowetz, A. (eds) (1982) *The Sociology of Deviance.* St. Martin's Press, New York.

Ross, B. and Walter, V. (2007) 'To Catch a Predator': A sting gone bad, *ABC News* (Sep 7) http://blogs.abcnews.com/theblotter/2007/09/to-catch-a-pred.html (accessed Mar 21, 2014).

Ross, E.A. (1896) Social control. *American Journal of Sociology*, 1 (5), 513–535.

Rutledge, L. and Donley, R. (1992) *The Left-hander's Guide to Life.* Penguin Books USA. Inc., New York.

Rytina, S. (2000) Is occupational mobility declining in the US? *Social Forces*, 78 (June), 1227–1276.

Salinger, S. (2002) *Taverns and Drinking in Early America.* Johns Hopkins University Press, Baltimore, MD.

Sanger, S. and McCarthy Veach, P. (2008) The interpersonal nature of suicide: a qualitative investigation of suicide notes. *Archives of Suicide Research*, 12, 352–365.

Scalen, W. and Payne, L.W. (2011) The transition of a Texas county from "dry" to "wet" and a comparison of DWI arrest rates before and after. *Southwest Journal of Criminal Justice*, 8 (1), 59–66.

Schick, V.R., Rima, B.N. and Calabrese, S.K. (2011) Evulvalution: The portrayal of women's external genitalia and physique across time and the current Barbie doll ideals. *Journal of Sex Research*, 48 (1), 74–81.

Schildkraut, J., and Muschert, G.W. (2014) Media salience and the framing of mass murder in schools: A comparison of the Columbine and Sandy Hook massacres. *Homicide Studies*, 18 (1), 23–43.

Schoenthaler, S.J. (1983) Diet and delinquency: A multi-state replication. *International Journal of Biosocial Research*, 5 (2), 70–78.

Schur, E.M. (1971) *Labeling Deviant Behavior: Its Sociological Implications.* Harper and Row, New York.

Schweitzer, N.J. and Saks, M.J. (2007) The CSI Effect: Popular fiction about forensic science affects the public's expectations about real forensic science. *Jurimetrics*, 47, 357–364.

Science Channel (2012) Lindbergh: American Nazi? an episode in *Dark Matters*, Season 2, Discovery Communications, LLC (July 14). http://science.discovery.com/tv-shows/dark-matters-twisted-but-true/videos/dark-matters-season-2-a-seriously-killer-song.htm

Seal, K.H., Bertenthal, D., Miner, C. *et al.* (2007) Bringing the war back home: Mental health disorders among 103,788 US veterans returning from Iraq and Afghanistan seen at Department of Veterans Affairs Facilities. *Archives of Internal Medicine*, 167, 467–482.

Shapiro, S.P. (1980) *Thinking about white collar crime: Matters of conceptualization and research.* US Department of Justice, National Institute of Justice, Washington, DC.

Sheldon, W., Hartl, E.M. and McDermott, P.P. (1949) *Varieties of Delinquent Youth.* Harper & Row, New York.

Shelton, D.E., Kim, Y.S. and Barak, G. (2006) A study of juror expectations and demands concerning scientific evidence: Does the "CSI Effect" exist? *Vanderbilt Journal of Entertainment and Technology Law*, 9 (2), 331–368.

Sherefkin, R. (2003) Lee Iacocca's Pinto: A fiery failure. *Automotive News* (June 16) http://www.autonews.com/article/20030616/SUB/306160770/lee-iacoccas-pinto:-a-fiery-failure (accessed Mar 11, 2014).

Sherman, L.W. and Berk, R.A. (1984) The specific deterrent effects of arrest for domestic assault. *American Sociological Review*, 49 (2), 261–272.

Sherman, L.W., Smith, D.A., Schmidt, J.D. and Rogan, D.P. (1992) Crime, punishment, and stake in conformity: Legal and informal control of domestic violence. *American Sociological Review*, 57 (5), 680–690.

Shermer, M. (1997) *Why People Believe Weird Things: Pseudoscience, Superstition, and Other Confusions of Our Time*. W.H. Freeman and Company, New York.

Sherwood, C.H. (2014) Becoming a minimalist: When having fewer possessions means living a better life. *SmartPlanet, Issue* 11, http://www.smartplanet.com/blog/pure-genius/becoming-minimalist-when-having-fewer-possessions-means-living-a-better-life/4331 (accessed Feb 28, 2014).

Shone, M, Esposito, R., Cole, M. and Greenwald, G. (2014) War on Anonymous: British spies attacked hackers, Snowden docs show. *NBC News* (Feb 4) http://www.nbcnews.com/news/investigations/war-anonymous-british-spies-attacked-hackers-snowden-docs-show-n21361 (accessed Mar 28, 2014).

Short, J.F. (1984) The social fabric of risk: Toward the social transformation of risk analysis. *American Sociological Review*, 49, 711–725.

Shugart, H.A.(2006) Ruling class: Disciplining class, race, and ethnicity in television reality court shows. *The Howard Journal of Communications*, 17, 79–100.

Silton, N.R., Flannelly, K.J., Milstein, G. and Vaaler, M.L. (2011) Stigma in America: Has anything changed? Impact of perceptions of mental illness and dangerousness on the desire for social distance: 1996 and 2006. *The Journal of Nervous and Mental Disease*, 199 (6), 361–366.

Skipper Jr., J.K. and McCaghy, C.H. (1970) Stripteasers: The anatomy and career contingencies of a deviant occupation. *Social Problems*, 17 (Winter), 391–404.

Smith, V. (2013) *Sociology of Work: An Encyclopedia*. Sage, Los Angeles.

Snowden, A.J. and Pridemore, W.A. (2013) Alcohol and violence in a nonmetropolitan college town: Alcohol outlet density, outlet type, and assault. *Journal of Drug Issues*, 43 (3), 357–373.

Spencer, H. (1889) *The Study of Sociology*. D. Appleton and company, New York.

Spencer, K. (2013) 'Mind if I smoke?' taking on a new meaning for D.C. hosts. *The Washington Post* (Jan 10) http://www.washingtonpost.com/lifestyle/style/mind-if-i-smoke-taking-on-a-new-meaning-for-dc-hosts/2013/01/10/d46b4dc6-4550-11e2-8e70-e1993528222d_story.html?wpmk=MK0000200 (accessed Jan 11, 2013).

Stack, M. (2000) Local and regional breweries in America's brewing industry, 1865 to 1920. *The Business History Review*, 74 (3), 435–463.

Stack, S., Bowman, B. and Lester, D. (2012) Suicide by cop in film and society: Dangerousness, depression, and justice. *Suicide and Life-Threatening Behavior*, 42 (4), 359–376.

Stack, S., Krysinska, K. and Lester, D. (2007) Gloomy Sunday: Did the "Hungarian Suicide Song" really create a suicide epidemic? *OMEGA: Journal of Death and Dying*, 56 (4), 349–358.

Stephenson, F. (1996) The Evil Gene. *Research in Review* (Spring), http://rinr.fsu.edu/spring96/features/evil.html

Stryker, S. and Whittle, S. (eds) (2006) *The Transgender Studies Reader*. Routledge, New York.

Stump, S. (2013) Jennifer Lawrence on 'Photoshopped' Dior ad: 'Doesn't look like me at all'. Today.com (Mar 1) http://www.today.com/style (accessed Mar 1, 2013).

Suarez, E. and Gadalla, T.M. (2010) Stop blaming the victim: a meta-analysis on rape myths. *Journal of Interpersonal Violence*, 25 (11), 2010–2035.

Substance Abuse and Mental Health Services Administration (2011) Drug Abuse Warning Network, 2009: National Estimates of Drug-Related Emergency Department Visits. HHS Publication No. (SMA) 11-4659, DAWN Series D-35. Substance Abuse and Mental Health Services Administration, Rockville, MD. http://www.samhsa.gov/data/2k11/dawn/2k9dawned/html/dawn2k9ed.htm

Substance Abuse and Mental Health Services Administration (2012) Results from the 2011 National Survey on Drug Use and Health: Summary of National Findings. NSDUH Series H-44, HHS Publication No. (SMA) 12-4713. Substance Abuse and Mental Health Services Administration, Rockville, MD.

Sudi, K., Öttl, K. Payerl, D. *et al.* (2004) Anorexia athletic. *Nutrition,* 20 (7), 657–661.

Sullivan, B. (2012) Exclusive: Hackers turn credit report websites against consumers. *NBC News* (Mar 26) http://redtape.nbcnews.com/_news/2012/03/26/10875023-exclusive-hackers-turn-credit-report-websites-against-consumers?chromedomain=usnews (accessed Mar 27, 2012).

Sullivan, J. (1997) Charges against Danish mother dropped. *The New York Times* (May 17), p. A23.

Sutherland, E.H. (1945) Is "white collar crime" crime? *American Sociological Review,* 10 (2), 132–139.

Sutherland, E. H. (1949) *White Collar Crime.*Holt, Rinehart, and Winston, New York.

Sutherland, E. and Cressey, D. (1978) *Principles of Criminology.* Lippincott, Philadelphia.

Sykes, G. and Matza, D. (1957) Techniques of neutralization: A theory of delinquency. *American Sociological Review,* 22 (Dec), 664–670.

Takada, S. (1999) *Contingency Cannibalism: Superhardcore Survivalism's Dirty Little Secret.* Paladin Press, Boulder, CO.

Tan, A.S. (1986) Social learning of aggression from television, in *Perspectives on Media Effects.* (eds J. Bryant and D. Zillmann), Erlbaum, Hilldale, NJ, pp. 41–55.

Tappan, P.W. (1949) Who is the criminal? *American Sociological Review,* 12, 96–102.

Taverner, W.J. (2011) *Taking Sides on Clashing Issues in Human Sexuality,* 12th edn, McGraw-Hill, Guilford, CT.

Teich, N.M. (2012) *Transgender 101: A Simple Guide to a Complex Issue.* Columbia University Press, New York.

Thompson, W. E. (1991) Handling the stigma of handling the dead: Morticians and funeral directors. *Deviant Behavior,* 12, 401–427.

Thompson, W.E. (2012) *Hogs, Blogs, Leathers, and Lattes: The Sociology of Modern American Motorcycling.* McFarland Press, Jefferson, NC.

Thompson, W.E. and Bynum, J.E. (2016) *Juvenile Delinquency: A Sociological Approach,* 10th edn, Rowman and Littlefield, Lanham, MD.

Thompson, W.E. and Harred, J.L. (1992) Topless dancers: Managing stigma in a deviant occupation. *Deviant Behavior,* 13 (3), 291–311.

Thompson, W.E., Harred, J.L. and Burks, B.E. (2003) Managing the stigma of topless dancing: A decade later. *Deviant Behavior,* 24 (6), 551–570.

Thompson, W.E., Hickey, J.V., and Thompson, M.L. (2016) *Society in Focus: An Introduction to Sociology,* 8th edn, Rowman and Littlefield, Lanham, MD.

Tillyer, M.S. and Tillyer, R. (2014) Violence in context: A multilevel analysis of victim injury in robbery incidents. *Justice Quarterly,* 31 (4), 767–791.

Timmermans, S. (2005) Suicide determination and the professional authority of medical examiners. *American Sociological Review,* 70 (April), 311–333.

Truman, J.L. and Langton, L. (2014) *Criminal Victimization,2013.* US Department of Justice, Office of Justice Programs, Bureau of Justice Statistics, Washington, DC.

Tonry, M.H. (1995) *Malign Neglect: Race, Crime and Punishment in America.* Oxford University Press, New York.

Transparency International (2013) *Corruption Perceptions Index, 2013.* http://cpi.transparency.org/cpi2013/results/ (accessed Mar 17, 2014).

Truman, J., Langton, L. and Planty, M. (2013) *Criminal Victimization, 2012.* US Department of Justice, Office of Justice Programs, Bureau of Justice Statistics, Washington, DC, http://www.bjs.gov/index.cfm?ty=pbdetail&iid=4781

USA Today (2002) Justice Department covers partially nude statues. *USA Today* (Jan 29), p.1A.

US Bureau of the Census (2010) *Statistical Abstract of the United States, 2010*, 129th edn, Table 1090, Washington, DC.

United States Department of Education. (n.d.) The Campus Safety and Security Data Analysis Cutting Tool [data file], ttp://ope.ed.gov/security/

United States Department of Justice (2010) *The National Strategy for Child Exploitation Prevention and Interdiction:A Report to Congress*. United States Department of Justice, Washington, DC, http://www.justice.gov/psc/docs/natstrategyreport.pdf

van Poppel, F. and Day, L.H. (1996) A test of Durkheim's theory of suicide – without committing the 'ecological fallacy'. *American Sociological Review*, 61 (3), 500–507.

Vare, E.A. (2012) *Love Addict: Sex, Romance, and other Dangerous Drugs*. Health Communications, Inc., Deerfield Beach, FL.

Veblen, T. (1899) *The Theory of the Leisure Class*. Macmillan, New York.

Venkatesh, S.A. (2009) *Off the Books: The Underground Economy of the Urban Poor*. Harvard University Press, Cambridge, MA.

Victor, J.S. (1996) *Satanic Panic: The Creation of a Legend*. Open Court Publishing, Chicago.

Vitale, S., Cotch, M.F. and Sperduto, R.D. (2006) Prevalence of visual impairment in the United States. *Journal of the American Medical Association*, 295 (18), 2158–2163.

Wall, D.S. (2001) Cybercrimes and the Internet, in *Crime and the Internet:Cybercrimes and Cyberfears*, (ed. D.S. Wall), Routledge, New York, pp. 1–17.

Watson, J. M. (1980) Outlaw motorcyclists: An outgrowth of lower class cultural concerns. *Deviant Behavior*, 2, 71–76.

Weber, M. (1904–1905, 1958) *The Protestant Ethic and the Spirit of Capitalism*. Scribner, New York.

Weber, M. (1947) *The Theory of Social and Economic Organization*. The Free Press, New York.

Weinstein, A. (2012) The Trayvon Martin killing, explained. *Mother Jones* (Mar 18), http://www.motherjones.com/politics/2012/03/what-happened-trayvon-martin-explained (accessed Mar 31, 2014).

Wheeler, B. (2012) The slow death of prohibition. *BBC News Magazine* (Mar 21), http://www.bbc.co.uk/news/magazine-17291978 (accessed Jan 3, 2013).

White, H.R.and Gorman, D.M. (2000) Dynamics of the drug–crime relationship, in *Criminal Justice 2000, Vol. 1: The nature of crime: Continuity and change*. US Department of Justice, National Institute of Justice, Washington, DC, pp. 151–218.

White, R.D. (1997) The making of American drug policy: A multimodel analysis of the Harrison Narcotics Act of 1914. *Commonwealth: A Journal of Political Science*, 9 (1), 1–20.

Wiegand, B. (1992) *Off the Books: A Theory and Critique of the Underground Economy*. General Hall, Dix Hills, NY.

Williams, W. (1986) *The Spirit and the Flesh: Sexual Diversity in American Indian Culture*. Beacon Press, Boston.

Windrem, R. (2013) Expert: US in cyberwar arms race with China, Russia. *NBC News* (Feb 20), http://openchannel.nbcnews.com/_news/2013/02/20/17022378- expert- us- in- cyberwar- arms- race- with-china- russia (accessed Feb 20, 2013).

Wolfgang, M. and Ferracuti, F. (1967) *The Subculture of Violence*. Tavistock, London.

World Health Organization (2013) *Global and regional estimates of violence against women: Prevalence and health effects of intimate partner violence and non-partner sexual violence*. World Health Organization, Department of Reproductive Health and Research, Geneva, Switzerland.

Wray, M, Colen, C. and Pescosolido, B. (2011) The sociology of suicide. *Annual Review of Sociology*, 37, 505–28.

Wright, J.P., Cullen, F.T. and Blankenship, M.B. (1995) The social construction of corporate violence: Media coverage of the Imperial Food Products Fire. *Crime and Delinquency*, 41 (1), 20–36.

Wright, R.T. and Decker, S.H. (1997, 2006) Creating the illusion of impending death: Armed robbers in action, in *In their Own Words: Criminals on Crime*, 4th edn, (ed. P. Cromwell), Roxbury Publishing, Los Angeles, CA, pp. 159–164.

Wu, Y. (2013) Robbery victimization among Asian Americans: A comparison with White and Black Americans. *Journal of Crime and Justice*, 36 (1), 35–52.

Young, K.S. and Nabuco de Abrey, C. (eds) (2011) *Internet Addiction: A Handbook and Guide to Evaluation and Treatment*. John Wiley & Sons Inc, Hoboken, NJ.

Zweig, J.M., Dank, M., Yahner, J. and Lachman, P. (2013) The rate of cyber dating abuse among teens and how it relates to other forms of teen dating violence. *Journal of Youth and Adolescence*, 42 (7), 1063–1077.

## Cases cited

*USA v. Blagojevich and Harris*, Criminal Complaint, (2008)

*State v. A.B. Rhodes*, 61 N.C. 453, (1868)

*Thurman v. City of Torrington*, 595 F.Supp. 1521, US Dist Ct (D. Conn. 1984)

*Nico Jacobellis v. State of Ohio*, 378 US 184 (1984)

# Glossary

**absolutist position on deviance**  Some things are right, others are wrong.

**achieved status**  A status based on something an individual does to earn it.

**active defense technology**  Retaliatory action by companies against hackers. See also *strike-back technology*.

**adultery**  Sex outside of marriage. See *extramarital sex*.

**aggravated assault**  An unlawful attack by one person upon another for the purpose of inflicting severe or aggravated bodily injury.

**alcohol dependence**  A medical condition involving a craving for alcohol, losing control of drinking, becoming physically dependent on alcohol and experiencing withdrawal symptoms, and increasing tolerance for alcohol so that more and more alcohol is needed to feel the same way. See also *alcoholism*.

**alcoholism**  See *alcohol dependence*.

**amputation**  The surgical removal of a body part.

**anorexia athletic**  Sport-related anorexia nervosa.

**anorexia nervosa**  Intentional, purposeful starvation.

**apotemnophilia**  A strong desire to amputate a healthy limb.

**ascribed status**  A status assigned to us by others through no effort on our part.

**adult entertainment**  Refers to businesses and jobs which provide sex-related products and is often viewed as synonymous with sex industry.

**adultery**  Sex outside of marriage. See *extramarital sex*.

**age-crime curve**  Illustrates that criminal offending increases as we age, peaks in the late teens/early twenties, and declines with age.

*Deviance & Deviants: A Sociological Approach*, First Edition. William E. Thompson and Jennifer C. Gibbs.
© 2017 John Wiley & Sons, Inc. Published 2017 by John Wiley & Sons, Inc.
Companion website: www.wiley.com/go/thompson

**aggravated assault**  An unlawful attack by one person upon another for the purpose of inflicting severe or aggravated bodily injury.

**altruistic suicide**  In Durkheim's typology, suicide occurring when a person's bond to society is too strong, when suicide becomes a duty.

**androgyny**  The blending of masculine and feminine traits.

**anomic suicide**  In Durkheim's typology, suicide occurring when social regulation is weakened or absent.

**anomie**  A state of social strain, normative confusion, or rapid change in norms or social structure which results in people no longer feeling constrained by conventional social norms.

**arson**  Any willful or malicious burning or attempting to burn, with or without intent to defraud, a dwelling house, public building, motor vehicle or aircraft, personal property of another.

**atavism**  A biological throwback to a more savage earlier phase of human evolution.

**beat**  A small geographical area that can be effectively supervised by an officer.

**bestiality**  Sex with an animal.

**BIID**  An abbreviation for *body integrity identity disorder*.

**bigorexia**  Abnormal eating, often combined with supplements and drug use, to achieve larger muscle mass. See also *reverse anorexia*.

**bisexuality**  Sex with members of both sexes.

**binge drinking**  Having at least five drinks in a row.

**black-collar occupations**  Jobs that are considered deviant and stigmatize those who perform them.

**blue-collar occupations**  Involve manual labor or factory work.

**body modification**  Any alteration of the body.

**body mutilation**  Extremely bizarre alteration of the body.

**branding**  Form of scarification that usually involves heating a piece of metal and burning the impression into the skin.

**bribery**  A payment to coerce someone in a position of power to overlook his or her duties.

**bulimia**  A cycle of binge-eating followed by purging through vomiting and/or using laxatives.

**burglary**  Unlawful entry of a structure to commit a felony or theft.

**child abuse**  Physical, sexual, or emotional abuse or neglect by a caregiver toward a person under age 18.

**child sex tourism**  Involves Americans traveling to foreign countries (usually poorer countries like those in Southeast Asia) to purchase children there for the travelers' sexual gratification.

**civil service**  System requiring hiring the best qualified candidates for the job.

**cohort**  A group of people who share something in common, like an age range.

**co-marital sex**  Couples in a committed relationship (usually marriage) who engage in sexual activities with others as a social or recreational activity. See also *swinging* or *the lifestyle*.

**come out**  Become open about previously hidden homosexuality.

**conflict perspective** Provides a macro-level analysis that focuses more on the values and origins of norms than on the deviant behaviors or deviants themselves.

**conformity** Adherence to norms.

**containment theory** This theory conceptualizes a double line of defense—inner and outer containment—that controls people's urges to commit deviance and encourage conformity.

**control theories** View deviance as a "normal" response to many social situations and believe that it is conformity that must be explained.

**corporate crime** Conduct of a corporation, or of employees acting on behalf of a corporation, which is proscribed and punishable by law.

**courtroom workgroup** The prosecutor, the defense attorney, and the judge.

**crackers** Type of cyber-trespassers who have no principles and may simply be anti-establishment.

**crime** Those acts that involve the violation of formally codified norms that we have previously defined as laws.

**criminology** The scientific study of crime and criminal behavior.

**cronyism** Jobs offered to friends regardless of their qualifications.

**cross-dressing** Dressing and acting in ways traditionally associated with the opposite sex. See also *transvestism*.

**CSI effect** Because of crime dramas like CSI, jurors expect definitive scientific proof and, at the same time, are more critical of the forensic evidence presented to them.

**culture** The learned set of attitudes, values, beliefs, norms, and material goods shared by members of a society.

**culture shock** Feelings of confusion and disorientation that occur when experiencing a different culture.

**cyberaggression** Unwanted, hurtful, harassing, and/or threatening interaction through electronic communication media that is not repeated (like cyberbullying). See also *online aggression*.

**cyberbullying** Repeated, unwanted, hurtful, harassing, and/or threatening interaction through electronic communication media.

**cyberdeviance** Harmful behavior or otherwise deviant activities that are somehow related to a computer.

**cyberpiracy** Using computer technology to copy digital goods that include software, documents, audio (including music and voice), and video for any reason other than to back up without explicit permission with intent to deny compensation to the copyright holder.

**cybersanctioning** Attempts to modify someone else's behavior usually through name-calling.

**cybersex** Using a computer for flirting, sex-talk, viewing pornography, and other forms of sexual stimulation through cyberspace.

**cyberstalking** The persistent tracking and harassment of an individual by another and the sending of obscene messages or even death threats.

**cyberwarfare** Involves the actions by a nation-state or international organization to attack and attempt to damage another nation's computers or information networks through, for example, computer viruses or denial-of-service attacks. See also *netcentric warfare*.

**dark figure of crime** Crimes that do not come to the attention of the police or make it into official statistics, especially when people do not report crimes.

**definition of the situation** During interaction people create a definition of social reality that is real in its consequences.

**demonology** The systematic study of the belief in demons or super humans that are not considered to be deities.

**deviance** The violation of norms.

**deviant career** A progression through various stages of deviance from novice to fully established deviant.

**deviant occupation** One that is stigmatized either because it may involve illegal, immoral, or simply undesirable activities.

**differential association theory** Asserts that people learn values, norms, and behaviors from people with whom they associate and interact.

**differential identification theory** Contends that an important variable in social learning is the extent to which a person identifies with a role model.

**differential reinforcement** Whether deviant behavior is positively reinforced or negatively sanctioned.

**"Dirty Harry" problem** See *noble cause corruption*.

**dirty work** The type of work that most people in society would rather not do.

**discrimination** Negative actions toward a category of people.

**disenfranchised** Occurs when a person is no longer legally eligible to vote or to receive certain benefits from the government because of a felony conviction.

**dysfunctional** When something threatens the overall well-being or smooth functioning of society.

**ecdysiasts** Women and men who remove their clothing (strip) for money.

**ecological fallacy** Applying macro-level findings to individuals.

**Edelhertz typology** Divides white collar crime into four types: (1) personal crimes; (2) abuses of trust; (3) business crimes; and (4) con games.

**edgework** Negotiating the boundary between chaos and order, or skirting the edge between danger and safety.

**egoistic suicide** In Durkheim's typology, suicide resulting from excessive individualism; the most common type of suicide.

**emaciation** Self-starvation leading to an extremely thin and bony body.

**euthanasia** See *physician-assisted suicide (PAS)*.

**extortion** Others give money or property to a political official because that official threatened the person.

**extramarital sex** Sex outside of marriage. See *adultery*.

**extreme deviance** Beliefs, behaviors, and activities that go well beyond the range of tolerance and often result in serious social sanctions.

**extreme lifestyle** An unconventional way of living that violates cultural values and norms and is considered deviant and possibly even dangerous by members of mainstream society.

**extreme pornography** Anything produced solely or principally for the purpose of sexual arousal which is grossly offensive, disgusting, or otherwise of an obscene character.

**extreme sports** Activities that involve a high level of danger and pose risks of severe injury or death.

**fat shaming** Making a person who is obese feel inadequate.

**fatalistic suicide** In Durkheim's typology, suicide occurring when there is too much social regulation; rarest type of suicide.

**fathers' rights groups** Groups that argue that sexual allegations against fathers are false and the penalty for the "malicious mothers" who make these claims is to give the fathers full custody of the "brainwashed" children; they typically do not advocate paying child support or spending time with children.

**feminist perspective** Studies, analyzes, and explains conformity and deviance from a gender-focused viewpoint.

**fetishism** Sexual arousal associated with a specific inanimate object (such as opposite sex clothing).

**folkways** Informal rules and expectations that guide people's everyday behavior.

**formal social control** Social control involving the criminal justice system or other official government agencies.

**free will** Self-determination.

**functional** When something contributes to the overall well-being or smooth functioning of society.

**functionalist perspective** Provides a macro-level analysis that examines broad social structures and society as a whole.

**gender** Refers to cultural and social understandings about what constitutes masculinity and femininity.

**gender bending** Actively transgressing prescribed gender roles for a person's sex.

**gender gap** The difference between men and women.

**gender paradox** Women are more likely than men to have suicidal thoughts and attempt suicide, while men are more likely than women to actually commit suicide.

**gossip** Small talk with social purpose.

**graft** Abusing political office for personal profit.

**Guardian Angels** An international, nonprofit citizen group dedicated to safety.

**hackers** Type of cyber-trespassers who have principles like believing all information should be freely accessible to the public.

**hate crimes** Crimes against persons or property based on race, ethnicity, religion, or sexual orientation.

**homicidal triad** Three characteristics that serial killers are said to have in common: (1) arson; (2) animal abuse; and (3) bedwetting.

**homophobia** Unnatural and unrealistic fear, hatred, and discrimination directed toward homosexuals.

**homosexuality** Sex between two people of the same sex.

**homosocial environments** Environments that have become social enclaves containing hotels, bars, restaurants, shops, and other businesses that are owned, operated by, and cater to the LGBT community.

**honest graft** Using positions of power – legally – to become personally wealthy.

**hot spots** High concentration of crime occurs at certain locations.

**human sexuality** The wide range of possible ways that people express themselves as sexual beings.

**human trafficking** Selling and buying humans for the purposes of sexual slavery, forced labor, or other illegal purposes.

**hundreds** Ten tithings.

**illegal occupations** Jobs that violate criminal laws.

**immoral occupations** Jobs that violate mores.

**informal social control** Social control involving society members unaffiliated with official government agencies.

**interactionist theories** View conformity and deviance as flexible and symbolic terms that are defined and redefined through the process of interaction.

**intimate partner violence (IPV)** When a husband, spouse or boyfriend/girlfriend uses violence against his wife, spouse, or boyfriend/girlfriend – his an intimate partner.

**jails** Short-term confinement facility housing offenders sentenced to incarceration for less than one year.

**labeling theories** See conformity and deviance as labels applied to certain acts and conformist and deviant as labels assigned to certain people.

**larceny-theft** The unlawful taking, carrying, leading, or riding away of property from the possession or constructive possession of another.

**latent functions** Unintended consequences.

**laws** Formal norms established and enforced by some government entity.

**liberation hypothesis** Deviance is increasing among females because as rigid gender roles become more flexible and more gender equity is achieved, girls and women have more opportunities to participate in deviant activities.

**looking-glass self** A person's self is a reflection of other people's perceptions of him or her.

**macro-level analysis** Examines broad social structures and society as a whole.

**manifest function** Intended consequences.

**mass murder** Intentional killing of at least three people during one event.

**master status** When one status somewhat overpowers or supersedes other statuses in a person's status set.

**medicalization** Occurs when human behaviors, activities, and events that previously were considered to be non-medical, become defined as health or disease related conditions.

**medical model** Compares deviance to illness or disease.

**Metropolitan Police Act of 1829** Piece of legislation that led to the creation of the first trained, professional civil police force in London.

**micro-level analysis** Focuses on the day-to-day interactions of individuals and groups in specific social situations.

**minimalism** The practice of living a simple, uncluttered, non-materialistic life.

**moral crusade** An effort to identify wrongdoing, inform others of its existence and potentially dire consequences, and establish rules or laws to eliminate the behavior and punish the wrongdoer.

**moral differentiation** The ability to promote some selected norms and values over others.

**moral entrepreneurs** Social reformers who are not satisfied with existing rules because they believe that some type of behavior is taking place that should be controlled or eliminated.

**moral panic** The belief that the very survival of society is threatened by a particular type of deviant or deviance.

**mores** Salient norms that people consider essential to the well-being of society.

**motor vehicle theft** Taking cars or other automobiles without the use of force.

**naturism** A lifestyle based on both private and public nudity. See also *nudism*.

**necrophilia** Sex with a human corpse.

**neighborhood watch programs** Involves citizens in crime prevention efforts in their own neighborhoods.

**nepotism** Jobs offered to family members regardless of their qualifications.

**netcentric warfare** See *cyberwarfare*.

**neutralization theory** Contends that much deviant behavior can be explained by people's ability to rationalize it and thereby neutralize their inhibitions about committing deviance.

**noble cause corruption** Using unethical means to justify good results. See also *"Dirty Harry" problem*.

**norms** Socially constructed guidelines that suggest appropriate behavior in certain social situations.

**nudism** A lifestyle based on both private and public nudity. See also *naturism*.

**occupational prestige** The relative ranking of occupations based on people's perceptions of them.

**official data** Crimes known to the police.

**online aggression** See *cyberaggression*.

**organic analogy** Viewing society as being like a huge organism comprised of interconnected and interdependent parts.

**ostracism** Excluding a member from the social group.

**parole** An offender released from prison can live in the community with frequent visits with the parole officer, but if the offender commits a new offense or violates the rule of parole, a judge may order the offender to return to prison.

**passing** Attempting to conceal the potentially stigmatizing attribute from others so that the person is not identified as being deviant.

**pathological** Irrational, unreasonable, or "sick."

**Penile subincision** Slicing the penis from the urethra opening down to the base for aesthetic purposes or sexual pleasure.

**period effects** Something historical happened like the latest recession.

**personal identity**  A person's image of self.

**phone sex**  Simulated sex or sex talk over a telephone.

**phrenology**  A system for studying the shape, bumps, and indentations of the skull in order to determine the cerebral functions that govern human behavior.

**physician-assisted suicide (PAS)**  Occurs when a doctor provides patients, typically those dying painfully, with drugs to end their own lives. See also *euthanasia*.

**pink-collar occupations**  To describe occupations dominated by women.

**plea bargaining**  An offender makes a deal with the prosecutor for a lesser charge or shorter sentence in return for a guilty plea.

**police misconduct**  Police use their authority inappropriately.

**political corruption**  Activities which take place either wholly within the public sphere or at the interface between the public and private spheres, such as when politicians use their privileged access to resources (in whatever form) illegitimately to benefit themselves.

**political intelligence**  Former politicians and staff members return to Capitol Hill to gather information that has not yet been made public to sell to Wall Street.

**polydrug use**  Using more than one drug in a short period of time.

**pornography**  Usually defined as explicit materials intended solely for sexual arousal.

**positivism**  A philosophy of science based on the assumption that true knowledge requires positive verification.

**prejudice**  Negative attitudes based on pre-judgments.

**premarital sex**  Sexual intercourse prior to marriage.

**prescriptive norms**  Tell us what we should do.

**primary deviance**  A situation in which a person violates norms, but does not internalize the self-concept of being deviant.

**prison**  A correctional facility housing those convicted to more than one year of confinement.

**probation**  A convicted offender can live in the community with periodic checks by a probation officer, but will revisit the judge for a harsher sentence if a new crime is committed during the term of probation.

**property crimes**  Taking others' possessions without the use of force.

**proscriptive norms**  Tell us what we should not do.

**prostitution**  Exchanging sexual favors for something of value (usually money) with no emotional involvement.

**pseudoscience**  A claim or belief system that is presented as scientific, but lacks the rigor of reliability, validity, and testability demanded by adherence to the scientific method.

**quasi-military**  Civilian body that follows the military courtesies and customs and adopts a military rank structure.

**range of tolerance**  A scope of behaviors that are considered acceptable and not considered deviant although they technically might violate a norm.

**rape myths**  Mistaken victim-blaming attitudes that excuse or minimize offenders' behaviors; prejudicial, stereotyped, or false beliefs about rape, rape victims, and rapists.

**recidivism** Reoffending.

**reverse anorexia** See *bigorexia*.

**ridicule** Mocking or teasing directed at individuals.

**ritualistic cutting** Designs may be carved into the face, arms, torso, or legs for cosmetic purposes or to denote social statuses.

**robbery** Occurs when an aggravated assault and a larceny-theft occur together.

**role** A set of expectations that are associated with that particular status.

**role distance** When people play a role but remain detached from it in order to avoid any negative aspects associated with the role.

**role embracement** Occurs when a person's sense of identity is influenced by the role.

**role engulfment** A situation in which a role becomes such an important part of a person's identity that it supersedes all other roles.

**role merger** An individual becomes the role.

**role-taking** The process of adopting and fulfilling the expectations associated with a particular status.

**role set** The different roles that accompany each of their statuses.

**sanctions** Ways of enforcing norms.

**scarification** Body modification that involves scratching, cutting, burning, branding, or otherwise permanently scarring the body.

**science,** Knowledge based on empirical evidence gained through direct, systematic observation.

**secondary deviance** When a person internalizes a deviant identity.

**self-harm** The intentional harming of one's body in order to reduce emotional pain and cope with overwhelming emotions.

**self-stigma** Internalizing negative beliefs that others will discriminate against the person with mental illness.

**serial killing** The murder of more than three people over a period of time.

**sex** Biological and physiological differences between males and females based on genetics and chromosomes.

**sex industry** Refers to businesses and jobs which provide sex-related products and is often viewed as synonymous with adult entertainment.

**sexting** Sending out semi-nude or nude photos over mobile phones.

**sexual deviance** Violating sexual norms.

**sexual norms** The multitude of folkways, mores, laws, and taboos that surround and attempt to regulate sexual behavior.

**shame** Emotional feeling similar to guilt or embarrassment.

**shire** Equivalent of today's county.

**shire reeve** The person who oversaw the groups of hundreds in his shire; equivalent of today's sheriff.

**snuff film** Depicts the actual or staged murder of a human being.

**social bond theory** Contends conformity relies on individuals developing a strong bond to society in the form of attachment, commitment, involvement, and belief.

**social control**  All of the processes by which people define and respond to deviant behavior.

**social identity**  The way a person is perceived by others.

**social integration**  The extent to which people feel that they are a meaningful part of society.

**social learning theories**  Contend that much human behavior, including conformity and deviance, is learned through social interaction.

**social pathology**  A social problem that potentially threatens the survival of society.

**social problem**  An undesirable issue (like racism or violence) that has damaging effects on members of a community.

**social regulation**  The extent to which society controls or regulates individual behavior.

**social threat theory**  Contends that efforts of social control are related to the perceived threat of social deviance to those in power.

**sociobiology**  A discipline that combines the scientific approaches of sociology and biology to combine the effects of nature and nurture in attempting to explain human behavior.

**sociological perspective on deviance**  Contends that there are no universal standards for normative behavior and, consequently, no rigid definition of either deviance or conformity.

**sociology**  The scientific study of society, social groups, and human behavior.

**sodomy laws**  Laws passed by individual states banning what was sometimes vaguely referred to as "unnatural sex acts," or in some cases were more explicit in banning oral sex, anal sex, and sex between unmarried couples.

**spearfishing**  Offenders try to elicit sensitive information from key government or military personnel by sending official-looking email messages with attachments that look legitimate but actually launch spyware programs.

**statistical anomaly view of deviance**  Looks at patterns of behavior, and determines what are the most common behaviors in a given social circumstance and declares them as constituting the norm. Anything deviating from the statistical norm is considered deviant.

**status**  A relative position in society that becomes part of our social identity.

**status set**  A combination of all of a person's different statuses.

**stereotypes**  Static and oversimplified ideas about entire categories of people.

**stigma**  Any attribute that discredits an individual from full social acceptance.

**stigma symbols**  Identifying marks or characteristics that provide hidden social information about a stigma.

**strain theories**  View deviance as a result of the tensions or strain experienced by people because of their position in and relationship to the larger social structure.

**strike-back technology**  See *active defense technology*.

**STOCK Act**  Legislation that prohibited insider trading among Congress people and executive branch members, expanded financial disclosures, and made politicians' trading more easily searchable by the public.

**subcultures**  Smaller cultures within a larger culture that adhere to most of the characteristics of the dominant culture, but share some set of distinctive norms that set them apart from it.

**suicide**  The intentional taking of one's own life.

**suicide-by-cop**  Law enforcement-forced-assisted suicide.

**suicide terrorism**  Terrorism where the perpetrator is willing to die during attacks.

**survivalism**  A social movement of groups and individuals who are actively preparing for the end of civilization.

**suspension**  Involves suspending a human body in the air from metal hooks placed in various parts of the body (most often the chest or back).

**swinging**  Couples in a committed relationship (usually marriage) who engage in sexual activities with others as a social or recreational activity (sometimes called *the lifestyle*).

**symbolic interaction perspective**  Views social meaning as arising through the process of social interaction.

**symbols**  Anything that represents something else.

**taboos**  Acts so repugnant that their commission is considered almost unthinkable.

**terrorism**  The threatened or actual use of illegal force and violence to attain a political, economic, religious, or social goal through fear, coercion, or intimidation.

**the lifestyle**  Couples in a committed relationship (usually marriage) who engage in sexual activities with others as a social or recreational activity. See also *swinging*.

**theory**  Refers to a set of interrelated propositions or statements that attempt to explain some phenomenon.

**tithings**  Groups of ten families.

**transgenderism**  Situations in which a person's gender identity does not correspond with his or her sex.

**transsexualism**  Generally refers to a person who no longer identifies with his or her biological sex, undergoes counseling and hormone treatments, and sometimes surgery to realign his or her physical appearance to fit the gender identity of the opposite sex.

**transvestism**  Dressing and acting in ways traditionally associated with the opposite sex. See also *cross-dressing*.

**trolling**  The attempt to hurt, humiliate, annoy, or provoke in order to elicit an emotional response for one's own enjoyment.

**turn out**  Introduce the new initiate to the world of prostitution.

**values**  Shared ideas about what is socially desirable.

**victimization data**  Records how many times people have been on the receiving end of criminal incidents during some time period, like the last six months.

**vigilantes**  People who bypass the police take criminal matters into their own hands.

**violence**  Use of force against another person, with the intent to harm.

**Wall's typology**  (1) cyber-trespass; (2) cyber-deception/thefts; (3) cyber-pornography/obscenity; and (4) cyber-violence.

**white-collar crime**  A crime that is committed by a person of respectability and high social status in the course of his occupation.

**white-collar delinquency**  Consists of computer crimes committed by juvenile offenders.

**white-collar occupations**  Generally involve office work, service work, or some other form of non-manual labor.

# Index

Page numbers in *italics* refer to illustrations

*Deviance & Deviants: A Sociological Approach*, First Edition. William E. Thompson and Jennifer C. Gibbs.
© 2017 John Wiley & Sons, Inc. Published 2017 by John Wiley & Sons, Inc.
Companion website: www.wiley.com/go/thompson